Mining Morality

PRAISE FOR *MINING MORALITY: PROSPECTING FOR ETHICS IN A WOUNDED WORLD*

"William P. George has written a wonderful book about an unlikely topic: the ethics of mining. It is an entrancing book, blending fact and law, philosophy and religion, all in the context of George's personal experience and ethical passion. No one reading it will doubt for a second that the ethics of mining is, after all, a matter of the highest importance." —**Mark Weston Janis**, University of Connecticut School of Law

"Mining is an essential part of modern life that takes place largely out of sight of those who depend on it. George has explored its possibilities under the earth, into space, and through the changing requirements of law, economics, and public policy. *Mining Morality* is informative, engaging, and a profound reflection on what it means to understand any human activity in moral terms." —**Robin W. Lovin**, Cary M. Maguire University Professor of Ethics Emeritus, Southern Methodist University

Mining Morality

Prospecting for Ethics in a Wounded World

William P. George

LEXINGTON BOOKS/FORTRESS ACADEMIC
Lanham • Boulder • New York • London

Published by Lexington Books/Fortress Academic

Lexington Books is an imprint of The Rowman & Littlefield Publishing Group, Inc.
4501 Forbes Boulevard, Suite 200, Lanham, Maryland 20706
www.rowman.com

6 Tinworth Street, London SE11 5AL, United Kingdom

British Library Cataloguing in Publication Information Available

Library of Congress Cataloging-in-Publication Data

ISBN: 978-1-9787-0792-4 (cloth)
ISBN: 978-1-9787-0793-1 (electronic)

Contents

List of Figures

Preface

I grew up in "The Treasure State," but as a child I didn't really know what that meant. I knew, from grade school civics, I suppose, that the words *Oro y Plata* (Gold and Silver) were on Montana's state flag, but I didn't fully grasp why that was so. I knew that, unlike other parts of the country, silver dollars were used all the time, but I thought that was just because we lived in the West and were different from other states. I didn't know it had everything to do with silver mining in places like Philipsburg, just seventy-five miles away. In the eighth grade or so, a friend talked about an awesome book (but we didn't say "awesome" then) called *The War of the Copper Kings*. But unlike Saint Augustine, I did not "pick up and read,"[1] and so I missed a chance to find out where I lived and who I was.

Mining was all around me in those days—but not right around. Compared to Butte or Anaconda, Missoula was not really a mining town. Mining was on my mind, but more at the edge than at the center, more on the surface than deep within. Yet it was there, with its subtle tug of fascination. One older neighborhood kid repeated rumors of abandoned mines, but no one seemed to know just where these old mines were. I thought it would have been neat, if a little scary, to find one, since I knew a lot about abandoned mines from episodes of *The Lone Ranger* and other westerns. Mine shafts were dangerous places where innocent people got trapped and saved, and where the bad guys hid. They were dark places where you needed a torch that might burn out at just the worst time.

The closest I came to actual mining was on family trips. On the way to Spokane and then Seattle to visit our oldest sister who had entered the convent, we would pass through Kellogg, Idaho, where waste from the mines turned the river that bordered the highway a melancholy gray. Perhaps the timing was wrong, but we never stopped in that town for lunch or gas.[2] On another trip, I recall not when or to where, we did pass through Butte and saw trucks with ten-foot tires crawling around like Tonka Toys in the monstrous Berkeley Pit. Near the town of Anaconda, down the road, we saw maybe the tallest smokestack in the world. I thought that was really cool. When I was eight, we took a train trip to Chicago. At the Museum of Science and Industry (you could see yourself on color TV!), we went into a coal mine where they told us about canaries and other things. I remember better the White Sox game we saw at night (the Sox beat the Senators, 10-4, with fireworks after the game), but I do recall the elevator ride into that sort-of-real mine.

In the summer of 2014, I returned to Montana with my wife, Susan, for a family reunion near Glacier National Park, where the ice recedes now more each year. We flew into Billings and then travelled to Bozeman and then south past Big Sky, a western refuge for the rich. After a day in Yellowstone Park, which I had last seen as a child, we drove to Butte, where we visited a high school friend. He told us a lot about Butte—for instance, how, with the help of a helicopter, they managed to put together the huge statue of Our Lady of the Rockies that overlooks the city from a mountaintop—a maternal complement to Rio de Janeiro's more famous *Cristo Redentor*, which we would see for ourselves a year later and then again on TV during the Summer Olympics of 2016.

The next morning, we drove through old Butte, passed the campus of Montana Tech's School of Mines and Engineering, and strolled the grounds of the World Museum of Mining, with lots of buildings and structures and a much else underground. Then, on our way out of town, we stopped and paid a few dollars for access to a viewing site above the Berkeley Pit. We were the only ones there. Many things struck me that day. Three stand out: (1) The stark and simple claim made in one of the museum displays that "Everything begins with mining"; (2) the realization that even though I grew up less than three hours away, I had never spent enough time in Butte to think much about its mining past; and (3) the fact that, with the pumps in the mines turned off years before, the Berkeley Pit was now a lake of toxic water, rising little by little each year.

On the way to Missoula, before heading north toward Flathead Lake and the reunion near the lake's upper end, we tested our rental car on a rough and mildly treacherous road up to Garnet, a restored mining town with a high ratio of bars to other buildings. Arriving there, we were surprised to see several parked cars and soon learned that they had come up from the other side. After our self-guided tour, we took that way ourselves and found pavement half-way down. Apparently, there are harder and easier roads to reach a present that converges with the past.

At this road's end, we met the two-lane highway on which I had travelled often with my family or others when I was young, maybe on the way to Great Falls, with Minute Man missile sites visible from the highway that passes through Lincoln where the Unabomber would be found. Closer to Missoula, the highway runs along the Blackfoot River that Norman MacLean remembered in *A River Runs through It* and where my siblings and I had fished with our father—dry flies only, just like in the book. Approaching Missoula from the east, the road runs through Bonner, where once stood the Anaconda-owned lumber mill that produced timber posts and beams and rail ties and other materials for that company's wood-insatiable mines. I remembered taking a tour of the mill when it still ran strong during my grade-school days and recalled the beveled cube-shaped wooden yardstick we were given at the end of the tour. I don't know what happened to that company-stamped ruler or whether it was ever used it to measure anything worthwhile.

Mining has been on my mind much of my life, but, as I say, more on the periphery than near the center. This was true as I moved away from Montana, that land of grizzly bears and bobcats, of gold and silver and copper and coal. Later, I would have the good fortune of spending two two-year stints in Zambia, mostly teaching in a secondary school. Shortly after first landing in that country, afflicted by war in Zimbabwe just to the south, I visited Kitwe in the Copperbelt, the life-blood of Zambia's economy. I then traveled to the Southern Province where I would reside mostly among the Tonga people, whose way of life was not mining but mostly cattle and maize. During those years, I was aware of the Copperbelt and its mines; references were frequent enough in the *Times of Zambia* or the *Daily Mail.* But I did not travel to Kitwe again.

Still, without knowing it, I carried Zambian copper into graduate school where I studied ethics and society. Almost out of the blue—but maybe not—I hit upon a dissertation topic about which I knew next to nothing at the time: the 1982 Convention on the Law of the Sea. My focus would be the robust debate over deep seabed mining, and who would have access to this newly accessible (or so it seemed), if not newly discovered, wealth: huge deposits of polymetallic nodules containing copper and other minerals lying on the ocean floor. With a focus on that sector of ocean space designated in the emerging law as humankind's "common heritage," my questions were something like "Who owns the earth?" and "How do we live together in the space between the world as it is and a world that might be?"

Occupied as I was with the ocean depths, one might assume that thoughts of a distant country like Zambia would recede. But I found that, like other land-locked, mineral-exporting countries, Zambia took a keen interest in what was happening in the various rounds of negotiations over the emerging sea law, asking who stood to gain or lose from the extraction of minerals buried in the abyss. So I discovered what I probably already knew: that mining has a way of connecting things and people and nations, and even something or someone beyond, if only we take the time to notice that this is so. Mining has a way of sundering the earth and relationships as well.

This book is an effort to bring mining closer to the center of moral consciousness. But the intended focus is not the author's consciousness or the kinds of reminiscences recorded above. Apart from occasional first-person comments to move things along, there are two exceptions to this third-person treatment of a taxing topic, a major one and a minor one. The major one is the second-person character of the work: An abiding implicit invitation to you, the reader, to examine and perhaps expand your own moral consciousness by turning your thoughts to mining and, in the process, contribute, in ways not found in the text, to crucial conversations and actions that begin with mining but do not end there. The minor exception, found in one chapter, is a self-reflective account of my introduction years ago to international law, in this case the Law of the Sea, with a special focus on seabed mining. But even there, the aim of this exercise in memory is to illustrate for the reader that what goes on in anyone's life, including one's interior life—in times of crises or of quiet—has connections to mining and other matters far beyond the self.

Still, if autobiography or memoir would distract or detract from a work such as this, some memories are surely appropriate as I recall those who have aided this project in ethical prospecting, extending to the various moral mining sites that, in the pages to follow, I have chosen to explore. One may find in the Catholic social tradition, to which I will turn, references to "the priority of labor," the notion that anyone's accumulation of capital—financial, social, intellectual—is dependent largely on someone else's prior labor. I see the truth of that in my own case. As the recollections recorded above would suggest, I have, of course, family to thank, each contributing, in his or her own way, to my well-being and more. For this project I am especially grateful to my brother, Tom, a mathematician and engineer long engaged in nuclear safety, whom I consulted for a chapter on uranium mining and, to use the language of that chapter, other "nuclear things."

Reaching back almost as far as family, I owe more than I can say to the Society of Jesus, especially the Oregon Province (now Jesuits West), for much of my education, in the fullest sense of the term, beginning in my youth but especially during the years I shared in their Company in the Northwest, in Zambia, and in other places. One benefit among many was exposure during philosophy studies to the thought of Bernard Lonergan, SJ, a lead "prospector" in the pages that follow. I have learned since then from other students of Lonergan. I think of Fred and Sue Lawrence; Patrick Byrne; Robert Doran,

SJ; Richard Liddy; Ken Melchin; Michael Vertin; John Haughey, SJ; and others who have welcomed me to many of the Lonergan Workshops at Boston College each June.

I have learned from others, too. With particular relevance to this investigation, at Weston School of Theology, Sister Mary Emil Penet, IHM, convinced me that anyone concerned with justice—say, in a labor dispute, but also between nations—must also worry about prudence. Both faculty and fellow students at the University of Chicago Divinity School advanced my thinking about ethics and other matters during my years in Hyde Park. Robin W. Lovin, with expertise in the thought of Reinhold Niebuhr and much else, directed my dissertation on the Law of the Sea. Duncan Snidal, of the Department of Political Science, introduced me to the world of international relations and regimes. Chris Gamwell, a third reader, helped me to be clear.

I owe special thanks to colleagues at Dominican University, a second home for the past twenty-four years, where the spirit of the Sinsinawa Dominican Sisters is widely shared. A grant of a semester's leave set me on track for this project, but the ease of conversation across the university has been at least as helpful. Department colleagues Hugh McElwain and Kathy Heskin (emeriti), Clodagh Weldon, Richard Woods, OP, Timothy Milinovich, and Anthony Suárez-Abraham have inspired me daily with their deep commitment to *caritas* and *veritas* (Dominicans' motto), so clearly evident in their teaching, scholarship, and service. Jeff Carlson, also a department colleague, has graced the life of the university, and me personally, with his administrative leadership as longtime dean of Rosary College of Arts and Sciences and now university provost and academic vice-president, but also with his abiding commitment to interfaith dialogue and practice.

The reader will find in this extended meditation on mining a brief reference to Xenophon, who records a dialogue that finds Socrates discussing with good reason the mines of Athens. That this reference reached me by way of Chris Colmo, professor emeritus of Political Science, is not surprising. Chris has been for years perhaps my closest conversation partner on matters philosophical, political, and so much more. He and Ann Colmo, also a political philosopher with much to teach, have been a blessing in my—and our—life.

I say "our" because I owe the most to my life-partner for nearly twenty-seven years, Susan A. Ross, for her constant support—and occasional prodding—during my struggles with a topic not easy to manage or finish off. Susan's help included reading with a critical eye drafts of the various chapters and giving her wise, scholarly counsel on questions that arose both from the process of writing and from life—sometimes with little daylight in between. I would say that I cannot repay her, but talk of payments seems not to capture what I mean.

Early encouragement to expand on a basic idea, captured by the title, came from Michael Gibson of Fortress Press. Neil Elliott, now of Lexington Books/ Fortress Academic, an imprint of Rowman & Littlefield, and assistant editor Gayla Freeman continued that support with their editorial direction and advice as the manuscript moved toward publication. My sincere thanks to each of them. I also thank Meaghan Menzel, and others unknown to me, for expert and cordial guidance through the production process. I am especially grateful for the thoughtful comments and questions of a reviewer of the initial manuscript. These added to the contributions from members of the University of Chicago Divinity School Writers Group that meets once each year and generously to read early chapters.

Although the main topic of the book is mining and morality, the theme of education, of teaching and learning, is clearly woven in. This is consistent with the gratitude expressed in the prefatory remarks above for what I have gained from others over the years. It would be difficult to single out one teacher that I—or others—have known, such that one's gratitude gives reason for the dedication of a written work. So, taking refuge in the rhetorical device of *synecdoche*, whereby one person or thing can stand for all the rest, and singling out two teachers rather than one, it seems fitting that this work be dedicated to two great teachers of an earlier generation—chronically, of the very same generation, it turns out, as they were born on opposite sides of the world a year apart. They never met in person, so far as I know, and one I have met only through a fraction of his many writings. But as the discerning reader may surmise (one will be discussed at length), they have met many times in my mind. So in gratitude for what each has given to me and so many others, this book is dedicated to James M. Gustafson, who taught many of us at the University of Chicago and elsewhere so much about theological ethics that never stopped there; and to the memory of Judge Christopher Weeramantry (1926–2017), who taught his students and the world about the kind of law—"ethics writ large," I call it—that can lead to a more just, sustainable, and peaceful world.

NOTES

1. Saint Augustine, *Confessions,* trans. Henry Chadwick (Oxford: Oxford University Press, 1991), Bk. 8, ch. 12.
2. In 1972, ninety-one miners would succumb to carbon monoxide poisoning from a fire in the nearby Sunshine Mine. Today, approaching Kellogg from the east, one can see the sculpture memorializing that disaster: a defiant miner hoisting a rock drill.

Acknowledgments

Cover Photo: Zambian copper miner. Photo by David Rose; used with permission.

An edited and expanded version of William P. George, "Learning to Love the Law of the Sea," chapter 4 of *In Search of the Whole: Twelve Essays on Faith and Academic Life,* ed. John C. Haughey, SJ, 51–72 (Washington, DC: Georgetown University Press, 2011) is published here by permission of Georgetown University Press; www.press.georgetown.edu.

Excerpts from Janet L. Finn, *Tracing the Veins: Of Copper, Culture, and Community from Butte to Chuquicamata* (Berkeley: University of California Press, 1998), are reprinted by permission of University of California Press (through Copyright Clearance Center, Inc.).

Excerpts from C. B. Glasscock, *The War of the Copper Kings: Greed, Power, and Politics: The Billion-Dollar Battle for Butte, Montana, the Richest Hill on Earth* (Helena, MT: Riverbend Publishing, 2002), are reprinted by permission of Riverbend Publishing.

Excerpts reproduced by permission of Oxford University Press Australia from *Nauru Environmental Devastation* by Christopher Weeramantry © Oxford University Press, www.oup.com.au.

Excerpts from the encyclical letter *Laudato si'* of Pope Francis, on Care for Our Common Home, May 24, 2015 (© Libreria Editrice Vaticana) are reprinted by permission of Libreria Editrice Vaticana.

Part I

GETTING READY

Chapter One

Introduction: Mining and Moral Consciousness

On August 16, 2015, a spill from an abandoned mine in Colorado released into the Animas River about a million gallons of toxic waste.[1] For a few days at least, images of a river turned a bright but poisonous gold captured the attention of many in the United States. Included in the TV reporting was the estimate of as many as 500,000 abandoned mines in the United States alone. In November of the same year, millions of gallons of waste from an iron mine in Brazil burst through a dam and flowed into the Rio Doce River, and eventually the Atlantic Ocean. The effects were judged to be catastrophic and will last for decades.[2] But then the news cycles moved on. Out of sight, out of mind. Until, of course, another mining dam burst in Brazil in early 2019, this time killing hundreds and wreaking environmental damage on an epic scale.[3]

This book is about moving mining from the periphery of moral consciousness and closer to its center. In this regard, the book's title, *Mining Morality*, is significant as it carries a double-meaning: On the one hand, this is a book about a certain kind of morality: *mining* morality, or the morality of mining—what's morally good about digging for copper or coal or rare earth elements, and what's not so good about it, in view of an overriding moral question, "How ought we to live?"[4] *Ethics* and *morality* are often used interchangeably, and that will sometimes be the case here. But to the degree that a distinction is maintained, it is a relatively simple one: ethics is understood as reflection, more or less systematic (often less), on the pre-reflective moral life.[5] From this point of view, the *ethics* of mining has to do with understanding, making judgments about, and then expressing in various ways—regulations and codes, but certainly not only there—the relationship between mining and morality.

This is a relatively neglected subject. After describing human suffering related to artisanal mining in Burkina-Faso, Shefa Siegel laments the "missing ethics of mining." Siegel explains:

> Mining is the material basis for life, making it difficult to exaggerate its significance. George Orwell called it part of the "metabolism" of civilization. Major divisions of history are named in accordance with their dominant mineral products: the Paleolithic and Neolithic Periods; the Copper, Bronze, and Iron Ages. More than ever, humanity relies on minerals to sustain its existence. The growth of population, speed of transportation, proliferation of electronic gadgets and games, and delivery of electricity all depend on the expansion of mining. And yet we are ready to discuss almost any other ethics before the ethics of mining. Some view the concept as a contradiction in terms, others are alarmed that mining continues to exist at all, or simply find the topic supremely boring. We have more faith in our capacity to restrain or end violence and war than to address the ethics of mining.[6]

This book is intended, then, as an attempt to hear Siegel's complaint, echoed by others, possibly to rouse the reader from his or her slumber about this ethical gap, and to pursue more broadly and deeply the "ethics of mining" as Siegel describes it here and as we will explore it below.

But if the book is about the morality of *mining,* it is also about the mining of *morality*. At least that is the hope. If subjecting the extraction of minerals and other elements to moral scrutiny helps us to see mining with its sometimes dark corners in a brighter light, the hypothesis is that explorations of mining will also help us to understand better, and possibly in new ways, that broader, more fundamental moral question, "How ought we to live?" even when activities other than mining are on our minds. After all, mining has been around for a very long time,[7] certainly long before Socrates uttered his maxim that "the unexamined life is not worth living."[8] My hope is that thinking about mining can help us—reader and author—better to examine, if not now then later, the many and varied moral dimensions of our lives. Surely, the one examination can teach us something about the other. By descending into the world of mines and mining,[9] we may in the process find ourselves getting a clearer view of a wider, if still very steep, moral path leading out of the cave, into the light, and to more authentic human action and passion in the world we share.[10]

MINING AS A METAPHOR FOR ETHICS

All analogies limp, and metaphors have a way of spinning out of control. But it may help to explain the intent of this book to consider how mining might serve as a metaphor for the project of ethics as reflection on the moral life.

For on the face of it at least, mining and ethics have much in common. There are, of course, other wonderful images for the moral life, such as a garden where all sorts of things grow if tended well or shrivel up without care. Or, one thinks of the farmer's field where tares may get mixed with the wheat (Mt. 13:24–30), a scriptural image dear to the American theologian and public intellectual Reinhold Niebuhr. Thomas Aquinas, for his part, looked to the growth of animals when considering growth in charity.[11] Still, there is value in mining the image of mining itself to see what it might teach us about the reflection on moral life.

First, as Siegel points out in the passage quoted above, mining is "the material basis for life." As a display at the World Museum of Mining in Butte, Montana, puts it, "Everything begins with mining." In other words, mining is something basic, something fundamental to human living. So, too, is ethics as reflection on how to live—or so Socrates is reported to have said as he was facing his death. Second, mining generally has to do with finding and recovering, for the sake of developing and putting to use, something buried, sometimes close to the surface, sometimes deep within. So, too, ethics is in part an effort to discover and develop the good, the right, the virtuous that may lie buried, waiting to be brought to the surface and into the light, that it might be affirmed, refined, and enfolded into practice. In this regard, ethics includes considerations of "conscience," of what transpires in the very depth of one's being, with implications for action in the world. An examination of mining may aid an examination of consciousness and conscience—personal, for sure, but communal as well.

Third, mining is highly particular even if it yields to generalities, categories, and abstractions. As Siegel rightly points out, "There is a maddening futility about speaking of 'mining,' as if it were singular or coherent. It is like talking about 'Africa' or addressing the 'international community' in the fashion of humanitarians, as if it is all one big thing. Rather, there are many mining industries, and each has its own culture, directives, structure, purpose, and pathologies."[12] With references to "directives, structure, purpose, and pathologies," Siegel is already moving mining in the direction of ethics. But even at the level of geology, not all mining is the same. Not only are there different ores and elements to be mined, but they are of different grades, in different mixtures, at different depths, in places remote and not so far, and on and on. They may be on the earth—perhaps on a mountain top or in a desert or on the deep seabed—or in outer space. These locales are hardly one and the same. So, too, ethics is in part a matter of attending to the particular case, the singular situation, the specific context, without altogether giving up on the question of how the particular comes under some more general norm, or partakes in a larger, more inclusive whole. Thinking about the singularities and generalities of mining may help us to approach with surer footing the profound problem the Greeks called "the one and the many" as it presents itself in the moral life with its multiple venues and concerns.

Fourth, mining is, or can be, a matter of problem-solving: how to recover embedded copper, how to reach down to the deep seabed, how to mine on asteroids cruising along at thousands of miles per hour. While it may seem a bit cold and heartless to compare ethics to engineering, I do not think the comparison is unwarranted or unbecoming. Engineers tend to be very inquisitive people, highly imaginative, asking how things work or can be made to work, how something difficult or dangerous, perhaps something seemingly impossible, can be done. Ethicists—"professionals," but also those simply serious about the everyday as it leans into the future, the primary audience for this book—are a bit like Socratic engineers, raising questions that seem worth pursuing even when, perhaps especially when, the answers are not right-away. Questions about living morally not only in the best of times but during a war, in the wake of an empire's collapse, or amidst the brutality of a concentration camp—and why wars, empires, and death camps exist at all—can test the wits of any academic or everyday ethicist who has the "knack" of an engineer.[13]

Fifth, and closely connected to thoughts of ethics-as-engineering, genuinely new ways of mining—new technologies—are developed precisely in response to problems to be solved. So, too, new ethical questions, approaches, theories tend to emerge to meet new, or seemingly new, moral challenges: the invention of the cross-bow, the "discovery" of the New World and its exotic peoples, the Siren song of eugenics, the horrors of Auschwitz, the birth of the Bomb. Here, the suggestion is that our aptitude for ethics, whatever that aptitude happens to be, will be advanced precisely as we consider mining with its peculiar problems, possibilities, and perils. Ethics advances through practice as new challenges are met and at least sometimes overcome.

This would include, it seems, practice of a very intimate sort. Again, Socrates thought that the unexamined life was not worth living. Presumably, that includes one's "interior life." But Thomas Aquinas argued that one could know one's own soul not "by its own essence," but only insofar as it was "in act"[14]—wondering, getting the point, making a judgment, reaching a decision. Thus, it may be that each reader might come to know a bit better his or her own "soul," not directly but rather in the process of attending to, of considering, of questioning what mining of various kinds is all about—yesterday, today, and tomorrow—and perhaps choosing and acting differently in the world as a result. In short, examination of mining might contribute to the examined life.

Sixth, and perhaps in sum, mining is a *human* endeavor. Mining does not just happen; human beings mine. The name "'49ers" may be given to a kind of pancake, but first it was given to those who rushed for gold. As a human endeavor, mining is a mother lode of meaning and value, and it has languages of its own that mix with other languages all the time. Mining is a constant case of noticing or overlooking, of seeking and finding, of asking and answering, of digging in or moving on, of buying and selling, of owning and owing, of producing and polluting, of truth-telling or cheating, of protecting a workmate, of falling asleep at the switch. It is a matter of succeeding and failing, of oppressing the weak, of rescuing the same, of risking and possibly losing all. It is a matter of dreaming or having one's dreams—or one's body—crushed or poisoned by a process that can be terribly cruel. It is a matter of life and death. Ethics asks about such things as well.

As a human endeavor, mining is perhaps most of all about relationships—to other human beings, surely, with their shovels and skills, their investments and inventions, their wit and their wily ways. But mining is also about relationships to plants and trees, to animals of the forest and the rocky crag, to the birds of the air and the fish of the sea, even to the extremophiles that inhabit the toxic ocean depths. It is about human relationships to that which the ancients thought to be quite basic: earth, air, fire, and water. It is about relatedness to the minerals beneath one's feet but also to elements existing in a galaxy far, far away. And, as we shall emphasize, mining may also be a matter of relationship to the divine.

Yes, mining is about relationships. No one, really, mines alone. Mining is about competition but even more about cooperation, of working with others, of working with rather than against the laws of physics as well as the statistical laws that insurance companies know so well. It is a matter of working together for ill or for well. The true "ill" or "well" of mining is just the sort of thing that ethics seeks to sort out. But here, at least, the sorting out will come not by abandoning mining as one might abandon a mine that is spent; it will not be a matter of quickly leaving mining behind and rising above it all as though the total cessation of all mining were an option open to us.[15] Rather, the wager here is that the ethical sorting, determining what moral responsibility means not only in the case of mining but in other cases as well, will come by respecting the ways of mining and following its byways, and in that manner possibly extricating oneself from the traps of the cave or the moral mineshaft and entering once again into the light.

A MODEST APPROACH TO THE ETHICS OF MINING

If this book's title suggests what the book is basically about, the subtitle signals its modest aim. I assume that the subject matter both of mining and of morality is so substantial, the questions so many, the subtopics so varied that the prospects of my writing a book with a presumptuous title like "The Ethics of Mining" are slim. My intention is to offer not a definitive text on the ethics of mining, but something closer to a "prospector's report" on what appear to be promising veins of ethical inquiry, some to be pursued later or by others whose grasp of such matters, often quite specialized, far exceeds my own. Recall that mining is a cooperative, collaborative enterprise. So, too, is reflection on the moral life. It can be no other way, or so it appears to me as it has appeared to others, for instance people of old who cited the maxim regarding justice, that *nemo iudex in causa sua* (no one is to be a judge in one's own case). I would hope that the reader might find worthy of further exploration questions opened chapter by chapter and in the book as a whole. As a "prospecting" effort, the book is thus closer to a prolegomenon to an ethics of mining than to a treatise on the subject. But, as some rather famous examples attest,[16] a prolegomenon can have its good purpose and its good effect if it leads to further exploration, discovery, refinement, and use. In the case at hand, that use may be in the field of mining itself, which, as Siegel notes, is in need of an ethics. But it may extend to inquiry of other kinds as well. Reflection on the moral life is certainly as wide as it is deep.

The context for the prospecting is "a wounded world." Surely, other adjectives would also be apt: a complex world, a threatened world, a traumatized world, a fragmented world—and more. But "wounded" seems to capture the theme of care—for humanity and, as we shall see, "our common home"—in need of grace and healing. This theme will run as a vein to be tapped repeatedly throughout the book.

This meditation on mining, if one may call it that, is limited in other ways. Even apart from wider meanings—one thinks of "mining the data," as a researcher might in "drilling down" to answer this question or that—in its industrial usage "mining" may be restricted to metals or industrial minerals, including, for instance, sand or gravel or clay, or it may extend to oil and gas.[17] For the sake of manageability, the direct focus here will be limited to certain minerals such as copper, phosphate, uranium, and platinum. Thus, critical issues such as hydraulic fracturing and its effects, or the geopolitical or climate-changing implications of oil, will not receive here the attention they deserve—even if they receive mention, hover over, or slip in between the lines of the pages that follow. Nor will we take up directly that obvious target of moral assessment, the mining of coal, although it will make a significant film appearance late in the book. With implications that run from black lung to the "company store" of Merle Travis and Tennessee Ernie Ford's "Sixteen Tons" (the theology in the song should not be overlooked), to the loss of community with the closing of mines, to connections between coal and climate change, coal mining no doubt deserves extensive treatment of its own—as, in fact, it has been receiving for some time. But even apart from the inevitable references to fossil fuels that will appear now and then, recall that this is an exercise in prospecting: what we learn from examining a small selection of sites may lead to recommendations about mining morality in other fields.

Another limitation of this foray into mining requires comment. This is not in any conventional sense an ethnographic study. There are possibly good excuses for this limitation (one might, for instance, plead lack of time, budget, and proper training), but I offer none here. Still, a few observations about this shortcoming may be in order. First, while I have not done proper fieldwork, presumably others have—this includes, in subsequent chapters, especially Janet L. Finn in the cases of Butte and Chuquicamata (chapter 3), and Gabrielle Hecht, writing about uranium mining and "being nuclear" in Africa (chapter 6). There is something to be said for valuing and learning from the work of others and not assuming one could do better oneself. In this regard, the reader might recall that Francisco de Vitoria, OP, gave important lectures on the treatment of indigenous people of the New World (*De Indis* and *De Jure Belli*), even though he had not traveled there.[18] But he was, in part, responding to what he had learned from his brother Dominicans and others on the sometimes cruel and bloody scene on the other side of the sea.

Second, in the case of mining today, one wonders just what ethnographic study should include: interviewing not only laid off coal miners but also the engineers and technicians building multi-million-dollar machines for seabed mining or miniature satellite probes for prospecting in space? This is to say nothing of up-close understanding of just how decisions are made in corporate boardrooms, whether we are talking about Standard Oil or the Anaconda Mining Company (chapter 3), or, today, Deep Space Industries or Planetary Resources (chapter 7). As the chapters below will more than suggest, mining is a vast enterprise involving many who might not think of themselves as miners at all. To anticipate an example from chapter 3, what went on in Judge Clancy's Butte, Montana, courtroom—and in Judge Clancy's head and heart—was arguably as important as what transpired in the mineshafts and workways below.

The aim of the subtitle will be apparent throughout the book. Each chapter will conclude with an interim prospector's report on mining morality, articulating a few findings on how an "ethics of mining" could and should be more fully developed, or suggestions as to how reflecting on mining at this or that site can help us better to understand the moral life. The book's conclusion will offer, in brief summary form, a prospector's report on ethics under the earth, on the ocean floor, and in outer space.

PROSPECTING TOOLS

"Prospecting," as the term is used here, involves investigating, in successive chapters, various "sites" to see what moral insights and lines of inquiry might be near the surface lie hidden below, or hover up above. But prospecting of any sort requires instruments or tools. The notion of "tools" may be problematic if the reference is to external objects independent of the inquiring subject, such as the reader. In fact, popular images in America of prospectors as bearded old geezers with their pans and pickaxes might reinforce such notions. But that need not be the case. As the philosopher of science Michael Polanyi points out, a "tool" may be quite personal, an extension of the self.[19] This is especially true in this case, since the tools to be employed here are largely cognitive and affective, replete with or seeking out meaning and value that can extend as far as the divine. In that respect, even the stereotypes in the old westerns aren't so far off: wizened old prospectors who were in fact wise, with their prospecting tools loaded on their beasts of burden (should we really burden animals so?) but loaded mostly in their heads. Still, if the reader finds it more helpful to think in terms of conceptual frameworks or sources for approaching the topic, there is no objection to that. But "frameworks" and "sources" can also limit and obscure one's search if they get detached from the dynamism that is the questioning human mind and desiring heart.

I realize, too, that "tools" other than my own might be employed, just as, today, extractive industries employ a number of different methods for finding what they seek.[20] I have chosen certain tools or means of investigation because they are closest to hand—or, more accurately, because they have been handed to or educed from me, in the process of my education. But they are also, I believe, effective—both powerful and sensitive at the same time. I will explain in more detail in the next chapter, and periodically thereafter, how these tools "work" and how I am drawing upon them. But here I can at least say what they are.

First, are key insights of the philosopher and theologian Bernard J. F. Lonergan, SJ (1904–1984), who in his many writings, especially the book *Insight,*[21] details and asks the reader to identify for himself or herself—and within himself or herself—a "generalized empirical method."[22] On the one hand, this method is not imposed on the "prospector," or questioning subject, whoever he or she might be. On the contrary, the subject encounters and affirms the elements of this method in the dynamic workings of his or her own mind and affectivity and may make this method more and more his or her own through a process of self-appropriation. On the other hand, as "method," the tools lead to "cumulative and progressive results."[23] In this case, the results may be the initial findings of this study. But they may lie still in the future, in the more fully developed ethics of mining that exceeds the bounds of the text. Furthermore, I cannot emphasize enough the open-ended nature of this method, inviting as it does not only, say, the insights of theologians in the Christian tradition which was Lonergan's own, but also the engagement of human thought and action, religious and other, quite beyond Christianity's bounds—which, it must be said, Lonergan himself willingly and adeptly crossed.

Other, related tools from Lonergan on which I will draw include the "functional specialties" integral to Lonergan's method in theology; the worldview called "emergent probability" (which has much to say, for instance, about mining and its related activities as a dynamic, cooperative enterprise);[24] the "scales of values" by which not only individual acts but also cooperative schemes and structures, such as mining, and even religious practice may be assessed; the prospects of human "progress" and "decline," along with the need for "redemption," due in large part to the devastating effects of "bias" and sin. I will also say something about Lonergan's deep excursion into economics, but along the lines of pointing to a "tool" that could and should be applied to the case of mining by others better equipped for the task than I.

Second, is the long, and still developing, Catholic social tradition (CST), generally referred to as "Catholic social teaching" or "Catholic social thought." But it can, and should, also include "social movements."[25] There are several reasons why CST provides a valuable set of tools for ethical prospecting. Let me mention three. First, are its ancient origins: While CST often refers narrowly to papal teaching starting with the first of the great "social encyclicals"—*Rerum novarum,* in 1891—CST has biblical roots and builds upon Christian teaching and thought and action over 2000 years and more.[26] If mining is an ancient enterprise, then it stands to reason that the moral reasoning with which it is engaged should have a long history as well. Next, while Catholic social thought is clearly rooted in a particular tradition, that tradition is, in principle, open to engagement of and by all others "of good will," for instance by way of its longstanding, theologically-grounded commitment to natural law. There is no reason why those of other traditions, religious and other, cannot gain from engaging Catholic social thought, even as they can surely advance that tradition through critique and by adding insights of their own. Finally, there is the sheer range and scope of CST's concerns, a range and scope that continues to grow. We will take up this topic below, but simply to point the way, consider how two critical issues closely associated with mining—labor and the environment—are also key aspects of "the social question," from beginning to end. Thus, the subtitle sometimes given to Leo XIII's 1891 encyclical *Rerum Novarum* is "On the Condition of Working Classes," and Pope Francis's 2015 encyclical on the environment, *Laudato si'*, pleads with humanity to care for "Our Common Home."

Third is law—or, more specifically, international law, which I first encountered in a serious way during doctoral studies when I explored the 1982 United Nations Convention on the Law of the Sea.[27] The relationship between law and morality or ethics is a contested matter, and the tendency to conflate or confuse can be problematic. I am not unaware of this problem. Yet, as will be explained in due time, international law is a rich and highly complex carrier of moral meaning and value, and thus the practice of international law may be understood as "ethics writ large." That is, international law is an ongoing, dynamic, often highly contested process of reflection and action on the question, "How ought we to live, how *can* we live, together on the same planet, even as, like Icarus (or maybe not), we sometimes seek to escape that planet's bounds?"

I would also add, as a fourth tool but also integral to the three discussed here, the virtue of prudence as understood by Thomas Aquinas. Arguably, most if not all questions of justice are in fact also questions of prudence. Since, as we shall see, mining has much to do with justice, including both intergenerational justice and ecojustice, an ethics of mining has much to do with prudence, including an international *jurisprudence* that extends to any number of critical issues.

We will discuss these "prospector's tools" at more length in the next chapter. But two further comments about them are in order here. First, different tools may be used differently, or more prominently, for different mining sites. Still, these tools are interactive, both complementing and strengthening one another. Taken together, they constitute, in this prospector's mind at least, one integrated, dynamic whole. For instance, understanding of the workings of international law may be advanced by turning to Lonergan and what he says about emergence and emergent probability.[28] Something similar may be said about linking Lonergan and the Catholic social tradition. In fact, some argue that Lonergan's forays into economics constitute a true advance of that tradition.[29] Conversely, considering international law, and the many "cases" with which it deals, can help one better to understand concretely and historically what both Lonergan and CST are about, even when, perhaps especially when, they become a little abstract.

Second, as noted above, just as different mining problems give rise to the need for better and different tools,[30] so it is possible that a focus on mining will reveal the inadequacy of the tools I have chosen. But something else may occur. Unlike drill bits that grow dull with use, or outdated mining machines that cannot keep up with the task, the tools employed here are such that, precisely with use, they can be sharpened and improved. So, what Lonergan says about "method" may be refined as that method—basically raising and answering questions of fact and value, leading to decision, and reflecting on that process in one's own case—is brought to bear on the issues that mining poses. And our mining explorations may advance CST beyond the references to mining that one already finds in its texts or more focused "teaching," such as the Philippines bishops' call in 2008 for a moratorium on mining and logging until indigenous peoples could be protected.[31] Finally, by turning to mining, one may envision the ways in which international law can and might need to grow to meet the ethical challenges posed by mining around the globe, and beyond the globe, day after day.

In other words, this is a book about "prospecting," about searching for veins of further inquiry so that a more adequate ethics of mining might be retrieved, developed, and refined. But as a happy by-product of that process, of interest to some readers, it may suggest how Lonergan studies can be further developed along untapped veins of inquiry, how Catholic social thought may further realize yet hidden potential, and how international law might be better appreciated, with the hope that established law with relevance to mining might be affirmed and new law might emerge. So, while the first audience of this work is those interested in the morality of mining or the mining of morality, and preferably both, it may also be of value to those who already have an interest or expertise, often exceeding that of the author, in the understanding and use of one or more of the prospector's tools. If readers less familiar with these tools find them of value and want to claim them as their own, then this will advance considerably the prospector's aim.

Given the complexity, nuance, and sometimes technical language attached to these tools, it is understandable if the reader might want to skip ahead to the interesting mining sites we will visit. Such skipping is quite possible, just as in, say, do-it-yourself home repair, one may jump right into the task and everything may work out just fine. You can learn as you go. But things usually work out better when one takes some time to the read the directions—even when they don't spell out everything in advance of the task. When it comes to repairing or healing a wounded world and building something new, it might pay to spend some time on a set—or a chapter—of directions, imperfect as those directions may be.

MODES OF MINING MORALITY

To this initial discussion of "tools," it will be helpful to add a few words about what theological ethicist James M. Gustafson says about "varieties of moral discourse."[32] For this, too, will help to introduce this book, not so much its intent and content as its approach and tone, as well as its limitations.

Gustafson understood a critical point: that when people think or speak of "ethics," or talk or write about "morality," they do not always think or speak the same way. For some, ethics, if it is to be worthy of the name, must be "prophetic," boldly naming a demon to be faced and presenting a vision of the way the world should be. "Speaking truth to power" is perhaps the typical way this is put today. For others, however, ethics must do more than denounce and announce. It must explain, often in precise and nuanced terms. "Fine," one can imagine those looking for moral clarity might say to the prophet, "we're all for 'justice' and against 'injustice' when it comes to mining, but can you step back for a moment—or step down from your pulpit—and tell us just what justice and injustice happen to be? For as people such as Plato[33] and John Rawls[34] attest, it's not so easy to say." Thus, we have the mode which Gustafson calls "ethical": "observer-oriented," systematic, careful, and detailed.

For still others, ethics is all about telling a story of weal and woe, and much in between, often in moving and nuanced ways. So "narrative," which embraces what theory often cannot—the subtlety of affections especially may be left out—becomes for some a privileged if not the only legitimate mode of reflecting on and expressing the meaning of the moral life. Feminist ethicists among others have good reason for according narrative its proper place. Or, one thinks of the power of slave narratives and everything they can teach. It is understandable that some who turn to the Bible with its dramatic stories and its parables find ethics and narrative so closely joined.

For yet others, these three modes may be fine and good—unless you are the one who, caught in a web of contingencies often beyond your control, must take the moral bull by the horns and make a decision in the concrete, when this person's job or that person's health or, to bring it a little closer to our topic, this particular mining operation, or even an entire industry, such as coal or nuclear power, is on the line. So, the "policy" mode is a fourth way in which ethics may be conceived and carried out. The policies at issue can aim low or high. They can be close to home or bear consequences thousands of miles away, and it must be stressed, far into the future: whether to go on strike or cross a picket line; whether to bail out a bank or a nation in economic free fall; whether to become a party to the 1982 United Nations Convention on the Law of the Sea or the Paris Agreement on Climate Change.

Gustafson's point is that each of these "modes" or "varieties" of moral discourse is necessary; none is sufficient on its own. While in practice they often conflict, they may also complement one another. Each has its weaknesses, and each has its strengths. In this book, not all will be represented in equal measure and, to be sure, none will be represented in full. For instance, this book cannot possibly match the prophetic or narrative power of

Elizabeth Barrett Browning's "The Cry of the Children," a poem with much to say about the "ethics of mining" (to say nothing of factories) during the Industrial Revolution; of George Orwell's *The Road to Wigam Pier*, about the plight of England's coal miners; or of John Huston's cinematic tale of greed to the point of murder in *The Treasure of the Sierra Madre*. But this "prospector's report" will recommend that prophetic and narrative—indeed, sometimes deeply religious—voices will be sorely needed for mining morality in the days ahead. One chapter at least leans heavily on one activist-scholar's commitment to hearing the often-muted life stories of those in the field, particularly women. In a chapter on space mining we will turn to films to aid our inquiry. But prophesy and narrative are not the only valid modes of moral inquiry and expression; this prospector's report will recommend the need for other modes as well. The reader may also gain a sense that, at some level—the level of the human subject that, in Lonergan's terms, inhabits multiple realms of meaning[35]—these various modes do share a common ground.

MINING SITES

After a chapter devoted to assembling and explaining in more detail the prospector's tools, the plan of the book is to turn our attention, and our tools, to five mining sites—four on earth (with one on the ocean floor) and one in space. In one case, the tiny island-country of Nauru, a key investigator refers to that site as a "microcosm." But to a greater or lesser degree, this might describe other sites as well. Each site is distinctive and is yet connected to the wider world of mining and of morals in multiple, often complex ways.

This is certainly true of the first site to be explored in chapter 3 on Butte, Montana—"The Richest Hill on Earth," but also "a moral morass." It is on the list because of its autobiographical proximity to home, but that is by no means the only reason. In remarkable ways, "the battle for Butte"[36] was, and to a certain extent still is, emblematic of and thus a good introduction to the morality of mining in its several intertwining facets: geological, psychological, economic, cultural, political, communicative, and religious—and more. The moral gamut of Butte in earlier years ran from the beer that flowed in its bars to the money that flowed, or not, from Wall Street and beyond. Murder and mayhem, law and lawlessness, pollution and populism, lewdness and labor strikes, renegades and railroads, racism and robbery, daring and despair, boom and bust, oversized egos and outrageous acts, guns and greed, crassness and corruption—but also idealism and ingenuity, honor and honest labor, ethnic pride, geniality and generosity of a profound sort, to say nothing of humor—were all on display in Butte. They were all mixed in, just as hubris and humaneness worked side by side there in the mines, with implications for the morality of mining today and tomorrow.

Furthermore, the battle for Butte, especially as the nineteenth century turned into the next, was at once local, territory- and later statewide, *and* national. Thus, if we are to consider only one mining site within the United States, Butte is not a bad choice. In many ways, it points to all the rest—from the Comstock Lode in Nevada to the coal mines of West Virginia. But the battle for Butte was in certain respects also international. The controversial role played by the Industrial Workers of the World, or "Wobblies," on Butte's mining stage is but one example. The involvement of one of Butte's "copper kings" in Canadian mining is another. The role of international finance in Butte's history is a third. Most significantly, perhaps, the story of Butte is also the story of a powerful transnational corporation which, as we shall see, both joined and split two great mining sites. So, our study of Butte turns into a consideration of Chuquicamata, Chile, the "World's Greatest Mining Camp." This expansion of issues and geography already makes us mindful of one set of "prospector's tools," namely, international law. It leads us nicely into consideration of the other sites to be explored, each beyond the borders of the United States.

That we have left Butte for another part of the world, in terms of geography, mining, and meaning, becomes clear in chapter 4 when we turn to the tiny Pacific island of Nauru, some 5,800 m./9,300 km. from Silver Bow County in Western Montana. Here, the major issue was and is devastation caused by phosphate mining during the colonial period and, later, the "mandate" system of the League of Nations and the "trustee" system of the United Nations. From "Pleasant Island to phosphate plunder," one might say. Christopher Weeramantry of Sri Lanka, at the time a law professor at the Monash University in Australia, was commissioned by the government of Nauru to lead an independent investigation of the environmental effects of phosphate mining with a view to seeking reparations for this damage through the International Court of Justice where Weeramantry would later serve as a judge and vice president. In his book-length report on the commission's work (which extended to ten volumes), Weeramantry observed that Nauru, with its complex of problems related to mining (ecological, economic, political, cultural), "presents in microcosm an unusual variety of the great historical currents that have shaped the course of human affairs."[37] To understand this case, then, is to grasp much about the ethics of mining, especially its international dimensions, in a changing world—for instance, a world of migrants and refugees, such as those turned away from Australia and held on the island of Nauru today amidst protests of human rights abuse.

This site also introduces us to Weeramantry himself, whose vision of "one world"[38] integrates ethics, questions of cultural diversity, interreligious dialogue, and international law in ways that are perhaps without equal today. Thus, our prospecting for ethics will arguably expose us to a moral miner worthy of emulation. We will also consider here the ways in which a teacher can pass on to his or her students critical perspectives on law and other subjects. This teacher-student relationship returns us to an ancient question: Can ethics, or at least virtue, be taught?[39]

Chapter 5 moves us from an island in the Pacific to the ocean floor. The monumental 1982 United Nations Convention on the Law of the Sea, the reigning if still problematic agreed-upon way to govern the oceans,[40] included deep-seabed mining among its many interconnected topics. Should mining sites below the water's surface fall under the auspices of an international authority and somehow benefit humankind as a whole—including countries less well off, and generations still to come? Or should nations or major corporations with the wherewithal and the willingness to risk be allowed to strike out on their own, and take the lion's share if not all of what they bring to the surface and into the free markets of the world? Or is there some middle way?

These sorts of questions both furthered and frustrated the emergence of a new sea law. The more explicitly ecological questions that seabed mining raises were not far behind and are prevalent today. Catholic social thought has, especially of late, stressed care for the earth. But even if the vision found in Pope Francis's encyclical on concern for the environment, *Laudato si'*,[41] is compelling, the way to realize that vision may be less sure. At the very least, moving from vision to implementation will require international law. For that reason alone, it will be worth turning to the Law of the Sea—the result of one of the largest and most complex negotiating processes in history, and a leap forward for international law—to see what lessons we can learn.

While in certain respects, this chapter is the most explicitly "global" (some regarded the 1982 Convention on the Law of the Sea a "constitution for the oceans," and it may even be construed as a "constitution for the world"), it is also perhaps the most personal. That is, using especially prospector's tools borrowed from Lonergan, I draw on my experience of writing on this topic many years ago, and reflecting upon it since, to connect interiority to the ocean depths. Hopefully, this semiautobiographical approach will assist and not impede the reader's own personal attempts at mining morality.

Chapter 6 is perhaps the most philosophical and theological, as forays into uranium mining in Africa, with the help of historian Gabrielle Hecht, lead into a question of "ontology," namely, what does "being nuclear" mean and with what ramifications? In "The Missing Ethics of Mining," Safel Siegel complains that "we have more faith in our capacity to restrain or end violence and war than to address the ethics of mining." Whether Siegel is right about this is debatable. But turning our attention to the mining of uranium surely urges us to ask how the ethics of mining and the ethics of war, especially nuclear war, might be joined. Thoughts about the morality of, among other things, the bombing of Hiroshima, and the Manhattan Project behind it, lead to a discussion of the relationship between morality and *time*. Thus, the title of this chapter: "Uranium in Africa and Beyond: A Matter of Being and Time."

Our final site, in chapter 7, is beyond the bounds of earth. In the historically based film *October Sky*, Homer Hickham and his young rocketeer friends turn away from the coal mines of West Virginia and turn their eyes to outer space. Werner von Braun and Homer's heroic but headstrong coal-mining father will, for a time at least, do battle for Homer's heart and mind. In the end, Homer leaves West Virginia for an education higher than, or at least different from, the education the mines can offer, and he eventually lands at NASA.

Of course, Homer did not really leave mining behind since spaceships and satellites remain fully under the law of Butte: "Everything begins with mining." But now we have come full circle. What we are facing today is mining in outer space. Since actual mining has yet to occur, this might seem to be getting ahead of ourselves. But as space mining ventures such as Deep Space Industries and Planetary Resources tell us, we are not that far away. As will be explained in chapter 5, extant international space law provided some of the legal guidance for the emerging ocean regime. A little like science fiction, space law raises some interesting and important questions about who we are, earthbound as we may be. Asteroid mining, it turns out, is especially effective in generating such questions. These speeding bodies hold promise of untold mining-generated wealth. But a spate of Hollywood disaster films, along with some very knowledgeable people, warn us that the prospects of an asteroid crashing into the earth are also real. So, our ethical prospecting will view asteroids both as *opportunity* and as *threat*, especially *moral* opportunity and threat. With the help of Hollywood, but our prospecting tools as well, we will ask whether a focus on asteroid mining might yield an ethics for space aliens or for us.

PROSPECTING REPORT

In keeping with the intent of this book, the closing chapter takes the form of a brief "prospector's report," some further reflections on what mining morality might mean, and where signs of ethics-in-act might have been found among the veins and even the tailings of the various sites we have visited. The closing pages, then, are less a conclusion than an encouragement to further reflection and investigation. To develop an adequate ethics of mining would be a formidable, if worthy, undertaking. Moral measurements are not so easy in any case. Given its history, its variety, its enormous complexity and connectivity to virtually every other human activity under the sun and away from the light, to take the full moral measure of mining would be a monumental task.

Whether or not it is true, as a proverb has it, that "God writes straight with crooked lines," the fact is that, for us mortals, there are plenty of crooked lines—and twisting veins—to contend with when it comes to the ethics of mining. Still, human minds and hearts are not always morally slippery; sometimes they can be morally supple. Aristotle reminds us of this with his simple example of the "leaden rule used in Lesbian construction work" to measure an uneven surface on a rough-hewn wall: Take a ruler fashioned from lead and bend it to the curves; thus, you will get the proper surface length and shape. Ethics, says Aristotle, or at least that element of ethics called equity, requires a flexibility of this kind.[42]

But if this small example from the ancient world points us in the right ethical direction, it also leads back to our topic. Aristotle's flexible rule has its hidden or taken-for-granted origins. Leaden rulers come from lead-producing mines.[43] Once again, "Everything begins with mining." The proposition I close with here is that maybe the "everything" of this claim includes not only materiality but also reflection on the moral life. In the next chapter, this proposition will come into clearer focus as this reflection on the morality of mining begins by assembling and understanding a set of prospector's tools.

NOTES

1. Jesse Paul, "Animas River Fouled by 1 Million Gallons of Contaminated Mine Water," *Denver Post,* Aug. 6, 2015, http://www.denverpost.com/2015/08/06/animas-river-fouled-by-1-million-gallons-of-contaminated-mine-water/.

2. Vincent Bevins, "As Brazil Mine Spill Reaches Ocean, Its Catastrophic Extent Becomes Clear," *Los Angeles Times*, Dec. 20, 2015, http://www.latimes.com/world/brazil/la-fg-brazil-spill-20151220-story.html.

3. Jason Daley, "Brazilian Mine Disaster Leaves 58 Dead, 200 Missing," Smithsonian.com, January 28, 2019, https://www.smithsonianmag.com/smart-news/brazilian-mine-disaster-kills-dozens-and-covers-town-mud-180971358/#D6EbeHXuYjbluEXg.99.

4. This question, of course, gives rise to related questions, such as "Who is the *we*?" and "Does *ought* imply *can*?" We will try to be mindful of these questions, too, as we proceed.

5. This corresponds but only in a very rough way to a common, often overstated, distinction as discussed by Robin W. Lovin: "*Ethics*, the study of the choices by which we try to live a good life, is sometimes distinguished from *morals,* the practices

and beliefs by which people live. Ethics, then, is about thoughtful, reflective, and self-conscious decisions. Morals are the rules people follow without thinking about them" (*Christian Ethics: An Essential Guide* [Nashville: Abingdon, 2000], 16–17). Lovin does not endorse this distinction, especially today, and he uses the terms *ethics* and *morals* interchangeably.

6. Shefa Siegel, "The Missing Ethics of Mining," *Ethics and International Affairs,* Journal of the Carnegie Council, February 14, 2013, http://www.ethicsandinternationalaffairs.org/2013/the-missing-ethics-of-mining-full-text/.

7. The editors of a text on mining engineering put the first "mining (at surface), by Paleolith humans" at 450,000 B.C.E., and the first underground mining at 40,000 B.C.E." See Howard L. Hartman and Jan M. Mutmansky, eds., *Introductory Mining Engineering*, 2nd ed. (John Wiley & Sons, 2002; reprint New Delhi, Wiley India Pvt. Ltd., 2007), 7.

8. Plato, *Apology*, 38a,5–6, in *Essential Dialogues of Plato*, ed. Pedro de Bals; trans. Benjamin Jowett (New York: Barnes and Noble, 2005), 295.

9. The image of descending into mines has its limits. When it comes to mining in space (chapter 7), there will be a lot of ascending before any descending can begin.

10. For Socrates' allegory of the cave, see Plato, *Republic*, trans Francis MacDonald Cornford (New York: Oxford, 1945), 514a–520a. As for mining, Socrates was not unaware of its economic importance. According to Xenophon, Socrates suggests that Glaucon, who aspires to rule the city but seems woefully ill-equipped for the task, would do well to visit the local mines to learn why their productivity has waned. See Xenophon, *The Memorabilia: Recollections of Socrates*, trans. H. G. Dakyns (Macmillan and Co., 1897), Book III, Chapter 12.

11. Thomas Aquinas, *Summa Theologica*, trans. Fathers of the English Dominican Province (New York: Benziger Brothers, Inc., 1948; reprinted by Westminster, MD: Christian Classics, 1981) Part II–II, Question 24, Article 6 (hereafter: *ST* II–II, 24, 6).

12. Siegel, "The Missing Ethics of Mining."

13. For a humorous but insightful take on this "knack" from the cartoon Dilbert, see and hear https://www.youtube.com/watch?v=Dx6HojLBsnw.

14. Thomas Aquinas, *ST* I, 87, 1–4.

15. See Daniel K. Finn, "Recycling Isn't Enough: A Defense of Responsible Mining," *Commonweal Magazine,* May 2, 2017, 12–14. Finn, an economist and theologian and a major contributor to Catholic social thought, is, I believe, making an argument analogous to that of his fellow economist Tibor Scitovsky, who wrote about the very real moral dangers of consumerism. The problem, Scitovsky points out, is not that we are consumers; how could we not be? The problem is that we are often *bad* consumers, leading to less than true human satisfaction. See Tibor Scitovsky, *The Joyless Economy: A Psychology of Human Satisfaction,* Revised Edition (New York: Oxford Unversity Press, 1976; 1992).

16. I have in mind here not only Kant's famous *Prolegomenon to Any Future Metaphysics*, but also the prolegomenon to Hugo Grotius's *De Jure Belli Tres Libres* (*Law of War and Peace: Three Books*), which had a significant impact on the jurisprudence of seventeenth-century Europe and beyond.

17. For a discussion of the various elements that may come under the umbrella term "mining," see *Introduction to Mineral Exploration*, ed. Charles J. Moon, Michael K. G. Whately, and Anthony M. Evans, 2nd edition (Malden, MA: Blackwell Publishing, 2006), 1–18.

18. See especially Francisco de Vitoria, *De Indis* (On the American Indians), in Francisco de Vitoria, *Political Writings,* Cambridge Texts in the History of Political Thought, ed. Anthony Padgen and Jeremy Lawrence (New York: Cambridge University Press, 1991), 231–92. As we shall see (chapter 4), Vitoria's "relections" have their own place in the ethics of mining.

19. "While we rely on a tool or a probe, these are not handled as external objects. . . . We pour ourselves into them and assimilate them as part of our existence. We accept them existentially by dwelling in them" (Michael Polanyi, *Personal Knowledge: Towards a Post-Critical Philosophy* [Chicago: The University of Chicago Press, 1958; corrected version 1962], 59).

20. Hartman and Mutmansky, *Introductory Mining Engineering*, 47–95.

21. Bernard J. F. Lonergan, *Insight: A Study of Human Understanding*, 5th ed. revised and augmented, Collected Works of Bernard Lonergan, Vol. 3, ed. Frederick E. Crowe and Robert M. Doran (Toronto: University of Toronto Press, 1992).

22. Ibid., 95–96.

23. See especially chapter 1 of Bernard J. F. Lonergan, *Method in Theology* (Toronto: University of Toronto Press, 1990).

24. Emergent probability is discussed most fully in chapter 5, on the Law of the Sea and seabed mining.

25. This point is central in Marvin L. Krier Mich, *Catholic Social Teaching and Movements* (New York: Twenty-Third Publications, 1998).

26. For one study of and contribution to CST that takes this long view, see Daniel K. Finn, *Christian Economic Ethics: History and Implications* (Minneapolis: Fortress Press, 2013). See also Michael Schuck, *That They Be One: The Social Teaching of the Papal Encyclical 1740–1989* (Washington, DC: Georgetown University Press, 1991), which stresses that the social encyclical tradition predates *Rerum Novarum.*

27. For the text of the convention, see United Nations Convention on the Law of the Sea, https://www.un.org/Depts/los/convention_agreements/texts/unclos/unclos_e.pdf.

28. See, for instance, William P. George, "International Regimes, Religious Ethics, and Emergent Probability," *Annual of the Society of Christian Ethics* (1996): 145–70.

29. Neil Ormerod, Paul Oslington, and Robin Koning, "The Development of Catholic Social Teaching on Economics: Bernard Lonergan and Benedict XVI," *Theological Studies* 73 (2012): 391–421.

30. For example, prospecting in outer space has required the development of new kinds of probes.

31. "Bishops Seek Ban on Mining, Logging," *The Manila Standard,* December 9, 2008, republished by MAC: Mining and Communities, December 12, 2008, http://www.minesandcommunities.org/article.php?a=8996.

32. The paragraphs that follow draw on James M. Gustafson, *Varieties of Moral Discourse: Prophetic, Narrative, Ethical, Policy* (Grand Rapids: Calvin College, 1988).

33. Plato, *Republic*.

34. John Rawls, *A Theory of Justice* (Cambridge, MA: The Belknap Press of Harvard University Press, 1971).

35. Lonergan, *Method*, 81–89.

36. The phrase is from the title of Michael P. Malone's highly regarded *The Battle for Butte: Mining and Politics on the Northern Frontier, 1864–1906* (Seattle: University of Washington Press, 1981), a key text for chapter 3.

37. Christopher Weeramantry, *Nauru: Environmental Damage under Trusteeship* (Melbourne: Oxford University Press, 1992), 1.

38. *Towards One World* is the title of Weeramantry's three-volume memoirs.

39. This is a key question in Plato's *Meno*.

40. Even the United States, which is not a party to the treaty, accepts the vast majority of the convention as codification of customary international law.

41. Encyclical Letter *Laudato si'* of the Holy Father Francis, Our Common Home, http://w2.vatican.va/content/francesco/en/encyclicals/documents/papa-francesco_20150524_enciclica-laudato-si.html.

42. Aristotle, *Nicomachean Ethics*, trans. with intro. and notes, Martin Oswald (New York: Macmillan Publishing Company, 1962), Bk V, Ch. 10 (1137b, 28–31), 142.

43. One thinks of the lead mines in Galena, Illinois. Ulysses S. Grant returned there after a war to save the union and to end slavery and its suffering—in the fields, surely, but also in the mines.

Chapter Two

Assembling the Prospector's Tools

The aim of this chapter is to assemble the prospector's tools. As suggested earlier, this might conjure up for some images of pickaxes, shovels, and meal pans (or "rockers") for separating the gravel from the gold. Actual prospecting is more complex than that, as are the instruments employed. To give but one example, geophysical approaches to mineral exploration today include airborne surveys, magnetic surveys, radiometrics, spontaneous polarization, induced polarization, continuous-wave electromagnetics—and on and on.[1] This list does not extend to prospecting in space.

With reference to certain of these instruments, less technically inclined readers might ask, "What is that?" But such questioning is very much to the point. As explained earlier, by "tools" are meant, following Michael Polanyi, extensions of the human subject in the exercise of capacities for attending to the case at hand, for questioning, for imagining, for getting the point, for testing that understanding, for making judgments, for reaching decisions—only to raise more questions, to take the next theoretical or practical step, in an ongoing, cumulative way. Such acts of understanding and decision-making are very personal matters. But they just as surely rely on others, present or long departed, and they may be a matter of cooperative efforts of astounding extent and sophistication. As we are reminded by voices from the past, if we see farther and do better, we stand on the shoulders of giants—and less than giants, too.

With both the personal and the communal in mind, the tools I have chosen—or, that have chosen me—are fourfold: (1) Key insights and developed ideas from philosopher and theologian Bernard Lonergan (1904–1984); (2) the intellectual, moral, and theological fruit of the Catholic social tradition, as drawn together in Pope Francis's 2015 encyclical, *Laudato si': On Care*

Figure 2.1. Gold-mining prospectors near Nome, Alaska.
Photo by Wilhelm Hester (1872–1947).

for Our Common Home; (3) key aspects of international law as "ethics writ large"; and (4) the virtue of prudence, as understood by Thomas Aquinas. Here again, there are severe limitations: each of these on its own represents a huge topic that cannot be covered in any real breadth or depth. Admittedly, that is a loss. But the gain is that more than one set of tools is brought to the task. Here, the aim is simply to give the reader who may not be familiar with all or even any one of these a clear enough grasp of them so that he or she can better join in the prospecting in the chapters ahead.

Furthermore, as noted above, these tools are "self-sharpening." That is, just as one's mind may be sharpened by working through difficult problems, so, too, the tools may be improved as the prospecting moves ahead. So, for instance, Lonergan's insights may be enhanced or revised by discussing topics he did not take up in any direct way,[2] in this case mining as well as international law. The tools also may be sharpened as readers expert in, say, Catholic social thought or international law or the virtue theory of Thomas Aquinas add their own insights, in some instances correcting my own. The tools are also, in a sense, "interlocking." While the four are surely distinct, when juxtaposed or put in dialogue with one another, they are mutually or multilaterally illuminative and critical. At least I have found this to be so.[3]

INSIGHTS FROM BERNARD LONERGAN

Each set of tools already involves a certain kind of "mining," namely, reaching into the past for the sake of retrieval. In that regard it may be helpful to recall one of the sources of Lonergan's own thought, John Henry Cardinal Newman (1801–1890), and, more specifically, simply the title of one of Newman's best-known works, *An Essay in Aid of a Grammar of Assent.*[4] For present purposes, it is the first part of the title—*An Essay in Aid of*—that is most pertinent, for it seems to capture the aim and tone of much of Lonergan's work, especially his best-known work, *Insight: A Study in Human Understanding.* That is, what Lonergan presents in this monumental study is a rich and challenging aid for the reader to grasp and to affirm for himself or herself just what he or she is doing when he or she is knowing, why that is knowing and not something else, and what he or she knows by doing it.[5] By gaining "insight into insight," but also "insight into oversight" (understanding and confronting in oneself and beyond oneself the problem of bias), the reader may begin to "appropriate," or take ownership, of his or her process of knowing and decision-making, with the hope of living more authentically. It may be fair to say that Lonergan's later writings stress not just questions about knowing—"an understanding of understanding"—but also questions regarding valuing and loving, about doing and being responsible. With that in mind, I would emphasize that the "prospector's tools" of most relevance here may not be those provided by Lonergan but rather those already available to the self-reflective reader as he or she engages in what Socrates called "the examined life."

But this "turn to the subject" is not meant to end in solipsism, subjectivism, self-absorption, or narcissism. On the contrary, insight into insight is meant to open one up to what lies beyond the self, to new vistas to be explored. As Lonergan famously puts it, *"Thoroughly understand what it is to understand, and not only will you understand the broad line of all there is to be understood but you will also possess a fixed base, an invariant pattern, opening upon all further developments of understanding."*[6] The "further developments" are to be pursued not on one's own, as crucial as solitude may be,[7] but rather in the company of others—or, to borrow a phrase from Michael Polanyi, as a member of a "society of explorers."[8]

Nor is getting "insight into insight" an escape from this world and its perils. As stated in the subtitle to this book, the context for our prospecting is a "wounded world." Sensitive as he was to the lighter and darker chapters of history (*Insight* was written with fresh memories of the Great Depression, Hitler and Stalin, and two world wars), Lonergan proposes that such insight provides a basis for understanding what counts as "progress" in history, just as "insight into oversight" offers some hope of understanding and thus intervening in the dynamics of decline—the very sorts of questions about "progress" and "decline" that arise when one asks what mining adds to or subtracts from not only the true "wealth" but also the true "health of nations."[9] Insight into oversight includes coming to grips with the problem of "bias," starting with oneself but not ending there.[10] There is "dramatic bias," where needed insights and judgments for living a dramatic, engaged, and storied life are stymied in part because the kinds of images that give rise to needed insights about self and world may be suppressed. It's the sort of bias that might be partly undone when an "intervention" by loved ones helps a person suffering from an addiction to understand the hurt and harm his or her behavior brings and a possible way to move ahead. There is "individual bias"—a failure of human intelligence to transcend one's own needs and interests—to ask not just what's in it for "me," but also what's in it for an expanding circle of both "us" and "them."

There is the often pernicious "group bias," whereby my country, my culture, my political party, my race, my gender, my school of thought, my religion is thought to have a corner on truth and goodness, while others are surely mistaken, "wrong without remainder,"[11] or even down-right evil. And there is "the general bias of common sense," a stubborn anti-intellectualism, affecting both individuals and groups, that has little desire or time to think through from every needed angle big problems (say, climate change) when a sound-bite, an aphorism, a political slogan, a bumper-sticker dogma would seem to do just as well.[12] The fuller implications of Lonergan's abiding concern about what he calls the vectors of progress and decline, along with the theologically rich vector of "redemption," wherein grace, faith, religious love play a dynamic role,[13] should become more apparent when we turn to Catholic social thought.

Method

The kind of "prospecting" undertaken here requires a method, and this is in fact what Lonergan helps human subjects—say, readers of this book—to discover within themselves. The opening chapter of *Method in Theology* reviews the fundaments of this "transcendental method," namely, a "basic pattern of operations" "leading to cumulative progressive results."[14] These operations together constitute four distinct yet related levels of conscious intentionality, which may be summarized as Experience, Understanding, Judgment, and Decision.[15] The method is normative—not extrinsically, as what the teacher or The Party or The Company might say, but intrinsically as the knowing and acting subject is urged from within to abide by the "transcendental precepts": Be attentive, Be intelligent, Be reasonable, Be responsible.[16]

In one respect, there is nothing mysterious about this. Lonergan points out that "in a sense everyone knows and observes transcendental method. Everyone does so, precisely in the measure that he is attentive, intelligent, reasonable, and responsible."[17] To illustrate Lonergan's point with reference to mining, one might as ask: How many mine accidents are a result of someone not paying *attention*, or of not *understanding* the risks, of bad *judgment* in failing to treat the risks as real when the evidence is clear, or of *irresponsibility* when something of lesser value is placed ahead of, say, human life or health? Or, more positively, how many days go by with no accidents because people are neither asleep nor neglectful of their duties. In short, mining operations, like so much else, are a matter of human subjects' cognitive operations that are not without their affective dimensions. Miners and others may be very good knowers and doers, very methodical, very responsible, even if they cannot give a full and detailed account of what knowing and doing is.

But then, Lonergan goes on to say: "[I]n another sense it is quite difficult to be at home in transcendental method, for that is not to be achieved by reading books or listening to lectures or analyzing language. It is a matter of heightening one's consciousness by objectifying it, and that is something that each one, ultimately, has to do in himself and for himself."[18] In a related footnote Lonergan points out that "I am offering only a summary, that the summary can do no more than present the general idea, that the process of self-appropriation occurs only slowly, and, usually, only through a struggle with some such book as *Insight*."[19]

Now, the reader will find neither in this chapter nor in subsequent chapters anything approaching even the sort of summary of transcendental method found in chapter 1 of *Method,* to say nothing of what one might find within oneself and for oneself by working one's way through "some such book as *Insight*." Rather, the suggestion—the hope—is that, in some limited but perhaps important ways, grappling with the enterprise of mining at various "sites," both close to home and far away, will involve the reader in the sort of heightening of consciousness, and reflection on or "objectification" of that consciousness, that Lonergan proposes.[20] In other words, bringing mining a little closer to the center of moral consciousness might make more likely, more probable, what Lonergan calls "self-appropriation"—an appropriation or self-possession that does not end with the self.

There is much else in chapter 1 of *Method* that is pertinent to mining morality, for example, the observation that "method in theology" is but a specification of a "transcendental method" the envisaged results of which "are not confined categorically to some particular field or subject, but regard any result that could be intended by the completely open transcendental notions [of being and value]."[21] Further: "Transcendental method offers a key to unified science."[22] These are bold claims that can be neither fully explicated nor tested here. But I cannot overestimate their importance. As we shall see, both Catholic social thought and international law, and even prudence, would seem to assume, or at least seek, some sort of "unified science" that makes possible dialogue across disciplines, fields, and traditions—religious and other. It must be stressed, however, that the "unifier" is not likely to be some set of universally shared, immutable concepts, as important as shared concepts and frameworks might be, but rather the concrete human subject in conversation and cooperation with other human subjects[23]—raising and seeking to answer questions about any number of important matters, including the matters of mining and morality.

Functions, Realms, and Stages of Meaning

In the "foreground" chapters of *Method* Lonergan identifies further the sorts of notional tools that may be brought to bear on the topic of mining. Again, we must be selective. There are, to begin with, the various "functions"[24] and "realms"[25] of meaning which we can call to mind when discussing mining. Meaning has its *cognitive* function as we move beyond the child's world of immediacy into a world mediated by meaning, with its past and future, a world of meaning filled with possibilities but also threatened by error and even lies. Meaning has an *effective* function when it enables people to get things done—securing a loan, constructing a mine or a smelter, but also reducing pollution or treating silicosis and other mining-related diseases. The *constitutive* function of meaning is evident whenever and wherever "social institutions and human cultures," for instance the culture of coal country, "have meanings as intrinsic elements." Meaning is also *communicative* as human beings engage one another "intersubjectively, artistically, symbolically, linguistically, incarnately." These functions are abundantly evident in the world of mining; they are also to be found both in the Catholic social tradition and in international law.

As for "realms" of meaning, there is the world of *common sense*, wherein we relate things to ourselves, but also the realm of *theory* that relates things to one another: Not just "Twinkle, twinkle, little star," but a world of light-years and theories of relativity and black holes invisible to the eye. Not just owing your soul to the company store, but complex economic theories and econometrics. There is the realm of *interiority*, where common sense and theory may be carefully distinguished and related. There is the realm of *transcendence* that matches "an unrestricted demand for intelligibility," a transcendence that "criticizes every finite good," that "goes beyond common sense, theory, and interiority and into the realm in which God is known and loved." These realms of meaning will also be encountered as we go about our prospecting at various sites.

Meaning also has its stages,[26] evident, for instance, in Socrates' search not just for examples of virtue but for an understanding of what makes virtue *virtue*, and not something else. The topic of "stages" is a matter of some complexity. Here, I want to make two simple points. First, if meaning is a matter of stages, then we should not assume that a child is less than human simply because he or she has to move, say, from arithmetic to algebra to calculus, from ABCs to linguistic theory, or that an island people is somehow less than human, or "uncivilized," because their highly integrated way of life does not match their "discoverers'" remarkable achievements, such as a differentiation of consciousness or a degree of specialization that may, when things go awry, result in fragmentation, rigid compartmentalization, or the overly comfortable silos of higher education.

Second, as we shall see, Pope Francis writes about conversion from a "technocratic paradigm" to ways of thinking more conducive to care for "our common home." Perhaps this, too, may count as an advance in the stages of meaning. International law also has its "epochs,"[27] its "paradigm shifts," to which those prospecting for ethics, say on the island of Nauru or in the uranium mines of Niger, must be attuned. We should not be surprised if new questions shift the meaning of "the social question" taken up over the years by Catholic social thought, or even what we mean by "international law."[28] In short, there is always the possibility of breakthroughs or at least advances in meaning. Given the problem of bias and, theologically, sin, neither should we be surprised if meaning as well as values can suffer serious breakdowns, possibly ushering in a world of entrenched tribalism in place of creative concord, of gleeful deconstruction without reconstitution, of repeal without serious thought of replacement, the strange and troubling world of "alternative facts," of *Animal Farm* and *1984,* the phenomenon that Lonergan calls the "longer cycle of decline."[29]

The Human Good and Emergence

Under the heading of "the human good," we should pay special attention to two things. First is the notion of value that, with the aid of feelings that go beyond mere cravings, draws the self-transcending subject beyond himself or herself to the truly good. We should note especially the scale of values, advancing "from agreeable to vital values, from vital to social, from social to cultural, from cultural to personal, from personal to religious."[30] We should stress that values may be true or false. Vital values include such things as health and a good night's sleep. Social values include such things as the good of order—maybe a complex healthcare system serving all. Cultural values, higher on the scale, have much to say about what *kind* of ordered society will prevail. German society under the Nazis was very ordered but *culturally* very Aryan. *Personal* value "is the person in his self-transcendence, as loving and being loved, as originator of values in himself and in his milieu, as an inspiration and invitation to others to do likewise."[31] One thinks of Dieterich Bonhoeffer or Martin Luther King writing from prison, able to inspire others because they had found "the deep-set joy and solid peace, the power and the vigor," the *religious* value "of being in love with God."[32] We should note that the scale of values, emphasized by Lonergan and others, has affinities to the "complete development" of the Catholic social tradition.[33]

With the mention of "cultural values" we should emphasize Lonergan's distinction between a "classicist" view of culture, defined as "a set of meanings and values that informs a way of life," as opposed to an "empirical" or "historically-minded one"[34] that does not lock us in to one particular culture's view of the way things are and ought to be. As we shall see, such a distinction is key both for *Laudato si'* and for international law—for instance, in the latter's references to "civilized" and "uncivilized" nations. But for the moment we return to the scale itself and stress that it can prove to be an important set of tools for prospecting for ethics in virtually any mining site.

Especially important under the heading of the human good is the "good of order," mentioned above as a "social value"[35]: not just one good lesson for this one child, but an entire school or school system that works, where, through their attentive, intelligent, critical, responsible thoughts and actions, day after day, bus drivers and teachers and administrators and counselors and school boards and coaches and caring parents and others conspire to help students thrive. The relevance to mining operations will, on the surface at least, be obvious. Think of coal or copper miners descending and ascending, day after day, so long as nothing goes awry or the target ore is not exhausted or there is no labor strike. But consider that cooperative schemes of recurrence, or the good of order, can serve morally questionable if not reprehensible ends or "terminal values," as is the case of child labor in the mines. Then the relevance of values and value judgments that inform the good of order is more to the fore.

A focus on the good of order provides an entry point for at least introducing the worldview that Lonergan calls "emergent probability," with its higher schemes of recurrence emerging from lower schemes, and with its defensive circles that provide stability but that can join with bias of various kinds to block the emergence of higher, liberative schemes.[36] To anticipate, such liberative schemes may be found in the integral ecology envisioned by Pope Francis,[37] or in a more just and effective international law to match. When it comes both to the morality of mining and to the mining of morality, emergent probability is a particularly powerful and subtle prospecting tool. Its full relevance to our topic will become more apparent when we turn in chapter 5 to deep seabed mining and the *emergence* of the 1982 Convention on the Law of the Sea. But it is applicable not only there.

The notion of emergence, the prototype of which is "insight" (which we must recall lest we lose sight of the human subject)[38] also provides an opening to discuss an issue prominent both in recent Catholic social teaching and in international law, namely, the question of *intergenerational* justice, or concern for future generations. This is an issue that Lonergan does not address directly, but it is an issue that his "understanding of understanding," with its *anticipatory* character, is arguably able to address at least in part.[39] But the notion of emergence also calls to mind another theme about which Lonergan was quite explicit, namely, "the emerging religious consciousness of our time."[40] This emerging consciousness, shared by multiple traditions even in their distinctiveness, yearns for a truly unified humanity in the midst of alienation and fragmentation. As will be suggested momentarily, what Lonergan has in mind here would appear to be consonant with Catholic social teaching as expressed in *Laudato si'*—with its appeals to people of all faiths and of none to contribute to conversations about and active care for "our common home." Furthermore, there is reason to believe that this emerging consciousness may be discernible also in the practice of international law.[41]

Functional Specialties

Keeping in mind the notion of recurrent or "cooperative" schemes—cooperative for good or for evil, but hopefully for good—we return to *Method in Theology* and recall that theology is itself a collaborative enterprise with its own recurrent or cooperative schemes. This is especially apparent when we consider a central, if not the central, feature of that method, namely, the notion of "functional specialties." But since that method is "general," since it seeks a "unified science," so, too, it may be applicable to or discernible not only in the theologically rooted and theologically informed Catholic social tradition, but also in international law.[42] But that is not all. The central notion of functional specialties may apply, in various ways, to the massive and complex reality of mining in relation to the moral life. To show how this is so requires a brief discussion of functional specialties.

For Lonergan, the enterprise of theology has two phases: a *mediated* phase (basically, what has come before and where we are now) and a *mediating* phase (given where we are, including the shortfalls and shortsightedness we have uncovered and sought to correct, where we might want to go, and how we might get there). Theologians—or those working in other fields—may work collaboratively through these phases in eight functional ways:[43]

In the *mediated* phase:

1. *Research* (corresponds to level of "experience") makes available the relevant data for investigation. For theology, this means such things as texts and artifacts. But it can mean more than that, especially when our concern is mining. I will suggest that it extends to such things as the "experience" of miners and their families (Chapter 3 will focus in part especially on women's narratives), the sources of Catholic social thought, and the primary and subsidiary "sources" for international law recognized in Article 38 of the Charter of the International Court of Justice.
2. *Interpretation* (level of "understanding") attempts to understand the data, putting it in context—an undertaking that Lonergan suggests is "replete with pitfalls."[44] In theology one thinks of all that has been said about interpreting the Bible, but laws about mining (the famous "apex rule" in chapter 3) and international treaties and Latin-phrased legal principles about property (e.g., *terra nullius*, *mare liberum*, "common heritage") are open to interpretation, too.
3. When it comes to *history* (level of "judgment") Lonergan distinguishes "basic" history (who? what? when? where? etc.), "special" history of movements or doctrines or disciplines (e.g. art, or, for our purposes, mining practices or international law); and "general" history, "perhaps an ideal," in which basic history is informed by special history. Notably, Lonergan insists that theology cannot ignore general history, which would include, for instance, relations among religious traditions—and, we may assume, such movements as Marxism, global capitalism, environmentalism, nationalism, and human rights, each with its own nuances and complexities—all of which are eminently relevant to mining.
4. *Dialectics* (level of decision) deals with conflicts, contradictions, insights as well as oversights, in the service of seeking a more comprehensive point of view, a critical task that is aided by conversion. Seeking to understand the tradition(s) of international law will involve one in dialectics, and, as we shall see, one scholar-activist places great emphasis on the "contra-diction" she finds in the case of women in mining communities now finding their voice.[45]

In the *mediating* phase:

5. *Foundations* (level of decision) entails the objectification of conversion, "a transformation of the subject and his world,"[46] which while personal can

also be communal—not a fundamental set of doctrines, but rather a transformed horizon which allows those doctrines to be grasped, not only in, say, churches, but also in a union hall or even the World Court. While there is much to be said about conversion in relation to foundations, one point to stress is that conversion is ongoing and, in a sense, always incomplete.
6. Following from foundations, *doctrines* (level of judgment) "stand within the horizon of foundations. They have their precise definition from dialectic, their positive wealth of clarification and development from history, their grounds in the interpretation of the data proper to theology"[47] or, we might add, proper to international law.
7. *Systematics* (level of understanding) pursues the further questions raised by doctrines, let us say the doctrine of the Trinity in theology, but let us also say, in international law, the recently emergent "doctrine" of R2P (Responsibility to Protect), or the doctrine of "strict liability" for damage done to a small Pacific island through years of phosphate mining (chapter 4).
8. *Communications* (level of experience) is concerned with external relations which, for theology, might involve education, engagement of the arts, or use of the media. In the case of mining, "communications" might include, as we shall see, company-controlled newspapers, lobbying, or telling the public, through a website, what asteroid mining is all about and why investment is encouraged. Of course, international law is in multiple respects a matter of communication, often crucially so.

How might these functional specialties serve as "prospector's tools"? First, engaging the specialties can be an enormously complex matter. To give but one example: "Dialectic" in theology might require a sophisticated grasp of contending theological perspectives, positions, schools—as would be the case if the specialties were applied to international law. Still—*and this is a crucial point for all that follows*—in some, often undifferentiated, "common sense," or even muddled ways,[48] it seems that relative success or failure in these specializations may be discernible wherever and whenever individuals, groups, institutions, industries, even nations or the United Nations reflect on where they have been, where they find themselves, what needs to change (conversion), and how they are now meeting or going to meet the future and its challenges.

In other words, just as Lonergan explains that, by honoring in practice the "transcendental precepts," everyone follows "method" even if they are not able to give a full account of knowing and decision-making, so, too, it might be argued that people are quite capable of undertaking the "functional specialties" if only operationally rather than explicitly. So, those who have sought to tell the story of Butte—and, later, Chuquicamata—may very well be engaged in at least some of these specialties in implicit ways—and likely all of them if they pose the further, future-oriented question: "Now, given what we know of its past, where does Butte, where does mining, where do we go from here?"

To put this more generally: some version of the "functional specialties" as Lonergan lays them out would seem to be operative—or ignored—whenever one asks, with regard to mining or anything else: "Where have we been? How did we get here? Where do we stand? What went wrong? What needs to change? What is the right path to take from here? How do we communicate that path to others?" But the flow of the specialties might run in both directions. Looking ahead, say, to mining in outer space that has not yet occurred (chapter 7), or letting others (even future generations?) speak to us before we preach or teach, might just as surely cause us to look back, to help to clarify, to understand, to re-evaluate where we have been and how we might need to change course or change ourselves. In short, by asking where we are headed, we might be coaxed to ask just where we have been—and take delight in, or positively cringe at, what we see in the rear-view mirror.

Functional specialties can, I think, assume the role of a heuristic framework, one that can be applied to the massive and complex subject of mining, just as students of Lonergan have drawn on functional specialties to propose climate-change strategies.[49] As the notion of "specialty" would suggest, collaboration is key. In that regard, we should recall that Lonergan was intensely interested in the collaborative process that is *education*, with its plethora of disciplines and pedagogies.[50] Education is central not only to Catholic social *teaching* but also to international law.[51] While the topic could be taken up elsewhere, a focus on education leads us to consider Lonergan's twofold understanding of development—from *below*, basically a matter of discovery on one's own, and from *above,* through the example of others, through belief, through the cultural wisdom of elders, through creeds, and, sometimes, by way of law in its pedagogical function.[52] Or, to return to the phrase from Michael Polanyi, we "dwell in" what is handed to us by parents and coaches that care, by teachers and scholars, by poets and artists, by established paradigms and the rules of the game, by the example of leaders in the field. We "dwell in" these, and by doing so we just might "break out" with something creative and new.[53] To Polanyi's point but especially to Lonergan's, such dwelling means most radically dwelling in the transforming love of God.

Lonergan's Economics

In mining operations of various kinds, some will be trained in the use of certain tools that remain beyond the skillset of other workers, even if those others have a general sense of what those tools are and what they might do. Such is the case here. Lonergan's important forays, over the years, into economics are beyond if not my reach at least my grasp. But if only to further my basic premise about prospecting rather than mining in full, relying on others I will make what I hope are a few relevant comments about this critical dimension of his work.[54]

First of all, Lonergan's early work in economics, 1930–1944, and then much later, 1978–1983, was spurred by deep concern for the plight of workers and others who suffered under various economic systems with their booms and busts and other failures that denied a decent standard of living for all. Second, while he shared the moral concerns of Catholic social teaching, he was convinced that such teaching must not be reduced to moralism. Rather, one needed to respect the relative autonomy of economics and develop a theory that would point to an economic system that was respectful of democracy and, when it came to economic choices, the freedom of the intelligent many and not just the powerful few. He was looking to find an economy that truly works because its theoretical underpinnings, its foundations, were truly sound.

Third, along with the inadequacy of liberalism, Marxism, and Fascism due to their materialism, and their failure to fully respect the full scale of values, including the personal and transcendent realms, Lonergan was convinced that even the best available economic theories fell short of pointing the way toward the kind of equilibrium needed in a highly dynamic, changing world. Fourth, in a manner consistent with the image of "dwelling in" and "breaking out," his dissatisfaction with past and current economic theory did not impede his deep study of those who had come before. On the contrary, he immersed himself in what they had said and done.

The crux of his own economic theory, a new paradigm if you will, revolves around the relationship between what he called a "basic circuit" having to do with production, which will raise the standard of living (e.g., of workers and their families), and a "surplus circuit," a withdrawal from production to find innovative and better ways to produce. As Paul St. Amour explains, one can imagine withdrawing from fishing for a time, and being supported in that withdrawal, to devise and make a net that will increase production that will flow into the community. The key is to find an equilibrium between these two circuits. Everyone producing for consumption with no one in research and development, or vice versa, will not do.

What Lonergan has in mind here is far more complex than these few words suggest. The role of finance, for instance, needs to be understood. But they may be enough to usher in a few points to consider. First, it would be surprising if mining did not present a superb test case, or exemplar, for his theory. Mining does not only produce for the market, say, the market in smart phones with their requisite rare earth elements; it also produces for itself, as in the form of, say, better and more efficient techniques or tools. In terms of equilibrium, or lack thereof, one thinks especially of the asteroid mining to be discussed in chapter 7. For a time, everything is on the side of investment and of innovation of an amazing sort. But there is, as of now, no real production, no retrieval of ores to feed demand for, say, platinum, and raise the standard of living for others. Such an imbalance of surplus circuit over the basic circuit is not likely to last forever. Investors may get impatient and go elsewhere with their funds.[55]

Second, those seeking to bring Lonergan's economic theory to the task of mining morality would need to answer, it seems to me, the question of how both circuits deal with the question of "externalities"—so crucial when it comes to the concerns of *Laudato si'*. If, in the "surplus circuit," stepping back to devise a net (Paul St. Amour's example) will bring a greater production of fish, then one should not be surprised if the development of sonar and refrigeration can lead to overfishing and disputes when long-range fishing excursions lead one nation's fishing crews into another nation's traditional fishing grounds. Or, to return to the preface of this book, consider the history of Butte's massive lake of toxic water called the Berkeley Pit—just who pays for that?

But apart from these sorts of questions perhaps the equilibrium between "basic" and "surplus" circuits mirrors the ideal relationship between knowing and acting in the world ("basic circuit") and arriving at an understanding of one's own understanding and doing what Lonergan calls "self-appropriation" ("surplus circuit") on the other. Such a question is not only with reference to Lonergan. Taking time to follow along with Aristotle as he discusses ethics, especially in relation to what he calls politics, might aid one—or, more importantly, the community—in living a good life. But this is not to say one should spend all one's times dwelling on Aristotle's *Ethics,* for such dwelling is not what Aristotle says the good life is about. Put more simply, perhaps, Lonergan's economics, with its emphasis on an equilibrium between surplus circuit and basic circuit, may counsel an equilibrium between withdrawal (say, to Waldon Pond) and return (say, William Wilberforce's return to the antislavery fray after a joyful conversion), between examining one's life and actually living that life in the world. The alternative may be solipsism, self-absorption, or narcissism, on the one hand, or an utterly unreflective life on the other. In either case of disequilibrium, one may become a danger to oneself or, especially if immense power is mixed in, to the world.

Conversion

Finally, we should make more explicit that which has been implied: the importance of conversion—intellectual, moral, and religious: intellectual conversion in coming to a thorough understanding of understanding; moral conversion when mere satisfaction gives way to apprehension and commitment to living by the scale of values; religious conversion when one's whole life is transformed by the love of God. For if the issue is progress and decline, if the vector of redemption is operative and conscious in an emerging manner, then the topic of conversion will be integral to mining morality. This may become more apparent as we pick up other prospectors' tools. In fact, we may anticipate what we will find there by announcing that, as Neil Ormerod and Cristina Vanin have argued, Lonergan's understanding of conversion, extended by Robert Doran's understanding of "psychic conversion," provides an excellent framework for interpreting Francis's call in *Laudato si'* for what he calls "ecological conversion."[56] The nature of conversion and its importance—as well as its lifelong character—should become more apparent as we take our prospecting tools into the field.

Healing and Creating in History

Summaries of extensive and subtle matters are rarely satisfactory, and that may well be the case here. But perhaps I can take one more pass at our topic by referring to one of Lonergan's shorter writings, an essay entitled "Healing and Creating in History,"[57] even if I can only highlight a couple of points. The first is the example Lonergan chooses to show the need for "creating" in history through a cumulative and self-correcting process of insights, judgments, and decisions that constitute real progress. His example is the challenge of huge multinational corporations operating beyond the reach of effective governing structures, and thus the need to "create" such structures—a very daunting task. I note his example (he could have chosen others) because when it comes to mining, some version of this problem has long been with us and still exists—whether it be the sprawling Anaconda Copper Mining Company, operating both in Montana and in Chile (as we shall see in chapter 3), Chinese corporations buying up and working the mines of Zambia but skirting the mining regulations of a weakened government,[58] or the privatization and commercialization of outer space (chapter 7).

Thus, the need for "creating in history." But creativity alone, without the healing that flows from a love unmixed with hatred, will not do. This is the second point. There must be "development from above," as when one falls in love with God, as well as "development from below," when people apply intelligence to a task. As Lonergan puts it, "Just as the creative process, when unaccompanied by healing, is distorted and corrupted by bias, so too the healing process, when unaccompanied by creating, is a soul without a body."[59] One might suggest that the dual emphasis on healing and creating provides a fitting point of transition to Catholic social teaching, and especially the teaching of Pope Francis, with his emphasis not only on *healing* "mercy," divine and other, but also on *creative* and effective responses to an ecologically and otherwise threatened world. Arguably, the typically Catholic dual affirmation of "faith" and "reason" is pointing to the same thing. It is sometimes said that the most important word in the Catholic tradition is "and." This would seem to be a case in point.

THE CATHOLIC SOCIAL TRADITION AS EXPRESSED IN *LAUDATO SI'*

The second set of tools to be considered is found in the Catholic social tradition. I use this term to embrace what is ordinarily meant by Catholic social teaching, comprising the now extensive body of papal encyclicals and other "official" documents, but also "Catholic social thought," to which many not identified with the Church's "magisterium" have contributed,[60] as well as what might be termed "Catholic social movements."[61] Given the vast range of what this tradition entails, there is no way to summarize it easily. One could, of course, list the basic principles, themes, or "building blocks" distilled especially from official teaching.[62] Such lists are variously numbered and described, and there is great value in that—not least of which is at the level of the functional specialty of what Lonergan calls "communications."[63] Or, one could turn to the *Compendium of the Social Doctrine of the Church*[64]—but that is hardly a short summary, and it has its own restraints, beginning, perhaps, with the contested term "doctrine." Here, the reader will find a different approach. Drawing largely on the assumption that papal teaching self-consciously builds upon previous teaching and, to greater or lesser degrees, on the wider social tradition, the focus will be on the tradition as reflected in Pope Francis's important 2015 encyclical *Laudato si': On Care for Our Common Home*.[65] Not only do familiar principles inform this encyclical, sometimes with enhanced meaning, but the very nature of the encyclical indicates that ethics in the double sense captured by the phrase "mining morality" is more than applying principles—regarding, say, the dignity of the human person, the common good, or subsidiarity—to specific cases.

To give but two examples: *Laudato si'* followed upon and is closely related to Francis's earlier lengthy "exhortation," *Evangelii Gaudium—The Joy of the Gospel.* This linkage suggests that ethics can also be a matter of *exhorting*, of *calling*, of *reminding*, of *preaching* through word and deed—even as the *content* of that exhortation remains crucial and open to critique, theological and other.[66] Second, as I will suggest below, as a tool—or set of tools—for mining morality, *Laudato si'* "interlocks" with Lonergan in terms of "emergent probability." But this is true not only in terms of the implicit *message* of the encyclical that, with a sense of urgency, we must act to shift the probabilities that ecological and climatological disaster will be avoided or minimized. Arguably, the very *timing* of the encyclical's publication in May 2015 was intended to shift the probabilities that the Paris Conference on Climate Change, to take place a few months later, would succeed.

Even as we assume that *Laudato si'* represents well the Catholic social tradition, the encyclical itself defies easy summary, and, in keeping with the notion of "self-sharpening tools," it is open to a level of critique not found in these pages.[67] Here, we will attend to key aspects of the encyclical with an eye to the ways in which this set of prospector's tools meets with key insights from Lonergan, on the one hand, and the general topic of mining morality on the other. We will also have something to say in anticipation of the encyclical's relationship to international law, the third set of prospecting tools to be considered here.

There is to be found in this encyclical plenty of language of indictment, what James M. Gustafson identifies as characteristic of a "prophetic" mode of moral discourse. Yet that is not its starting point. Reaching back to his namesake, St. Francis of Assisi, the pope's starting point is praise of God for "our common home," which, by way of mediation gives us access to the divine (9). Thus, the profoundly theological and, indeed, sacramental character of the encyclical is immediately to the fore—a mediational, or sacramental, starting point that renders "nothing in this world . . . indifferent to us" (3). This introduction foreshadows prominent themes and emphases to be found in the pages that follow: the need for a "global ecological conversion" (5); the need for all to unite in common concern (7f.) in the face of, among other challenges, a structurally dysfunctional economy (6); nature, and all that it includes, as viewed by St. Francis, "as a magnificent book in which God speaks to us and grants us a glimpse of his infinite beauty and goodness"; the need for a conversation "which includes everyone," each contributing "according to his or her own culture, experience, involvements, and talents"[68] (7); and the critical role of science, but also a strong critique of "new forms of power derived from technology" (16).

What Is Happening to Our Common Home?

In chapter 1: "What is happening to our common home?" Francis sets out to provide "a fresh analysis of our present situation." The picture is not encouraging. Perhaps best captured by his observation that "the earth, our common home, is beginning to look more and more like an immense pile of filth" (21), Francis discusses at some length various aspects of our situation: pollution and climate change—including the claim that climate itself is a "common good" (23); the huge and complex issues surrounding water, and the claim that *"access to safe drinkable water is a basic and universal human right"*—and, with reference to our topic, how mining practices pose a threat to that right (29, emphasis in original); loss of biodiversity (32–42); the fate of the oceans (40); the decline in the quality of human life and the breakdown of society—in the course of which he discusses "the throwaway culture" (43); the loss of contemplation and, by contrast, "true wisdom, as the fruit of self-examination, dialogue and generous encounter between persons" rather than "a mere accumulation of data which eventually leads to overload and confusion, a sort of mind pollution" (47); and the fundamental and seemingly intractable problem of global inequality, in the context of which mining again receives mention. As the reader may imagine at this early point, most, if not all, of these themes may be related to the practice of mining in some way.

But analysis of our situation is not enough. So, in this early chapter Francis begins to discuss responses—weak inadequate ones, mostly, due to an unconverted culture, lack of political will internationally, sheer denial of the problems besetting us, and sometimes war (57). In terms of interlocking elements from Lonergan, one can discern here—as throughout the encyclical—the spiraling dynamic of experience, understanding, judgments of fact and of value, moving toward decision. If one level seems especially prominent in this opening chapter, it is that of experience—of attentiveness to the givens, the data, of our situation. On the other hand, the turn to experience is already driven by a *question*: "What is happening to our common home?" In short, as is the case for Lonergan, and as was the case for Lonergan's great mentor, Thomas Aquinas, the spirit of inquiry is at the heart of the matter.[69]

Creation and Our Common Home

The opening of chapter 2 is remarkable for its candor: "Why should this document, addressed to all people of good will, include a chapter dealing with the convictions of believers?" (62). Francis is aware that his religious views are not shared by all, sometimes to the point of dismissal or disdain. Still, he is convinced that "science and religion, with their distinctive approaches to understanding reality, can enter into an intense dialogue fruitful for both" (62). So, in this chapter he presents a biblically based view of creation with its basic themes: We are not God; we are called to cooperate with God in caring for creation; each and every creature manifests God (85); the goods of the earth are meant for all; creation and Christology are intimately linked.

With reference to Lonergan, we might stress the importance of a more adequate interpretation of scripture to counter misinterpretations of past and present.[70] Given the emphasis on revealed truth found here—whether accepted by all or not—we should also recall Lonergan's emphasis on "development from above."[71] In this respect, this chapter is eminently Catholic (capital "C") in its approach: both faith and reason are affirmed, with dialogue open to all and in need of all, serving as the nexus. While this point would need to be developed, it seems consistent with this encyclical, with Lonergan's thought, and with the Catholic tradition to see "dialogue"—for example, the dialogue between science and religious traditions—as a locus of grace.

Leaving the Technocratic Paradigm Behind

In a manner that recalls Lynn White's classic *Science* article "The Cultural Roots of Our Ecological Crisis,"[72] chapter 3: "The Human Roots of the Ecological Crisis" presents perhaps Francis's most critical remarks on what another insightful writer, Robert Heilbroner, called "the human prospect."[73] This section focuses on one of the roots, if not the root, of our arguably dire situation, namely, an unreflective commitment to the "technocratic paradigm." We are moving headlong into the future with little regard for the devastating effects of technology—not least of all on the human spirit. "A tendency to believe that every increase in power means 'an increase of progress itself'" (105) has led us to where we are. This paradigm, to the degree that it prevails, begs for its reversal.

Clearly, Francis is not espousing a new Udditeism, for "[t]echnoscience, when well directed, can produce important means of improving the quality of human life," including art and beauty (103). The problem is lack of proper direction, a symptom—but also a cause—of which is a "practical relativism" which fails to grant that "we are not God." Thus, Francis's concern is to steer us toward a new (but arguably also old) paradigm which is a Christian anthropology, a true humanism, properly understood, to replace the errant anthropocentrism which modernity has bequeathed to us. This anthropology will include, among other things, a dimension of human living so central to the Catholic social tradition, namely, the proper place of work and employment—threatened in so many ways in our time (124f.). Francis closes this section with a focus on a specific kind of technology that has become problematic, namely, biotechnology. No doubt this focus of the encyclical deserves comment, but in light of our overall topic, let me say that this chapter could just as easily have taken up the range of technologies tied directly or indirectly to mining, such as "fracking." To make that point in abbreviated form, let us not forget that in one case at least, that of uranium mining (the topic of chapter 6), the technologies at issue are tied to nuclear power and to weapons of mass destruction more devastating than the bombs dropped on Hiroshima and Nagasaki.

There are further ways in which, at this point, the "prospector's tools" found in *Laudato si'* interlock with key insights or themes from Lonergan. Here, I note a theme that pertains to the encyclical as a whole, but that is especially close to the surface here. The "technocratic paradigm" that so concerns Francis would seem to lend itself to discussion under the heading of "the longer cycle of decline," the fruit especially of the "general bias of common sense," with its short-term and surface-level thinking and acting. If this Lonerganian reading of *Laudato si'* is anywhere near the mark, then it provides enlightenment for a way forward in a project focused on mining morality: simply propose some ways to slow or reverse this decline. But in this suggestion, there is little cheer. For Lonergan asks in *Insight,* "Why, then, is it that the longer cycle is so long? Why is the havoc it wreaks so deep, so extensive, so complete? The obvious answer," Lonergan submits, "is the difficulty of the lesson that the longer cycle has to teach."[74] If Lonergan is correct about this, then this points up the profound challenge with which Francis is dealing. As he stresses in the next section, "everything is connected," and for proper care of "our common home" everyone must be on board the dialogical train. But this is no easy task. We may learn the lessons we need to learn only the hard way. Perhaps it is the law of the cross.[75]

Everything Is Connected: "Integral Ecology"

It would seem that chapter 4: "Integral Ecology" is meant to tie everything together. Here, Francis stresses that "we are faced not with two separate crises, one environmental the other social, but rather one complex crisis that is both environmental and social." Thus, "Strategies for a solution demand an integrated approach to combating poverty, restoring dignity to the excluded, and at the same time protecting nature" (139). In accord with what Lonergan stresses about a *scale* of values, sheer economic growth is not the answer. What is needed is an "'economic ecology' capable of appealing to a broader vision of reality" (141). Such a vision includes civic virtue and law. In anticipation of our third set of prospecting tools, international law, we note Francis's insistence that loss of respect for law undermines the common good. A deep respect for cultures, especially local cultures, is also integral to this vision and strategy.[76] As Francis points out, "Culture is more than what we have inherited from the past; it is also, and above all, a living, dynamic and participatory present reality, which cannot be excluded as we rethink the relationship between human beings and the environment" (143). Nor can we exclude from our sphere of concern what Francis calls "the ecology of everyday life" (144–152), threatened as it is by inadequate housing, poor transport, unstable neighborhoods with no breathing spaces, and a fundamental lack of respect for the body and thus a proper environment.

If the earlier parts of *Laudato si'* emphasized attempting to *understand* our dire situation, an understanding theologically informed, chapter 5: "Lines of Approach and Action" presents "an outline of the major paths of dialogue which can help us escape the spiral of self-destruction which currently engulfs us" (163). Returning to Lonergan, we might say that the emphasis now is on the fourth level of conscious intentionality, namely, decision and action—or, it might be linked to those "functional specialties" that tell us where to go from here. And immediately Francis turns to the international realm and the dialogue needed there, stressing that "[b]eginning in the middle of the last century and overcoming many difficulties, there has been a growing conviction that our planet is a homeland and that humanity is one people living in a common home" (109).

Here, we note a congruence with Lonergan's thoughts about an "emerging religious consciousness" that is also a consciousness of a movement toward a common humanity. Indeed, in keeping with Lonergan's notion of emergent probability, the pope states that "interdependence obliges us to think of *one world with a common plan*" (163, emphasis in original). Such a plan will, among other things, guide us toward "enforceable international agreements" and "global regulatory norms [that] are needed to impose obligations and prevent unacceptable actions, for example, when powerful companies dump contaminated waste or offshore polluting industries in other countries" (173). Given the ineffectiveness of current regulations, for example regarding the oceans, "what is needed, in effect, is an agreement on systems of governance for the whole range of so-called 'global commons'" (174). Due in part to the weakening of the traditional nation-state in the face of prevailing economic and financial sectors, "it is essential to devise stronger and more efficiently organized international institutions, with functionaries who are appointed fairly by agreement among national governments, and empowered to impose sanctions" (175).

Since these proposals might raise for some the specter of a "world state," it will be good to pause at this point and address this issue both from the point of view of the encyclical itself and with reference to Lonergan. In terms of the encyclical, it must be said, first of all, that what Francis is proposing is in accord with what previous popes, notably Benedict XVI and, earlier, John XXIII had said (175).[77] Second, while Francis does not use the term "subsidiarity," so central to Catholic social teaching, this notion—that the higher levels of government are to be subsidiary to the lower levels, exercising authority when the lower levels are unable to address challenges on their own—is arguably kept in view. So, we have Francis's deep concern about respecting the integrity of local communities. We also note that he is not calling for the complete abandonment of national sovereignty (175). Indeed, immediately after his call for new and better forms of international government comes a similar call for "dialogue for new national and local policies" (176–181). Third, and most important, Francis's call for global governing structures cannot prescind from what might be summarized as "ecological conversion" (140–143) and all that that entails. Arguably, this kind of conversion will be nurtured to the degree that other "lines of approach and action" urged in this section of the encyclical are undertaken. These "other lines" include "dialogue and transparency in decision-making" (182–188); "politics and economics in dialogue for human development" (189–198); and "religions [note the plural] in dialogue with science" (199–201).[78] These are hardly descriptors of a "world state," especially of any dystopian kind.

What might be some connections to Lonergan? There are many, a few to which I have already drawn attention; others will surface as we proceed. But here, with regard to legitimate concerns about the emergence of an oppressive "world state," we note Lonergan's stress on the importance of conversion will be increasingly important the more that power, coercive and other, is involved. To the degree that emergent probability is relevant here—as more comprehensive governing structures emerge from lower schemes of recurrence—it should be recalled that there is no guarantee that schemes of recurrence, serving the good of order, will be in the service of values rather than disvalues. Thus, the scale of values, which are arguably congruent with "ecological conversion," must be kept fully in view at all levels, including the international or global. Furthermore, as Patrick McKinley Brennan argues in his discussion of Lonergan and law,[79] the transcendental precepts (Be attentive, Be intelligent, Be reasonable, Be responsible) are at the core of law that truly serves the human community—the kind of law that Francis has in mind. This may be as true for "enforceable international agreements" and other forms of international law (custom, widely accepted legal norms) as it is for law at the national and other juridical levels. [80] Finally, one might at least hypothesize that Francis's attention to "another form of progress and development" bears an affinity to the kind of "progress" envisioned by Lonergan, one that relies not only "healing" but also, as Francis stresses (191), "creativity" in history.[81]

A Closing Ray of Hope

Pope Francis concludes his encyclical with reflections on "Ecological Spirituality and Education." That the two are treated together is significant. At the heart of this section is the call for an "ecological conversion" in the face of immense challenges that seem insuperable. Francis laments a consumerist lifestyle that has benefited neither the rich nor certainly the poor. But then in a manner echoing Lonergan's thoughts on the three vectors operative in history (progress, decline, and redemption), Francis offers this ray of hope:

> Yet all is not lost. Human beings, while capable of the worst, are also capable of rising above themselves, choosing again what is good, and making a new start, despite their mental and social conditioning. We are able to take an honest look at ourselves, to acknowledge our deep dissatisfaction, and to embark on new paths to authentic freedom. No system can completely suppress our openness to what is good, true and beautiful, or our God-given ability to respond to his grace at work deep in our hearts. (205)

Ecological conversion will, in Francis's view, both require and enable a new ecological lifestyle (203–208), and it will also mean "educating for the covenant between humanity and the environment" (209–215). Such education will go beyond attention to science and consciousness-raising to include, among other things, critiques of modernity's views on progress, and efforts to find ecological equilibrium at various, interconnected levels (210). It will also entail education in the virtues required to abide by the demands of this covenant (211)—virtues the practice of which make a difference even when they are mostly unseen, for instance, within the life of the family (213). The fruits of this conversion will be joy and peace, but also "civic and political love" (228–232). The encyclical ends on high theological notes, stressing the sacramental—especially Eucharistic, Trinitarian, and Mariological meaning and grounding of all that has come before (233–242). This theology extends to two prayers, which Francis offers as the final words of a lengthy reflection that has been "both joyful and troubling" (243). Notably, the first is meant for "all who believe in a God who is the all-powerful creator," while the other is explicitly Christian—another sign of Francis's appeal to an "emerging religious consciousness" that exceeds Christian bounds.

INTERNATIONAL LAW

The third set of "prospecting tools" is gleaned from the world of law, and within that world, international law. If the aim of the project is prospecting for ethics at various moral mining sites, then it must be acknowledged that the relationship between law and ethics in general, and international law and ethics in particular, is a problematic one. But since the intent here is not some finished ethical treatise on mining, but rather the more modest aim of prospecting for ethics, there are to be expected questions left unanswered or not properly asked—or questions posed for the sake of future exploration, extraction, and refinement.

There is another problem, of course. International law, both as a "normative system" (with its principles, norms, rules) and as an "operating system" (treaty negotiation, political processes, institutions, etc.) to generate norms and render them effective, has a long and complex history that may be quite unfamiliar even to its practitioners.[82] Thus for present purposes the need to be selective and tentative should be clear as I focus on only certain aspects of international law that, in ways to become more apparent as we proceed, pertain to mining morality. I will also be especially attentive to ways in which international law interlocks with the other prospecting tools we have discussed.

International Law as "Ethics Writ Large"

First, the need to distinguish law from ethics notwithstanding, it is reasonable, I believe, to think of international law as "ethics writ large."[83] By that I simply mean that, if ethics has to do with reflection—more or less systematic—on the basic question, "How ought we to live?" with some hope of actually living in that way, then arguably international law represents one ongoing, sometimes unfolding, sometimes stymied attempt to answer that question with regard to border crossings of various kinds and a vast range of issues: human rights, including the possible rights of future generations; the peaceful settlement of disputes; war when peace-making fails or is barely tried; trade and commerce; labor; travel; communications; the "global commons" and their governance; technology of all kinds; the environment; global climate change—and more. So, too, does the breadth of international law become apparent if we consider its "sources"—numerous multilateral and bilateral treaties; "custom," with all the messiness this term conveys; widely recognized legal principles; and, in a subsidiary way, court decisions and the writings of leading legal scholars.[84] Of course, international law sometimes deals quite directly with mining,[85] or extractive industries, but just as it has been said that "everything begins with mining," so also does the "moral life" have to do with topics of all kinds. Thus, even though our focus is mining, international law in its broader sweep is our real concern.

Second, as just proposed, international law in its own way raises and seeks to answer the question "How ought we to live, here and now, but also as we race into the future?" In fact, as any good textbook in international law will show, international law is, at root, a matter of asking and answering all sorts of questions—many of them quite open-ended and often hotly contested.[86] So, if international law has something to do with ethics, and if it may be related to the other prospecting tools discussed above, then the primary connection will be not some abstract framework but rather human "subjects," individually and together, capable of raising and answering questions as they emerge in the concrete: questions about the Richest Hill on Earth (Butte, Montana), linked by a giant company named Anaconda to the Greatest Mining Camp in the World (Chuquicamata, Chile) (chapter 3); about a small island devastated by years of phosphate mining at the hands of foreign powers (chapter 4); about who should lay claim to and benefit from mineral resources on the ocean floor (chapter 5); about the uranium of Africa that, once processed, ends up in nuclear power plants and nuclear weapons (chapter 6); about asteroid mining and the commercialization of outer space (chapter 7). Since we are stressing the questioning *subject*, it is worth noting that international law places great stress on who, in international law, counts as a "subject": individual countries or "states" only? international organizations? transnational corporations? the individual? While arguably states remain, quite problematically, the primary subjects of international law,[87] it is worth noting one very lengthy, and historically and philosophically sophisticated, argument that the category of "international legal personality" most certainly extends, or should extend, to *the individual person*.[88]

Of course, international law could be, too, and no doubt sometimes is, a matter of casting aside important questions, of suppressing or failing to meet them due to bias of various kinds. For instance, it is not without good reason that women and others underrepresented in the world of international law have had to make their voices known.[89] As we shall see, a law student involved in the Nauru case would later argue that international law has yet to shed its imperialistic past.[90] In any event, with sustained juxtaposition to Lonergan and to Catholic social thought as expressed in *LS*, the connections become increasingly apparent. Here, I will focus all too briefly on five ways in which international law may interlock with Lonergan and, in the process, with Catholic social thought as well: (1) International law and theology, including theological ethics, share a common method; (2) that common method deals with—or fails to deal with—progress and decline; (3) international law can be understood in terms of emergence and emergent probability; (4) its "secular" character notwithstanding, international law may express what Lonergan called "the emerging religious consciousness of our time"; (5) key to the emergence of more effective law will be conversion.

A Common Method

Here we recall what Lonergan means by *method* in theology, both in the sense of human subjects operating consciously but often unreflectively on the four levels of conscious intentionality, and in the fuller sense of self-appropriation.

Thus, we can simply say that those engaged in international law (lawyers, but others as well) engage in method, too, yielding the "cumulative and progressive results" we call international law. That is, they attend or fail to attend to the relevant data; they interpret that data badly or well; they make judgments, both of fact and of value, about the soundness of those interpretations; and they make decisions of various kinds. It is also quite possible to discern in the extraordinarily complex workings of international law the various functional specialties around which Lonergan argues theology may be understood[91]—just as it would be possible to use the eight specialties as an organizing principle to read and interpret what is moving forward in *Laudato si'*. Any of these specialties might be discussed at length. Think, for example, of the relationship between "research" and the "sources" of international law, or "interpretation" as applied to treaties. In fact, we will have occasion to show how two individuals, each in his own way, engaged that method by applying themselves to critical cases at hand.[92]

Here may be singled out, with slightly less brevity, two functional specialties. One is the profound role that "dialectics" plays in international law, so much so that one prominent legal scholar has judged international legal argument to be inherently unstable, vacillating as it does between the "utopian" claims of universally binding norms, on the one hand, and the "apology" that international law actually responds to the realities of international politics, on the other.[93] Even in the case of this eminent scholar and practitioner of international law, there would appear to be on his part a more fundamental desire to settle this matter—or at least making peace with it—for the sake of establishing solid foundations for moving international law forward.[94] Other differences, related or not, include the basic, if quite complex, conflict between "natural law" and "positivism," as well as the various methods[95] and theories[96] employed by scholars and others, especially more recently. This includes Third World approaches to international law (TWAIL), as well as feminist approaches which, we will see, also come into play when considering copper mining in Butte, Montana, and in Chuquicamata in Chile.

The other functional specialty is what Lonergan calls "communications." I stress this because, in terms of method in *theology*, it is here that, for Lonergan at least, engagement of carriers of meaning and value other than theology (e.g., academic disciplines, cultures, practices) is paramount. Furthermore, it may be argued that "communications," in a broad sense, is a *raison d'etre* of international law itself. International law provides a language (stable yet subject to change), a means, a practice for states and other international actors to engage one another, to cooperate, to avoid or at least lessen the chances that wars or other calamities will occur. If to this is added the possibility that international law provides a "suprastructure" for an underlying "emergent religious consciousness" that seeks unity among all peoples (to be discussed below), then international law might even be construed as a kind of "practical theology."

Finally, we should recall Lonergan's point about method in relation to a "unified science." This is a topic too extensive for comment here, but it may be enough to stress that international law lends itself—indeed, requires—interdisciplinarity. As the eminent jurist Manfred Lachs stressed over thirty years ago, "International law has entered into fields of a scientific and *theological* character, and it cannot be made, interpreted or applied without taking into account almost all the sciences; from physics, chemistry and biology to spheres concerning communications and transport. While all of them need law's guiding hand, they may play an important part in assisting and inspiring the law-making process."[97] Surely, Lonergan's understanding of method and of the human subject can both affirm and inform Lachs's as well as Francis's assessment of the interdisciplinary boundary-crossing needed today.

Emergence and Emergent Probability

The general topic of international law and emergence deserves more discussion that it can receive here. Here I simply stress that, since mining, together with its many effects (climatological, ecological, economic, political, sociological, etc.), has its lower and higher schemes of recurrence in the service of values as well as disvalues, and since mining has much to do with international law, then emergent probability should prove to be a useful tool for ethical prospecting, and for mining morality. How so?

International law is a dynamic reality, an arena of slow developments, of breakthroughs and breakdowns, of expansion and sometimes contraction. In short, it is a matter both of emergence and of probabilities for that emergence and the sustainability of that which emerges. Consider, for instance, the lower schemes of cooperation that can give rise—or not—to an important treaty, let us say the 1982 Convention on the Law of the Sea,[98] or on the climate change that occupies Pope Francis in *Laudato si'*. Or, think of the law-generating United Nations Charter, emerging from the ashes of the Second World War, a multilateral treaty designed, in part, to shift the probabilities that "succeeding generations" would be saved "from the scourge of war." Or, again, think of the emergence of the Universal Declaration of Human Rights, the emergence of which was by no means assured but was made more probable by the convergence of just the right conditions at just the right time.[99] The "lower schemes" in question can be low-level meetings or formal rounds of negotiations, or, in the case of customary law, the behavior of states. But at a more fundamental level the schemes in question are the recurrent and cumulative spiral of insights, judgments, and decisions that condition the emergence of new laws and institutions and programs—an emergent international criminal court, or a regional seas program of the United Nations Environment Program. As a reminder that these lower schemes can serve disvalues as well as values, that international law can court decline as well as progress, we might note that international law includes a kind of norm called *jus cogens*, or peremptory law, to serve as a check on the wayward legal actions of states. We might note, too, that evident "progress" in international law, for instance the establishment of the right to self-determination, may have unintended consequences, such as a fragmentation of the world that threatens not only order but the very justice that everyone seems to want. I will return the connections between emergent probability and international law in chapter 5.

With regard to progress and decline, it may be appropriate at this point to return to a question posed above regarding "stability" in ethics and in international law. One might ask whether there should be at the level of decision, of enacted policy, of established law (*lex lata*), certain "settled points" so that we can build upon these and move on. So, for instance, Francis looks for such stability when he says that policies need to outlive the governments that enacted them, if they are to do their work (181), and there is something similar found in international law: "states" are more permanent than particular "regimes." But there is a downside to this: future generations can be saddled with the sins of their elders—for example, when one regime takes all the money, leaving succeeding regimes with massive debt.[100] This is not to resolve the problem of stability and change; it is to recognize it as a problem continually to be addressed. It is a problem to be addressed in part when, we ask, in relation to the "ends" of mining—in this case of uranium (chapter 6)—whether it is possible to settle, once and for all, the question of the legality ever to use or threaten to use weapons with unspeakable power to destroy.

International Law and Religious Consciousness

International law is a largely secular matter, part and parcel, it would seem, of what Charles Taylor has called a "secular age."[101] There is no denying this—at least on the surface. But without turning back the clock to the age of Vitoria, Suárez, and even Grotius, when religion and law were closely joined, it may yet be possible to detect or discern within the workings of international law—that is, among the "subjects" of international law—signs of an underlying emergent religious consciousness. Put in Lonergan's terms, it might be possible to view international law as a "suprastructure" expressive of an underlying prereflective "infrastructure" of an emerging religious consciousness that, in the face of alienation, is consciousness of a common humanity.[102]

At least one leading expert on law and religion has affirmed this line of thinking. Toward the end of his review of Mark W. Janis and Carolyn Evans, *Religion and International Law*, the late Harold Berman posed a question: "In a multicultural, multireligious world, what, if any, common faith can provide a basis for legal institutions that will support world peace against potential aggressors, and universal human rights against oppressive governments?" He then turned to a contribution in that volume from the present writer for one answer, which was, in Berman's words, "surprisingly," the proposal of "a common faith in the underlying 'global ethic' of international law itself."[103] After discussing this "one answer" at some length, he closed the review in this way:

> This, indeed, may be the final word in the analysis of the interaction between religion and international law in a multicultural, multireligious world: that not only Roman Catholicism and Protestantism, as in the Grotian paradigm, but all great faiths, including some forms of humanism, may unite in affirming the presence of a transcendent spiritual element—a holy spirit—in the processes of making, interpreting, and applying international law itself.[104]

If this is in fact the case, if international law has its tacit religious or transcendental dimensions, and if international law is a suitable tool for prospecting for ethics at selected sites, then perhaps this most secular carrier of meaning and value might bring closer to the surface of consciousness the religious dimensions of both mining and the moral life.

International Law and Conversion

The theme of conversion—or, better, conversions—is central to Lonergan's writings, and it clearly plays a central role for Francis and Catholic social thought. As we have seen, *Laudato si'* is an invitation, or exhortation, to a new way of thinking and acting and loving in the world. It is not that conversion, in any explicit sense, is foremost on the minds of international legal practitioners and scholars. But one might argue that there is no reason to assume that, as a matter of fact, such practitioners are any less converted—intellectually, morally, even religiously—than, say, the readers of *Method in Theology*. At the very least, there is no reason to assume that international lawyers are consistently inattentive—for instance, to human suffering—or devoid of recurring insights, of sound judgments, of responsible decisions as though they lacked intellectual conversion. There is no reason to assume that, when it comes to international law, immediate satisfactions always win out over values, as though its practitioners lacked moral conversion, or that there is nothing like religious consciousness, with its transvaluation of values, that animates at least some of its practitioners if not all.

PRUDENCE AND ITS PARTS

It may be argued that most if not all issues of justice are in fact issues of prudence, for prudence is that virtue that enables us to achieve the ends of the moral virtues in the concrete.[105] I introduce it here as a fourth tool, but also one that I believe is integral to each of those described above in ways that we shall see. Let me say a few things about prudence here and say more when we move to various mining sites—especially in chapter 6, which has a particular focus on *time.*

First of all, there are for Aquinas what I have come to call "spheres of prudence."[106] So, for instance, Aquinas distinguishes the prudence of the householder, of the military commander, and of the political authority.[107] Each of these persons may or may not be prudent, but within a particular sphere. What Aquinas does not mention, but what is both important and problematic, is how these spheres might or might not conflict, sometimes radically. So, while Aquinas's *domestic* prudence may counsel that leaving one's family to serve in Iraq or Afghanistan is not a wise thing to do, the prudence of the *military commander* might dictate that what is needed are more boots on the ground. There is no reason to assume that the military general and the civilian commander in chief, both prudent let us assume, will see eye to eye. As we shall see, this question of congruent or conflicting spheres will arise repeatedly in the case of mining at various sites.

Second, while Aquinas is attentive to what prudence is all about, he is also fully aware of what he calls vices against prudence—just as Lonergan was concerned, in *Insight,* when it comes to practical reasoning, not just with "insight into insight," but also with "insight into oversight." Of special note is the attention that Aquinas gives to vices *resembling* prudence, for the resemblance might leave such vices unexposed and thus more pernicious. It might be suggested, for instance, that what might seem like "prudence" is anything but if individual agents and agencies are operating according to the "technocratic paradigm" that undercuts truly just consideration of the poor, the earth, and the common good with its own complex plurality of spheres.

Third, for Aquinas prudence is no simple matter, reducible to the warning "Better go slow," or "Let's be careful out there." Rather, prudence consists of eight "quasi-integral parts"[108] that in the prudent person or group conspire to make for prudent—and thus truly just, or temperate, or courageous—decisions and actions in the concrete. I will stress in chapter 6 that some if not all of these "parts" are "time-sensitive."

1. So, prudence is a matter of *memory*: "Think back to what happened last time we tried that." "Remember the debacle of Vietnam." "Remember

what got us into Great Depression and why we couldn't get out." "Remember that slavery is very much a part of our past, and we cannot pretend it is not." Or, to anticipate a later chapter, consider this article title: "Can deep-sea mining avoid the environmental mistakes of mining on land?"[109] But memory for Aquinas is no easy matter; as the philosopher Josef Pieper explains, it is "true to being" memory that we are after.[110]

2. Prudence includes *understanding*, an implicit but firm grasp of and constant adherence over time to first principles, such as the physician's first rule, "Do no harm," a rule that must impinge upon the physician's consciousness the entire time the patient is under his or her care. For Aquinas, understanding may come close to what Lonergan means by the *notion* of being or of value—not some abstraction, or concepts passed off as "eternal verities," but an *operative* notion leading one to seek, in this context or that, the true and the truly good. Or, if it is a grasp of first principles, "understanding" may mean being attuned to the "transcendental precepts" intrinsic to human knowing and deciding: Be attentive, Be intelligent, Be reasonable, Be responsible, Be loving, and, if necessary, Change.
3. Prudence requires *docility,* or "teachableness," an eagerness to learn from others, to get needed input when we are out of our depth, to consult specialists in this area or that, to at least listen to what an intergovernmental panel on climate change has to say before making judgments about whether or not climate change is human induced and, if so, how we might best respond. But we might also ask what it might mean to seek out those on the margins for their input—including, through imagination, those *temporally* on the margins, namely future generations. Arguably, in his call for wide dialogue across disciplines and traditions, his concern for the poor, and his attention to future generations, Pope Francis has in mind docility of this kind.
4. But in a complementary way, prudence also includes *shrewdness,* an ability to quickly cut to the chase, to grasp just what is at stake and which road to take, to recognize when calling for "another study" is just a stall tactic we might use when we are loath to change the way we live our lives. Shrewdness is "an alacrity on hitting on the middle term"[111]: Harming our common home is bad; this practice is clearly an instance of harming our common home (middle term); thus, this practice is bad and must be addressed.
5. Prudence involves what Aquinas calls *reason*, a willingness and ability to think things through, taking the time to go beyond bumper sticker ethics that would reduce complex moral problems to a few words: "Guns don't kill people, people kill people." "My country, right or wrong." "Make America Great Again." For unlike angels (on Aquinas's analysis), human

beings do not know everything all at once, in a single moment, a single insight. Human beings get to the truth step by step, or in roundabout ways.[112] Finding the truth, including moral truth, can take *time*—sometimes, a lot of time.

6. Especially important for our topic, prudence includes *foresight*, a regard for what Aquinas calls future contingents—that is, future events, consequences, realities dependent, at least in part, on what we do now: "What will happen if we take this course of action rather than that?" "What are the chances that this strategy will succeed or fail?" With regard to foresight it is worth stressing that the Latin word for foresight is *providentia*, or "providence." Furthermore, we might ponder the proposition that some of these "future contingents" will be "future persons."
7. Prudence also demands *circumspection*, an attention to circumstances: But we should not underestimate the conceptual and practical difficulties here. If, as Pope Francis insists, "everything in the world is connected," then don't we have to take "everything" into account before reaching good decisions, about mining or anything else? Aquinas is not unaware of the problem. An objection states that "one's surroundings . . . are of an infinite number, and cannot be considered by the reason wherein is prudence." To this objection Aquinas replies: "Though the number of possible circumstances be infinite, the number of actual circumstances is not; and the judgment of reason in matters of action is influenced by things which are few in number."[113] While by "few" Aquinas might mean "*relatively* few," the difficulty of ascertaining what circumstances are relevant in this case or that is not so easily dismissed, and it is not made easier by the fact that some of these circumstance are a matter of time—such as the "half-lives" of toxic nuclear waste materials that lie buried, and are meant to stay buried, long after the uranium from which they sprung was mined.
8. Finally, prudence is a matter of *caution*: Not only concern about what bad things might happen if we're not careful—for example, an EPA cleanup effort of an abandoned mine gone wrong—but caution about what we might become if we choose to act this way rather than that. So, we might ask not only what will happen to uranium miners if they are not protected from radiation poisoning, but what will become of those, morally and spiritually, who have failed to find out if workers are at risk?

In short, for Aquinas at least, prudence is right at the heart of moral decision-making, and, most explicitly in terms of memory and foresight but not only there, it has much to do with *time*—a point of emphasis to which we will return.[114]

PROSPECTING TOOLS: ONGOING ASSEMBLY REQUIRED

Prudence dictates that it is time to conclude, or, better, suspend for now, this assembling of the prospector's tools. Over the next several chapters, the reader is invited to consider what is of value here and extend that in the direction of a more complete and coherent ethics of mining. Such employment of tools may occur in the quiet or disquiet of the heart, but also, and especially, in the company of others who challenge and console. A turn to particular "moral mining sites" should aid in that personal but also communal endeavor. If in the process the reader arrives at a better understanding or articulation of the tools to be employed than has been presented here, or is reminded of other suitable tools that may be added along the way, then that is all to the good.

NOTES

1. This list is taken from the table of contents outline for John Milsom, "Geophysical Methods," in Charles J. Moon et al., eds., *Mineral Exploration*, 127–54.
2. Frederick E. Crowe explains the manner in which those who bring Lonergan's thought to bear on matters he did not take up (his example was feminism) must add insights of their own. See Frederick E. Crowe, "The Genus 'Lonergan and' . . . and Feminism," in Cynthia S. W. Crysdale, ed., *Lonergan and Feminism* (Toronto: University of Toronto Press, 1994), 13–32.
3. See, for instance, William P. George, "Catholic Theology, International Law, and the Global Climate Crisis," in Jaime Schaefer, ed., *Confronting the Climate Crisis: Catholic Theological Perspectives* (Milwaukee: Marquette University Press, 2011), 177–200; and "International Law as Horizon," in Frederick Lawrence, ed., *Lonergan Workshop*, vol. 23: *Ongoing Collaboration in the Year of St. Paul* (Boston: Boston College, 2012), 195–226.
4. John Henry Newman, *An Essay in Aid of a Grammar of Assent*, intro. Etienne Gilson (New York: Doubleday and Company, 1955).
5. On these three questions with regards to factual knowing, see Patrick Byrne, *The Ethics of Discernment: Lonergan's Foundations for Ethics* (Toronto: University of Toronto Press, 1916), 38–73.
6. Lonergan, *Insight*, 22. Neither the "fixed base" nor the "invariant pattern" should be confused with a set of immutable concepts. Rather, it is the knower's own dynamic capacity continually to raise, and answer critically, questions of fact and value. Denial of such a "base" or "pattern" may result in a "performative contradiction," as the denier affirms in practice what he or she rejects in theory. See Lonergan, *Method*, 20–21.

7. William P. George, “Learning Alone: Solitude and Undergraduate Education,” *America Magazine*, Sept. 15, 2008, 16–18.

8. Michael Polanyi, *The Tacit Dimension,* Chapter 3: “A Society of Explorers” (Garden City, New York: Doubleday & Company, Inc. 1966), 53–92.

9. See Daniel K. Finn, ed., *The True Wealth of Nations: Catholic Social Thought and Economic Life* (New York: Oxford University Press, 2010). The phrase “the health of nations” is inspired by Philip Allott, *The Health of Nations: Society and Law beyond the State* (Cambridge: Cambridge University Press, 2002).

10. On the problem of bias, see Lonergan, *Insight*, chapter 7.

11. I owe this phrase to Todd Whitmore, a theologian and ethicist at the University of Notre Dame.

12. Some version of this bias may be captured in what I have called “angelism,” the mistaken notion that, unlike angels in the thought of Thomas Aquinas, human beings do not grasp everything in a single insight. Human beings must learn, sometimes slowly and painfully. See William P. George, “Angelism and Its Devilish Effects on Education,” *Chicago Studies* 29 (2000): 194–210.

13. Lonergan, *Method*, 52–55; 117.

14. Ibid., 4.

15. Lonergan identifies these operations as “seeing, hearing, touching, smelling, tasting [level of “experience”], inquiring, imagining, understanding, conceiving, formulating [level of “understanding”], reflecting, marshaling and weighing the evidence [level of “judgment’], deliberating, evaluating, deciding, speaking, writing [level of “decision”]. I have indicated within brackets the distinct levels (*Method,* 6). It is not clear to me that this list is exhaustive, especially when it comes to dealing with the “data of consciousness,” for example, the feelings which apprehend values.

16. Lonergan, *Method*, 20.

17. Ibid., 14.

18. Ibid.

19. Ibid., 7, n. 2.

20. For an excellent discussion of what Lonergan means by consciousness as self-presence, see Fred Lawrence, “The Fragility of Consciousness: Lonergan and the Postmodern Concern for the Other,” *Theological Studies* 54 (1993): 55–94.

21. Lonergan, *Method*, 14.

22. Ibid., 24.

23. A similar emphasis on conversation especially across cultures may be found in Kwame Anthony Appiah, *Cosmopolitanism: Ethics in a World of Strangers* (New York: W.W. Norton, 2006).

24. Lonergan, *Method,* 76–80.

25. Ibid., 81–84.

26. Ibid., 85–101.

27. See Wilhelm Grewe, *The Epochs of International Law,* trans. and rev. by Michael Byers (New York: Walter de Gruyter, 2000).

28. In his conclusion to *Justice among the Nations* (Cambridge, MA: Harvard University Press, 2014), Stephen Neff says that “if there is any lesson to be drawn from our juridical voyage, it is that there cannot be any such thing as a history of

international law as a single unitary thing. The reason is that conceptions of what international is have changed so much over time" (481).

29. Lonergan, *Insight,* 251–67.

30. Lonergan, *Method*, 39.

31. Ibid., 32.

32. Ibid., 39.

33. See especially Paul VI, *Populorum Progressio: On the Development of Peoples* (Libreria Editrice Vaticana, 1967), http://w2.vatican.va/content/paul-vi/en/encyclicals/documents/hf_p-vi_enc_26031967_populorum.html.

34. Lonergan, *Method.*, xi. Note that this statement about a shift in the understanding of culture constitutes the very first words in *Method in Theology.*

35. Ibid., 48–49.

36. Lonergan, *Insight*, 146–151. On Lonergan's understanding of emergent probability, see Kenneth Melchin, *History, Ethics, and Emergent Probability: Ethics, Society and History in the Work of Bernard Lonergan* (Lanham, MD: University Press of America, 1986; and Cythia Crysdale, "Revisioning Natural Law: From the Classicist Paradigm to Emergent Probability," *Theological Studies* 56/3 (1995): 464–84. Given my inclusion of Thomas Aquinas's understanding of "prudence" as a prospecting tool, especially noteworthy is Patrick H. Byrne, "The Thomistic Sources of Lonergan's Dynamic World View," *The Thomist* 46 (1982): 108–45.

37. Pope Francis, *Laudato si'*, Chapter 4: Integral Ecology (pars. 137–162). For a discussion of Lonergan and climate change that not only contributes much to an understanding of *Laudato si'* but also emergent probability, see Richard Liddy, "Changing Our Minds: Bernard Lonergan and Climate Change," in Jaime Schaefer, ed., *Confronting the Climate Crisis*, 253–275.

38. Lonergan, *Insight*, 506.

39. William P. George, "Anticipating Posterity: A Lonerganian Approach to Contingent Future Persons," in Jan C. Heller and Nick Fotion, eds., *Contingent Future Persons: Philosophical and Theological Challenges*, Theology and Medicine Series (Kluwer Academic Publishers, 1997): 191–208.

40. Bernard J. F. Lonergan, S.J., "Prolegomena to the Study of the Emerging Religious Consciousness of our Time." In *A Third Collection*, ed. Frederick E. Crowe, S.J., 55–73 (Mahwah, NJ: Paulist Press/London: Geoffrey Chapman, 1985).

41. For my early thoughts on this matter, without any reference to Lonergan's essay on religious consciousness but with attention to Lonergan's concern for the "subject," see William P. George, "Looking for a Global Ethic? Try International Law," *Journal of Religion* 76/3 (1996): 353–82; reprinted with slight emendations in Mark W. Janis and Carolyn Evans, *Religion and International Law* (The Hague: Martinus Nijhoff Publishers), 483–504.

42. George, "International Law as Horizon."

43. For a summary of these specialities, see Lonergan, *Method*, 124–45; the specialties are discussed in detail in the second half of the book.

44. Ibid., 127.

45. See chapter 4.

46. Lonergan, *Method*, 130.

47. Ibid., 132.

48. "Now, in everyday commonsense performance, all four levels [by which the specialties may be distinguished] are employed continuously without any explicit distinction between them. In that case no functional specialization arise, for what is sought is not the end of any particular level but the cumulative, composite result of the ends of all four levels" (Lonergan, *Method*, 133–34).

49. John Raymaker with Ijaz Durrani, *Empowering Climate-Change Strategies with Bernard Lonergan's Method* (Lanham, MD: University Press of America, 2015). For my attempt to apply both insights from Lonergan and Aquinas's understanding of prudence to the issue of climate change, see. William P. George, "Catholic Theology, International Law, and the Global Climate Crisis," in Jaime Schaefer, ed., *Confronting the Climate Crisis*, 177–200.

50. Bernard J. F. Lonergan, *Topics in Education*, ed. Robert M. Doran and Frederick E. Crowe, *Collected Works of Bernard Lonergan,* vol., 10 (Toronto: University of Toronto Press, 1993).

51. See Manfred Lachs, "Teachings and Teaching of International Law," in *Collected Courses of the Academy of International Law* (Leyde: A.W. Sijthoff, 1978): 3:160–252. For my own reflections on the relationship between international law and Catholic higher education, see William P. George, "Why Catholic Universities Should Engage International Law," *Journal of Catholic Higher Education* 27/1 (Winter 2008): 173–93.

52. For a lawyer and theologian's perspective on law as a moral teacher in an American context, see Cathleen Kaveny, *Law's Virtues: Fostering Autonomy and Solidarity in American Society* (Washington, DC: Georgetown University Press, 2012), xi, 7, 28–33.

53. Polanyi, *Personal Knowledge*, 195–202.

54. Here, I am drawing on the introduction by editors Frederick G. Lawrence, Patrick H. Byrne, and Charles C. Hefling Jr. to *Lonergan's Macroeconomic Dynamics: An Essay in Circulation Analysis*, Collected Works of Bernard Lonergan, vol. 15 (Toronto: University of Toronto Press, 1999), as well as Paul St. Amour, "An Introduction to Lonergan's Macroeconomic Theory," Marquette University Lonergan Colloquium, February 28, 2013.

55. I raise this question because, in fact, this may be what is happening with regards to space mining—tremendous enthusiasm and production of such things as prospecting probes, but now some drawbacks in company commitments due to funding difficulties.

56. Neil Ormerod and Cristina Vanin, "Ecological Conversion: What Does It Mean?" *Theological Studies* 77/2 (June 2016): 328–52.

57. Bernard J. F. Lonergan, "Healing and Creating in History," in Frederick E. Crowe, S.J., ed., *A Third Collection: Papers by Bernard J. F. Lonergan, SJ* (New York: Paulist Press, 1985), 100–109.

58. Human Rights Watch, "Zambia: Workers Detail Abuses in Chinese-Owned Mines," Nov. 3, 2011, https://www.hrw.org/news/2011/11/03/zambia-workers-detail-abuse-chinese-owned-mines.

59. Lonergan, "Healing and Creating," 107.

60. One thinks, for instance of Jacques Maritain, who influenced Paul VI, among others; of Dorothy Day, with her commitment to nonviolence and the poor; of numerous lay theologians around the world today, increasingly from underrepresented or marginalized groups; or of Lonergan himself, whose commitment to economics was motivated in part by what he perceived as the need to address a shortcoming in Catholic social teaching.

61. See Mich, *Catholic Social Teaching and Movements.*

62. See, for example, seven key themes as listed by the United States Conference of Catholic Bishops, http://www.usccb.org/beliefs-and-teachings/what-we-believe/catholic-social-teaching/seven-themes-of-catholic-social-teaching.cfm. For an excellent treatment of the recent Catholic social tradition, see Kenneth Himes et al., eds., *Modern Catholic Social Teaching Commentaries and Interpretations*, 2nd edition (Washington, DC: Georgetown University Press, 2018).

63. Lonergan, *Method,* 355–69.

64. *Compendium of the Social Doctrine of the Church,* http://www.vatican.va/roman_curia/pontifical_councils/justpeace/documents/rc_pc_justpeace_doc_20060526_compendio-dott-soc_en.html.

65. The paragraph, or section, numbers will be placed in parentheses in the text.

66. Compare, for example, the content of *Evangelii Gaudium* with that of another famous exhortation—Pope Urban II's rousing call to Christians to take up the cause of a crusade.

67. For an insightful and critical commentary, see Christiana Zenner Peppard, "*Laudato si'*," in Himes et al., eds., *Modern Catholic Social Teaching*, 515–52.

68. Here, we cannot overemphasize in *Laudato si'* the pope's desire to promote dialogue that includes everyone, whether "believer" or not. A specific example would be the well-known writer on climate change and capitalism Naomi Klein's invitation to speak at a Vatican press conference regarding *Laudato si'.* See Naomi Klein, "A Radical Vatican?" *The New Yorker*, July 10, 2015, http://www.newyorker.com/news/news-desk/a-visit-to-the-vatican.

69. We should not underestimate the importance of the *quaestio* at the very heart of scholastic theology and philosophy from which Lonergan learned so much, a spirit of inquiry hardly restricted to the medieval university. See, for instance, the opening book of Augustine's *Confessions*, where questions flow as though from an inexhaustible spigot.

70. See Lonergan, *Method*, chapter 7: "Interpretation."

71. This is not unlike what one finds in the opening of Aquinas's *Summa Theologica*. Why, Aquinas asks, is not human reason—development from below—sufficient? Because, for one thing, even that which can be known through unaided reason "would be known only by a few, and that after a long time, and with the admixture of many errors" (*ST* I 1.1).

72. Lynn White Jr., "The Historical Roots of Our Ecological Crisis," *Science* 155/3767 (10 March 1967): 1203–7.

73. I refer to Heilbroner because he understood years ago the huge price to be paid for not attending now to ecological and other looming threats to humanity, threats that might require solutions that will be painful at best. See Robert Heilbroner, *An Inquiry*

into the Human Prospect, Updated and Reconsidered for the 1980s (New York: W.W. Norton and Company, 1980; 1974).

74. Lonergan, *Insight*, 258.

75. See Mary Gerhart, "Bernard Lonergan's 'Law of the Cross': Transforming the Sources and Effects of Violence," *Theological Studies* 77/1 (2016): 77–95.

76. This is a central concern of chapter 4, on Nauru.

77. Benedict XVI, Encyclical Letter, *Caritas in Veritate* (29 June 2009), 67.

78. Fears on the part of some of a "world state" recalls a theme in *Insight* that is relevant here. In his discussion of "cosmopolis," Lonergan is careful to distinguish cosmopolis from a police force, or a United Nations, as good and necessary as these might be. See *Insight*, 263–67. It would be worth asking whether, in *Laudato si'*, Francis is inviting readers to enter something like "cosmopolis."

79. Patrick McKinley Brennan, "Asking the Right Questions: Harnessing the Insights of Bernard Lonergan for the Rule of Law," *Journal of Law and Religion* 21 (2006): 1–38.

80. William P. George, "Neither Apology nor Utopia: A Lonerganian Approach to International Law," paper delivered at the annual meeting of the Society of Christian Ethics, January, 2014.

81. See Lonergan, "Healing and Creating."

82. For Stephen Neff's attempt to rectify what he perceived as a lack of attention to international law's history, see his *Justice among Nations*.

83. At least one prominent thinker, John Stuart Mill, would seem to agree. In his inaugural address as rector (president) of the University of St. Andrews, Mill says: "To these studies I would add International Law; which I decidedly think should be taught in all universities, and should form part of all liberal education. The need of it is far from being limited to diplomatists and lawyers; it extends to every citizen. What is called the Law of Nations is not properly law, but a, part of ethics: a set of moral rules, accepted as authoritative by civilized states." See John Stuart Mill, "Inaugural Address Delivered to the University of St. Andrews," February 1, 1887 (London: Longmans, Green, Reader, and Dyer, 1867), 73.

84. For an authoritative statement on sources, see Article 38 of the Statute of the International Court of Justice, https://www.icj-cij.org/en/statute.

85. See, for example, George (Rock) Pring, "International Environmental and Human Rights Law Affecting Mining Law Reform," Presented at the Mining Law Seminar Northern Institute for Environmental and Minority Law (NIEM) Arctic Centre, University of Lapland Rovaniemi, Finland, 25–26 September 2008; and Eric L. Garner, "International Treaties Governing Mineral Exploration," *Environmental and Engineering Geology*, Vol. III, http://www.eolss.net/sample-chapters/c09/E6-65-05-04.pdf.

86. See, for instance, the "Notes" at the end of each topic in the multiple editions of Westlaw's *International Law: Cases and Materials*—notes which are, in fact, mostly a series of questions, often with no easy answers.

87. Antonio Cassese, "States: Rise and Decline of the Primary Subjects of International Law," in *Handbook of International Law*, ed. Bardo Fassbender and Anne Peters (Oxford: Oxford University Press, 2012), 49–70.

88. Janne Elisabeth Nijman, *The Concept of International Legal Personality: An Inquiry into the History and Theory of International Law* (The Hague: T.M.C. Asser Press, 2003).

89. See, for instance, the chapters on "Feminism" and "Third World Approaches" in Andrea Bianchi, *International Legal Theories: An Inquiry into Different Ways of Thinking* (Oxford: Oxford University Press, 2016), 183–204; 205–26.

90. Antony Anghie, *Imperialism, Sovereignty, and the Making of International Law* (Cambridge: Cambridge University Press, 2004).

91. George, "International Law as Horizon," 195–226.

92. The two are former vice president of the World Court, C. G. Weeramantry, in the case of phosphate mining on the island of Nauru, on the one hand, and the legality of using or threatening to use uranium-based nuclear weapons, on the other (chapters 4 and 6); and Arvid Pardo, in the case of deep-seabed mining and the Law of the Sea (chapter 5).

93. See Martti Koskenniemi, *From Apology to Utopia: The Structure of International Legal Argument* (Cambridge: Cambridge University Press, 2006).

94. William P. George, "Neither Apology nor Utopia: A Lonerganian Approach to International Law." Paper delivered at the meeting of the Society of Christian Ethics, January, 2014.

95. Steven Ratner and Anne-Marie Slaughter, eds., *The Methods of International Law* (The American Society of International Law, 2004).

96. Andrea Bianchi, *International Law Theories.*

97. Manfred Lachs, "The Grotian Heritage, the International Community, and Changing Dimensions of International Law," in *International Law and the Grotian Heritage: A Commemorative Colloquium*, ed. T.M.C. Asser Instituut (The Hague: T.M.C. Asser Instituut, 1985), 204–205 (emphasis added).

98. See chapter 5 below.

99. Mary Ann Glendon, *A World Made New: Eleanor Roosevelt and the Universal Declaration of Human Rights* (Random House, 2001).

100. On this and related shortcomings of international law that adversely affect the poor, see Thomas Pogge, "Divided against Itself: Aspiration and Reality of International Law," in *The Cambridge Companion to International Law,* ed. James Crawford and Martti Koskenniemi (Cambridge: Cambridge University Press, 2012), 373–97.

101. Charles Taylor, *A Secular Age* (Cambridge, MA: The Belknap Press of Harvard Univeristy Press, 2007).

102. Lonergan, "Emerging Religious Consciousness," 65–66.

103. Harold J. Berman, Review of Mark W. Janis and Carolyn Evans, eds., *Religion and International Law*, in the *American Journal of International Law* 94/4 (October 2000): 802. His reference was to George, "Looking for a Global Ethic? Try International Law."

104. Ibid., 803.

105. Aquinas, *ST* II–II 47, 6 and 7.

106. The phrase is inspired by Michael Walzer, *Spheres of Justice: A Defense of Pluralism and Equality* (Basic Books, 1989).

107. Aquinas, *ST* II–II 48.

108. Ibid., 49, 1–8.

109. Carol J. Clouse, "Can deep-sea mining avoid the mistakes of mining on land?" *The Guardian*, June 28, 2017, https://www.theguardian.com/sustainable-business/2017/jun/28/deep-sea-mining-environmental-mistakes.

110. Josef Pieper, *The Cardinal Virtues* (New York: Harcourt, Brace, & World, Inc., 1965), 15.

111. Aquinas, *ST* II–II 49, 4 ad. 1.

112. See George, "'Angelism' and Its Devilish Effects on Education."

113. Aquinas, *ST* II–II, 49, 7, ad. 1.

114. See chapter 6.

Part II

PROSPECTING FOR ETHICS ON EARTH AND IN OUTER SPACE

Chapter Three

Butte, Montana: "The Richest Hill on Earth" and a Moral Morass

With its massive deposits of copper and other minerals, Butte, Montana was once known as "the Richest Hill on Earth," and fittingly so.[1] But it garnered other titles—for instance, "the perch of the devil."[2] I refer to it here as "a moral morass." For mining morality in this corner of the world turns out to be a muddy and sometimes a muckraking affair.[3] It is also a matter of entanglement, of attempting to sort out the really good from the really bad, the not so good from the not so bad. This is made especially difficult since, for the most part, we are dealing with what Lonergan calls the ever-fluid realm of "common sense," what others might call "the everyday" or, since we will be travelling to Chile later on, "*lo cotidiano*," that most familiar but also perplexing dimension of life that does not sit still. Morally, the story of Butte can be at times as bewildering as the miles of mineshafts and workways beneath this small and then not so small town in the west. It can also be as troubling as the Granite Mountain mine disaster of 1917, taking 168 lives, or, in "safer" times, the 40 billion gallons of toxic water in the Berkeley Pit that continues to rise.

One way to sort things through would be to name the moral issues embedded in Butte and try to assess them one at a time. One thinks, for instance, of how Thomas Aquinas dealt with "theft," carefully distinguishing and connecting as he went along.[4] Without leaving aside such issues (theft is hardly peripheral to ethical prospecting in Butte), the approach here will be somewhat different. Recall what was said above about "method" in relation to functional specialties and the basic dynamic of questioning—"Where have we been, where are we now, and where will we, where should we, go from here?"—that may inform those specialties and their interconnection. Recall, too, caveats about expectations of neatness or differentiation with regard to the specialties. This will help to explain the character of this chapter. That is, we will consider

Figure 3.1. Prospectors in Butte, Montana, c. 1860s.

here three distinct but not totally separate accounts of the story of Butte—where Butte has been and, to a lesser extent, where it is going. The three accounts, or retellings, are C. B. Glasscock's once popular *The War of the Copper Kings: Greed, Power, and Politics: The Billion-Dollar Battle for Butte, Montana* (1935);[5] Michael P. Malone's highly regarded *The Battle for Butte: Mining and Politics on the Northern Frontier, 1864–1906* (1981); and Janet L. Finn's provocative *Tracing the Veins: Of Copper, Culture, and Community from Butte to Chuquicamata* (1998),[6] the title of which signals that the story of Butte extends beyond the borders of Montana and of the United States.

As contributions to moral mining, each account in its own way exemplifies an attempt to tell a complex story such that the author's own moral horizons become apparent, sometimes implicitly, sometimes (as is the case with Finn) with an honest effort to articulate for the reader not only what those horizons are but also how they have shifted over time. In that sense, each author is telling his or her own story. But of course, that is not their primary aim. As self-transcending subjects (to use Lonergan's terms), they are telling a story beyond themselves—the story of mining, the story of Butte, of "independents" and of a giant "amalgamated" aptly named Anaconda, of laborers and labor, of Montana and America, of Chile and the world. By considering these retellings, the reader may mine morality in perhaps new ways. So, too, a brief and surely inadequate updating on Butte today, with special reference to a remarkable person one might call a modern-day "copper king," is meant to expose further the veins of moral inquiry waiting to be mined.

THE WAR OF THE COPPER KINGS

Written in the midst of the Great Depression and when Butte still had legitimate claim to its "richest hill" title, C. B. Glasscock tells the story of *The War of the Copper Kings.* It is an engaging, insightful, sometimes appalling, sometimes humorous story based largely on available sources and interviews with those who lived through a tempestuous time in a truly remarkable place. There is, it might be noted, not a footnote to be found.[7]

To discuss this "war" all too briefly but in ways that serve our purpose, it may be best to start where Glasscock begins, with an opening chapter entitled "Civilization at Scratch," the first sentence of which reads: "A group of ragged, bearded, weary men, fleeing from hostile Indians, made camp beside an alder-lined creek high in the mountains in 1863."[8] The place later became Bannack, some eighty miles from Butte, where

> latent in the surrounding ground were the makings of more than one hundred murders, more than a score of hangings without process of law, more than two billion dollars in material wealth, a corporation designed to rule the electric light and power of the world, battles of giants in the depths of the earth and in the capital of the nation, and a financial panic that staggered the country in 1907.[9]

Throughout his book, Glasscock refers repeatedly to "civilization," sometimes sincerely, sometimes facetiously, but with a consistency sufficient to suggest that it signals Glasscock's own understanding of what Lonergan might mean by "progress," and it arguably reveals Glasscock's own foundations for assessing the history he records. Such progress would include the move away from a lawless society where some of its heroes were vigilantes, one of whom would serve as Montana's first elected senator. It would also include a retrospective, pained consciousness, on Glasscock's part at least, that Butte's brief, almost comically "heroic" role in the Nez Perce War was in fact Butte's participation in "one of the blackest marks in the whole black record of American 'civilization's' treatment of the savages"[10]—hardly a minor point given the treatment of indigenous peoples in the history and present practice of mining.[11] In other words, the "war" to which the book's title refers is in the first instance between and among certain principal actors, the "copper kings," but it is a war on many fronts, including, it would appear, the author's own grappling with what counts as "civilization"—or progress—in Montana, in America, in the world.

In the 1860s Butte was a small, relatively isolated mining camp, or town, which showed some promise for yielding gold and silver. To this town came William Clark, "a driving, grasping, truly ambitious youth of truly astonishing energy, and business ability near to genius."[12] Before and after his arrival in Butte, he amassed an immense fortune in ways that included but were by no means limited to mining. Banking, it should be stressed, was one of his early and consistent endeavors. Marcus Daly, an Irish immigrant, educated in the mines of Nevada and elsewhere, arrived in Butte nine years later and, with almost preternatural prospecting skills, saw Butte's great potential for the mining of copper—increasingly in demand with telecommunications and electrification. With the backing of outside money, he shrewdly bought several mines, became fabulously wealthy in his own right, and started the town of Anaconda (the name of one his mines) a few miles from Butte. There he built a smelter, in part to alleviate the pollution problems in Butte. In all of this, Daly never lost touch with the miners who, in certain respects, remained his equals. For reasons that are not entirely clear—at least in terms of initial causes—Clark and Daly became bitter, lifelong rivals. Thus, one reason for Glasscock's title: *The War of the Copper Kings.*

These two mining giants were joined by F. Augustus ("Fritz") Heinze, who brought with him training in mining and metallurgy. Years younger than Clark and Daly, he would one day "wring their souls and cut into their profits to cries of 'Napoleon! Napoleon!'."[13] If there is a hero in Glasscock's story—and this is a guarded "if"—it would appear to be Heinze. For as the years passed, Heinze took on, almost single-handedly, a fourth copper king, arriving on the scene about the same time as Heinze—not an individual but rather a corporation: New York based Standard Oil, founded by John D. Rockefeller, of "shrewd brain and tractable conscience."[14] For Glasscock and surely others, Standard Oil was the epitome of nineteenth- and early twentieth-century capitalism. In fact, Standard Oil was not directly involved in the Butte mines, but certain of its principals were—namely, Henry Rogers and William Rockefeller, the elder Rockefeller's son. There were other players, too, such as the financial backers of Daly and Clark, and the Boston financiers who turned their attention from their profitable mining interests in Michigan to the riches of Butte. For a time, the Rothschilds of banking fame were investors as well.

Butte as the Apex of Underhandedness

The "war" was economic, political, and cultural, in ways that are difficult to separate. On the one hand, it was simply a fight to see who could gain control of the copper industry and profit the most. Daly's strategy was amalgamation of several mines, and this strategy led him eventually to join forces with the Eastern investors associated with Standard Oil. Heinze, by contrast, is portrayed by Glasscock as the independent par excellence, a David who stood up against the Goliath of big business. He did this in cunning and sometimes devious ways. Heinze's strategies included stalling the opposition's mining advances with countless—and enormously costly—legal battles, most often fought in the court of a Heinze-backed judge, William Clancy, who periodically awoke from his apparent courtroom daydreaming either to spit tobacco or to rule in Heinze's favor.[15]

Because it leads one to ponder, if not resolve, questions about the role of law in relation to ethics, and because it signals an issue of fundamental importance in Catholic social thought and beyond—namely, the issue of property—of special interest here is Heinze's reliance on the "apex" rule in mining law, a rule that made its way into federal legislation. This rule stated that a claim that included the "apex" (or peak) of a vein extended to the whole of that vein, even if, somewhere below the surface, the vein crossed the boundary of another's claim. Since continuity of veins could be devilishly hard to track, this rule invited much legal mischief, and Heinze was quick to accept the invitation. In one instance, he staked a claim of a few square yards next to his rivals' claims, but a claim with supposedly "apex" status.[16] He thus tied up his rivals in court for years. No less potent were his efforts to stem Standard Oil expansion through clever minority stockholder schemes. His minions would buy stock in his rivals' publicly-traded companies and then, using their minority status, block mining purchases that would hurt Heinze's interests. A larger point here is that the morality of mining can be equally a matter of geology and of high finance and economics.

Of course, Heinze was not alone in his underhanded strategizing—amounting on occasion to outright theft of his adversaries' ore and leading to war of a more literal kind as Heinze's miners dangerously clashed with Amalagamated miners underground. But to a great extent, this is Glasscock's point: Heinze was the underdog fighting the industrial giant, but with the giant's own power-grabbing tools. For, in Glasscock's words, "he found himself fighting the greatest, most powerful, most ruthless and conscienceless trust on earth."[17]

The war had other fronts as well. As Montana moved toward statehood, the war of the copper kings included an enormously costly battle to see which town would be elected to be state capital, with Heinze's allegiance to Helena pitted against Daly's beloved Anaconda and a few other candidate cities of modest size. In the end, Helena won out. If the vast sums of money spent on that campaign—in effect, buying state capital status—was tainted at best, William Clark's unbridled ambition to secure a U.S. senate seat, through bribery of state convention delegates (popular election of senators did not come until 1913), attained the level of an unmitigated national scandal.[18] While

Figure 3.2. Augustus Heinz, 1910.

it is too complex to examine here, these highly partisan battles had a profound effect on the dynamics of party politics, with the powerful pull of populism directed mainly against big business very much a part of the mix.

The role of bribery in the story of Butte, of Montana, and of the copper kings, provides an opening to discuss briefly Glasscock's assessment of what might be termed the moral status of Butte.[19] Many besides Glasscock have chronicled the wild side of Butte as it grew, with it numerous bars, its guns and occasional gunfights, its gambling, its prominent red-light district. For Glasscock, Butte, during the time of the copper kings, appears to have been a place which teetered between "high culture"—for example, theater and visiting Broadway Stars—and debauchery, between the "high heart" and the "low morals" of its beloved madams, between a level of moral maturity to match such civilizational advances as running water, on the one hand, and the depravity of an uncivilized world, on the other.[20] Put otherwise, what Lonergan calls the "scale of values" was in full play. In any event, in Glasscock's telling, with the lure of the red-light district "catering to the worst instincts of the community, moral fiber was breaking down. And only on that premise can one account for the state-wide toleration of political bribery and corruption which was to follow."[21]

Whether or not such loose behavior accounted also for another topic discussed in this same chapter, namely, the paltry level of taxes paid by wealthy mine owners (Daly, Clark, Lee Mantle, and others), Glasscock does not say. But it is clear enough that, for Glasscock, morality is at least as much about bribery and political corruption as it is about the prostitution, adultery, and addictions[22] that can hasten a downward moral spiral. Put in Lonergan's terms, one might say that Glasscock was attuned to how accepting morally questionable behavior of one kind can shift the probabilities that bad behavior of another kind will prevail and be tolerated as well.

Labor Caught in the Crosshairs

Another battle front, of course, was labor.[23] We will have more to say about this when we turn to other tellers of the story of Butte, but here one aspect of Glasscock's account should be stressed. Heinze portrayed himself as the friend of labor, standing against the giants of Standard Oil who are depicted as ready to swoop in and own not only the miners' labor but their very lives. After one of Heinze's legal victories against Amalgamated, it seemed clear to the industrial giant that they stood to lose to "a general of such Napoleonic qualities and Al Caponic methods as F. Augustus Heinze."[24] In other words, Heinze was fighting Standard Oil with weapons of their own kind.

But Standard Oil was used to winning, and so it responded to the injunction levied against them by immediately shutting down all their operations.

Twenty-thousand employees in Butte, Great Falls, Anaconda, and elsewhere—roughly 80 percent of the Montana workforce—were thrown out of work. Clark and others who were now firmly in the embrace of Standard Oil reviled Heinze, in Glasscock's words, as a "Moses pretending to lead the miners out of Egypt, out of bondage under the Pharaoh of Standard Oil."[25] In the short term, Heinze, who had become a great orator, was able to assure a hostile crowd that they should stick with him, as he announced that their adversaries had "filched the oil wells of America, and in doing so they trampled on every law, human and divine." Warning of a repeat in the mines of Butte, he left a freezing crowd of ten thousand convinced that he "was as Christ and the Standard Oil Company as his crucifiers."[26]

That was the short term. In the longer term, winter and other hardships weakened the workers' resolve. With the suffering of idle laborers and their families as leverage, the Amalgamated pressured the governor to call a special session to pass legislation having to do with change of venue for adjudicating mining disputes in the holding company's favor. So, as one chapter heading puts it, "Montana Bows to the Trust."[27] In fact, under the circumstances, the governor had little choice. As the nation's newspapers looked on, only those who saw big business as the bringer and savior of civilization, Glasscock points out, "failed to report the incident as the coercion of the state."[28]

In the end, then, big business won out. The Almalgamated assumed the name the Anaconda Copper Mining Company and, Glasscock reports, lived up to its name, not only coiling around and squeezing Montana but slithering off beyond the borders of Montana and the nation, most notably into Chile and its copper-rich mines. In time, off in New York away from the gaze of the Butte populace, Heinze would sell out to the holding company for a huge price, see his efforts to gain more through New York banking efforts backfire on him in the panic of 1907, and, after a life of hard-living and hard-drinking, die young at forty-one.

Recalling the basics of our prospector's tools—most notably for present purposes the dynamics of method with its functional specialties oriented implicitly around the questions "Where have we been, where are we now, and where are we going?"—Glasscock's summary judgments are instructive. He appears, at the level of "foundations," to concede that the war of the copper kings, even as it resulted in the virtual subjugation of a state to a giant corporation, had its merits. The copper kings got most of the money, but the world got copper, other metallic riches, and the efficiencies of the modern corporation. In terms of the scale of values, "vital values"—the basics for life—may have been secured for many (but surely not all), even if other values (cultural, personal, transcendent) were in doubt. Recalling Lonergan's essay on "Healing and Creating in History," we might say that the copper kings may indeed have "created in history," but they were arguably short on real "healing" in that time and place.

The Heroic Individual

But for Glasscock, it is not big business that deserved the credit for this material advance. Most striking is Glasscock's landing spot: "What of the individual?" he asks. Heinze "wrested ten and one-half million dollars from the greatest trust of the America of his day. In so doing he revealed opportunity to thousands," bringing affluence to some and a better life to others. Daly, "untrained in any school except that of hard work and experience, saw opportunity in a blue-gray rock, and took millions from it in the twenty-five years of life which remained to him."[29]

Interestingly, Clark, generally regarded as the most notorious of the three, receives more comment than the others. Glasscock writes:

> Clark accumulated capital simply by grasping every opportunity and improving upon it. Farm boy, country school teacher, miner, merchant, banker. Still, not a man to be admired? Perhaps. Certainly not a man of tender conscience. But just as certainly a vivid exemplification of definite accomplishment in a day *when Americans stood upon their own feet, without fear or favor*.[30]

Clark is commended especially for his banking practices, whereby his millions stood behind his clients' deposits. Clark's bank remained private, thus enabling him to skirt state and federal regulation. Through economically troubling times, depositors never lost confidence in W. A. Clark & Brothers, Bankers, and, as a result, others prospered. Clark was "convicted of political practices so outrageous that the United States Senate refused him the seat to which he had been elected. Two years later, he marched down the aisle, and took that seat." After death he was memorialized by the people of Montana in glowing terms. All of which leads Glasscock to conclude *The War of the Copper Kings* with these final words: "That could happen in America."[31]

That cryptic closing phrase raises a host of questions: That *could* happen in America, but why? Could "progress" or "civilization," as Glasscock sees it, have come in some other way? If it could happen once, "when Americans stood upon their own feet, without fear or favor," could it happen again? *Should* it happen again? If it could happen *in America* (but perhaps not elsewhere), what was it, or is it, about America, especially the America that was Butte and Montana, that is so special—or so problematic? These are open questions. But it may be that while Glasscock—with his selected sources, his interpretation of those sources, his history of Butte and Montana and Wall Street and America, his focus on the dialectics that he calls "war"—is, for the most part, telling us where we have *been*, he may also be pointing ahead to where he thinks we should go, establishing and communicating to us the ground, the foundations, the doctrines for how we ought to, how we can, live. If his closing comments

Figure 3.3. "What a fuss they made about us." Senator William Clark of Montana, with money bags, and Senator Quay of Pennsylvania.
Photo: Library of Congress.

are any indication, he places great faith in the individual man[32] of great daring and bold genius. In certain respects, the vision for an America (and the world?) which he suggests is at odds with the moral vision of *Laudato si'*. For Pope Francis, the unbridled pursuit of wealth, especially if it means crushing the vulnerable in the process, is a monumental moral problem.

In his critique of big business, represented by Standard Oil, Glasscock would appear to side fully with the robust populism of the day and sympathize with those most in danger of getting squeezed. But it is not so clear that Glasscock put any more trust in "the people" than he did in the Trust that was Standard Oil and its ilk. When describing the way in which Heinze and Clark turned the people of Butte against Daly after he had sold out to big business, Glasscock tells of how Heinze, now a great orator, swayed the masses, but then adds that "[t]he ignorant majority of Montana voters were as ready in 1900 to believe any demagogic outbursts against trusts and capitalism as voters of their character are today."[33] For Glasscock, it would seem, it is neither the rapacious corporation nor the easily swayed masses that will move civilization ahead. In Glasscock's America, at least, only an amalgamation, real or only apparent, of daring and genius in the heroic individual can hope to do that. Make way, over a hundred years later, some might say, but others most surely not, for Donald Trump.

THE BATTLE FOR BUTTE

In his preface to *The Battle for Butte,* historian Michael P. Malone, who later served as president of Montana State University[34] in Bozeman (about eighty-five miles from Butte), distinguishes himself from Glasscock and his "heroic personalized approach."[35] Rather than simply retelling the story related by

Glasscock and another popular writer, C. P. Connelly, Malone points out that "both men relied heavily on oral history and that neither attempted to approach the subject with the *detached objectivity* that relies upon thorough research in primary and secondary sources,"[36] many of which were not earlier available.

Of Objectivity and the Earth

This prefatory remark is noteworthy because it raises at least two questions. First, what is meant by "objectivity"—especially in morality, broadly understood to include judgments and decisions reached by mining magnates, stock brokers, judges (recall Judge Clancy), politicians running for office (Clark), newspaper editors serving the interests of their papers' owners (i.e., the copper kings or their supporters), mine operators or individual miners faced with a safety or health issue or contemplating a strike? This is not so easy to pin down. For Lonergan, at least, "objectivity" is hardly a matter of simply taking a good look, for that's not what knowing is. Nor is it a matter of knee-jerk "common sense" on which so many politicians and others tend to want to take their stand today, since common sense is often mixed with common nonsense, is closely tied to particular time and place, is prone to rash judgment, and is but one realm of meaning, albeit a crucial one. Most problematic of all, common sense cannot rise above itself. Rather, for Lonergan, "objectivity" is a question of "authentic subjectivity," a difficult, ongoing matter of raising questions, of seeking "insight" and overcoming "oversight" engendered by biases of various kinds. Put otherwise, "objectivity" is a matter of following, in every endeavor, in every conceivable walk or aspect of life, the "transcendental precepts," Be attentive, Be intelligent, Be reasonable, Be responsible, and, much in tune with Pope Francis, Be loving. If necessary, Change.

Second, the notion of "objectivity" in the scholarly realm in which Malone moves is a special matter for discussion—for example, in terms of sources: Which—or who—are the "sources" that garner the scholar's attention? Whose story gets told, and from what angle? To what, or to whom, is the scholar "attentive"? As we shall see, such issues emerge in significant and interesting ways in the case of our third teller of the story of Butte, since Janet L. Finn's work, without leaving theoretical frameworks behind, relies heavily on interviews, especially of women. As for Malone himself, he tells us that he is less interested in the "good and bad copper kings than in the political-economic forces which they created, and which created them."[37] One might say that his focus is more on the structural than on the personal, and we will keep this in mind as we touch on several topics that Malone explores.

For all his interest in political and economic forces, however, the starting point for Malone is not political maneuvering or financial backing for early mining ventures in Butte or other locales. Nor does he begin, as Glasscock does, with highway robbers and vigilantes in an untamed land, or even with the lives of early placer miners. Rather, Malone's starting point is the geology "that made this isolated valley such a remarkable place."[38] This may seem an obvious place to start. But it is also significant, given our prospector's tools. For instance, Lonergan's notion of emergent probability pertains to world processes that are a matter of natural history (how did this gold get here, anyway?) as well as of human history (mining ventures, railroads, banking systems, stock markets, nations engaged in trading or war, etc.).[39] Of course Pope Francis's "common home" fully includes the flora and fauna of Butte, given by God as a gift.[40]

Malone quickly moves beyond geology as prospectors arrive on the scene, but geology is never left completely behind. While he is not offering a history of mining, Malone presents the early days of Butte as a dynamic interrelationship between the earth, with its secrets and its mix of refractory ores, and those human actors who arrived, first to a small mining camp that showed modest promise and then to what would become "the Richest Hill on Earth." No doubt a mining engineer or geologist who is also a historian could tell the reader more about the various challenges miners faced and how they were met—or not—but Malone is not inattentive to such things. Nor does he ignore the many connections between mining in Butte and the mining that came before, in such places as Nevada and Colorado.

Such connections include the "self-correcting processes" (Lonergan) of teaching and learning,[41] whether that education occurred in a Nevada operation, preparing Marcus Daly to become "one of the greatest practical miners and mine developers who ever lived," or at the Columbia University School of Mines or the University of Freiburg, where Fritz Heinze's studies made his future exploits possible.[42] In other words, the processes to which Malone attends are of various kinds, and they occur in various venues—local, state, regional ("the northern frontier" of Malone's subtitle), national, international, above the ground but also in the bowels of the earth. They occur over time. For Malone, the story of Butte is the story of much previous mining, in the Western United States and elsewhere. But it is also the story of the earth itself.[43]

"Boom Town" and Beyond

Many would say, and Malone would surely agree, that in the period under discussion there was no place in America, perhaps the world, quite like Butte. Yet, even when the focus is fully there, as in a chapter entitled "Boom Town," the connections beyond Butte are many. To begin with, Malone stresses that Butte was a town of immigrants, with all the bonding and conflict that came with it. Malone identifies the bonds that united the populace, notably the (largely Irish) Catholic faith, on the one hand, and labor, on the other. Yet, religion and labor were themselves prone to bitter ethnic conflict,[44] as Italians and Eastern Europeans, often Orthodox Christians, faced frequent discrimination that sometimes turned violent. The "white prejudice" in Butte resulted in discrimination not only against blacks, who were relatively few in Montana, and Native Americans, who were not, but also, Malone points out, against Chinese immigrants.[45] Labor unions, it must be stressed, offered no guaranteed remedies for this discrimination. On the contrary, anti-Chinese policies could rise to the level of union demands.[46]

The question of class distinctions is somewhat perplexing. On the one hand, as is clear from any account, the gap between the fabulously wealthy and the miner working below ground for $3.00 or $3.50/day (other labor paid a bit more) was as vast as the gap between Marcus Daly's magnificent Butte mansion and the squalor in which many miners, single or married with children, lived. On the other hand, Malone describes, in the early years especially, a kind of individualistic egalitarianism that embraced rich and poor alike. Yes, there was in those early days "desolation, fatalism, and despair," but there was also to be found "a characteristic get-rich-quick attitude, an unassuming democracy, and an unquestioned tolerance of one's fellow man" such that "[m]illionaires, bums, working stiffs, well-groomed ladies, and whores all bumped elbows on common terms."[47] In this atmosphere, an "unrestrained individualism" prevailed. Not only did Butte have its "characters," but valorization of the individual seems to have extended even to particular horses, dogs, cats, mules, and "the 'Centerville Bull,' which roamed the upper hill."[48]

I want to return to this emphasis on the individual, but since Malone is eager to stress political and economic forces, it is important to note the care with which he discusses the complex matter of party politics surrounding the state-capital campaign and Clark's scandal-plagued U.S. senatorial campaigns. Especially notable here is the way that populism, with the demagogic encouragement of Heinze, cut across party lines, and the way in which mining and populism came together in the "free silver" movement championed by William Jennings Bryan.

As we saw above, Glasscock ascribed to the miners of Butte the view that "Heinze was as Christ and the Standard Oil Company as his crucifiers." Perhaps in the back of Glasscock's fertile mind was the historical fact of Bryan's famous "Cross of Gold" speech, to which Malone refers in the course of his chapter on "Politics: The Clark-Daly Feud."[49] In any event, Bryan and what he stood for are key components of Malone's account of political forces shaped by and shaping the copper kings. Attention to Bryan shows that the politics of Butte and of Montana were clearly linked to politics at the national level. At the same time, those politics were clearly contextualized by mining in Montana. The populism that stood behind the free silver movement was meant to protect small businesses and especially farmers from powerful business interests. But populism in Butte and in Montana (which did yet not have the populist-leaning agricultural sector it would later have) was, of course, tied to silver because Montana was a silver mining state. Deflating the value of silver in relation to gold from 16/1 to 32/1 could be devastating not only to those who owned but also to those who labored in the mines.

But for our purposes, it is noteworthy what Malone does not discuss: Bryan not only as a political figure but also a turn-of-the-century religious figure who, contrary to the popular view of him as simply a fundamentalist fool (compliments of the play and film *Inherit the Wind*), in fact was deeply worried about a commitment to science that ends in social Darwinism.[50] To put this another way: Glasscock reports that Heinze, that great champion of the common laborer standing against the evils of Standard Oil, at least until he pretty much sold out to the same, came to Butte after "the advantages of civilization [had trained him] in the scientific theories of mining engineering and metallurgy." One might therefore ask with Bryan, not only here but throughout this extended meditation on mining: To what extent does science and technology serve all the people, especially those most vulnerable, and to what extent does it serve only the strong and the few?

Of Robin Hood and Robbers

This, of course, is the sort of question that Pope Francis might pose in the context of his "technocratic paradigm." But within the context of Malone's own telling of the battle for Butte, it is also raised by the figure of Heinze. As he moves toward the conclusion of his retelling the story of Butte, Malone asks just what motivated the technologically, business, and legally savvy Heinze to battle so long and as hard as he did against those from the East bent upon taking over the mines of Butte, including his own. While some saw in Heinze a "Robin Hood of copper," Malone cannot help but conclude that "Heinze had really aimed all along primarily at forcing the trust to pay him an exorbitant price for his holdings. This is not to say," Malone continues, "that his antitrust crusades were altogether insincere, only that he was an especially virulent example of the ruthless capitalists of his time."[51]

With this judgment in mind, Malone's comment on an earlier phase of Heinze's life is intriguing for reasons both immediate to the story Malone tells and beyond that story to larger questions of mining morality especially critical today. For a couple of years, Heinze left Butte for Trail, British Columbia, where he bought a newspaper to serve as his mouthpiece, established a smelter in the area (thus saving shipping costs), and became a champion of the region and its people against the oppressive Canadian Pacific Railroad—only to abruptly leave the area after selling his holdings to the Canadian Pacific. "Did he seriously intend to develop the Rossland district?" Malone asks. "Or was he simply posing as the champion of the area in order to shake down the Canadian Pacific and to extract profitable land grants from the provincial and national parliaments?"[52] For Malone, the latter is the more likely case.

For the larger purpose of mining morality, Malone's assessment of Heinze raises very basic questions of intentionality, motivation, and personal integrity, as well as transparency in communicating to others what one is planning to do. These are the sorts of questions that anyone might raise about the actions of others, but as importantly about actions and plans of one's own. But questions at the personal or intersubjective level may lead one to ask about the relationship of such intentionality and integrity to identification with, or resistance to, particular institutions, groups, or movements and their constitutive meanings and values.[53] Recall that Malone is less interested in the "good and bad copper kings than in the political-economic forces which they created, *and* which created them" (emphasis added). So, which is it? Did the copper kings create the forces that shaped and overwhelmed Butte; or were the copper kings simply the products of these larger forces?

If this chicken and egg dynamic is not easily resolved, it is at least illumined and perhaps complicated by other characters in Malone's account, namely, the principals of Standard Oil, Henry Rogers and, later, John D. Ryan, who relocated to Butte and assumed the presidency of Anaconda. Malone points out that Rogers exemplifies "the schizoid nature of the business titans of his generation": "Virile, arrogant, ruthless in business, magnetic and witty in society, Rogers still had a lunar dualism—dark on one side, bright on the other." As for Ryan, he seemed to "admiring businessmen" to be "beyond reproach, a devout Catholic and devoted family man," professionally adept and dedicated. To the critics of big business, however, he "personified the worst traits of corporate capitalism," leading one to comment that "organized greed could teach him nothing in selfishness and no awakening conscience disturbed the dreams of his avarice."[54]

Apparently, Malone himself does not think this sort of split moral personality, if we can put it this way, is inevitable or justifiable. When discussing the political-economic forces that led Montana down a bribery-ridden path to national scandal, Malone lists the names of the four lone Republican state legislators who did not succumb to corruption. Leaving aside his historian's "detached objectivity"—or not?—he tells the reader: "The names of these men deserve to be remembered," just as Malone remembers the former vigilante Wilbur Sanders, in his castigation of Republicans who bowed to Clark, as "the Diogenes of the GOP." [55] Clearly for Malone, the fact proves the possibility: corrupting forces need not sully every soul; the individual moral agent can stand firm. Toward the end of his tale, after conceding that much necessary good came out of the consolidation of the mines, he counts the costs of the bribery, the violence, the corruption, the endless legal wrangling, and he offers a general judgment on the battle for Butte, if not a lament: "It need not have been this way." Other great mining districts took a smoother path to consolidation, for instance, negotiating around the "silly" "Apex" law. Butte was a "tortured and complex situation," involving a "ruthless group of Wall Street manipulators" coming up against two unscrupulous independents, Clark and Heinze. "In the process," he says, "they disgraced themselves and injured thousands, living and unborn."[56]

Beyond the Battle for Butte

It need not have been this way, perhaps, but it was this way. Writing some seventy-five years later, Malone himself appears to share the editorial judgment of *The Nation* that appeared in 1906: "Nobody comes out of the contest with clean hands, but at any rate there is hope of now ending it."[57] In the last pages of his book, Malone focuses on a central if not the central issue: the implications for the future—that is, post-1906—of the battle for Butte. Put in terms of emergence, one might say that, for Malone, *how* something—a town or city, a mining industry, a utilities company, a new member state of the United States—emerges is as important as the fact *that* it emerges. Political-economic forces, but also persons with their intentions and plans, their avarice and their hopes for a better future, conspired to make not only Butte but also Montana into what it would be after the 1864–1906 battle for Butte was through. The emergence was such that, in the wake of the battle, a mining company, together with its sister utility company, Montana Power, could for many years hold a state in its thrall.

The grip had an especially deleterious effect on labor relations. In time, Butte moved away from the "baronial benevolence" of the early days when the many unions "tended to identify with and cooperate with management in a climate of harmony."[58] With the concentration of power and a thus greater distance from the workers (unlike in the days of Clark, Daly, and Heinze), many workers were attracted to the wave of "leftist radicalism and socialism" that was becoming prevalent in the West. This led to a split among Butte miners, some more conservative and aligned with the "company," others impatient and ready to side with the Industrial Workers of the World—a move toward amalgamation of another kind. The result was violence and, in time and with the intervention of federal troops, a crushing of unionism during World War I, a blow from which it would not recover until Montana workers regained the closed shop in 1934 with the New Deal. Even more pernicious, in Malone's view, was Anaconda's manipulation of Montana politics. Joined with its "Siamese twin Montana Power" which "ruled the roost as a giant faction in a small commonwealth—wielding precisely the kind of naked power that James Madison had long ago feared and would now have understood."[59]

Malone cautions against "overly dramatic and Manichaean" descriptions of the spirited, often harsh and even violent dialectic (our term) that was Butte and Montana, pitting corporate interests against "the rest of the population which feels it has no stake in the Company's prosperity,"[60] even if such descriptions are truer than not. The Company's power was never absolute, and, in time, it, too, was not "immune to the forces of history." This included not only the panic of 1907 but also the diminishing returns from the labor-intensive copper mines of Butte. With the purchase of the American Brass Company, Anaconda expanded into manufacturing and, to satisfy internal demand for copper, bought a major interest in the Guggenheims' mines in Chile, "the largest single purchase that Wall Street had ever seen."[61] This gave Anaconda access to the vast deposits of low-grade ore at Chuquicamata high in the Andes, about which we will hear more below. Back in Butte, the future of mining was tenuous. In 1955, Anaconda would turn to more economical open-pit mining. After some twenty years, driven to near bankruptcy by the nationalization of the mines in Chile, it sold off its assets to Atlantic Richfield (ARCO), causing Butte to breathe a sigh of relief that its mining future would be once again secure, even as it dealt with new challenges such as increasing environmental concerns. This optimism was to be short-lived; by the time Malone concludes his narrative, the new owners had shut down its two smelters and the days ahead were not so sure.

In his discussion toward the end of his book of William Clark's tainted and relatively uninspiring single term in the U.S. Senate, Malone turns to Clark's own words. "In rearing the great structure of empire on this Western Hemisphere," Clark told the Senate as he was leaving, "we are obliged to avail ourselves of all the resources at our command. The requirements of this great utilitarian age demand it. Those who succeed us can well take care of themselves."[62] Given Malone's sensitivity to how complex historical events and developments, such as the battle for Butte, can cast a long and sometimes dark and ugly shadow over the future, and given Malone's own horizons and "foundations," it would be hard to find more damning words than these. Just as, for Glasscock, "Clark Leaves Heinze to Hold the Bag" (the title of chapter 27), so, for Malone, Clark left not only Heinze but also future generations to "hold the bag," to fend for themselves, and to pay dearly for the sins of

Figure 3.4. Butte union hall meeting.
Farm Security Administration—Office of War Information Photograph Collection (Library of Congress).

those who had gone before. In this respect at least, the horizons against which Malone tells the story of Butte have much in common with our prospector's tools, which urge us to look out for future neighbors and their weal and woe.

A Side Trip into Canada and International Environmental Law

If, in delving into the past, Malone is alert to the future—often ill—effects of decisions, actions, and movements occurring during the years 1864–1906, it may be in accord with his intentions to bring one aspect of his narrative forward in ways that he himself does not. It has to do with Fritz Heinze's two-year excursion into Canada. As explained above, Heinze left Butte for Trail, British Columbia. There he built a smelter in 1895. He soon sold his interests in that venture and returned to Butte. Over the years, pollution from that job-producing smelter was accepted by the local community as a sign of prosperity. But it crossed the border into Washington State where it did significant damage and was not so well received. Redress was sought through arbitration, and the case turned out to be an early landmark in what would later become international environmental law.

This is partly so because the novelty of the border-crossing claim required the arbitration tribunal to search for models to guide its judgment. They found one in the United States Supreme Court's attempts to deal with damage claims made by one state against another.[63] One might say that at the very time that Montana, a territory whose claim to statehood owed so much to mining, was emerging as a state, international environmental law was emerging as well—and one of the Montana copper kings initiated the damages that spurred its growth. On the surface at least, our retellings of the story of Butte so far have had little apparent connection to international relations and law, and, especially perhaps, to the *transnational* corporations discussed by Lonergan in "Healing and Creating in History." But such connections were already implicit in the early history of Butte (think, for instance, of the immigration issues with which Butte dealt), and in time they would become fully apparent. They are more than apparent in the third retelling to which we now turn.

CONTRADICTIONS AND CONTRA-DICTION IN BUTTE AND CHUQUICAMATA

In his telling of the story of Butte, Michael Malone aspired to a "detached objectivity" that he did not find in Glasscock and others. On first reading, at least, one might suggest that Janet L. Finn's *Tracing the Veins: Of Copper, Culture, and Community from Butte to Chuquicamata* runs in the other direction. She seems hardly "detached." Rather she is engaged, passionate, politically committed. As for "objectivity," not only does she show an intense interest in the intimate, "subjective" experience of others, but her own subjectivity is quite visible to the reader. But such an easy contrast would be unfair. Each in his or her own way might be said to be responsive to what Lonergan has termed the "transcendental precepts" that take one beyond oneself in the direction of truth and the truly good.

A Tale of Two Cities

Finn both changes and expands the focus of the story in important ways. We will consider only a few of these and, unfortunately, not in the detail they deserve. First, of course, this is not really one more telling of the story of Butte, but rather "a tale of two cities": Butte, "The Richest Hill on Earth," and Chuquicamata, Chile, "The World's Greatest Mining Camp." The two are bound together by mining, mostly of copper, and, more to the point of the story, by the Anaconda Copper Mining Company, which, as we saw from our two earlier accounts, grew up in Butte but expanded to Chile in the early 1920s. Anaconda relinquished the Chilean mines with nationalization in 1971, a blow to the company that led in part to Anaconda's sale of assets in Butte in 1977. Given the challenges of such a study, including the fact that Finn is a native of one locale (Butte) and not the other, the depth and nuance of her study is remarkable, signaled by her reluctance to call it a "comparative" study since easy comparisons can be misleading. She wants to drill down, to transgress boundaries, to tell a more complex tale.

Second, unlike Glasscock and to an extent Malone—but not unlike Lonergan—Finn is from the outset concerned about "method," at least in the sense of setting out to "build upon and critique a theory of practice as I grapple with the questions of cultural politics."[64] This theory, she points out, "seeks to grasp the dynamics of structure and human action as they unfold over time." This approach, which draws on the work of Karl Marx and Max Weber, insists that human beings are both constrained by structure but are also agents for building them. Add to this the ways in which human actors are themselves changed in the process, and you have "a 'triadic' approach, one that attends to the mutual constitution of the constraining structures, the human action that critiques and makes structures, and the "making of social actors as they reproduce and change the system."[65]

Now, in some respects this would seem to be not all that different from what Malone was after in *The Battle for Butte*, when he tells us he is less

Figure 3.5. Copper on a loading dock in Chuquicamata, Chile.

interested in the "good and bad copper kings than in the political-economic forces which they created, and which created them."[66] That is, powerful human agents are creators of but also creatures of "forces" or, in Finn's term, "structures." Certainly, concerns about "meaning" and "power" are evident in Malone's account. But there are significant differences. For one, as just noted, Finn is more explicit about and detailed in the approach she is taking, the method she is applying. Second, she is not focused only on the action of people like Clark, Daly, Heinze, Rogers, and Ryan. She is at least as focused, if not more so, on the actions of those not at the top, especially women as they grapple with meaning and power—for instance, during a prolonged mining strike. If we may put it in terms of "healing and creating in history," for Finn, those on the underside of history—those often thought to be "disposable," for Pope Francis—can be and often are healers and creators, too. Third, Finn is acutely aware of how she herself is at once constrained and enabled by structures and yet faced with the responsibility of helping to reshape or transform them—and of how she has been changed in the process.

Contradictions from Top to Bottom

The approach that Finn takes in this book leads her to uncover multiple "contradictions" that people face in their lives. As one might expect in a study guided by a theory informed at least in part by Marxism, these are contradictions of global capitalism, but if this is so, they are manifest at the low, often intimate level of community and even family life. In this respect, one might say that Finn is engaged in the functional specialty "dialectics," and in the process is struggling to find solid ground, new foundations from which to move forward. But it is not the dialectics found in competing theories (although she is not unaware of these), so much as it is the experience of everyday life in Butte, in Chuquicamata, and beyond. In this manner, she sharpens our prospector's tools. The functional specialty of "research," linked to the level of "experience," may not be the first instance of the establishment of which texts to read (although she has clearly made choices about this) but of whose experience to listen to, say, around a kitchen table.[67]

In her narrative, which includes forays into what Lonergan would term the "theoretical" realm of meaning, or what James Gustafson would call the "ethical" mode of moral discourse, with its carefully defined terms and distinctions, without getting lost in these realms, Finn "dig[s] beneath the surface to disrupt images of wholeness, revealing," for instance, a "complicated history of collaboration and conflict."[68] This is evident in her review, in chapter 2, of Anaconda's presence and operations in the two locales over the course of a century. While there is much similarity between Butte and Chuquicamata,

Finn seeks to go beyond surface comparisons.[69] Such an approach involves attending to the interplay of structure and agency as residents of both locales face dilemmas and double binds of dealing with a corporation that both gives and takes away.

The contradictions continue. Butte miners were highly skilled, took great pride in their work—*pace* Marx, who pegged them as alienated from it[70]—and were ready to risk their lives. Yet they could not seem to manage their own affairs, especially money and alcohol. "In short, they say that Butte boys needed their mothers," Finn reports, "and their mothers often obliged, much to the resentment of many wives."[71] As for those wives, they stood by their men in labor disputes, and yet there was inequality at home. So, their lives were complicated and contradictory, too.

A Complex Feminine View from Above

Finn has much else to say about gender roles (and were she writing now would probably have a more complex story to tell), but for our purposes one stands out because it reaches into what Lonergan would call the "transcendent" realm of meaning, a realm which, of course, permeates *Laudato si'* and the rest of Catholic social thought. I refer to Finn's reporting on the role and complex meaning of the Virgin Mary in both communities, where she stands as "the embodiment of the ultimate feminine contradiction: virgin and mother."[72]

In Chuquicamata, celebration days included dance troupes associated with the Virgin of Guadalupe that expressed meanings outside the narrative of Anaconda. But Butte presents a particularly interesting case. There, in Finn's narrative women represented, as they did in Chuquicamata, the trinity of virgin, mother, and prostitute in this heavily Catholic city. But it was mostly men who conceived of and then overcame great challenges to put a ninety-foot Lady of the Rockies on a mountaintop overlooking the city. What began with a man of Mexican heritage being counseled to seek the aid of Our Lady of Guadalupe to help his wife recover from an illness turned into a five-year community project. The story of its building, as told in various media, "offers an intriguing mythology that pits man against nature (and government bureaucracy), and faith against doubt."[73]

In ways that may approach both Pope Francis's openness to other faiths in *Laudato si'* and Lonergan's notion of an emerging religious consciousness that crosses religious lines, the statue, so rooted in Catholic piety, was named "Our Lady of the Rockies" in order to "include all religions and faiths because we will need them all to finish this project."[74] This watchful figure, in Finn's telling, joins in fascinating ways capitalism and cosmology. Our Lady of the Rockies is also "a complex entity." "For some, she symbolizes community hope; for the more skeptical, she represents the feminizing of Butte's labor force. Perhaps she embodies a struggle for a sense of order, and enduring presence in time of uncertainty, and immutable representation of motherhood."[75] Here we might add that, for both communities, Mary or the Virgin provides a particularly rich vein for prospecting for ethics. For instance, liberation theologians have much to say about this feminine figure that might add to Finn's reflections and sharpen our prospectors' tools.[76]

Consumption

In "Crafting the Everyday," Finn explains further that the convergence of corporation, paternalism, and patriarchalism shaped but did not determine women's identity. The women of Butte negotiated these contradictions as they crafted the everyday, especially during hard times. In the process, they formed their own critical consciousness. They faced and dealt with the "collective depression" found in Butte, even as they we were often left behind when the men in their lives searched elsewhere for work. Banding together, they founded a shelter called Safe Space, where they dealt with life in the mines, with its fears of danger and unemployment sometimes manifested itself in domestic violence. In both Chuquicamata and Butte, women as well as the miners themselves lived in a toxic, health-harming environment, and were consumed by worries about family finances and much else. In fact, "consumption"—another name for the silicosis that plagued the miners—is for Finn a fitting metaphor for life in these mining centers.

The shift to open pit mining in Butte in the 1950s quite literally consumed parishes and sections of old Butte. On the outskirts of Butte the beloved Columbia Gardens, William Clark's one great contribution to that town, was eventually consumed as well. In Chuquicamata, some women as well as men were consumed by depression and alcoholism, but this was lived out in a culture of denial. As they were consumed by the desert and its winds, they also suffered from isolation. Nor did children escape this consumption. Just as men hid their fears behind bravado, so children grew up in an atmosphere of "danger and defiance."[77] Slag heaps were their playgrounds and copper ponds that rotted their clothes were their swimming holes. In Finn's account of the more recent history of these two communities, while the mines in many ways consumed the workers and others, the community became consumers of fast food and other marks of the good life. In the process, they may have consumed their own values.

The theme of dealing with contradictions, successfully or not, is taken up anew as Finn turns to matters of "trust, betrayal, and transformation" in her penultimate chapter. The focus here is primarily gender imagery and relations in the stories of Butte and Chuquicamata. In Butte it was often a case of "workingman's wisdom . . . being steeped in trust and betrayal." Over the years, laborers encountered secrecy within the Anaconda Company's practices, which included infiltration of the unions—a practice which often led to mistrust of the unions more than of the company. Thus the "little guys" got squeezed by both.[78] For instance, unions got the blame for specialization that did not prepare them for the multivalent workforce that would later be touted by the modern corporation, when in fact some workers attested that it was the company that, earlier on, had demanded just such monovalent or specialized labor in and around the mines.

In the late 1970s, when Anaconda was purchased by Atlantic Richfield Corporation (ARCO), workers felt like they dealt with the new owners in good faith, only to see the mines close, with devastating effects. Then again when the mines were reopened in 1986 under new ownership, workers again felt they acted in good faith, only to see the mining operations resume union-free. While the reopening of the mines was greeted by many as great news, lifting the community from its "collective depression," perspectives on the process were actually complex, with a great deal of suspicion on the part of workers. This extended to the environmental cleanup that was now the order of the day, an effort that was viewed by many as a process that profited only outside experts who seemed unable to set aside their jargon and answer long-time community members' questions about what, exactly, was going on. Environmental groups brought their own perspectives and suspicions regarding not only the efforts and rhetoric of ARCO, but also the complicity of the community through their willingness to put up with environmental threats of various kinds. In November 1995, a flock of geese alit on the rising waters of the Berkeley Pit. The 342 that were later found dead "have become symbolic of the palpable risks that Butte people face each day."[79] In the midst of such a situation, the people of Butte did not know whom to trust.

The people of Chuquicamata had their own struggles with ambiguity and contradictory narratives. Those interviewed had problems with Anaconda, but absent the strong sense of betrayal found in Butte. The Chuquicamata stories bespoke more "transparency of corporate power," where distinctions were out in the open, although further inquiry suggested more intrigue beneath the surface, such as those in power secretly shifting gold out of the country. It was stories of the Popular Unity governments, the dictatorship (of Pinochet), and the current mine management that reveal betrayals of trust. The new regimes, both left and right, could be heavy-handed, not fully respectful of the miners' experience. The new order, critical of the paternalism of the Anaconda days, was meant to be participatory, but, in the miners' view, it really was not. The affirmation that young, expert managers

Figure 3.6. The Berkeley Pit.
Photo courtesy of NASA.

received was "a slap in the face to many workers, whose life experience was reduced to contamination by the capitalist order that made them pollutants of the new order."[80]

Deep Play with Contradictions

Finn offers a particularly interesting comment on a study that criticized past social work practices. The study reflected many of Finn's own views on social work (her field of specialization), but she comments that "the authors' political and ideological position obscured their view of the nuances of a life built both because and in spite of fifty years of capitalist domination."[81] This leads her to wonder if her own political views have blinded her to the actual lives of those she has encountered. Unfortunately, the many nuances that Finn does capture in her review of the various regimes are lost in brevity here. It will have to suffice to say that whether the mining regime was the paternalism of the Anaconda Company, the socialism of Allende, the dictatorship of Pinochet, or the more recent running of the mines up to the time of Finn's writing, the narratives of those in charge did not quite match those of the ones who labored in and around the mines. Meanwhile, as Finn points outs, neither racism nor corruption have gone away.

To make some sense of all this, Finn turns to the notion, first put forward by Jeremy Bentham and then refined by Clifford Geertz, of "deep play." Deep play, which refers to "a game one seemingly cannot win but can't not play," Finn says, "captures the practical essence of the problems posed to workers by the capitalist contradiction."[82] Occasionally, however, by their participation those who stand inevitably to lose might change the rules of the game. Such has been the case, for instance, when gender lines have been crossed, with women getting involved in labor strikes and relations, and with men cross-dressing to escape brutal treatment at the hands of strike breakers. Finn has in mind this notion of deep play as she looks to the future, not only of the women of Butte and Chuquicamata but her own future as well.

The shifting ground of gender relations, whereby women's roles are expanding with new imagined futures, takes place in Butte under the watchful eye of Our Lady of the Rockies. Finn sees such structures, erected in times of crisis, "not as reflections of stability but formidable efforts to create a sense of immutability in the moments of profound transformation."[83] Chuquicamata women, too, are engaged in transformation, but it is not a sure thing. They are invited by Corporatión National de Cobre (CODELCO)-Chuqui to tell their stories, but at least some activists know that such participation requires that they strategize "to change the rules of the game through their participation and to demand answers and accountability in the process."[84] Moreover, certain formal distinctions or "Rolls"—supervisors (A), salaried employees (B), and laborers (C)—may have been abandoned. But they remain in fact, for instance, between the direct employees of the mines and the contracted laborers who live in the *poblacions* (poor neighborhoods), where women, often abandoned by the men in their lives, join together in their own struggle for a better future.

In both Butte and Chuquicamata, the rhetoric and reality of "reclamation" are both prevalent and complex. On the one hand, there is, especially in Butte, the huge task of repairing the damage done from mining over the years, while there is also the question of whose histories will be reclaimed and how. So, "in both locales, diverse and at times competing claims to history are being made in the interest of present and future community survival."[85] Here again, the role of "back-talk" to counter the dominant stories of those in power emerges as a theme. As Finn points out, "These practices of reclamation reflect the Spanish meaning of the word *reclamer*: to claim, demand, or protest." It has been one of Finn's goals to ensure that women are engaged "in the process of reclamation with new imaginings of and claims for communities of connection and concern."[86]

The ending of Finn's narrative—or, one might say, her critical collation of narratives—is particularly germane to mining morality. It would seem to signal the sort of "self-appropriation" that lies at the heart of Lonergan's generalized empirical method. On the last pages of *Insight*, Lonergan discusses his own experience of grappling with the writings of Thomas Aquinas in the light of Pope Leo's 1879 call to "augment and perfect the old by means of the new" (*"vetera novis augere et peficere"*):

> After spending years reaching up to the mind of Aquinas, I came to a two-fold conclusion. On the one hand, that reaching had changed me profoundly. On the other hand, that change was the essential benefit. For not only did it make me capable of grasping what, in the light of my conclusions, the *verita* really were, but also it opened up challenging vistas on what the *nova* could be.[87]

Tracing the Veins is not the fruit of engaging a profound thinker from the past. Finn's "texts" were hardly the same. Yet the result is not so totally different. Finn professes that "this work has transformed my life. It has brought me face-to-face with the depth of human brutality and the wells-spring of human courage, hope, and possibility."[88] One might say that, for Finn, too, her research opened "challenging vistas" as she looks to the future. Attuned as she is to "the confines of [people's] social and critical circumstances," she asserts that "the notion of an intentional human subject has been soundly trounced in the poststructural and postmodern move to discursively constructed subjectivities and fragmented identities."[89]

Perhaps so, but this depends on what one means by "intentional." For in the next breath she acknowledges, "As I listened to a wealth of stories, I became more convinced of the power of humanness, the search for meaning, and the desire to render coherence in the face of contradiction."[90] Is this all that different from what Lonergan refers to as "dialectic," a sorting through of contradictions in search for meaning, or for a larger whole? Is her concern with "mining feeling" and "the structure of feelings" she encountered so concretely totally removed from the more abstract but no less sincere turn to the feelings that apprehend values that one finds in the later Lonergan, or the more visceral encounter with feeling one finds in Pope Francis? Does not "the power of humanness" that Finn detects in those caught in a web of contractions and pain come close to what Pope Francis says in *Laudato si'*—quoted earlier, but worth repeating here? Francis writes:

> Yet all is not lost. Human beings, while capable of the worst, are also capable of rising above themselves, choosing again what is good, and making a new start, *despite their mental and social conditioning*. We are able to take an honest look at ourselves, to acknowledge our deep dissatisfaction, and to embark on new

> paths to authentic freedom. *No system can completely suppress our openness to what is good, true and beautiful, or our God-given ability to respond to his grace at work deep in our hearts* (205, emphasis added).

Or, to anticipate a topic to be discussed later, is the future-orientation of Finn's last chapter, where she finds herself committed to "a game we seemingly cannot win, but can't not play," so different from the attitude of some international lawyers who focus not only on *lex lata*, law as it is, but also on *lex ferenda*, law as it might or could be? It may be that postmodernism and poststructuralism have not "trounced" the "intentional human subject" after all.

We will return to this and other possible ties to our prospector's tools, but for now it should be noted that, perhaps more than Glasscock and Malone, Finn is facing the future, as concerned, if not more so, about where we are headed as she is about where we—and the often-silent voices she has sought to hear—have been. In fact, upon further reflection she says she has been writing the "next chapter of this history from the moment I began the project."[91] It is future that is focused on community, but one that is transnational as well as local, one that sees "the need for imagining new forms of community in order to confront the challenges posed by the shifting forces of global capitalism."[92]

A NEW COPPER KING AND MONTANA POWER

In the latter part of *Tracing the Veins*, Finn discusses the more recent history of Butte, including the familiar sorts of suspicions surrounding the "new owner" of the Anaconda Company/ARCO mining operations. She also notes earlier that "a Montana businessman announced plans to resurrect mining in Butte" two months after "Our Lady began her permanent vigilance over Butte" on December 20, 1985. Finn does not name the "new owner." This seems curious, if not inexplicable, for this "Montana businessman" was—and is—in his own way a bigger-than-life figure, not unlike the copper kings of more than a century ago.

If America's Horatio Alger myth contains any truth at all, then Dennis Washington may be cited as living proof.[93] Washington was born in Spokane, Washington; spent part of his youth in Missoula, Montana, and other places; and then returned to Missoula in his late teens. Not unlike Marcus Daly, he was educated on the job rather than in college. He became a highly successful construction worker as a late teen, overseeing major jobs in his early twenties, and was vice president of the company by age twenty-six. At twenty-nine, he struck out on his own, with a $30,000 loan for a caterpillar tractor, and built a highly successful construction company. His first major contract was road-building in Glacier National Park, before the glaciers began noticeably to melt away due to climate change. Over the years, he has branched out into railroads, tugboats, mining, and, pertinent to this evolving story, more recently environmental reclamation.

In 1985 he purchased the Anaconda/ARCO Company at a time when the copper market was severely suppressed, and it resumed mining in the Continental Pit. Shortly after the purchase, copper prices rose significantly. As we saw from Finn's account, this turn of events was viewed by some as almost divine intervention, while for others it was yet one more cause for suspicion and the experience of capitalism's contradictions. From the point of view of business leaders, Washington was, and is, an extremely hardworking, shrewd risk-taker—an example of capitalism at its best, to say nothing of a realization of the American Dream. Washington reopened the mines as union-free, having secured workers' agreements to take pay cuts but, in exchange, to share in company profits. With some setbacks and a short-term shut down, the mining operations have continued, employing about 350 at a high salary level. Furthermore, Washington Companies boasts a remarkable safety record compared to a very dangerous past, and the company claims to be fully committed to sound environmental practices as well environmental reclamation—which, it should be stressed, is a business opportunity.[94] Just as Marcus Daly had his racehorses in the Bitterroot Valley, so Washington's favorite pastime appears to be refurbishing fabulous yachts.[95] But together with his wife he is also a committed philanthropist, giving generously especially to education with, among other outlets, the aptly named the Horatio Alger Montana Undergraduate Scholarship program.[96]

In short, Washington appears to embody at the top the kinds of contradictions to which Finn is so attuned through her engagement with those at the bottom—capitalism takes but can also give. Here, an extremely wealthy, "self-made" capitalist takes a sizable business risk that may lift a community out of "collective depression." But this is a story older than Finn's account. Surely, Glasscock is aware of contradictions, of "double binds." He recounts the moral shortcomings of the copper kings even as he extols their achievements and all the wealth and jobs they brought to others. So, too, Malone is keenly aware of how laborers were caught in the middle, and very probably simply used, in the battle for Butte. But in the process, some no doubt contradicted those who would mistreat them or hold them back.

To show that the contradictions, or at least the ambiguities, persist, we might return to another "character" in the story of Butte discussed by Malone, namely that "Siamese twin" of Anaconda, the Montana Power Company. Now, in Finn's retelling, "power" tends to spell trouble, at least for those who do not have much of it. No doubt Montana Power, which together with Anaconda pretty much owned the State of Montana, might be cast in a purely negative light. Yet, in keeping with themes of contradiction and ambiguity, this particular story of "power" is not so simple. From one point of view the story of Montana Power is another chapter in the story of how big business got the best of a state, but it seems also to be, in part, a story of a big company having served the citizens of that state fairly well. CBS's *Sixty Minutes* begins a February 2003 report in this way:

> For nearly 90 years, the Montana Power Company exemplified the very best of American capitalism. It provided cheap, reliable electricity for the people of Montana, excellent benefits for thousands of employees and generous, reliable dividends for its stockholders. Everyone was happy, except for the corporate officers and their Wall Street investment banking firm who decided there was more money to be made in the more glamourous and profitable world of telecommunications. The result exemplified the worst of American capitalism.[97]

The report goes on to claim, among other things, that the corporate officers pushed for deregulation, not in order to benefit consumers through increasing competition, but rather to increase the value of their assets before selling them off. If this was indeed the case, then one is reminded of Heinze's maneuvering against the Amalgamated, not so much to protect the workers from the wolves of Wall Street, but to ensure the maximum price when he sold out to them.

What exactly is the truth of the matter in the case of Montana Power, which was founded by John D. Ryan, president of Anaconda, I am not prepared to say. But let us assume that CBS's assessment to that point (more recent history is another question) is correct: that Montana Power, a company that was allowed by the State of Montana to remain a monopoly because the state controlled the price of its product to consumers, represented "the best of American capitalism." At this point, one might add to the mix Montana Power's earlier excursion into the strip-mining of coal, with all its environmental downsides, to fuel its new power plants. From a later point of view, say, of *Laudato si'*, the best of American capitalism might not have been so good or great after all. So, we are back to a world of contradictions, apparent or real, superficial or truly profound—contradictions that one prospecting for ethics, at least the present writer, can point out, but may not be quite able fully to resolve. The ethical prospector or moral miner that is the reader is encouraged to take up the task.

INTERIM PROSPECTOR'S REPORT

As should be clear, the story of Butte is not one story. It is not even the story of one place. The retellings discussed here—there are many others—by no means give us everything we need if we are to engage in "mining morality."

But certain prospects for that mining have emerged, and I would like to focus on a few, noting that other promising veins may surface in other chapters, and some of what I say here will be said again, perhaps in another manner befitting other moral mining sites. Let me frame this ethical prospector's report and set of recommendations under the heading of "lines, loyalties, and spheres—and contradictions arising therefrom."

To a great extent, ethics is about lines and where to draw them—bright lines, crooked lines, dotted lines—or failing to draw them at all. In the story of Butte, there are lots of lines, starting with the miners' surveyed claims on side-hills and in valleys, and in the codes that emerged to adjudicate these claims. This includes the infamous "apex rule," which Malone at least found to be "silly" and downright devilish, as Fritz Heinze proved again and again. But if this rule, made federal law, was inane, why was it so? What are we to say about property lines—about "ownership," about "dominion"? What is reasonable, what is not? We have said little directly about property, but this does not mean that much cannot or should not be said. In fact, in a subsequent chapter (chapter 5) we will be asking a property question of no little moment: Who, if anyone, owns the ocean and its depths? Or, for that matter, who owns the asteroids that speed through space (chapter 7)? The Catholic social tradition, for its part, has said much about property, insisting that neither an absolute right to "ownership" nor no rights whatsoever will do.[98] If a right to private property is affirmed, it is within the context of a prior truth about the universal destination of goods, and about stewardship, rather than domination, as a proper understanding of dominion. Moral mining will require, among other things, continuous reflection on questions of ownership, of property—including, not least of all, "intellectual property," in increasingly complex circumstances and times.

Another line to be considered has to do with what is morally acceptable to a community and what is not, and, if morally unacceptable, whether it can or should be eradicated at all costs. Glasscock appears to be weighing in on this question when he observes that even in a city famous for its toleration of vice, certain practices, including bribery, crossed a moral line and was too much to bear. More generally, Thomas Aquinas and others have asked whether every vice could or should be "against the law." Recalling Lonergan's notion of "emergent probability," we might ask whether other means, such as education, might be more fitting and effective than laws in shifting the probabilities that moral behavior and attitudes might be moved in the direction of virtue rather than of vice, assuming we know what counts for each. This sort of question is especially important when it comes to "politics"—and there was plenty of politics surrounding Butte and Chuquicamata, including, in the latter case if not the former, "geopolitics."

At a professional meeting I once listened to a paper with the clever title "Immanuel Kant Had Clean Hands. Immanuel Kant Had No Hands." Does politics lie somewhere in between? Dirty hands but not too dirty? We saw in the case of Fritz Heinz that he used the morally questionable tools of Big Business to battle Big Business, ostensibly for the sake of the unnamed miners of Montana. At what point does such imitation turn into identity? At what point has one gone "too far"? After all, Malone stresses that the copper trust so readily seen as a division of Standard Oil in fact "had no corporate connection to [Standard Oil] at all, only to its executives." While often "blamed for the sins of his proteges," John D. Rockefeller himself strongly disapproved of the emerging trust "and later censured the boys when they got in trouble."[99] At least in the person of the elder Rockefeller, even Standard Oil had its standards.

There is also the question to consider of moral levels, or, perhaps better, moral spheres—along with complex questions about conflicting loyalties and roles, even the "contradictions" to which Finn constantly draws attention. This is not a new problem. Antigone was torn between human decrees and the laws of the gods about burying the dead, and in his underappreciated treatise on the "order of charity," Aquinas asks, for instance, whom we should love more—those who have benefited us or those who will benefit tomorrow from what we do today?[100]

Or, recall another aspect of Catholic social thought and one of our prospecting tools—Aquinas's discussion of prudence[101] which, as explained in chapter 2, operates in various "spheres."[102] What might seem prudent to a person operating in one sphere, say, the family, might not seem so prudent to decisionmakers in another sphere, say, a mining operation of considerable size. In Butte, such conflicts to the point of "contradictions," in the language of Finn, seem to abound, for instance in labor relations. Interestingly, as the mines of Butte were being woven into one "amalgamated" company, over the objections of the "independents," so, too, were the many distinct labor unions joining forces. So, small may be "beautiful," à la E. F. Schumacher,[103] but neither labor nor management seemed always to concur as spheres of power seem to centralize and expand.

In any event, the story of Butte is the story of interlocking, sometimes conflicting spheres: the family; the ethnically identified parish; the otherwise racially or ethnically specified groupings (from the Irish and Italians to Eastern Europeans to Native Americans to the immigrant Chinese); the labor unions; the independent mine at odds with the amalgamated "company"; the cities (at least two with copper king patrons) vying to be the state capital; the county (of which Montana has fifty-six); the broad and booming State of Montana, barely born before tasting corruption; political parties, sometimes at odds with themselves; the "people" as in "populism" in its various forms;

the United States as one of—or "exceptional" among—many other nations; the world—with at least one great mining company crossing national lines; various faith traditions, sometimes local or national, sometimes extending to a Roman power suspect by the dominant Protestant religion of the realm. Today, we see more clearly—or not—that the spheres the moral miner must consider include other species and the planet, our "common home," under ecological threat, and a cosmos enveloping all. Especially with a rising etho- and economic-nationalism at odds with globalization of various kinds, the moral miner cannot escape the challenge of conflicting spheres, tugging at the consciences of some individuals and groups, if not all.

Sorting all this out will be no easy task, no matter what Pope Francis says about "everything being connected." It will require, individually and with others, starting from wherever one finds oneself and contending with biases of various kinds. It will require ensuring that the scale of values is played to the full and on key. Theologically, I can offer some possible consolation along the way. One is Thomas Aquinas's observation that while everyone is called to imitate God, not all are called to do so in the same way.[104] A city councilor is not the mayor, and the mayor is not a governor and need not believe himself or herself to be so. Each may "imitate God" but in distinctive ways. But isolation in one's own sphere is no option. Being aware of other spheres, and working with those engaged there, is an essential if difficult matter of working for the "common good," not just of my group, but of ever larger wholes. In the U.S. context, one only need utter the phrase "states' rights" to recognize the challenge. If the reader wishes to advance in mining morality, one step forward might be to begin sorting through and connecting the various spheres in which he or she lives and acts.

Second, and in a related way, is the double truth to be found in Catholic teaching about "subsidiarity": (1) that when it comes to governance and problem-solving, matters should be dealt with at the lowest level possible; and (2) that sometimes low-level problem-solving is not feasible or even possible—sometimes state or federal aid or, as we shall see in later chapters, some international organization such as the United Nations must play a crucial if subsidiary role. This again is a challenge. After all, "subsidiarity" is a central tenet of the European Union, a tenet tested by the message of Brexit: "We're better off going it alone." When, each of us must ask, are we really "better off" in this way?

Third, the moral miner should understand, again, that he or she is not the first to have grappled with the problem of "contradictions," of being morally torn in two or more directions. The "casuistry" of traditional moral theology in the Catholic tradition, but not only there—Rabbinic as well as Sharia reasoning are in some ways similar—may have its limits and is subject to abuse and a descent into legalism or laxism. Pascal's *Provincial Letters*, a humorous but deadly serious attack on Jesuit casuistry, are worth reading even today. But casuistry can also be read as honest attempts to help people live up to the demands of conscience in morally ambiguous, even contradictory times.[105] Furthermore, the history of casuistry is itself a reminder that, on occasion, reasonable people may reasonably disagree about right and wrong, and for different reasons. Thus, we may be back to the question of differing moral horizons, not only within each "sphere" (those vying for a Senate seat in early Montana had sharp differences) but also within any of the various groupings the mining moralist may put forward: race, gender, ethnicity, class, to name a few.

These are the sorts of groupings of which Finn is particularly aware, and yet her own attentive, intelligent, reasonable, and responsible inquiry discloses that not everyone on the bottom, or for that matter at the top, thinks or acts alike—even as his or her "social location" may be more or less the same. Those seemingly at odds with one another may have differing horizons—beliefs, understandings, convictions. The difference in horizon may indeed be "radical," such that conversion by one, both, or all parties may be required. Or they may be complementary, contributing to a community's rounded view. Or they may be developmental, as, say, children develop intellectually and morally over time.[106] When it comes to prospecting for ethics, we must certainly be attuned to the structural, the systemic, the "technocratic paradigm" of Pope Francis, the cooperative schemes of recurrence of which Lonergan writes. Yet, as attention to both the inflated figures of individual copper kings and the individual, overlooked women encountered by Finn reminds us, mining morality is a highly personal, delicate, and obscure matter, too. Heinze was not Daly, and Daly was not Clark; the woman at one kitchen table in Butte or Chuquicamata was not the woman next door. Maybe ethics, or mining morality, is best understood as a delicate matter of discernment, as one prominent Lonergan scholar has argued insightfully and at length.[107] If, in the course of mining morality our judgments, especially judgments about the actions of others, must be bold, they need not be, perhaps must not be, final in every respect.

I offer this prospector's recommendation about boldness tempered by a certain tentativeness or even tenderness, a recommendation to which I will return (especially in chapter 6), for reasons arising from the prospector's tools I have chosen. If context counts, it is important to regard the "ultimate" context within which these sometimes congruent, sometimes conflicting spheres, perspectives, and horizons exist, and our best judgments about these: not only the justice but also, as Pope Francis reminds us, the mercy of God—at least within the Christian tradition, but I think not only there. This appeal to mercy should not be read as the "cheap grace" about which Dietrich Bonhoeffer warned in his own morally perilous and, by some accounts, all too familiar times. Nor does it mean shying away from the task of arriving at the best moral judgments we can, responsibly communicating these to others, and holding ourselves and others to account. Rather, as we seek out the morally right, the morally good, in this situation or that, the mercy of God is a basis of hope for us all—whether it is the "sinner" frequenting the brothels of Butte, the "tax-collector" in the boardrooms of nationalized or neocolonial mining companies, or the countless miners and others caught in a maze of contradictions from which there is no easy escape. This is a hope that human agents on their own can neither promise nor provide. But it may be available to all.

NOTES

1. In 1902, the Butte mines produced about one-fifth of the copper in the United States.
2. C. B. Glasscock, *The War of the Copper Kings: Greed, Power, and Politics: The Billion-Dollar Battle for Butte, Montana, the Richest Hill on Earth* (Helen, MT: Riverbend Publishing, 2002), 71.
3. See Dennis Schwibold, *Copper Chorus: Mining, Politics, and the Montana Press, 1889–1959* (Helena: Montana Historical Society, 2006).
4. *ST* II–II 66. For some reflections on what students and others can learn about ethics by taking such questions seriously, see William P. George, "Murder, He Wrote: Introducing Christian Ethics through One Question in the *Summa*," *Teaching Theology and Religion* 11/4 (2008): 222–29.
5. Glasscock, *War of the Copper Kings*.
6. Janet L. Finn, *Tracing Tracing the Veins: Of Copper, Culture, and Community from Butte to Chuquicamata* (Berkeley: University of California Press, 1998).
7. This in itself should not disqualify the work. A text written during the very period Glasscock discusses, and which is highly relevant to our topic, is also bereft of scholarly apparatus. See Thorstein Veblen's 1899 classic, *The Theory of the Leisure Class*.
8. Glasscock, *War of the Copper Kings*, 1.
9. Ibid.
10. Ibid., 54.
11. See especially chapters 5 and 6. Recall that, in terms of our "prospector's tools," the fate of indigenous peoples and local cultures is of grave concern to Pope Francis. The context suggests that Glasscock's language here ("savages") is intentional, a judgment on past attitudes.
12. Glasscock, *War of the Copper Kings*, 26.
13. Ibid.
14. Ibid., 28.
15. Ibid., 135–37.
16. Ibid., 132–33.

17. Ibid., 201.
18. Ibid., 146–76.
19. For a history of bribery and the ethical and spiritual toll it can take, see John T. Noonan, *Bribes: The Intellectual History of a Moral Idea* (Berkeley and Los Angeles: University of California Press, 1984).
20. Glasscock, *War of the Copper Kings*, 72.
21. Ibid., 81.
22. I think it is safe to say that Glasscock would not have regarded as "diseases" rather than moral failings the alcoholism and drug addiction, enabled by the local pharmacies, to which he refers. This aspect of Butte's legacy haunts us to this day.
23. At least thirteen unions were well established in Butte by the 1890s.
24. Glasscock, *War of the Copper Kings*., 253.
25. Ibid., 255.
26. Ibid., 217.
27. Ibid., 262.
28. Ibid., 265.
29. Ibid., 286.
30. Ibid., 287, emphasis added.
31. Ibid., 289.
32. Apart from madams, prostitutes, and an alleged adulterer, women are mostly absent from his narrative.
33. Malone, *Battle for Butte*, 180.
34. It may seem tangential to note that this institution features prominently in Robert Pirsig's classic *Zen and the Art of Motorcycle Maintenance*, published six years before *The Battle for Butte*. But Pirsig's book has deep connections to our topic. Not only is it an "inquiry into values" (the subtitle), but it is in part a reflection on the relationship between spirituality and technology, which is not at all beside the point of mining morality, or of Pope Francis's critique of the "technocratic paradigm."
35. Malone, *Battle for Butte*, xix.
36. Ibid., emphasis added.
37. Ibid.
38. Ibid., 3.
39. For a helpful discussion of emergent probability as it pertains both to natural processes and to human history, see Liddy, "Changing One's Mind."
40. This intersection of natural and human processes, of geology and human activity, is apparent when "fracking" to recover gas and oil results in increased numbers of earthquakes.
41. Lonergan, *Insight*, 197–98; 311–12.
42. Malone, *Battle for Butte*, 52–53.
43. As we shall see, related chapters of that story involve asteroids, to be discussed in chapter 7. It is striking that, on the very first page of his two-volume *Ethics from a Theocentric Perspective*, James M. Gustafson tells the reader: "[I]t has become clear to me how much undergraduate interests in sociology and cultural anthropology, *geology (especially earth history)*, and physical anthropology shaped some of my basic outlooks" (1, ix, emphasis added).

44. For instance, the Catholic social teaching of its time, such as the important work of John A. Ryan, might have held some sway with Catholics, urging justice for workers. But this was more likely if the workers happened to be Irish. As one scholar puts it, "The Hibernians *had* learned well the Catholic social teaching that arose out of *Rerum Novarum*—but they applied its countercultural proscriptions with a fine ethnic selectivity" (David M. Emmons, "The Socialization of Uncertainty: The Order of Hibernians in Butte, Montana, 1880–1925," in Robert R. Swartout, ed., *Montana: A Cultural Medley* [Helena: Faircountry Press, 2015], 161).

45. Treatment of Chinese immigrants is an important and troubling chapter not only in the history of Butte, but, of course, in the history of the United States. For one account with particular references to mining, see Robert R. Swartout, "From Guangdong to the Big Sky: The Chinese Experience in Frontier Montana, 1864–1900," in Swartout, ed., *Montana: A Cultural Medley* (Helena: Faircountry Press, 2015), 94–120.

46. Malone, *Battle for Butte,* 85, quotes the *Anaconda Weekly Review*, Nov. 8, 1888: "Thousands of laborites turned out for [Clark's] rallies and cheered Chinese-baiting promises 'to keep the Mongolian race from our shores' and 'to give the poor, struggling white woman the washing and daily housework which will enable her to earn an honest livelihood.'"

47. Ibid., 71.

48. Ibid., 72–73.

49. Ibid., 107.

50. Gary Wills, *Under God: Religion and American Politics* (New York: Simon and Schuster, 1990), 101, 108, 118.

51. Malone, *Battle for Butte*, 188.

52. Ibid., 52.

53. Lonergan, *Method*, 78, 178, 180, and *passim*.

54. Malone, *Battle for Butte*, 167.

55. Ibid., 119–20.

56. Ibid., 189.

57. Ibid.

58. Ibid., 207.

59. Ibid., 210.

60. Arthur Fisher, "Montana: The Land of the Copper Collar," *The Nation* 26 September 1922 (quoted by Malone, 210–11).

61. Malone, *Battle for Butte*, 214.

62. Ibid., 195–96.

63. For a brief discussion of this case, see Lori Damrosch et al., eds., *International Law: Cases and Materials,* 4th ed., American Casebook Series (St. Paul: West Group, 2001), 1517–19.

64. Finn, *Tracing the Veins*, 10.

65. Ibid., 11.

66. Ibid., 1.

67. In this respect, she may be challenging Lonergan more than Pope Francis, who insists that the experience especially of the poor be taken very seriously. Where she seems to challenge both is in terms of greater attention to the experiences of women.

68. Finn, *Tracing the Veins*, 12.
69. I understand her to mean here comparisons *and* contrasts.
70. For Finn's comment on this point, see *Tracing the Veins*, 119.
71. Ibid., 116. One wonders, of course, whether this depiction of men, especially during the period under discussion, is limited to the mines. A male icon of the 1950s and 1960s, who traded a hard life in the mines of Oklahoma for the major league ballparks of America, would seem to epitomize this bundle of contradictions. See Jane Leavy, *The Last Boy: Mickey Mantle and the End of America's Innocence* (Harper Collins Publishers, 2011). Whether Mantle's family was related in any close way to Lee Mantle, a major figure in the story of the copper kings, I have not been able to determine.
72. Finn, *Tracing the Veins*, 128.
73. Ibid.,130.
74. Ibid., 132, quoting the main project backer.
75. Ibid.,133.
76. See, for instance, Ivone Gebarra and Maria Claire Bingemer, *Mary, Mother of God, Mother of the Poor,* Theology and Liberation Series, trans. Philip Berryman (Maryknoll, NY: Orbis Books, 1989).
77. Finn, *Tracing the Veins*, 185.
78. Ibid., 203.
79. Ibid., 208. Twenty-one years later, about ten thousand snow geese would alight on the Berkeley Pit. Thousands perished as a result. See Ben Guarino, "Thousands of Montana snow geese die after landing in toxic, acidic mine pit," *Washington Post*, December 7, 2016, https://www.washingtonpost.com/news/morning-mix/wp/2016/12/07/montana-snow-geese-searching-for-pond-land-in-toxic-mine-pit-thousands-die/?noredirect=on&utm_term=.3281a40f33f6.
80. Finn, *Tracing the Veins*, 210.
81. Ibid., 212.
82. Ibid., 219.
83. Ibid., 222.
84. Ibid., 223.
85. Ibid., 225.
86. Ibid., 229.
87. Lonergan, *Insight*, 769.
88. Finn, *Tracing the Veins*, 231.
89. Ibid., 233.
90. Ibid.
91. Ibid., 243.
92. Ibid., 248.
93. See Dennis Washington—Biography, Washington Companies, http://www.washcorp.com/doc/DennisWashington-FullBio.pdf.
94. For Montana Resources' own statements on worker safety, sound environmental practices, and community life, see Montana Resources, https://www.montanaresources.com/.
95. Louisa Kroll, "Dennis Washington, Owner of Quarter Billion Dollar Yacht, on His Passion for Boats," *Forbes*, November 14, 2016, https://www.forbes.com/sites

/luisakroll/2016/11/14/dennis-washington-has-spent-hundreds-of-millions-countless-hours-on-his-beloved-boats/#3806c4677881.

96. Dennis and Phillys Washington Foundation, https://www.dpwfoundation.org/.

97. David Kohn, "Who Killed Montana Power?" CBS *Sixty Minutes*, February 6, 2003, accessed at https://www.cbsnews.com/news/who-killed-montana-power-06-02-2003/.

98. For an overview of the Catholic social tradition on private property, see Daniel K. Finn, *"Centesimus Anno,"* in Himes et al., eds., *Modern Catholic Social Teaching*, 459–62. Other contributions to this volume also comment on traditional but evolving teaching on property.

99. Malone, *The Battle for Butte,* 135.

100. *ST* II–II 26, 11–12.

101. That prudence is very much a part of Catholic social teaching is evidenced by the American Catholic Bishops' 2001 statement on climate change. See USCCB, "Global Climate Change: A Plea for Dialogue, Prudence, and the Common Good," http://www.usccb.org/issues-and-action/human-life-and-dignity/environment/global-climate-change-a-plea-for-dialogue-prudence-and-the-common-good.cfm.

102. As noted earlier, I have borrowed this term from Walzer, *Spheres of Justice*. I will return to this topic especially in chapter 6.

103. E. F. Schumacher, *Small Is Beautiful: Economics As If People Mattered* (London: Blond and Briggs, Ltd., 1973).

104. *ST* II–II 64, 4, ad. 1.

105. See Albert R. Jonsen and Stephen Toulmin, *The Abuse of Casuistry: A History of Moral Reasoning* (Berkeley: University of California Press, 1986).

106. Drawing on Lonergan, Cynthia Crysdale provides a very helpful corrective to those who would see all differences as a cause for celebration, on the one hand, or cause for coercive elimination, on the other. Rather, she distinguishes different kinds of differences: developmental, complementary, and radical. See Cynthia Crysdale, "Horizons That Differ: Women and Men and the Flight for Understanding," *Cross Currents* 44/3 (Fall 1994): 345–61.

107. Patrick Byrne, *Ethics of Discernment*: Lonergan's Foundations for Ethics (Toronto: University of Toronto Press, 2016).

Chapter Four

Nauru: From Pleasant Island to Phosphate Plunder

The news cycles swirling around the early days of the Trump administration included a contentious phone conversation in early February 2017 between President Trump and Australian Prime Minister Malcolm Turnbull, during which Trump complained of the Obama Administration's "dumb" deal to consider accepting into the United States refugees kept by Australia on the tiny island nation of Nauru and other islands.[1] News items such as this can have backstories little known or forgotten, at least by those little affected or far away. Such it is with Nauru, a small dot in the Pacific, one of the smallest countries by area in the world.[2] When we consider that two nations smaller are Vatican City (a city-state), with its long and morally mixed history, and Monaco, with gambling and international banking abound, clearly lack of size is no impediment to offering lessons on mining morality.

If everything begins with mining, then in the case of Nauru everything, or at least a great deal, begins with the mining of phosphate. In its more recent history, that is, shortly after independence in 1968, Nauru was, per capita, one of the wealthiest countries in the world, even boasting its own small airline. More recently, its populace has been underemployed, economically at risk, and registering one of the highest obesity and diabetes rates in the world. Nauru's political history since independence is, by certain accounts, one of frequent regime changes and corruption, including extensive money laundering. But Nauru has remained in the news off and on beginning in 2001, since Nauru has served Australia as a holding place for those seeking asylum by sea (those arriving by air are treated differently), a practice that has given rise to claims of human rights abuses.[3]

So, the ethical prospector might ask: How did Nauru begin as Pleasant Island and, due to mining and its attendant abuses, end up as something else?

Who is responsible for this? These are the primary questions of this chapter, and the answers, incomplete as they are, may shed light on a further question: Having learned from the past, where are we now and where does Nauru—where do we all—go from here? What does Nauru teach us about mining morality for the sake of generations to come?

ENVIRONMENTAL DAMAGE AND BROKEN SACRED TRUST

In December 1986, with a view to bringing a case before the International Court of Justice (ICJ), the government of Nauru established an independent, three-person Commission to investigate and report on the first of two briefly-stated and related questions:

- [Which] government or organization should accept responsibility for rehabilitating the areas of phosphate land worked out in the periods covered by the German administration, the League of Nations, the Japanese occupation, and the United Nations trust; and
- The cost and feasibility of any proposed rehabilitation.[4]

The Commission was headed by Christopher Weeramantry, a professor of law at Monash University in Australia, but originally from Sri Lanka, where he served on the Sri Lankan Supreme Court.[5] The report was submitted to the government of Nauru in 1988, on the basis of which Nauru presented its case for reparations to the ICJ in 1992. Australia's objections that the Court lacked jurisdiction were denied. But before the case was heard, the Court was informed that Nauru and Australia had reached a settlement, and so the case did not move forward.

But this does not mean that, for the ethical prospector, the Nauruan reparations case is now devoid of meaning or importance. The major focus of this chapter will be on the Commission's inquiry into the question of responsibility for the environmental damage due to phosphate mining, which, we shall see, involves other sorts of damage and other veins of inquiry. The substance of this case clearly echoes the concerns of *Laudato si'* with regard to at least three interconnected issues: (1) environmental devastation; (2) economic injustice; and (3) disruption of and disregard for local cultures. We can also say that the focus of the inquiry—the question of responsibly for and the cost of repairing damage done—has much to do with what Lonergan called "healing and creating in history."

Figure 4.1. Karst following phosphate mining on Nauru.
Photo courtesy of U.S. Department of Energy's Atmospheric Radiation Measurement Program.

Without leaving Lonergan's insights or social Catholicism aside, this chapter will highlight especially the ethical prospector's tools of international law. In the case of Nauru, the question of "trusteeship" or "tutelage" is central. A key—perhaps the key—question in this case was whether certain nations abused their role of "trustees" over the island of Nauru and its people. As we shall see, the notion of trusteeship has been considered by some to be "sacred," thus leading us perhaps into what Lonergan calls the "transcendent" realm of meaning. But with its implied paternalism, it can also be problematic. We will deal with that. But since in this case the notion of trusteeism is construed in terms of parenting, of stewardship, of fiduciary responsibility, and helping others to assume responsibilities of various kinds, it raises a perennial question for the ethical prospector: When it comes to morality, what exactly is the role of teaching, of passing on meaning and values, of development "from above" (as Lonergan puts it), as well as from below? Put simply, can ethics be taught? For that reason, among others, in the latter part of this chapter I explore one facet of that question, the relationship between a teacher and his student, both of whom were intimately involved in this case.

The Case for Reparations

To begin engaging the Commission's inquiry, it will be helpful to mark key moments in Nauru's history. The report itself lists over fifty such moments from the time of "discovery" to independence; here we must limit ourselves to far fewer.[6]

In November 1798, Captain John Fern came upon the island and called it "Pleasant Island." As a result of an 1886 treaty between Germany and Great Britain regarding "spheres of influence" in the Pacific, in 1888 Nauru fell under the control of Germany, which, in turn, granted to Jaluit Gesellshaft (called Jigglestaff by unfriendly British traders) exclusive rights to mine Nauruan phosphate, important especially for fertilizer. About the same time, the first Christian missionary arrived on the island. In 1900 the English Colonial Office granted the Pacific Island Company rights to mine Ocean Island, a similarly phosphate-rich island which later became a British Colony—a distinction that would bear great legal significance. In 1905, German authorities transferred the right to exploit phosphate in the Marshall Islands from Jaluit to the Pacific Island Company, which later became the Pacific Phosphate Company. Mining began in 1906, with a Pacific Phosphate Company paying the Nauruan landowners a royalty of .5 dinari (pence) per ton—about 1/700 of the phosphate's market value. In 1914 Germany surrendered administrative authority over the island, and with the culmination of World War I the United Kingdom, New Zealand, and Australia began negotiations over control of Nauru, agreeing in 1920 as partner governments to acquire the assets and rights of the Pacific Phosphate Company.

By this time, the League of Nations had become involved, conferring "mandate" status on the island in 1920 and appointing a mandate administrator. Seven years later, a Council of Nauruan Chiefs was established, but with advisory authority only. Significantly, the Commission lists among key historical moments the anthropologist Camilla Wedgwood's 1932 report on the island—some twenty years after the first anthropologist, Dr. Kretzschmar, had studied the island and its people. Then, once again, Nauru was affected by war. In 1942, after bombing raids and the evacuation of most Europeans and Chinese (brought to the islands to work the mines), the Japanese attacked and then occupied the island. They built an airstrip and, after heavy bombing by the Allied forces, in 1943 deported to Truk Island 1,200 Nauruans—one-third of whom would die in the next two years. The Japanese surrendered to Australian forces in 1945, and in 1946 civil administration was reintroduced. In 1947 the United Nations Trustee Agreement was reached, with a basic premise that Nauru would be helped to secure independence. After several rounds of negotiations, conferences, and the election of the first Nauru Legislative Council in 1966, Nauru gained its independence in 1968. Significantly, questions of responsibility for damage due to mining were integral to the independence process and were discussed, but they were not resolved.

After independence, the report explains, Nauru maintained close, favorable ties with Australia, including the adoption of its currency and access to the Australian judiciary. Nauru also began benefiting directly from mining operations, which it now controlled, and, as noted above, in the process gained enormous per capita wealth. But as the report also points out, as of the late 1980s, "there [was] a need for substantial change, for, whatever the resources of the country, the people need goals and activities towards which to strive both as individuals and as a nation. Such goals and activities will not suddenly and spontaneously evolve on the cessation of the phosphate economy. They must be planned for now."[7] One might assume that this was especially the case since the Nauruans themselves were not fully participants in the mining, and were in fact victims of discrimination on their own island home when it came to employment.[8] Beyond the report, we should note that, whatever "goals" might have been in view, "activities" since 2001 have included, off and on, the housing of asylum seekers on the Island—activities that have given rise to no little controversy. Thus, at the time of the report, the question of Nauru's future was still open.

To gain some purchase on that open question, with its ties to other questions of mining morality, we will explore further certain aspects of the Commission's report. In the view of the Commission, Nauru was on firm legal ground, and certainly firm moral ground, in asking that those nations engaged in phosphate mining over sixty or so years bear responsibility for the immense environmental damage wreaked upon the tiny island. Inquiring just how this conclusion was reached should advance our ethical prospecting, exposing rich veins—legal but also moral—to be mined for the sake of a better future. For instance, even though the report, authored by then Professor and later Judge Weeramantry, is subtitled simply "Environmental Damage under Trusteeship," it may be argued that Weeramanty and his colleagues treated the terms "environment," "damage," and "trusteeship" as exceptionally rich in meaning—quite in keeping with the realms of meaning and the scale of values to which our prospecting tools are sensitive. Put in another way, phosophate lies on or near the surface, and so phosphate mining has much in common with strip mining. It seems fair to say that the commission was asking what else besides phosphate was stripped away over the years from the island and its people.

Inevitably, prospecting in the case of Nauru must be selective. So, we will limit our inquiry to certain themes or patterns that run through the report as so many layers of meaning and value. Taking our lead from *Laudato si'*, which stresses that everything is connected, we can perhaps bundle these themes together and ask: From the time of discovery until the time of Nauruan independence, were the Nauruan people, their culture, and their land justly treated? It might be easy enough to answer in the negative, at least on the whole. But it would be a mistake to overlook exceptions, counterpositions, ambiguities, or what Janet Finn, discussing Butte and Chuquicamata, might call "contradictions." According to Lonergan, "the good," as a transcendental notion, is not some abstraction. Rather, it is "concrete"—the good "in its every aspect and its every instance."[9] But this is not to say that the case of Nauru, or any case for that matter, will exemplify the total opposite: that the treatment of Nauru was *bad* in every instance or in every respect. In the case of Nauru, we should not overlook the vector of genuine legal and moral progress exerting its pull alongside the vector of decline, even if the latter arguably has had the upper hand.

There are several ways to ask whether the island of Nauru and its people were well treated by those who arrived on the island from the outside. We may begin with the simple reminder that the Nauruans were already on the island when the island was discovered, and that the more remote origin of the Nauru people is unclear. On the face of it, then, the island was hardly *terra nullius* (land belonging to no one), to invoke a legal term of no little import, when people from the West arrived. The fact that the inhabitants' language was distinctive suggests they had been on the island for a very long time.

Early on, a few Europeans settled on the island, intermarried and died there. But a consideration of early German trading practices in the Pacific sheds light on early (middle 1800s) interactions between Nauru and the West. While the guano these islands could provide was highly valued by the Germans, the islanders had few needs that the traders could meet in exchange for this valuable resource. The obvious answer was to create needs for such things as firearms, alcohol, and tobacco. While "smoking schools" were apparently successful in teaching the islanders to appreciate the great value of tobacco, "less success was had at first in making the islanders feel the need for European clothes."[10]

But, of course, central to the story is phosphate and its extraction. As noted above, Germany had early control of the island, and Jaluit Gesellshaft had been given rights to the work the deposits. Not unlike the wily copper kings of Butte, the Pacific Islands Company recognized but wanted to keep secret the mining potential not only of Nauru but also of Ocean Island, which was in British hands. In both cases, stealth was required to gain access: Neither the islanders nor those holding the rights must know the full value of what was under their feet. So moves to secure mining rights included "secret prospecting" in the form of surreptitious "walkabouts" to confirm the company's projections of just how valuable the islands might be.[11] As it turns out, this lack of full disclosure on the part of those with economic interests would be a constant in the story of Nauru under international trusteeship.

The report explains that the company obtained the necessary consent and cooperation of the islanders in very different ways. On Ocean Island (Banaba), the company entered into a formal agreement with the chiefs. It included clauses regarding (1) sole rights to extract and ship the rock; (2) the right to erect buildings and whatever else might be necessary for the mining venture; (3) the agreement not to mine in the areas where coconuts or other fruits were growing; (4) the sole right to establish a store from which Banabans could make purchases and sell their goods at a set price; (5) the agreement to pay the Banabans fifty pounds per annum; and (6) the term of the agreement: 999 years.[12] The result of this agreement? Exploitation leading to displacement of the Banabans, who were forced to abandon their mined-out island and resettle on the Fijian island of Rabi (pronounced Rambi).[13]

As for Nauru, under German administration there was no such agreement. Rather, they simply explained to the islanders the way things were and would be. Albert F. Ellis, who had negotiated the agreement with the Banabans, writes, with surprising candor:

> [The Nauruans] were told that it had been found that the rocks and soil on the high portion of the island were useful to the white men, and that the company whom we represented would pay them for the phosphate at a stated rate. The chiefs were gravely interested; one of them thought it was hardly the thing for the white men to have to pay for rocks, and another suggested that when they were being removed, we might leave behind sufficient for them to make the special stone sinkers they use for their fishing-lines. *They must have had some prophetic insight into the white man's thoroughness.*[14]

In commenting on this encounter, Weeramantry remarks that "not acquainting the Nauruans with the full value of their phosphate was seen as good policy then and it remained good policy throughout the period of mining."[15] This period commenced when the Pacific Phosphate Company began its operations on the two phosphate-rich islands in 1907. From 1907 to 1913 the yield from these operations on Nauru was worth £945,000. Over this period, the Naurans were paid £1320—about .0014 percent of the Company's take.[16]

The onset of World War I spelled the demise of the Pacific Phosphate Company, but mining was not interrupted for long. Australia, New Zealand, and the United Kingdom seized on the opportunity to exploit Nauru, and soon created, as part of the Nauru Island Agreement (to which the report gives extensive attention), the British Phosphate Commissioners. These Commissioners—legally, an unincorporated body—were answerable to their own governments. They had charge over the island mining, and, in accord with the agreement, would sell all the mined phosphate to their own countries and to no one else. Meanwhile, however, the League of Nations was emerging, which the report views as in tune with "the rejection of concepts of colonialism and annexation by the idealism succeeding World War I."[17] In keeping with this move toward a new world order, under the mandate the British Phosphate Commissioners were answerable to the League. As the report points out, "Article 22 [of the League's charter]" required that "to peoples not yet able to stand by themselves under the strenuous conditions of the modern world there should be applied the principle that the well-being and development of such peoples form *a sacred trust of civilization.*"[18]

More specific questions may be raised about the obligations of the partner governments—for example: whether the Commissioners could insulate themselves from the oversight of the League-appointed administrator; whether they could continue to sell only to the member states, at reduced cost, when "another obligation lying on the partner powers was to secure equal opportunities for the trade and commerce of other members of the League";[19] and whether the entire cost of running the island could come from the mining profits. The report points out that Australia and New Zealand showed little interest in such questions, but that such questions *were* raised in the Parliament of the United Kingdom, with particular concerns about future injustices towards Nauru. The questions were many, in part because the Nauru Island Agreement, negotiated and signed by the three mandate nations even before that mandate was granted, was so problematic. To put it in the succinct language of a chapter subheading, it was a case of "Cheap Phosphates versus Trust Obligations."[20] To give a couple of examples: With regard to the importance of the Nauru Island Agreement to the Covenant and the League, when considering the Agreement one member of the House of Commons complained that "many of us who took part in recruiting during the War and who fought overseas believed that we were in this war with clean hands and that we were not anxious to secure any material benefit and yet we have had Honorable Members supporting this agreement because *it is good business*."[21] On the apparent self-interested nature of the Agreement, Parliament member Mr. Thomson sharply warned that the Agreement must not give the rest of the world cause to say that England "did not go into the war to save Belgium but that she went into it for what she could get for ourselves."[22]

The point here is not to enter an exhaustive discussion of what the League was asking of the countries granted mandate status over Nauru, and whether that request was normatively adequate. Rather, in keeping with what we have said about "dialectics," my aim is simply to point out that there were dissenting voices, questioning voices (in this case, in the British Parliament), when it came to the colonial-like plunder of Nauru. Even prior to World War I, during the time of German occupation of Nauru, it was not a case of plunder without reservation. The German notion of *Schutzgebiete* ("a protected area") was, in fact, the equivalent of colonization. Yet, there was in Germany at this time a degree of strong anticolonial sentiment, and, among both the Social Democrats (SPD) and the Catholic Centre Party, increasing humanitarian concerns, resulting in "reform of the entire colonial policy . . . based on the notion of trusteeship." As a result, mining on Nauru "was not lawless and haphazard at the whims and fancies of the authorities but strictly regulated by mining law as introduced by the statute." The German law differed from Nauruan customary law (considered below), but at least under the German law "the rights of landowner and miner were regulated." Significantly, the statute included an obligation to "restore the land mined to a usable condition."[23]

The Life and Law of the Nauruans

To a great extent, these developments were taking place far from Nauru itself—in Germany prior to the war, in the halls of the British Parliament, or at Versailles, where the mandate system was being worked out. But laws on the books of Germany or in Parliament are one thing; compliance with such laws on a tiny Pacific island is another. So, it is important to return to the island to discuss two points: First, the social impact of phosphate mining, and, second, the customary law of the Nauruans which, the report insists, should have been taken fully into account during the mining period, but was not. *Laudato si'* expresses general concern that local cultures be respected when economic endeavors are pursued. The Nauru investigation brings that concern down to the level of one sad case.

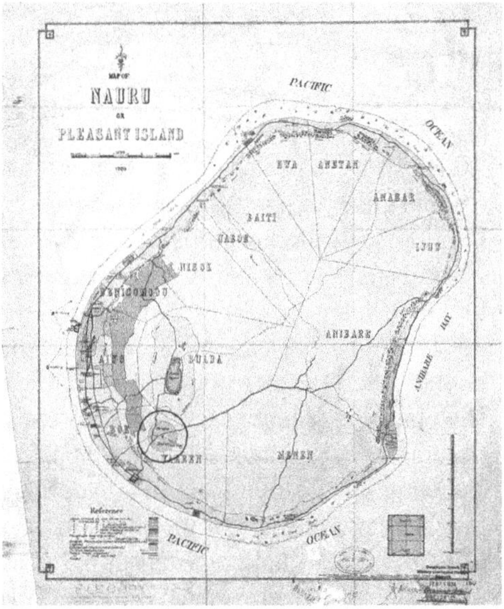

Figure 4.2. Pleasant Island/Nauru, 1926.
Photo: Library of Congress.

According to the report, phosphate mining had an immense impact on the life of the Nauruan people. With the arrival of the Germans and later the partner nations, the Nauruans moved from a subsistence culture centered on the fruits of the land and the sea to dependence on a cash economy. Imported foods became preferred to the traditional diet. Traditional arts and games decreased, and "foreign music displaced the ancient Nauruan chants which had performed an important narrative, historical and social purpose." So, too, Nauruan cosmic and cultural myths and legends were swept away by the cultural change. Traditional skills, especially fishing skills, also disappeared. The report concedes that a degree of cultural transformation—or Westernization—would have occurred in the absence of mining, but "the scale of the phosphate industry was worldwide in comparison with the miniscule size of the island and the strength of the industry was overwhelming when compared with the traditional subsistence economy of Nauru."[24]

Of particular importance was the Nauruans' relationship to the land itself. Geographically, Nauru has the appearance of an inverted saucer, with a fertile coastal area and a central phosphate-rich plateau called Topside. The partner governments tended to separate Topside from the coastal perimeter, which in their view was the Nauruans' true home. But even though the Nauruans did not live on that part of the island, they most certainly considered it their home, a place of great practical and symbolic meaning. A song composed in the 1910s or early 1920s laments:

> By chance they discovered the heart of my home
> and gave it the name phosphate.
> If they were to ship all phosphate from my home
> there will be no place for me to go.
> Should this be the plan of the British Commission
> I shall never see my home on the hill.[25]

As might be expected, it was not only the Nauruans' attachment to the land (in this case Topside) that was adversely affected by the mining. Much in keeping with the concerns of *Laudato si'*, the land itself suffered from the "disastrous effects and almost total disruption of island ecosystems."[26] So, too, the phosphate-induced meeting of the Pacific island with the West pretty much spelled the end of the once healthy diet of the Nauruans—no small matter when we consider the extreme health challenges that the islanders have faced in recent years. In short, "the problem of responsibility for mining damage is compounded when we consider the extent of the cultural, social and ecological damage cause to Nauruans and their inheritance."[27]

Since law, at least for our purposes, is central to mining morality, of special concern is the "vital importance in this inquiry" of Nauruan customary law.[28] The team of investigators was especially intent on ascertaining whether in fact, prior to Western incursion, the Nauruans possessed a legal system that newcomers were obliged to take into account. Since the case had to do with environmental damage, Weeramantry and his colleagues were especially interested in "the sanctity attaching to land under Nauruan customary law."[29]

Drawing on the observations of German officials, early anthropologists on the island, and others, the Commission concluded that, indeed, the Nauruans had both a sophisticated organized society and a developed legal system, including complex rules of family law. Individual ownership was a clearly established principle. "Indeed," the report points out, "it went much further than the European concept of ownership in the sacrosanct nature it attached to land, making it almost a *res extra commercium* [a matter outside of commerce altogether]. To the average Nauruan it was inconceivable that land should be the subject of sale like any physical chattel." Nauruans had a strong sense of obedience to law, and solid reasons for such obedience. According to diverse and perhaps opposing academic definitions (the sort of definitions of law which the World Court or another international tribunal might entertain), law might be a matter of some external force, or it might be "internalised within the minds and consciousness of the people."[30] From either point of view, the report concludes, the Nauruan legal system would qualify as law.

Traditionally, this system was diverse as to its content (covering land, reefs, trees, animals, family, inheritance, etc.) and sophisticated in character. It was especially detailed when it came to ownership, including ownership of Topside, with sophisticated signs and marks of such ownership. The concept of lease, as applied to land, was well established, as was the distinction of ownership of the soil and ownership of trees planted in that soil, such that one islander's land might be the site of another's trees. Ownership rights also extended to "certain incorporeal possessions," perhaps calling to mind later Western views on intellectual property rights. As the report explains at some length, the Nauruans most certainly had a strong sense of individual ownership that could become a highly complex matter, and that land ownership extended "to all that went with it—whether above it, like the trees, or below it, like wells. . . . [I]t is most unlikely that the Nauruans would have been of the view, had they been asked, that anyone but the landowner had rights to the minerals that lay below the surface."[31]

More could be said about this system, but the salient point is that both German law and British law contained within itself the need to respect the legal systems of indigenous peoples. For instance, "time-honoured doctrine in British colonial law ordained that even in captured territory the indigenous laws remained until expressly displaced by those of the conquerer."[32] This, of course, is hardly a justification of colonialism, but it is at least an acknowledgment that indigenous people are not lawless people incapable of ruling themselves.

But high regard for indigenous ways, legal and other, hardly prevailed in this as in so many other cases. As the report points out, "In areas of colonial expansion, the pursuit of wealth was . . . too powerful an urge to be constrained by such traditional concepts [e.g., regarding property]. Where great mineral wealth was involved, this was particularly the case."[33] Now, one might protest that the Europeans, at their best, were simply acting in ways that seemed reasonable and fair to them at the time. But as Weeramantry shrewdly points out,

> If European conduct in the past can only be judged fairly by European standards of that time, Nauruan reactions must also be judged by Nauruan standards at the relevant time. . . . By Nauruan standards the transactions into which the Nauruans were being forced to enter were incomprehensible and diametrically opposed to their cultural traditions.[34]

Since it is relevant to questions of ethics as well as of law, we should note the attention the report gives to "the myth of certainty."[35] It is often assumed that, unlike "primitive" legal systems, "developed" systems are marked by "precision and certainty as opposed to the generality and vagueness" of the "primitive" systems. Relying especially on legal scholar Julius Stone, the report challenges this assumption. "Developed" systems aren't so "precise and certain" as is often assumed; "primitive" systems, for their part, are surprisingly more "precise and certain" than one might think.[36] This point is particularly relevant since the international law to which we are giving considerable attention is itself often characterized as "primitive" compared to the developed systems of domestic (national) law, a characterization that is open to challenge.

Under the heading of Nauruan customary law, Weeramantry's team also considered the Nauruan concept of "wardship or tutelage—that is, of the concept of looking after the property of another over whom one has power and control."[37] As noted above, this is an important but also problematic topic. The report makes clear that tutelage—or trusteeship—would have been well understood by the Nauruans or similar custom-based people because the Nauruans valued highly the care and nurturing of children. Given their commitments to property and inheritance rights they surely knew what it meant to care for the property of their offspring.[38] Nauruan customary law regarding land, the report reports, is also flexible with regard to ownership and use. That is, Nauruans were quite familiar with the fact that use of the land might be given over to others without relinquishing ownership. Thus, the report finds a congruence between Nauru culture and the concept of trusteeship. To say that the Nauruans were familiar with this concept because they were familiar with child-raising (and thus holding a child's property in trust) may be true enough, but it may also be problematic in that it might appear to treat the Nauruans themselves as children vis-à-vis the European nations operating under the mandate of the League. But before simply drawing that conclusion, let us look more closely at the mandate system as applied to Nauru.

The Mandate System

The primary purpose of the mandate system, designed in part by Woodrow Wilson and General Smuts of South Africa, was, in Weeramantry's words, "to protect and develop the welfare of the natives of the mandated territories."[39] Quite in contrast to a sharing of the spoils of war (that is, in the case of World War I, German colonies and territories), the mandate was meant to be not a privilege of those carrying out the mandate, but rather a burden of responsibility to do so without seeking gain. But this burden was too easily set aside or not taken up at all. As the report notes, General Smuts's own contributions to the development of the system "were perhaps not entirely disinterested [as he] was intent on the acquisition by South Africa of the neighboring territory of South West Africa."[40]

The notion of a mandate was hardly new. The report places its philosophical origins at least as far back as the early sixteenth century with Spanish incursion into the New World. Weeramantry and his team note especially the role of the Salamanca school of theology in developing this concept, with special mention of Francisco de Vitoria, OP, to whom we will return. Vitoria, Weeramantry reports, argued for extending the right of dominion to the indigenous peoples themselves, except when such people were totally incapable of managing their own affairs. But even then, in the words of Vitoria quoted in the report, "any such intervention [must] be for the welfare and the interests of the Indian and not merely for the profit of the Spaniard. For this is the respect in which all the danger to soul and salvation lies."[41] Humanitarian movements in the eighteenth and nineteenth centuries further advanced international law, with "increasing recognition that subject peoples should be treated with humanitarian considerations and that their property rights were entitled to respect."[42] Edmund Burke, Jeremy Bentham, Immanuel Kant, and others began to question colonialism itself, just as various movements brought an end to the slave trade in the face of great opposition and potential economic loss.

Meanwhile, the report continues, the notion of tutelage took deeper root in British soil as their empire was expanding. Germany, too, recognized the principle, as did certain strains of law dealing with indigenous peoples of the United States and Canada. As the twentieth century unfolded, the notion of tutelage grew further. The aftermath of World War I brought a widespread determination to halt the sorts of tyranny that the War was supposedly to end, and so when nations gathered at Versailles to establish the League of Nations, the emergent mandate system "embodied the new idealism that emerged after World War I." Furthermore, "Nauru, perhaps the smallest of the mandated territories, provided a textbook example of how the world community through its international machinery could protect the weak against the strong and husband their resources against the day when the former would come into their own and manage their own affairs."[43]

The concepts of mandate, tutelage, and trusteeship are embedded in Article 22 of the Covenant of the League of Nations.[44] The article includes the following points: The beneficiaries are "peoples not yet able to stand by themselves under the strenuous conditions of the modern world" and "the principle that the well-being and development of such peoples form[s] a sacred trust of civilization" (22.1). "[T]he tutelage of such peoples should be entrusted to advanced nations" (22.3). "[T]he character of the mandate must differ according to the stage of the development of the people" and its "circumstances" (22.3). Thus, while certain peoples, such as those of the former Turkish Empire, "have reached a stage of development where their existence as independent nations can be provisionally recognized" (22.4), "[o]ther peoples, especially those of Central Africa, are at such a stage that the mandatory must be responsible for the administration of that territory" subject only to the maintenance of public order and several other conditions (22.5). But, the Article continues, there are also "territories, such as South West Africa *and certain of the South Pacific Islands*, which, owing to the sparseness of their population, or their small size, or their remoteness form the centres of civilization, or their geographical continuity to the territory of the mandatory, and other circumstances, can be best administered under the laws of the mandatory as integral parts of its [that is, the mandate country's own] territory . . . in the interest of the indigenous population" (22.6, emphasis added). Finally, the article makes clear that the mandatories are subject and answerable to the League in terms of reporting (22.7) changes of authority, control, or administration (22.8).

In the case of Nauru, at least some of this Article requires modest elaboration. First, the content of 22.6 is noteworthy. The people of Nauru were placed at the lower end of the development curve. Thus, Nauru was designated a "C" category entity: not quite an "annexed" entity (as Australia desired in the case of Nauru, or as South Africa pushed for in the case of Southwest Africa[45]), but not self-governing either. The League deemed that such peoples "can be best administered under the laws of the mandatory as *integral parts of its territory*" (emphasis added). This clause turned out to be quite controversial, as it left to interpretation (as Stone might have predicted in terms of "certainty") just where sovereignty should be located—in the mandatory power or in the people under the mandatory nation's care? Second, the Covenant stresses (in 22.7–8) that the mandatories are subject to the League. In Nauru's case, this precept was not well heeded, at least in this sense: Nauru had a League-appointed administrator who was supposed to be independent of the Commissioners who oversaw the mining. But in effect, the administrator had little real authority; the Commissioners, whose interest was profit from the mining for their respective countries, pretty much had a run of the island, with the administrator often doing their bidding rather than the other way around.

With the general notion of trusteeship as its context, the Commission of inquiry also investigated finances under the mandate and the trust. We cannot discuss this in sufficient detail, but a few things should be noted. First, as the investigators point out, reporting requirements notwithstanding, the financial arrangements and activities of the mandatory powers were often veiled in secrecy and featured less than stellar accounting practices. Second, the overarching concern on the part of the League and then later the United Nations was that the Nauruan people were not getting a fair share of the profits from the phosphate mining. Over the years, this situation improved due to international pressure. "Still, even at independence," the report notes, "the Nauruans were receiving less than half of the sale proceeds of their phosphate."[46]

Key to the notion of trusteeship, whether under the League or later the United Nations, was the aim of preparing those under the mandate for independence. In the case of Nauru, such preparation involved, at the very least, two interrelated issues: First, responsibility for post-mining, and, second, the question of resettlement of the Nauruans in the event that the island could not be sufficiently restored, as was the case with the Banan people of Ocean Island. The first question was unresolved prior to independence, and the second was both unacceptable to the Nauruans and at odds with the notion of trusteeship. While the partner governments argued that the Nauru Phosphate Agreement, reached in 1967 and thus prior to independence, was sufficiently "liberal" in its terms, the investigating committee judged otherwise. They found the shifts in control of phosphate mining over the years to be unsatisfactory in several respects, including some legally questionable developments. But put more fundamentally, the Nauruans were being asked to pay to take over an industry built up from the profits accruing from sale of resources which had belonged to the Nauruans all along.

There was also the question of the partner nations attempting to link independence with terms favorable to the partner nations. It should have been axiomatic, Weeramantry and his colleagues point out, that with independence "control over the phosphate industry would automatically pass to them, for the phosphates and the right to manage them had always in law belonged to the Nauruans. Yet at the independence discussions the control of the industry was treated as though it were a benefit being granted to the Nauruans by the trustee power rather than a case of the Nauruans coming into control of their birthright."[47] It must be said again, by the time independence came, the question of rehabilitation had not been settled even though rehabilitation was a clear legal responsibility. In *Laudato si'*, Pope Francis warns about the need for continuity in governance over time lest no one be held accountable for past actions and promises made.[48] The case of Nauru appears to represent a cruel twist on the principle of continuity: the Nauruans, who had benefited little from the mining, inherited the phosphate industry, but more than anything they inherited the devastation that this industry had wreaked on their once pleasant island.

Relevant Legal Principles

Since international law holds a privileged place in this meditation on mining, it will be helpful, finally, to review briefly the Commission's discussion of "some relevant legal principles."[49] Let us begin with the principle of acquired rights. This principle, quite in accord with *laissez faire* capitalism (the sort of capitalism arguably on display in Butte, Montana; Chuquicamata, Chile; and elsewhere) ensures that agreements will outlive the regime under which the agreements were made. For who wants to invest in a country if a change of regimes might put contracts in jeopardy? The principle solidified over time. But legal principles can also undergo change—a point which the ethical prospector should carefully note. In this case, challenges to colonialism exposed the need for limitations on this principle, lest parties external to the emerging state, rather than the newly independent state and its people, would continue to benefit from agreements that were arguably unjust from the start.

The mining of copper should be a familiar topic, so it is worth noting the Commission's prime example of such an injustice: copper mining in Zambia, a country which the Commission says has (or, had at the time of the report) roughly a quarter of the world's known copper deposits. Cecil Rhodes and his British South African Company obtained mining rights in the 1890s (about the time that things in Butte were heating up) "from illiterate Zambian chiefs 'through a combination of force threats of force, deceit and downright robbery. For articles of little value, the chiefs were made to give away right over their natural resources. In fact there was no legal right for the chiefs to give away the patrimony of the people to foreigners of any race.'"[50] The company ruled Zambia only until 1920, but held these rights until 1964, continuing to collect rents and royalties. Only when the government took majority interest in the mines in 1969 were these rights restored to the state. "Thus, far from receiving aid from the developed countries '. . . Zambia has been a donor, the beneficiaries being the developed nations, principally the United Kingdom, the United States and South Africa.'"[51]

In short, in this and other cases the acquired rights principle was hardly a guarantee of justice for indigenous peoples. The Commission's examination of the Nauru case during German, mandate, and trustee phases led to the conclusion that, for numerous reasons (lack of consultation with the Nauruan people; powerlessness of the Nauruans to resist; the failure of the Germans and others to rehabilitate the land), the early contracts need not be honored by the Nauruans.[52]

In reviewing the case of Nauru, the Commission also considered "supervening principles of international law." Four such principles were taken into account: (1) "the mandate/trust obligation which places the mandatory/trustee under and obligation to give primary consideration to the interests of the territory and its people"; (2) "the principle of permanent sovereignty over natural resources"; (3) "that provisions of the Covenant of the League and the Charter of the United Nations take priority over all other obligations" (which the Commission found "perhaps most compelling of all"); and (4) "the mandate and trustee agreements by which the powers concerned solemnly pledged to the world community that they would as mandatories and trustees look after the interests of the Nauruan people."[53] The violation of any one of these principles would have been sufficient to thwart the claim of acquired rights. In the event, the Commission found that all these principles applied in the Nauru case and overrode the principle of acquired rights.

Under the heading of relevant legal principles, the Commission also took up the question of colonialism and permanent sovereignty over natural resources. This included reviewing the notion of mandate and trusteeship in relation to permanent sovereignty.[54] It also included the emerging principle of self-determination prior to World War II, and the development of the principle after the war. Again, the Commission found that these principles obtained in the case of Nauru, and that the partner states had failed to heed them, at least sufficiently. For instance, the Commission observes that "the partner governments, at the time of the mining, did intend some day to restore the mined-out land to a usable condition," but then lost sight of this obligation, a failure which was "no different in effect from that in which a trustee deliberately damages trust property with no intent of restoring it."[55]

Notably, the Commission points to the (then) present legal status of permanent sovereignty over resources, quoting the International Law Commission: "emanating as it does from the *jus cogens* principle of self-determination, [the permanent sovereignty principle] is a fundamental principle of contemporary international law" (327). I say "notably" because the notion of *jus cogens* is an important international legal principle—one that we will see again in the cases of both seabed and asteroid mining. *Jus cogens*, or peremptory law, refers to an overriding legal principle from which there is no derogation. Thus, for example, a treaty whereby State A agrees to sell to State B some of its citizens as slaves would be invalid on its face since it runs counter to laws against slavery. To be sure, *jus cogens* is a highly contested principle in international law,[56] and, as the Commissioners point out, in the Nauru case not all would agree that the principle of permanent sovereignty over resources had attained *jus cogens* status. But in terms of the larger question of prospecting for ethics, wherein international law may be viewed as ethics writ large, *jus cogens* proposes for our consideration the possibility of real clarity, of bright lines, of stability in a world that might seem always in a state of becoming (or ceasing to be), always in flux, with no solid legal (or moral) ground on which to stand. As we shall see in chapter 6, when we discuss the shifting "ontologies of nuclearity," questions about constantly changing concepts or categories are not without practical implications.

The Commission also considered a growing body of environment law, both international and national. The 1972 Stockholm Declaration on the Human Environment, a watershed for international environmental law, provided a

Figure 4.3. Trusteeship Council Reviews Conditions in Nauru and New Guinea 18 June 1954.
Photo: UN Multimedia.

baseline. The declaration states, for instance, that "the natural resources of the earth including air, water, land, flora and fauna and especially representative samples of natural ecosystems must be safeguarded for the benefit *of present and future generations* through careful planning and management" (Principle 2).[57] Australia's own contribution to the drafting of the Declaration is worth noting: ". . . when such damage has occurred, the State, activities within which were responsible for the damage, should rectify or compensate for the damage and co-operate in the development of procedures for settling disputes which may arise."[58]

In *Nauru*, Weeramantry goes on to cite other aspects of international law, one of which recalls the sidetrip from Butte to British Columbia by one of the copper kings, Fritz Heinze. "The *Trail Smelter* arbitration," the Commissioners points out, "provides clear authority that international tribunals may require payment of compensation for past pollution damage. . . . The same Principle would apply to other forms of environmental damage where such damage is caused by one country to the territory of another."[59] Nauru was not, in a strict legal sense, a "country" when the damage was done, but it was on its way to independence, and the status and quality of that independence, the Commission states, would clearly be "pre-empted" in numerous ways (limited freedom, threats to health, adverse budgetary effects, displacement of priorities, etc.[60]) by the mess created through the actions of others.

From Phosphate Plunder to Emergent Law

Recalling especially Lonergan's emphasis on *emergence*, here the Commission provides us with a superb example of the dynamic character of international law. In discussing the "rehabilitation obligation," the report cites an earlier international legal case regarding payment for damages, based on the U.S. "government's acceptance of *moral responsibility* for the harmful consequences of the [nuclear test] blasts [on Pacific islands] despite the lack of proven fault." Thus, it is "an important illustration of the role played by a sense of *moral* obligation in the evolving international law of the environment."[61] But even apart from moral obligation, the Commission points out that international *law* is moving toward new standards, in this case "strict liability," that is, liability in the absence of intent. Again, the *Trail Smelter* case is cited. What is at stake here, then, is "an emerging doctrine." True, such principles may be in "a formative stage—*lex ferenda* rather than *lex lata*"—but they go beyond the principle of strict liability, with its exceptions, that one finds in the common law.[62]

Similarly, although "unjust enrichment" has its weaknesses as a principle of international law, earlier arbitration cases show that the general formula

Jus suum cuique tribuere—"to each his own"—has gained international traction.[63] So, too, the doctrine of "abuse of rights" has such wide acceptance in domestic law that it, too, "offers an additional principle at international law on which the responsibility to rehabilitate can be rested."[64] We might add at this point that the refusal of the Commission to accept the acquired rights principle, as it applies to contracts, as some sort of absolute, is quite in keeping with the general view of Catholic social teaching. Just contracts are hardly just simply because people agree to them.[65] In this case, it is doubtful that even the bar of "agreement" was attained.

Some Preliminary Conclusions

What are we to make of this extended foray into international law? How has international law functioned as an ethical prospector's tool in this case of moral mining? First, the findings of the Commission, summarized in some four hundred pages, slowly build an exceptionally strong legal case regarding the responsibility of the partner countries to pay for damages due to the long years of mining. Exactly how strong is another question; international lawyers, representing one or more of the partner nations, might point out some weaknesses. But the findings of the Commission were certainly strong enough to move Australia to settle before the case could come before the International Court of Justice. In 1993, Australia agreed to pay Nauru 107 million Australian dollars in full settlement of the case.

Second, the Commission could build a strong legal argument because there was a tremendous reservoir of extant law, both international and domestic (for example, German mining law), on which to build. It is hardly the case that, during the colonial and early postcolonial era colonial powers were free to operate, and, in effect, plunder places and peoples, without legal restraint or accountability. Put otherwise, this case shows that international human rights law clearly predated the 1948 Universal Declaration of Human Rights.

Third, along with law there were *institutions* to which the Nauruans could appeal, directly or implicitly, for relief—the ICJ, to be sure, but other institutions as well, such as the British Parliament, the defunct (but in some ways still continuous) League of Nations—even an arbitration tribunal such as the one that ruled in the *Trailer Smelter* case in way off British Columbia. I cannot stress too strongly the "cumulative and progressive" (Lonergan) nature of law in general, and of international law with its institutions in particular, for gaining a sense of what "mining morality" might entail. Mining morality is not about a single insight, a single judgment, a single decision by a single actor, such as the reader—no matter how "brilliant." Rather, just as the miners descending on Butte (one thinks of Marcus Daly) in its early days brought with them skills and innovations developed elsewhere and by others, so anyone hoping to say something meaningful about mining morality on Nauru or anywhere else must be prepared to ask—as Weeramantry and his colleagues were so prepared, to the tune of ten volumes—what others, near and far, yesterday as well as today, have already said and done.

Fourth, although the Commission appeals to existing law of various kinds, clearly international law was, at the time of the Commission's work, undergoing change and development—for instance, in the areas of international environmental law and human rights. New law was—and is—emerging, and there is reason to believe that the Nauru case—with Weeramantry and his colleagues paying special attention to this small piece of "our common home"—was itself a contribution to that change. But change sometimes comes slowly. So it should not be surprising that some, at least, find international law flawed at a basic level, and thus in need of more than a simple course correction. For instance, it might be suggested that the notion of tutelage, as applied to the relationship of colonizers to colonized, leads too easily to a view of indigenous people as children who are not quite full human beings. As we shall see momentarily, it has been argued that the very purpose of modern international law, beginning in the late fifteenth and early sixteenth centuries, was not to set aside but rather to put into place and to protect a colonial world order.

Fifth, I have suggested that international law can serve the ethical prospector in part because it is, in a sense, ethics writ large—an attempt to answer the question, "How ought we to live together in one, interconnected world?" In the Nauru case, more than once the gap between law and morality begins to narrow. Appeals to *moral* if not strictly *legal* obligations are hardly deemed irrelevant to the case at hand. But even if legal arguments are carefully distinguished from moral arguments, it remains that law is, or can be, informed by an entire range or scale of values quite recognizable to someone such as Bernard Lonergan or Pope Francis—or the reader himself or herself.

Finally, it is no deflection from a focus on laws and institutions simply to remember that both are generated—and followed or skirted—by human subjects with their insights and oversights, their breakthroughs and biases, their broad and not so broad moral horizons, their aspirations for true progress rooted in values, their capitulations to decline. Perhaps in the Nauru case these subjects are not as visible or colorful as the copper kings of Butte or as approachable as the women of Chuquicamata, but they were and are certainly present and active in parliaments, in law schools, in mining company boardrooms, at the mining site called Topside, in the dwellings found on Pleasant Island. Here, we want to look at two individuals very much caught up in the Nauru case to see what more we might learn about mining morality: the lead investigator himself, Christopher Weeramantry, and his student and assistant in this case, Antony Anghie. If Heinze and Daly and Clarke were "copper kings," then maybe we can view Weeramantry and Anghie as "phosphate philosophers" with a practical bent—or something akin to that.

C. G. WEERAMANTRY: MORAL MINER AND TEACHER FOR OUR TIME

In his Commission report, Christopher Weeramantry writes that "Nauru presents in microcosm an unusual variety of the great historical currents that have shaped the course of human affairs."[66] In the second volume of his three-volume memoirs, *Towards One World*,[67] Weeramantry discusses his involvement in the Nauru case in similar terms: "Nauru," he writes, "contained in microcosm the vast range of rich world/poor world issues which constituted a center theme of my later work and, in fact, the essential core of the bulk of world problems today."[68] But we might say something else: Weeramanty, who died in January 2017, was the ideal person to investigate the case of Nauru. His own life and work intersected with the "historical currents that have

Figure 4.4. Christopher Weeramantry.
Photo by Henning Blatt.

shaped the course of human affairs." More than that, as an astute observer of these currents and their diverse directions, as a lawyer, a humanist, an educator, a religiously informed global citizen, he eased the flow of some of these currents and sought to reverse or change the course of others.

There is no way to summarize adequately C. G. Weeramantry's decades of service, legal and other, to the cause of humanity and its "common home," so here I will simply highlight briefly four themes pertinent to moral mining: (1) the relationship between his life story and his deft use of the self-sharpening prospector's tools, especially international law; (2) his exemplification of what Lonergan calls "the emerging religious consciousness of our time"; (3) the deep resonance between his work and the vision of *Laudato si'*; (4) his commitment to education for peace and justice. In a continuation of these themes, in chapter 6 we will have an opportunity to take a brief look at another focal point of his work: a judgment on the legality of using or threatening to use the nuclear weapons that, like everything else, "begin with mining"—in this case the mining of uranium.

Weeramantry was born in Ceylon. His place of origin says much about who he was and, over the years, who he became. For Ceylon was, historically, a meeting place or crossroads for diverse cultures and religions. Born into a Catholic family, from an early age Christopher also enjoyed the riches and rituals of other traditions—for instance, the Buddhism of his extended family. He was also born into a family of educators. His mother was his primary school teacher who loved philosophy, art, and music, and his father was a superb mathematician who was deeply committed to advancing math education in the secondary schools in which he taught—Buddhist, Catholic, and Muslim. Under the British colonial system Chrisopher received a classical education, with ample doses of Shakespeare and other English language authors, but also the rich literature of other traditions. This wide and deep appreciation for traditions other than his own would rise to the surface in his later voluminous writings and even his court briefs. That his education would be multicultural and multireligious stands to reason; he reminds us that the Buddhist centers of learning in his homeland predated the universities of Europe—for instance, the one in Salamanca which will prove important below.

Not unlike Mohandas Gandhi, Weeramantry received some of his legal education in England before returning home to Ceylon and, in a profound sense, to a world on the move—not least of which was the move from colonialism to a postcolonial age, as Ceylon became Sri Lanka in 1948. The title and subtitles of his three-volume memoirs provide a sense of the widening sweep of his life: *Towards One World* is the overall title and, it seems, the very aim of his life as it passed through its various phases: *The Sri Lanka Years* (vol. 1), during which, after a rich family formation, he became an expert in the law of contracts (a topic of no little irrelevance to the Nauru case) and served on the Sri Lankan Supreme Court; *The Australian Years* (vol. 2), when he taught at Monash University, entered deeply into the world of international law—in part because it was not being given sufficient attention at Monash—and, of course, was invited to lead the investigation into the Nauru case; and, finally, *The International Court of Justice and Thereafter,* a period of nine years in The Hague, where he contributed significantly to key cases, followed by his many activities "thereafter," especially in peace education.

What one finds in Weeramantry's memoirs is an ever-expanding life of experience, of accumulated insights and judgments, of sometimes mundane, sometimes momentous decisions—such as his decision to step down from the Sri Lankan Supreme Court and to take up the more intellectually and geographically expansive life as a distinguished professor of law, now much freer to roam the world by books and boats and planes.[69]

In the process, he was contributing to that world, seeking bit by bit to make it *one* world. This should be apparent from our discussion of what Weeramantry called "the Nauru story," which, he explains, "has a significance reaching well beyond the tiny coral island which was the subject of [the] inquiry."[70] In assembling and bringing to bear upon the case of Nauru a vast and varied body of law, especially international law, he was asking us—the Nauruans, the Mandate partner countries, the League of Nations, the United nations, all of us—to think about how we ought to live, and where we have fallen short. In the process, he was sharpening those tools, bringing new relevance to ancient principles and old law, and helping that law to grow and serve the human family as a whole. Indeed, in one of his major works, *Universalising International Law*, Weeramantry advocated for wider adherence to the rule of law, but also for a transformation of that law into something it is not yet.[71] He advocated for education in international law, making its principles accessible even to children.[72]

Put in other terms, Weeramantry's life's work seems to be continual employment of "method," with its "functional specialities" (Lonergan). Looking to the past together with others, he identifies the relevant sources (research), interprets their meaning (interpretation), traces their history (history), deals with differences (dialectics), seeks solid ground to move ahead (foundations) with new or revised legal doctrines (doctrines) to be further explicated as to their meanings (systematics) so that these might be communicated broadly (communication) for the sake of newly emergent law in a newly emerging world that seeks to heal the wounds of the past. In seeking "one world," the ethical prospector's tools of human intelligence and affectivity, on the one hand, and international law, on the other, are joined.

Just as Weeramantry's life and work, especially in international law, may be construed as a movement toward "one world," they also exemplify what Lonergan called the "emerging religious consciousness of our time," a consciousness intimately bound up with "a thrust towards world community in contemporary consciousness."[73] Unlike many international lawyers who simply dismiss religion as "something we used to have,"[74] Weeramantry found religion and international law highly compatible. So, for instance, in 1988 he published a book on Islamic jurisprudence from an international perspective to counter the ignorance and lack of appreciation for that tradition that he found among his law students, but also to emphasize Islam's contribution to international law.[75] A decade later, in response to a suggestion from a colleague that he write a book out of his own tradition, he published through an American Catholic press, *The Lord's Prayer: Bridge to a Better World*,[76] a work that obviously dovetails with his life's theme of "towards one world"—the very orientation that Lonergan says marks the emerging religious consciousness of our time under the heading of "world community."[77]

The Lord's Prayer, on Weermantry's reading, has to do with such things as economic justice, war and other kinds of violence, and human rights of all kinds—the very sorts of topics, that in one form or another, occupy international lawyers and might come before the World Court where Weeramantry served as judge and vice president. The further titling on the book's cover is also germane: *A Vision for Personal and Global Transformation.* If "mining morality"—on Pleasant Island or in underground Butte—necessarily involves the systemic, the institutional, the complex schemes of recurrence about which Lonergan writes, it is also about the person as "originating value," about "interiority," about conscience, where Weeramantry's Catholic tradition says the individual person "is alone with God, whose voice echoes in his [or her] depths."[78] It is also about conversion—and it is not necessarily conversion to Christianity. Even as *The Lord's Prayer* is written from the perspective of a Roman Catholic, Weeramantry insists that "the rich and varied nuances that impregnate the Christian scriptures can sometimes receive a new radiance through rays of inspiration coming from other scriptures, just as those others can be lighted up by inspiration from the Christian"[79]—a statement that captures the essence of the dialogical practice of what some call "comparative theology."

Legal Counsel to Pope Francis and the World

In chapter 6, we will have another brief opportunity to consider how Weeramantry uses the tools of international law on a moral and legal issue of no little moment, the use or threat to use nuclear weapons. For now, I would at least note the significant overlap between Weeramantry's work and Catholic social thought, as expressed in *Laudato si'*. In fact, if Pope Francis were seeking a good lawyer to deal with the legal implications of *Laudato si'*, Weeramantry, even posthumously, would be high on the list. First, there is the shared concern for the environment. Even to compare the titles of two works is instructive. On the one hand, of course, is Pope Francis's *Laudato si': On Care for Our Common Home*; on the other is Weeramantry's 2009 book *Tread Lightly on the Earth: Religion, the Environment and the Human Future.*[80] While the two works stress the interconnectedness of all things,[81] we can be more specific than that and say that they complement one another in terms of religious focus and grounding. *Laudato si'* is written from a Christian perspective but insists that everyone's voice is needed if we are to care effectively for our common home; *Tread Lightly on the Earth* seeks not just in Christianity but in major religious traditions (Hinduism, Judaism, Buddhism, Christianity, and Islam) principles and other resources for achieving if not the identical at least a very compatible end: "illuminating an area of deep concern to the human future—namely the rights of future generations and the conservation of the environment."[82]

The clear convergence of the two on concern for future generations cannot be overstated: the term itself appears eleven times in *Laudato si'*, and "future" many more times than that. This should be no surprise. Future generations had increasingly become a topic of Catholic social teaching prior to *Laudato si'*. As for *Tread Lightly*, together with care for the environment, the rights of future generations are the central focus of the work, a 340-page report of the World Future Society, an organization to which Weeramantry was deeply committed. Pope Francis and Weeramantry clearly share a common concern for future generations, but Weeramantry is more explicit than Francis in locating this concern in *all* the major religions. Thus, we can say that, for Francis and even more so for Weeramantry, the religious consciousness that is emerging in our time includes a vital concern for future neighbors.

There are other intersections between the two works that could be explored, such as concern for the poor, arguably more pronounced in *Laudato si'* than in *Tread Lightly*, but most certainly present in *The Lord's Prayer*. Threats stemming from advanced technology, not least of which is nuclear weaponry, also occupy Weearamantry's attention. In fact, a closer comparison of *Laudato si'* and *Tread Lighly,* joined with other of his writings, would very likely confirm the hypothesis that Weeramantry is in basic agreement with Francis's worries about the "technocratic paradigm."

The two works complement others in yet another way. If, as suggested in chapter 2, international law is a necessary if not sufficient requirement for the vision of *Laudato si'* to be realized or even advanced, then the beginnings of that effort are visible in *Tread Lightly*. There, Weeramantry makes pertinent points about international law, such as the problem of its largely secularized Eurocentrism, and he appeals to international organizations such as the United Nations, the International Court of Justice, and the Intergovernmental Panel on Climate Change to move us forward. Most notably, perhaps, an appendix records Judge Weeramantry's dissenting opinion in *The Gabčíkovo-Nagymaros Project,* a prominent environmental case brought before the ICJ in 1997. We should also keep in mind that, as the Nauru case alone suggests, *Tread Lightly* is, one might say, but the tip of a melting iceberg when it comes to the international legal world that Weeramantry brings into conversation with *Laudato si'*.

Phosphate Philosophers: A Student and His Teacher

Finally, a word about Weeramantry as educator. As noted above, Weeramantry was born into a family committed to education, and one of his brothers chose teaching as a career. As also noted, Weeramantry's decision to leave the Sri Lankan Supreme Court for the classroom was for him a liberating experience, allowing him to travel widely and expand his horizons in diverse directions. His impact on his law students was no doubt significant, but, so, too, was his impact on others, and these wider educational efforts, especially for peace, were rightly recognized by UNESCO.[83]

But something else deserves stress. There is, in the Catholic moral tradition, if not only there, an emphasis on law not only as restraining or compelling, but also as educating. This arguably includes international law. It can teach us how to live—how to treat one another and how, in the language of *Laudate si'*, to treat "our common home." In fact, given perhaps the greatest challenge to international law—the problems of compliance and the frequent lack of coercive backing sufficient for some at least to admit that it is even "law"—international law still gives us some direction on how we *ought* to conduct ourselves on the earth, beneath the sea, and, as we will see, beyond the earth's bounds—even if we fail to learn our legal lessons when it comes to practice. Thus, as he sought to retrieve, to revise, and help new law to emerge, Weeramantry was among those who, Aristotle says, seek to educate the community by seeking to make good laws.[84] Had Weeramantry never entered the classroom, this would still have been true. He would still have been an educator. But, happily, it is also true that he had students in the more traditional sense of the term. To one of these we now turn.

In 2004, a law professor at the University of Utah, Antony Anghie, published *Imperialism, Sovereignty, and the Making of International Law*, a work that received considerable critical attention. In his acknowledgments, Anghie explains:

> Christopher Weeramantry inspired me by his example to take up the study of international law and he has been unstinting in his support and concern ever since I was his student. His vision of international justice, his integrity, his erudition and wisdom establish the standards to which I will always aspire but never attain.[85]

In the introduction, Anghie further writes:

> The themes and concerns that animate this book *emerged* from my experiences as a research assistant working for C. G. Weeramantry who was then Chief Commissioner of an Inquiry established by the Government of Nauru to examine the history of the phosphate mining that took place on the island.[86]

As Anghie's testimony suggests, we have here an example of how mining morality can involve the relationship of teacher and student, of mentor and mentee, of partnership in a common endeavor larger than the teacher-student relationship itself. In the classroom and in the Nauru case, Weeramantry introduced Anghie to the world of international law that long-predated both. To invoke again the image from Michael Polanyi, together they "dwelt in" this world in order to "break out" with something new—the partial healing, through their efforts, of a devastated island-world. To return to the language of Lonergan, the relationship of teacher to student shifts the probability that in some small incremental way, the "one world" envisioned by teacher, and now student, may begin to emerge. Furthermore, it may be that the work that Weeramantry and his student shared was informed by the "emerging religious consciousness of our time." Such consciousness embraces a body of law, both settled (*lex lata*) and emerging (*lex ferenda*), to help "heal and create in history," in this case the history of Nauru but also far beyond.

But to say that teacher and student "dwelt in" international law together is not to say that they have "broken out" with the same new thing. Anghie's *Imperialism, Sovereignty, and the Making of International Law* was a major, and contested, contribution to the literature of international law. But rather than simply reiterating his mentor's international jurisprudence, Anghie takes it a step further—as in a moment we shall see. The fact that he had mentors other than Weeramantry no doubt accounts in part for that. Indeed, Anghie tells of his "great good fortune of having *two* extraordinary teachers,"[87] the other of whom was David Kennedy, "the principle figure" in the "critical legal studies" movement,[88] a movement that arguably takes a more conflictual and pessimistic view of international law than one finds in Weeramantry.

The point here is not to trace in every respect the lineage between mentor and student, or even between "school" or "movement" and someone like Anghie drawn into it—for schools and movements themselves are not so easy to pin down.[89] Rather, a more modest observation is in order. Teachers may provide certain conditions of possibility for the emergence of new insights and judgments about international law (or other subjects, of course) as they teach by example and pass on what they know. In this way, they provide bases for development "from above." But they may also encourage development "from below," inviting their students to make their own discoveries. Scholars and practitioners such as Anghie can learn to write and speak in their own voice, a voice that is distinctive and new, even as no one—neither student nor teacher—starts from intellectual or, one might add, affective scratch. Anyone who has even perused perhaps the most famous "classic" of international law, Hugo Grotius's *De Jure Belli ac Pacis, Tres Libri* (*The Law of War and Peace, Three Books*), will see that this is so. Not only did Grotius build upon the work of familiar "forerunners" such as Thomas Aquinas and Francisco de Vitoria,[90] but he also appealed to ancient sources the very names of which escape the memory of many readers today.

There is another point to be made. While there is need to stress the way in which international law progresses, with Anghie's advance on his mentors' work as an example, we must not assume that all is "progress." Along with insights and sound judgments that move the wheel of method toward "cumulative and progressive results," influential, often charismatic teachers may pass on to their students their oversights, their biases of various kinds—oversights that distort students' vision and impede their undertaking of the task of mining morality, of seeking the best answers to the question, How ought we to live? Such biases may become systemic. For instance, highly regarded textbooks may simply repeat without question the questionable claim that Grotius was bent on liberating international law from religious traditions, sources, and consciousness—the very sort of traditions, sources, and consciousness that someone like Weeramantry, against the grain, wants to recall and retrieve.[91] In any event, Anghie's thoughts and convictions are clearly his own, but they are just as clearly conditioned by others, both as immediate as the living teachers he thanks in his book and as remote as the many Latin terms that recur in international legal discourse, reminders of a distant intellectual and at times tempestuous past.

What are those thoughts and convictions as presented in *Imperialism, Sovereignty and the Making of International Law*? At the risk of oversimplifying, Anghie's advance on previous work appears to be this: Given his encounter with Weeramantry but also with others and his own extensive review of the history of international law, Anghie concludes not simply that international law, with the notion of sovereignty at its center, was in the past limited by its Eurocentricity and thus closed to those on the margins until such time as new nations emerged and could take their rightful place in the ordering system of sovereign states. Rather, he wants to show that international law is in fact the product of encounter between colonizer and colonized, such that the very notion of sovereignty central to international law was developed and defined in such a way that those outside the system were viewed as less than sovereign because they were less than "civilized." This suppression of the other was not only characteristic of the early "making of international law" located in the violent encounter with peoples of the "new world"; it has been maintained through its various phases—for example, the "mandate" system exemplified in the case of Nauru. This fundamental defect in international law remains today.

Now, there is no hope here of examining Anghie's claims in the depth they deserve. But at least a few observations pertinent to this exercise in ethical prospecting are in order. First, is Anghie's starting point for international law's road to suppression of those on its margins, clearly stated in the title of the opening chapter: "Francisco de Vitoria and the Colonial Origins of International Law." Anghie acknowledges that Vitoria, rather than the later Hugo Grotius, is rightly credited by some as the true originator of modern international law, and he concedes that he is a "an extremely complex figure." On Anghie's reading of Vitoria's famous "relections" *De Indis* and *Ius belli*, Vitoria reinterpreted established legal concepts, or invented new ones, that treated the indigenous peoples as equal, but only in theory. In fact, he was not dealing with the question of order between and among sovereign states, but rather "the problem of creating a system for relations between societies which he understood to belong to two very different culture orders, each with its own ideas of propriety and governance."[92] The problem emerges full force when Vitoria enunciates as one of the legitimate reasons for conquest the failure to allow the sort of communication (or trade) sanctioned by the natural law. "Vitoria's apparently innocuous enunciation of a right to 'travel' and 'sojourn,'" Anghie writes, "extends finally to the creation of a comprehensive, indeed inescapable system of norms which are inevitably violated by the Indians," thus giving rise to what the Spaniards (or others) might perceive as legitimate grounds for war.[93] In short, the international law that Vitoria develops is, in fact, hardly a law of de-facto equals but rather one that legitimates the domination of peoples that comes under the name of colonization—or, to give it more specificity, the kind of "trade and commerce" that befell the not-yet-sovereign, not-yet-independent Nauruans over the years.

Surely, Anghie is not alone in his critique of Vitoria. Years before, for instance, Carl Schmitt, in *The* Nomos *of the Earth,* discussed Vitoria at length and made clear that the Dominican friar did not condemn conquest altogether.[94] There may be detailed rejoinders to Anghie, but I will not attempt them here. What I will do is reference observations of two reviewers, and then return to our "prospecting tools."

One reviewer—a self-described blogger—makes an interesting point: for all of Anghie's concern to honor diverse cultures, by focusing on Spain's encounter with the indigenous peoples of the Americas, he seems to place a lot of weight on *this* particular meeting of cultures. Could he not have asked, for instance, about European expansion elsewhere in the world? In other words, is there not more than one telling of international law's origins, one not so concentrated on Europe's encounter with the indigenous people of what is now the "Western" hemisphere?[95] After all, China and India receive explicit treatment in the early pages of Stephen Neff's history of international law, and other writers have stressed international law's non-Western origins.[96] The reader might recall from the previous chapter Michael Malone's observation about Butte: "It need not have been this way." Just as other mining centers did not go the way of Butte and its copper kings, so, too, other instances of an expanding Europe may not match exactly the sad and infuriating story of the *consquistadores*. This does not negate Anghie's theory, but it at least complicates it. For instance, international law may not be simply an ongoing shield for *Western* imperialism. Other imperialists now operating within the system of international law may be implicated as well.[97]

A second reviewer's point is along the same lines. What Anghie gives us, Dan Danielsen explains, is an alternative disciplinary reading of international law that joins other alternative readings, such as those offered by feminist scholars. This leads one to ask whether in fact international law is inherently pluralistic but falsely packaged under claims to universality. As Danielsen puts it:

> Anghie's book is important precisely because it illuminates the partiality of the traditional disciplinary narrative *and also of his own*. By pluralizing the historical and doctrinal narratives of the discipline, it becomes easier to see the international legal order not as a single-coherent normative system to be defended or critiqued in toto, but rather, as a complex, often incoherent governance regime made up of multiple and diverse legal orders and normative systems opening new space for further engagement and contestation.[98]

But then Danielsen goes on to point out:

> Surprisingly, however, Anghie ends his book with a renewed hope for a "truly universal international law that promotes a compelling vision of international justice" (p. 360). Yet Anghi's book stands as one of the most compelling testaments I know to the partiality and risks of any attempt to transcend difference

> with a universal vison of law or justice, even when couched in the most laudable, humane, or altruistic terms.[99]

In other words, Anghie seems to long for that which, armed with the tools of David Kennedy and others of a more "critical" or "deconstructive" bent, he has shown is not really feasible. In this longing, he seems to be the student of Weeramantry, who, in his hope-filled writings seeks "one world" and "the universalizing of international law."

But to return to our prospecting tools, what if the basis of the striving for universal justice is not some frozen set of concepts, or one specific way of defining or understanding international law, but rather the self-transcending human subject himself or herself, in dialogue with other human subjects near and far, seeking the true and the good in accord with what Lonergan has termed "transcendental" precepts? What if that vision is finally one that, à la Pope Francis, or even Portia in Shakespeare's *The Merchant of Venice*, seeks universal justice but also knows of human failure, sometimes on a massive scale, and thus the universal need for a mercy "that is not strained"?[100] Given the widespread oversights or biases that grease the wheels of disasters that strike with the suddenness of a mining accident or more slowly like a melting icecap or an increasingly degraded Pacific island or coral reef, is not such mercy needed today and by all?

Still, to long for universal justice tempered by mercy need not, cannot mean denial of the particular case—of copper beneath the hills of Butte, of phosphate on the Topside of Nauru—or of particular judgments and decisions that must be reached. It cannot mean denial of the individuals and groups involved. The human spirit seeks the intelligible and the good, and, heads toward judgment and decision—do this and not that. Sometimes the way is clear, but sometimes it takes ten volumes to build a case and reach a decision. Recalling again a major contributor to both the Catholic social tradition and international law, Thomas Aquinas, what is arguably required is an international juris-*prudence.* Such a jurisprudence will be animated by *understanding*, a heuristic, heart-felt grasp, of "first principles" such as "do good and avoid evil," even as the good in this or that case is not yet entirely clear. Practitioners of this juris-prudence will look to the past with, so far as possible, undistorted *memory*, and in a spirit of *docility*—an eagerness to learn—will consult others: legal scholars, past and present, anthropologists, the people of Nauru—maybe even future generations. Such practitioners will regard the *circumstances* of this case, as complex as they might be as they *reason* to a good decision. With *foresight* they will look ahead. The longing for universal justice may be the animator. But, as Thomas Aquinas puts it, the "chief act of prudence is to command" to act—in this case, or in that.

This again raises the question of stability in international law. True, international grows and emerges. Some of it has the character of *lex ferenda* and some of it is "soft law." It may even, as Martti Koskenniemi insists, ever vacillate between a Utopian set of universal norms and the pragmatics of self-interest. Still, it is not totally fluid and unstable, constantly changing, totally unreliable from one day to the next—as though there were no established sources (treaties, custom, legal widely accepted principles) on which to build. Not everything is constantly up for grabs. Someone, somewhere, must make a judgment, in this case about who is responsible for cleaning up the mess made of Pleasant Island, with larger implications for judging who is responsible for cleaning up, or "healing," other messes around the world. As we have seen in the case of Nauru, there is a lot of law in place on which to stand. In further chapters we will return to the question of law's stability in an unstable world, including a court decision, not only about the "ends" of mining—in this case the mining of uranium—but about the end of so much else, when the specter of a nuclear exchange reshapes our discussion about who is "civilized" and who is not.

INTERIM PROSPECTOR'S REPORT

The reader might consider a simple experiment: Show people a sea-level sketch of an island and ask them to draw what the island looks like below the waterline. Some (apparently, even a few who live on islands) might draw lines that join at some point beneath the surface, leaving the island to look like a floating iceberg. Others, unsure, might draw lines that run outward beneath the surface, but then just trail off, say, with dotted lines. Still others will indicate, correctly, that an island is really like a mountain peak. Not only is it not "free-floating"; it is a part—sometimes, as in the case of Nauru, a very small part—of the one landmass that, in our case, is the mostly stable crust of Planet Earth.

Examining the case of Nauru is a little like that. We may not realize what lies beneath the surface of a once pleasant, then devastated island, in terms of meanings and values, until we inquire with the help of others experienced in asking the right kinds of questions. Here, our main line of inquiry has been international law and the light it can shed on the question "How ought we to live?" Since we are talking about law, we might recall what, in an earlier instance, some saw as "bad law" and see if, in this instance, it can become "good law." I refer again to the "apex rule" whereby the tiny island of Nauru is the "apex" of veins of inquiry that extend beneath the phosphate-rich surface—not only downward through the spirals of history but outward across the globe.

This is perhaps another way of restating Weeramantry's point about the case he was assigned: that "Nauru presents in microcosm an unusual variety of the great historical currents that have shaped the course of human affairs." If, in Janet Finn's apt phrase, we "trace the veins" beneath and beyond Nauru, we can see, even from our limited prospecting, that the "apex" called Nauru is connected to such diverse and complex issues as colonialism and neocolonialism; the emergence of the League of Nations and its successor, the United Nations; two great wars; the Peace of Versailles; anthropological studies on Nauru and elsewhere; fertilizer and its uses; customary laws of the Nauruan people; domestic laws of Germany, Australia, Great Britain, and even the United States; the displacement of entire populations; South Africa and Southwest Africa (and, by extension, the system of apartheid); the Salamanca School of theology and philosophy, as well as other philosophical schools; and the very nature of international law, both settled and aspirational.[101]

Thus, a first recommendation to the reader seeking to mine morality would be to consider—or "trace"—further than I have done one or more of the various "veins" of inquiry that reaches its apex in this case, to see where it might lead—historically, intellectually, and, I would suggest, affectively. Surely, one cannot pursue every vein of moral inquiry. The point would be to focus on one or perhaps a few, but with a peripheral vision that take other issues, other disciplines, other persons or people (including future generations), other veins of inquiry into account. Mining morality might mean, for instance, exploring the perennial and profound question of war that so affected Nauru, or the failure to appreciate cultures other than one's own.

Or, it could mean delving more deeply into key aspects of international law. Let me suggest a few of those aspects relatively near the surface. First is the challenging set of questions posed by a key phrase in Article 38 of the Charter of the International Court of Justice—perhaps the most authoritative site for a listing of the "sources" of international law. Along with treaties and custom, the statute lists as a primary source "the general principles of law recognized by *civilized* nations;" (Art. 38.1.c emphasis added). Judgments about "civilized" and "uncivilized" were surely at issue in the Nauru case when it came to the "mandate" and "trustee" systems. Even the little said above about Antony Anghie's critique of the history of international law as being, in effect, a long-standing cover for Eurocentrism and colonialism, should make apparent why "civilized" is such a contested term. As it was in the case of C. B. Glasscock's *The War of the Copper Kings,* so questions of "civilization" have been central to international law.[102] Mining morality may mean pondering such questions, even when the focus is not Nauru. Reaching into our prospecting tools, one might be helped by considering Lonergan's distinction between a "classicist" and an empirical notion of culture. The former is more likely to equate "civilized" with "European" or any other limited set of meanings and values taken to be normative for all; the latter is inclined to take each culture on its own terms, even if, as with every culture, those terms need to be tested over time.

Second is the question of "bright lines" connoted by the appeal to *jus cogens* (peremptory) norms in international law, norms from which there can be no "derogations" or exceptions. Such norms regard such matters as torture or, especially in light of the Convention on the Rights of the Child, the execution of minors.[103] When it comes to morality, one sometimes asks: Are there any "absolutes"? Is *everything* "subjective" or relative to one's culture, one's religion, one's group?[104] The presence of *jus cogens* in international law suggests that the question of "absolutes" is alive here as well. If international law is in any meaningful sense "ethics writ large," then mining morality will mean grappling with this question.

Third is the fact that international law is integral to institutions of various kinds, and institutions are, in turn, integral to international law. This is apparent when it comes to formally designated "international organizations," such as the United Nations, the UN High Commission for Human Rights, the International Organization of Labor, and, as we shall see in the next two chapters, the International Seabed Authority and the International Atomic Energy Agency. But it is often true also of the international NGOs that now number in the tens of thousands—with their various, often conflicting agendas. So, too, are domestic institutions, such as judicial systems, affected by international law in complex and contested ways. One might consider the U.S. Constitution with its clauses that relate to international law, or ponder U.S. Supreme Court Justice Gray's famous words in the *Paquette Habana* case: "International law is part of our law, and must be ascertained and administered by the courts of justice of appropriate jurisdiction as often as questions of right depending upon it are duly presented for their determination."[105] Of course, such pondering might quickly lead to the realization that Justice Gray's words may be famous but, especially in light of strong nationalist claims, also open to rebuttal, as they were in his own day.

Fourth, without in any way denying the importance of the institutional, the structural, the organizational, I have emphasized in the case of Nauru also individuals with moral horizons that embraced law and institutions and so much else—especially Christopher Weeramantry and, with briefer attention, his student, Antony Anghie. One might have considered more fully the moral point of view of other characters in the story of Nauru, for instance Prime Minister Hughes of Australia, who heaped derision on President Wilson for his idealistic view of the League of Nations.[106] Or, one might regard more closely the convictions and positions of Wilson himself, charting his insights but also his serious oversights, especially on questions of race.[107] Whatever further investigating the reader might pursue, the point is to ask just where he or she stands as he or she regards the island of Nauru—and with questions of teaching and learning, of long traditions and multiple institutions in mind, just how he or she got to this standpoint and where to go from here.

Clearly, such questions have to do with moral mining sites other than a tiny dot in the Pacific. Yet we can learn from this case. No man—or woman—is an island. We have heard that so often, it must be true. Yet, we are in fact very much like islands: distinctive, set apart, each with our very own social location, our own identity, our own situation, our own gifts and talents, our own strengths and weakness, our own name. Much the same could be said for the various groups or locales to which we belong. Nauru was and is not Ocean Island despite their similarities, and neither is Ellis Island or the Isle of Crete. So, when it comes to mining morality, we should again recall Shefa Siegel's comment about mining itself: "There is a maddening futility about speaking of 'mining,' as if it were singular or coherent."[108] Mining morality cannot overlook differences. But, like every island in every pond or lake or sea, we are also connected—at least below the surface if not above—to some larger whole, to some common good. In the next chapter, we will focus on the 1982 Convention on the Law of the Sea, which has a great deal to say about islands. But we will mostly look below the surface where mining was, and is, a contested issue. From the ocean floor and perhaps the depths of moral consciousness, questions about our having something in common, some common heritage, will emerge.

NOTES

1. "Trump Disparages 'Dumb' Deal with Australia on Refugees," National Public Radio, February 2, 2017, http://www.npr.org/sections/thetwo-way/2017/02/02/513012395/trump-disparages-dumb-deal-with-australia-on-refugees.

2. Nauru is 21 square kilometers/8.1 square miles. To put this in some perspective, Butte-Silver Bow (now chartered together) is listed at 747 square miles, a very small slice of Montana's 747,000 square miles.

3. For a journalist's critical assessment of Nauru's present situation with a brief recital of the history leading up to this state of affairs, see Ben Doherty, "The Nauru Files: A Brief History of Nauru, Australia's Dumping Ground for Refugees," *The Guardian,* August 9, 2016, https://www.theguardian.com/world/2016/aug/10/a-short-history-of-nauru-australias-dumping-ground-for-refugees. The Australian Broadcasting Corporation tells a similar story, but with more of the burden for the Nauruans' plight since independence placed on the Nauruans themselves. See Kerri Phillips, "How Nauru Threw It All Away," RN, March 11, 2014, http://www.abc.net.au/radionational/programs/rearvision/how-nauru-threw-it-all-away/5312714. Certain

online comments on this story reflect a more acute sense of history, reminding readers of Australia, New Zealand, and Great Britain's role on the island. For another overview, see "Nauru," *Encyclopedia* (online), https://www.britannica.com/place/Nauru.

4. Christopher Weeramantry, *Nauru: Environmental Damage under Trusteeship* (Melbourne: Oxford University Press, 1992), xiii.

5. He was joined on the Commission by Mr. R. H. Challen and Mr. Gideon Degidoa.

6. Weeramantry, *Nauru*, x–xii.

7. Ibid., 13.

8. Ibid., 110–12.

9. Lonergan, *Method*, 35.

10. Stewart Firth, "German Firms in the Western Pacific Island," *Journal of Pacific History* 8 (1973): 14, in Weeramantry, *Nauru* 33. How, in this instance, needs-creation might relate to theories of "comparative advantage" from David Ricardo (1772–1823) onward is a question awaiting discussion. Since we are talking about sea trade, perhaps more to the point is Hugo Grotius's conviction, expressed in his famous treatise on "the free sea" (*Mare Liberum*), that God intended that nations would have diverse resources and arts so that none would claim self-sufficiency, and that "human friendship" would be maintained through trade. "Now it cometh to pass," he writes, "that one nation should supply the want of another by the appointment of divine justice, that thereby (as Pliny saith) that which brought forth anywhere might be seen to be bred with all" (Hugo Grotius, *The Free Sea,* trans. Richard Hakluyt with William Welwood's Critique and Grotius's Reply, ed. David Armitage [Indianapolis: Liberty Fund, 2004], 10).

11. Grotius, *The Free Sea*, 18–19.

12. This raises a significant question we cannot pursue here, namely, how different conceptions of time might affect the interactions of and agreements between people from diverse cultures.

13. Weeramantry, *Nauru*, 19.

14. A. F. Ellis, *Ocean Island and Nauru* (Sydney: Angus & Robertson, 1935), 124, quoted by Weeramantry, *Nauru*, 20 (emphasis added).

15. Weeramantry, *Nauru*, 20.

16. Ibid., 23.

17. Ibid., 1.

18. Ibid., 27 (emphasis added).

19. Ibid.

20. Ibid., 57.

21. Ibid., 60 (emphasis added).

22. Ibid., 62.

23. Ibid., 39–40.

24. Ibid., 28–29.

25. Ibid., 30.

26. Ibid., 26. The exact source of this quote is unclear, as Weeramantry cites here a number of scientific studies.

27. Ibid., 31.

28. Ibid., 154.

29. Ibid., 157.
30. Ibid., 158.
31. Ibid., 169.
32. Ibid.
33. Ibid., 165.
34. Ibid.
35. Ibid., 175–77.
36. Ibid., 176–77.
37. Ibid., 177.
38. The report cites a typical example recorded by the German explorer P. Hambruch: "Since Deie is still very small, Anin will take over guardianship of Deie in the case of the death of his brother Kenemei and will possess the rank of chief of the clan until Deie's coming of age. (This happened in 1911)." P. Hambruch, *Nauru: Results of the South Seas Expedition*, ed. G. Thilenius (Hamburg: L. Friedaricksen, 1914), 300, in Weeramantry, *Nauru*, 178.
39. Weeramantry, Nauru, 84.
40. Ibid., 84. South West Africa reappears in chapter 6, which takes up mining of uranium in Africa. For now, it stands as a signal that the mandate system may have been problematic from its inception.
41. Ibid., 78.
42. Ibid., 79.
43. Ibid., 85–86.
44. For the text of the Covenant, see The Covenant of the League of Nations (Including Amendments adopted to December, 1924), http://www.iilj.org/wp-content/uploads/2016/08/The-Covenant-of-the-League-of-Nations.pdf.
45. The report recalls that General Smuts "wanted South Africa to be permitted to annex the neighbouring German colonies in Africa on the ground that the region was 'inhabited by barbarians, who not only cannot possibly govern themselves, but to whom it would be impracticable to apply any idea of political self-determination in the European sense'" (*Nauru*, 9).
46. Weeramantry, *Nauru*, 239.
47. Ibid., 265.
48. *Laudato si'*, 81.
49. Weeramantry, *Nauru*, 307–60.
50. U. O. Umozurike, *Self-Determination in International Law* (Connecticut: Anchor Books, 1972), 220, in Weeramantry, *Nauru*, 310. If, as Pope Francis insists, "everything is connected," it is worth noting that Rhodes Scholarships may be connected to mining in Zambia, and the connection is not morally appealing.
51. Umozurike, *Self-Determination*, in *Nauru* 310.
52. Weeramantry, *Nauru*, 313–14.
53. Ibid., 315–16.
54. Ibid., 322–23. In their discussion of the principle of permanent sovereignty over natural resources, the Commission discusses at some length the similar case of uranium mining in Namibia, a case that anticipates the topic of chapter 6.
55. Ibid., 337.

56. See, for instance, Hillary Charlesworth, "Law-making and Sources," in *Cambridge Companion to International Law*, 190–92.
57. In Weeramantry, *Nauru,* 337, emphasis added.
58. Ibid., 72.
59. Ibid., 342.
60. For a complete listing, see Weeramantry, *Nauru,* 342–43.
61. Ibid., 347, emphasis added.
62. Ibid., 348.
63. Ibid., 357.
64. Ibid., 360.
65. Daniel K. Finn points out, for instance, the ways in which U.S. contract law falls short of Catholic social teaching on just contracts, with the emphasis on justice, not simply on agreement. See Daniel K. Finn, "The Unjust Contract: A Moral Evaluation," in *True Wealth of Nations*, 143–64.
66. Weeramantry, *Nauru*, 1.
67. C. G. Weeramantry, *Towards One World: The Memoirs of Judge C. G. Weeramantry,* 3 vols. (Moratuw: OPRO Printing and Publishing Solutions [Pvt] Ltd.) Vol. I: *The Sri Lankan Years* (2010); Vol. II: *The Australian Years* (2012); Vol. III: *The International Court of Justice and Thereafter* (2014).
68. Weeramantry, *Towards One World*, Vol. II: *The Australian Years*, 204.
69. Weeramantry, *Towards One World* ,Vol. I: *The Sri Lankan Years*, chapter 28 "The Move to Australia," 417–25.
70. Weeramantry, *Nauru*, 8.
71. C. G. Weeramantry, *Universalising International Law* (Leiden: Martinus Nijhoff Publishers, 2004).
72. "The principles underlying international law are based upon universally accepted values and moral standards. They can be understood by every schoolchild. When children are informed about them their eyes light up with appreciation that the international world is governed by principles which are so acceptable to them" (Judge Christopher Weeramantry and John Burroughs, "International Law: A Peace Lesson," Peace Lessons from around the World, 2005, a web-based part of Hague Appeal for Peace, www.haguepeace.org).
73. Lonergan, "Emerging Religious Consciousness," 65.
74. David Kennedy, "Images of Religion," in *Religion and International Law*, ed., Mark W. Janis and Carolyn Evans (The Hague: Kluwer Law International, 1999), 146. Kennedy is lamenting an attitude prevalent among his colleagues.
75. C. G. Weeramantry, *Islamic Jurisprudence: An International Perspective* (Kuala Lumpur: The Other Press, 1988).
76. C. G. Weeramantry, *The Lord's Prayer: Bridge to a Better World* (Ligouri, MO: Liguri/Triumph, 1998).
77. Lonergan, "Emerging Religious Consciousness," 65.
78. Vatican Council II *Pastoral Constitution on the Church in the Modern World: Gaudium et spes*, promulgated by Pope Paul VI, December 7, 1965, no. 16, http://www.vatican.va/archive/hist_councils/ii_vatican_council/documents/vat-ii_cons_19651207_gaudium-et-spes_en.html.

79. Weeramantry, *The Lord's Prayer,* 47.

80. C. G. Weeramantry, *Tread Lightly on the Earth: Religion, the Environment and the Human Future*, A Report for the World Future Council (Pannipitiya, Sri Lanka: Stamford Lake [Pvt.] Ltd., 2009).

81. For Weeramantry, *Tread Lightly,* see 38, 39–40, 131–33, 181–83, 233–34, 252.

82. Ibid., 1.

83. See "UNESCO Peace Prize for Judge Weeramantry," *Oneindia News*, June 3, 2006, https://www.oneindia.com/2006/06/03/unesco-peace-prize-for-judge-weeramantry-1149334513.html.

84. Aristotle, *Ethics,* Bk I, 2.

85. Antony Anghie, *Imperialism, Sovereignty, and the Making of International Law* (New York: Cambridge Press, 2004), xiv.

86. Ibid. (emphasis added).

87. Ibid. (emphasis added).

88. Stephen Neff, *Justice among Nations: A History of International Law* (Cambridge, MA: Harvard University Press, 2014), 459.

89. The Finnish scholar and practitioner Martti Koskenniemi is sometimes cited as "another prominent adherent" of the "critical legal studies" movement (see Neff, 459). But in a remarkable ten-page letter to the editors of the *American Journal of International Law* in response to a request to discuss this movement—on the assumption that he identified himself with it—he explains why he refuses to be identified with any one school. See Martti Koskenniemi, "Letter to the Editors of the Symposium," *AJIL* 93/2 (April 1999): 351–61.

90. Carl von Kaltenborn, *zur Geschitche des Natur- und Völkerrechts sowie der Politik*, vol. 1: *Die Vorläufer des Hugo Grotius auf dem Gebiete des Ius naturae et gentium sowie der Politik* (Leipzig: Verlag von Gustav Mayer, 1848).

91. William P. George, "Grotius, Theology, and International Law: Overcoming Textbook Bias," *Journal of Law and Religion* 14 (Winter 2001): 101–25.

92. Anghie, *Imperialism,* 16.

93. Ibid., 21–22.

94. Carl Schmitt, *The* Nomos *of the Earth in the International Law of the Jus Pubicum Europaeum* (New York: Telos Press Publishing, 2003), 101–25.

95. Elliot Conway, "Review of Antony Anghie, *Imperialism, Sovereignty, and the Making of International Law,*" https://classicliberalchap.wordpress.com/.

96. See, for instance, R. P. Anand, *Development of International Law and India*, Published under the auspices of the Max Planck Institute for European History, Frankfurt, Germany (Frankfurt, 2005; New Delhi 2007).

97. The West's off-and-on commitment to some sort of universalistic "natural law" extending to all humanity (the sort of claim one finds in Vitoria) may be problematic. But other empires, such as the Chinese empire, arguably viewed the world without any such pretense of respect for a "universal" humanity beyond their own borders. That is, the Chinese way is the *only* truly human way to live and to think. See Neff, *Justice among Nations,* 32–33. Those highly critical of Eurocentrism might take note.

98. Dan Danielsen, Review of Antony Anghie, *Imperialism, Sovereignty and the Making of International Law, American Journal of International Law* 100/3 (July 2006): 760 (emphasis in original).

99. Ibid., 761.

100. Shakespeare, *The Tempest*, Act 4, Scene 1, https://www.poets.org/poetsorg/poem/merchant-venice-act-iv-scene-i-quality-mercy-not-strained.

101. This represents only a tiny fraction of the hundreds of topics (many with multiple subtopics) listed in the index to Weeramantry, *Nauru.*

102. See Liana Obregón, "The Civilized and the Uncivilized," in *The Oxford Handbook of International Law*, ed. Bardo Fassbender and Anne Peters (Oxford: Oxford University Press, 2012), 917–42.

103. I cite this convention because it is the most widely endorsed human rights treaty on record (the United States is almost entirely alone in not being a party). It thus testifies to wide agreement on not only legal but also important moral issues, even though questions of cultural relativism remain. Notably, for our purposes, as the International Organization of Labor points out, the problem of child labor is especially pronounced when it comes to mining. See ILO, "Learn more about child labour in mining," at http://www.ilo.org/ipec/areas/Miningandquarrying/MoreaboutCLinmining/lang—en/index.htm.

104. While "subjectivism" and "relativism" are often used interchangeably, as the philosopher Mary Midgley points out, they may in fact be diametrically opposed. "Subjectivism" grounds norms in the individual; "relativism" grounds them in group identity, as in "cultural relativism." See Mary Midgley, "Trying Out One's New Sword," in *Heart and Mind* (New York: Palgrave Macmillan, 1981), 80–87.

105. The Paquette Habana, 175 U.S. 677 (1900).

106. Prime Minister Hughes to Governor-General, 17 January 1919, NLA, Novar Papers, M 696/2756, quoted in Weeramantry, *Nauru*, 44. The question of "idealism," extending to visions of a world government, versus state-centered "realism" will come up again in chapter 5, on deep seabed mining.

107. See Dick Lehr, "The Racist Legacy of Woodrow Wilson," *The Atlantic*, November 27, 2015.

108. Siegel, "The Missing Ethics of Mining."

Chapter Five

Seabed Mining: From Insight to International Law

On April 20, 2010, about 40 miles off the coast of Louisiana, the Deepwater Horizon disaster in the Gulf of Mexico took the lives of eleven and soon gained the dubious distinction of being the worst oil spill in history.[1] By July, nearly five million barrels of crude oil would pour into the gulf, and at least 1,100 miles of coastline and countless sea creatures would be affected. If there was ever a sobering reminder that it matters what happens in the ocean, on the ocean floor, and even some eighteen thousand feet into the crust below, the Deepwater Horizon horror story would seem to be it. If such things as off-shore oil-drilling are included in what counts as mining, then surely Deepwater Horizon should warn us that we may not be able to undo every harm to our common home, or—as we watched on our TV screens day after day—even to stop the underwater bleeding of a wounded world.

Not unlike the case of Nauru, prospecting for ethics and mining morality require that we ask about this massive spill: "Where have we been, how did we get here, what needs to change, where do we go from here?" Yes, like the case of Nauru, there have been postmortems to assign blame and to mete out compensation, and there have been efforts to repair damage done and to put in place safeguards for the future. But it seems hardly enough. It took a lot of creating in history to set up those rigs and to drill down so far. But when it comes to *healing* in history the wounds brought about by creativity gone awry, moral impotence and other impediments seem to leave us a bit short.

No doubt we could learn a great deal about mining morality by spending more time on this undersea disaster. It was at least for a time, a "hot topic," "a teaching moment"—one hopes that it still is. But in this chapter, we will take up a different case of mining that also has the sea as its site—the recovery from the ocean floor, and from its sulfide vents, minerals such as manganese

Figure 5.1. Deep Water Horizon.
Photo courtesy of United States Coast Guard.

and copper and zinc. Since the timeframe to be considered mostly predates Deepwater Horizon by years and even decades, the case may seem cold—like the ocean depths themselves. The starting point for the discussion in the pages below does not take place at sea at all, but rather in a quiet library. But, educationally at least, it can be good to consider topics that are cold. That way, when those topics become hot—like a warming ocean or an oil rig on fire—there may be a better chance of knowing what to think and do. Sometimes it is worth recalling quiet times alone, even when big, even global issues are at stake. As a prominent professor of international relations once pointed out to me, "It's amazing how many problems you can solve if you just go into your room and think about them."

THE LIBRARY AND THE LAW OF THE SEA

If there is wisdom in the old precept, "No one is to be a judge in one's own case," then autobiographical approaches to ethics are likely to suffer from the blind spots of the author. Still, autobiography may be illuminative if only to help others see their own case in a new light or from a different angle. We saw an example of this in the case of Janet Finn's self-reflection on her encounters with women and others in Butte and Chuquicamata. One of the leading ethicists of our time turns to his own life experience to elucidate "participation" as a promising way to think about religious ethics.[2] It may further our discussion of mining morality, then, if I begin this chapter on seabed mining and much else by explaining how I came to be interested in one set of prospector's tools, namely, international law, and then how I later turned to insights from Bernard Lonergan better to understand this enormously complex carrier of meaning and value especially as it relates to the 1982 United Nations Convention on the Law of the Sea (LOS), with seabed mining one of its most contentious issues.

This approach may bring closer to the surface at least three characteristics of mining morality. First, in my initial encounters with the LOS, mining was not the central focus, for the LOS dealt with many things. In fact, I wandered—or waded—into the LOS itself as I was looking for something else. So, while it may be true that "everything begins with mining," sometimes it takes a while, and several steps, to get back to where everything begins. Second, I hope these pages will offer some insight into insight. But they also say something about insight into oversight, as I realize now, in an exercise of *memoria*, that my thoughts on the LOS years ago may not be sufficient today—perhaps a little like needing to retell the story of Butte a second or third time. Third, the dangers of subjectivism notwithstanding, I hope to provide evidence that it is quite possible to be at once subjective and expansive, to be attentive to the recesses of one's own mind, on the one hand, and to worlds as least as wide and deep as the ocean and all that it holds, on the other. As Saint Augustine and others have stressed, attention to one's inner thoughts and passions may even offer suitable ways to think about and even encounter the divine.[3]

For many if not most doctoral students, the choice of a dissertation topic is a matter not only of importance but, until the choice becomes clear, also of some obscurity. So, at least, it was for me. Late in the first year of my program of studies in the late 1980s, I had yet to settle on a general topic that would shape my remaining course work and outside research. Having spent some time in Zambia, and with a background in philosophy and theology, largely but not exclusively in the Catholic tradition, I entered the University of Chicago Divinity School's program in Ethics and Society with vague ideas about exploring natural law, or property rights, or especially some aspect of international economic justice. Perhaps I would explore the ethics of international debt. But nothing seemed quite right.

Then one evening as I was thumbing through political science indexes (no internet search engines then) looking for material for a paper on military intervention on humanitarian grounds, I chanced upon entries on a very different topic: the 1982 United Nations Convention on the Law of the Sea. This was a topic about which I knew next to nothing at the time. Yet, almost out of the blue, it suddenly but quietly dawned on me that this would be—not could be but *would* be—the topic of my dissertation. Not everything was clear. There was much to learn and much to do. But that I had found my general topic I was sure.

In the months that followed, I began to see striking continuities and discontinuities between this experience and what had gone before. On the one hand, despite my lack of familiarity with the LOS, the topic did not emerge from nowhere. Rather, it embraced, in one way or another, the very subject matter (natural law, property rights, international economic justice, environmental issues, war and peace, and more) that I had been mulling over for some time. But there was at least this point of discontinuity: before I entered the Regenstein Library that evening I did not have a dissertation topic, and when I left I did.

This single, simple experience pointed me in new directions, leading to intellectual landscapes (or seascapes) and personal relationships I could not have anticipated even days or weeks before. Among the many memories of that period, two pertain especially to our topic. One was the attempt at what Mark Morelli calls "horizonal diplomacy"—the movement back and forth between significantly different horizons.[4] Within a few months of the library epiphany, I found myself immersed in things international—law, relations, economics—through courses, readings, and discussion groups. A political scientist (later one of my readers) with an interest in international cooperation introduced me to game theory and the then burgeoning work on international regimes.[5] Twice a week one term, I crossed the Midway—a tract of land that separates the Law School from the Divinity School and the main campus of the University of Chicago—to attend a class in international law. Later, I frequently made the same trip to settle on the sixth floor of D'Angelo Law Library where texts and journals in international law were shelved.

Especially at first, it was like moving into an uncharted world. In fact, it was while reading a text on international regimes that I first came across the inscription found on the margins of ancient maps: "*Cave! Hic dragones*" (Beware! Here be dragons.). Crossing over from theology, where I felt more or less at home, to international law, where I did not, was like reaching the edge of my intellectual map. Yet, deeper down, it seemed not so totally foreign or strange, as I began to ask myself something that, in these pages, I have assumed: Whether international law might be, in some sense, ethics writ large. I asked further, might there not be something theological in it after all?

A second related memory is the reaction of a person removed from academic life when I told him, in response to his query, that I was writing a dissertation on the Law of the Sea. "You mean the Holy See?" he asked. For, in his mind, what else could a divinity school dissertation be about? In misunderstandings, there are meanings to be found. So this misunderstanding of a single word is worth keeping in mind, for it helps to clarify further the approach to mining morality one finds in this and other chapters. That is, two sets of prospecting tools—insights from Lonergan, on the one hand, and the Catholic social tradition, with its papal documents such as *Laudato si'* on the other, are indeed Catholic—that is, Roman Catholic—in their origin and character. Lonergan, for instance, stresses at the end of *Insight* that he had spent years "reaching up to the mind of Aquinas," most certainly a Catholic theologian. Yet, they are arguably catholic, too, in the root sense of "catholic" as "universal." As we have seen, Francis's *Laudato si'* is a plea for dialogue and action across religions, cultures, and disciplines, and he fully expects that some will dismiss or reject his theological premises. Lonergan's thought has its universal thrust as well, for instance, in terms of a "generalized empirical method," an "emerging religious consciousness" that seeks a common humanity, an "unrestricted desire to know" that is by no means confined to Christianity or any other religious tradition.

True enough, there may have once been a "Catholic conception of international law," as one of the founders of the American Society of International Law, James Brown Scott proposed.[6] But Christopher Weeramantry, a Catholic layman, whom we met in chapter 4, was persistent in his engagement of multiple religious traditions and multiple cultures. So, he arguably presents a Catholic—or catholic—*re*-conception of international law to replace an earlier conception associated especially with Francisco de Vitoria, to whom Weeramantry refers in *Nauru* and of whom Weeramantry's student, Antony Anghie, was quite critical. In short, the prospecting for ethics undertaken here and in other chapters is at once Catholic and catholic, with permeable borders and multiple meeting points.

While my library experience might be interpreted in more ways than one, Lonergan's description of "insight" is surely apt. Insight, he writes, "(1) comes as a release to the tension of inquiry, (2) comes suddenly and unexpectedly, (3) is a function not of outer circumstances but inner conditions, (4) pivots between the concrete and the abstract, and (5) passes into the habitual texture of one's mind."[7] This chapter could include a careful analysis of the insight, or cluster of insights, I reached in the library that night and the manner in which that experience included each component of Lonergan's description. Autobiographically, that might be appropriate, since Lonergan's "understanding of understanding" (the subtitle of *Insight*) has helped me to understand myself in relation to ever-expanding and changing worlds. But the intent here is not simply autobiographical. Or, to be more precise, if it is autobiographical, it is along the lines of another element of Lonergan's thought that has shaped my understanding not only of the LOS but also of other matters of fundamental (one might say, with qualification, "metaphysical"[8]) importance. I refer to what Lonergan calls the "isomorphism," or dynamic correlation, that exists between cognitive operations of the knowing subject, on the one side, and the object of his or her inquiry, on the other.[9] So, in the present instance one may posit a correlation, or one might say a proportionality, between the operations of the knower—and, I would add, the decider[10]—and that which is to be known or engaged in concrete ways, in this case the LOS and the particular case of mining morality it presents.

A MATTER OF EMERGENCE

A major focus of this chapter, then, is isomorphism or correlation between the dynamics of my own thinking and acting, on the one hand, and the dynamics of international law, and especially the LOS, on the other. To understand one is to better understand the other. But to sharpen the focus, I need to add to the above description of insight another element discussed by Lonergan which we have seen elsewhere—the notion of emergence. "Add" is not quite the right word, for, as Lonergan explains, insight is the "prototype of emergence."[11] Autobiographically, the matter of settling on a dissertation topic was a matter of emergence. I did not have a dissertation topic, and then I had one—at least in inchoate form. The topic was not known to me, and then it was: it emerged. But emergence pertains to the *topic* of the dissertation in another crucial sense. Prior to December 10, 1982, there was no United Nations Convention on the Law of the Sea open for signing. Then there was. Over a period of some fifteen years, and even centuries (note the Latin phrases such as *res communis* or *res nullius* that informed the debate over ocean territory), it had emerged. More specifically, the existence and development of international law itself—as well as its breakdowns—may be understood within the framework of emergent probability, the rudiments of which have been previously discussed.[12]

Emergence, then, is a controlling or heuristic theme for much of what follows. But to this I must yet again add—or simply emphasize, for it is not foreign to the notion of emergence—another feature, that of *uncertainty*. I suppose "contingency" would serve as well, as perhaps might "fragility" or "vulnerability." Or, we might even say "woundedness," as in "a wounded world." In any event, what I am emphasizing is the absence of a guarantee in international law as in any number of other spheres of life, including both mining and morality, that emergence will occur or that a new reality that emerges will endure. There is no absolute guarantee that children will really learn, that families will thrive, that a mining venture will succeed, that a mining community will be sustained, or that nations or glaciers will endure.[13] For emergence is a matter of conditions being met, and this "meeting" may or may not happen. So, in the library incident described above, if certain "inner conditions" had been absent, for instance, if I had fallen asleep, or had no interest in or prior understanding of a range of issues, the event—the insight—could not have taken place.

Furthermore, a single insight will not do. Not only are insights "a dime a dozen," subject to verification in acts of judgment,[14] but insights along with judgments and decisions also accumulate.[15] As we have seen, for Lonergan at least, "method"—basically, the collaborative and effective functioning of questioning minds and all that that entails—yields "cumulative and progressive results," and this has much to do with the "assimilative" capacity of the mind.[16] There is a huge difference between a bright idea for a dissertation and a completed work, and it is a fact, sometimes sad, that many dissertations and other such projects languish for years or never quite get finished at all. Much more could also be said at this point, for example, about the ways in which *conversion*—intellectual, moral, psychic, religious—or its absence, may affect emergence and its uncertainty. But here I simply wish to push the point that international law, with the LOS as a key aspect of that law, is subject to myriad conditions that may or may not obtain. Our consideration of the Nauru case already gave some evidence that, when it comes to international law, there are no real guarantees of international law's effectiveness, especially when "compliance" is factored in, even as—and this is a crucial point—the very existence of law and its effectiveness may be made more or less probable. Here, with deep seabed mining as an emergent focal point, we will dive down a little deeper to see why this is so.

International Law and the Dialectics of Emergence

Since it happens that the work of Lonergan and international law share a common, if only partial, mooring in the thought of Thomas Aquinas,[17] it may be appropriate to begin a discussion of the dialectics of emergence with a phrase familiar to anyone who has read even a few articles from the *Summa Theologica*, each of which begins (Objection 1): "It would seem . . ." In this case, "It would seem that international law has little merit." Or, as it was once put to me by a civil rights lawyer, "International law is a joke." This complaint against or dismissal of international law takes various forms. It is proposed, for instance, that international law is simply what a superpower such as the United States says that it is; that no one obeys international law; that it is all theory and no practice; that, because it has no real coercive backing, international law is not real law and that international lawyers are not real lawyers.

While these and similar criticisms of international law may cause problems for the apologist, they are not insuperable. Or, at the very least, sharp criticism is not allowed simply to stand. So, for instance, an important book entitled *The Limits of International Law*[18] is met in part with a spirited response: *The Power and Purpose of International Law.*[19] Both are published by the same reputable press. If one considers the generally recognized sources of international law—namely, treaties, custom, and general principles accepted by the world's major legal systems[20]—it is easy to show that the body of international law is considerable and growing. Our consideration of the Nauru case demonstrated as much. As a system of norms and as an operating system,[21] international law daily, and usually silently, governs, among other things, international travel, trade relations, space exploration, disaster relief, the conduct of war and its preparation (including the development of weapons of mass destruction), care for the environment (more broadly, "our common home"), and an increasingly wide range of human rights.

Surely, it must be conceded to deniers and sceptics that international law is far from perfect and that compliance is often more than problematic, but to dwell only on its imperfections is to overlook the remarkable fact of its achievement. This achievement could be spelled out at length, but perhaps a succinct, oft-quoted statement from a leading international lawyer of the last century can suffice for now: "It is probably the case," wrote Louis Henkin, "that *almost all nations observe almost all principles of international law and almost all of their obligations almost all of the time.*"[22] In short, the criticisms of international law can be valid but overstated, or they may be myths to be debunked. International law is problematic in many ways. Yet, it is real, and in multiple forms it has emerged.[23]

Still, the claims of international law's deniers or despisers should not be so quickly dismissed. The availability of responses to the most extreme challenges to international law notwithstanding, there is no denying the uncertainty inherent in the dynamics of the emergence and sustenance of international law. For instance, Geoffrey Best concludes from his study of war and law since 1945 that the international legal record, while in some respects remarkable, has been anything but stellar at least in terms of compliance.[24] Since our focus is sea law, we should note the dismal record of compliance with international laws on the high seas.[25] The Nauru case, in its own way, strikes a familiar chord. While I stressed there the considerable body of law, including international law, that was in place to protect the people of Nauru, high regard for or even grudging compliance with such law was often woefully lacking. I will introduce further examples of how uncertain or fragile the emergence of international law can be, but first it will be helpful to review and expand on the notion of emergence in general and emergent probability in particular.

Emergent Probability

A key to emergence is the notion of conditionality: if certain conditions are met, then something (perhaps an insight) may occur. But that "something" may be not a single event but rather an entire scheme of recurrence. As Lonergan puts it, "if A occurs, then B, and if B then C, and if C then D, and if D then A again."[26] The simplicity of this A-to-D-to-A chain is for the sake of explanation only; the limited number of terms should not obscure the enormous complexity of the many schemes in which human beings actually participate[27]—both in the natural world (e.g., biological evolution, or the nitrogen and hydrological cycles) and in human history, say, the history of mining.

In terms of human history, conditioned in so many ways by matters studied by physicists, chemists, biologists, seismologists, meteorologists, and so on, think of all the further conditions that had to be met for Butte, Montana, to become in fact and not just in someone like Marcus Daly's dreams, "the Richest Hill on Earth." Think about the miles and miles of shafts and underground workways, the railroads, the smelters, the lumber mills, the housing and entertainment for workers, the financial agreements reached in Butte or in Boston, the labor unions with their meetings, the courthouses and court proceedings. None of these things were on the scene or on delivery, at least on the scale needed. Then they were. They all emerged, sometimes by hook and sometimes by crook. My reporting on others' accounts of the story of Butte—and Chuquicamata—barely hint of the complexities involved. Furthermore, as those accounts attest, not everything that emerged endured. The future of Butte was not assured. Not even the Anaconda Copper Mining Company was spared.

Now, for Lonergan, emergent probability is the worldview wherein higher, more inclusive schemes of recurrence are understood to emerge, according to schedules of probability, from lower schemes. Remember, Glasscock begins his *War of the Copper Kings* not in the bustling city of Butte, but seventy-five miles away in the small town of Bannock. But from small beginnings, from a concert of lower schemes involving engineering and skilled labor and shipping and so much else (vigilantism in the case of Butte may even be included) a great mining center grew up. In speaking of recurrent schemes, we must not overlook or underestimate those hidden from view in the creative, innovative and often scheming minds of a Marcus Daly or a William Clarke or a Fritz Heinze, or what transpired in the minds and hearts of the sometimes "contradicting" women of Butte or Chuquicamata, bent on keeping their families together and fed.

The emergence of higher, more inclusive schemes from lower schemes is a matter of probability: the probability jumps when the conditions for the emergence of the higher scheme(s) are met, and it jumps again when the higher scheme does in fact emerge.[28] Mining operations may be difficult to get up and running, but once the obstacles have been cleared at the lower levels (the financing secured, the claims made, the environmental impact statements filed—at least today—the contracts and subcontracts signed, the work carried out, and on and on), the odds of emergence are greatly increased. It is easier to maintain, say, a mine elevator that goes up and down, day after day, than it is to build one. But increased probability is not inevitability. The initial emergence is not guaranteed and neither is the sustenance of the schemes that do emerge. Much is required at the lower levels to make emergence more likely. Iron-clad guarantees of success—or sustainability, especially as the term is used today—are rare. As noted earlier, there are in the United States alone, thousands of abandoned mines, not all of which, one might assume, remain friendly to "our common home." The reconstructed mining town of Garnett, Montana, likely recalls other such towns that are no more, without even ghosts to be heard whispering in time's wake.

There are at least four further, critical aspects of "emergent probability" to be noted, if not fully explicated, before returning to international law, the Law of the Sea, and seabed mining. The first is that of "defensive circles." Lonergan explains that, in almost paradoxical fashion, recurrent schemes that could condition real progress "bind within their routines the material for the possibility of later schemes and thus block the way to full development."[29] In other words, the very thing that gives schemes their stability may also impede the emergence of new schemes. Now, in some instances defensive circles may be highly desirable. For example, a working immune system can stave off the emergence of disease. But the defensive circles may also be undesirable, as in "circle the wagons" to protect groups, organizations, church hierarchies, institutions in urgent need of transparency and reform. At this point I leave to the reader's imagination the relevance of such "defensive circles" that inhibit the emergence of agreements in labor disputes when miners go on strike.

This draws attention to the second point: schemes of recurrence contribute to, and in certain respects constitute, the "good of order"[30]—not just food for a day, but the developed means of growing, harvesting, processing, and delivering the food. But as stressed above, the good of order is not the good in its entirety. There is also the question of the values (or disvalues) served by the scheme(s).[31] The daily movement of black miners in South Africa to and from gold or uranium mines, governed by pass laws under apartheid, may have been orderly and predictable, but, from the point of view of the scale of values, would hardly be judged by everyone as good.

Third, the notion of a good, or set of goods, that transcends the good of order calls attention to something noted earlier—that emergence and emergent probability in human affairs are conditioned in part by conversion (intellectual, moral, psychic, religious) or its absence. This is a huge topic,[32] but it may at least be said that various kinds of bias—dramatic, individual, group, and the general bias of common sense—will impede or skew the emergence of new schemes that actualize human authenticity.[33] Dramatic bias may block the images and then insights needed to escape one's own narrow, wounded, sometimes severely traumatized world. Individual bias may impede insights into how one's plans and actions affect others. Group bias may feed the lie that my group, my party, my religion has a corner on the truth, thus diminishing civil discourse or honest debate—what one might call a fruitful dialectic. General bias may mock any attempt to ask big questions as out of touch, as ivory-towerish, as a denial of "good old common sense"—which, unfortunately, cannot on its own distinguish common sense from common nonsense, cannot see that the common sense of one household or company is not necessarily that of the house or business across the street, and cannot even explain what is meant by common sense.

To give an example that brings us back to international law, one may consider the manner in which racism, a deeply embedded and pernicious form of bias, especially group bias, could support the defensive circles that sought to defeat the emergence of nascent human rights laws proscribing the slave trade with its particular "good of order."[34] We saw how group bias affected life in Butte, with its discrimination on ethnic lines. We shall see in the case of uranium mining in Africa (chapter 6) that apartheid had deleterious effects on the "good of order" that characterized various mining operations. More generally, if the human subjects engaged in schemes of recurrence at various levels lack conversion, or if that conversion is only partial, then this will decrease the probabilities of emergence of a "better world" for miners or others. Or, if emergence does occur, the likelihood is lessened that the schemes to be sustained will be truly humane.

Finally, I have stressed the manner in which lower schemes condition development in the form of emergent higher schemes. Here, the emergence that takes place recalls that which occurs in cognitional processes when, successively, a novel experience gives rise to questioning (What is it?), insights into that experience beg for criticism and judgment (Is it really so? Are our insights, our suppositions, our hypotheses really sound?), and settled matters of fact urge sound decisions about the good to be pursued (Given what we know, and given our commitment to values over mere satisfactions, what should we do?). But it should again be stressed that such development is also promoted from "above," for instance in the form of an affectively moving visionary agenda, inherited values, or especially the experience of falling in love that radically shifts one's horizons.[35] There is no reason to assume that "top down" and "bottom up" cannot be operative at the same time.

For present purposes, development from above is especially important to keep in mind for at least two reasons. First, we should not underestimate the way in which international law, with its long and in some respects venerable tradition, develops from top down, as well as from bottom up, as new practitioners "learn to love the law" passed on to them by their teachers both living and long dead. So, for instance, a young Antony Anghie could be inspired by his teachers Christopher Weeramantry and David Kennedy, similar to the way in which a graduate student in economics could write with great admiration and even brilliance about the "worldly philosophers" that bequeathed to him his field of study.[36] Second, when it comes to international law, religion can play, and has played, a crucial role in providing the visions, the values, and even—or especially—the unrestricted love, that can aid in that development from above.[37] The possibility that love, manifest in praise for all that is, can inspire one to act and act well would seem to be a fundamental assumption of Pope Francis's *Laudato si'*, and surely that assumption is not his alone.

A Return to International Law

The point thus far has been simply to say enough about emergent probability to provide a basis for suggesting how international law fits within this framework and is at the same time marked by a degree of uncertainty or vulnerability. Consider, then, a few examples. The first is the League of Nations as an operating system for international law. As is regularly pointed out, the catalyst for the growth of international law is often the horror of war.[38] So, in briefest terms, the disaster of the First World War gave rise to the emergence of the League, which was to be guided by international law and was to advance that law, with, for instance a judicial arm (the Permanent Court of International Justice). It was also to be a security regime established to protect its weaker members. In short, as Christopher Weeramantry and his colleagues made clear in the Nauru case, the League was expressive of post-war hopes for a better world. With a strong push from Woodrow Wilson, the League was established—it did emerge. But it could not be sustained. One of the reasons, it might be suggested, is that "defensive circles" operative within the U.S. Senate and elsewhere blocked support for this later, "higher" regime informed by Wilson's vision. There were other reasons, of course. Again, as we saw in the Nauru case, some, such as Prime Minister Hughes of Australia, regarded the League as idealism run amok. But the point about defensive circles is that effective schemes of recurrence, because they "work" and work well, can be resistant to the emergence of something truly new. This is something to be kept in mind by anyone with cheerful thoughts of a New World Order that is truly just, or of a quick and easy shift away from the "technocratic paradigm" that Pope Francis believes has the world in thrall.

A second example regards the League's successor, the United Nations—an institution again integral to international law as both an operating system and a generator of new norms, such as those of a regime for governing the seas. From a certain point of view—namely, a robust egalitarian one—the United Nations is hardly a perfect institution (as periodic attempts at reform would more than suggest). Part of this is due to the original design of the organization, especially with the veto power of the "Big Five" in the Security Council.

Now, at its inception, such an imperfect arrangement was hardly satisfactory to certain "idealists." But it might be argued that the conditions for an alternative were simply not in place. This, at least, was the "realist" view of theologian Reinhold Niebuhr at the time. Those who envisioned a new world order without any inequality, without any necessary "balance of power," were in Niebuhr's view, "naive children of light" who did not understand that a new initiative of this magnitude could not be produced by fiat—for example, through the drawing up of a "constitution for the world."[39] Put in terms of emergent probability, it might be suggested that Niebuhr understood that the schemes of recurrence (related to what he called "social tissue") were not sufficiently developed to give rise to an institution and global good of order that would fully satisfy the idealists. The emergent institution could not run ahead of the lower schemes that made its emergence probable or, indeed, possible. Or, put in Lonergan's rather than Niebuhr's terms, it might be suggested that the truly worthy "ideal" is not something unattainable, but rather "the next stage in the development of the concrete"[40]—for the good is always concrete.

A third example regards the emergence of international human rights law, which is eminently relevant to the ethics of mining. Surely, this area of law has seen remarkable development since the arrival on the international scene in 1948 of the Universal Declaration of Human Rights. This document has conditioned or inspired the emergence not only of the two great human rights covenants,[41] but also a slew of declarations, conventions, tribunals, NGOs, institutes, academic courses, books and scholarly journals, internet websites, and more. One might add to the list the now full endorsement and defense of human rights by Catholic social teaching.[42] The importance of these developments—this complex of emergences—should not be underestimated. To give but one example, the Convention on the Rights of the Child is the most widely accepted human rights treaty existing today; virtually everyone apart from the United States is a party. This treaty has great relevance to the practice of mining as it intersects with child labor and child welfare overall.

Yet, neither should the uncertainty or fragility of existing human rights regimes be denied. As Mary Ann Glendon has shown, the emergence of the Universal Declaration was in part a matter of taking advantage of a small window of opportunity—a set of conditions—that might have been missed.[43] The groundbreaking declaration was thus no sure thing. Neither has the success of subsequent human rights efforts been assured. East-West and other ideological splits required that the Declaration be advanced through two separate covenants (or treaties), and these have yet to gain full endorsement. As importantly, issues of compliance and enforcement on a day-to-day basis continue to hinder advancement of human rights. Of course, the philosophical grounding for universal human rights remains a question for many.[44]

These examples surely require more thorough and more nuanced discussion, but they may be sufficient to intimate the heuristic potential of emergence and emergent probability for understanding the dynamics of international law, a potential that might be qualified as uncertain or fragile. This intimation may be advanced by a closer examination of the LOS.

Emergence of a New Ocean Regime

I began this chapter with a personal instance of insight-as-emergence and then introduced the notion of an isomorphism or correlation between the emergence that occurs on the side of the individual subject—such as the reader—and an emergent reality to be explored and possibly known, in this case the LOS. The dissertation itself did not employ directly either Lonerganian terms or the notion of emergence.[45] Rather, the focus of this work was the theological character of a key and contested principle in the 1982 Convention, the "common heritage of mankind."[46] This principle had much to do with mining, in this case mining on the ocean floor.

The study involved three Christian thinkers, the "Christian Realist" Reinhold Niebuhr (just mentioned), the theologically minded philosopher Jacques Maritain, and Gustavo Gutiérrez, a founder of "liberation theology," in a thought experiment, asking what each might make of the "common heritage of mankind," a critical and contested legal concept or principle in the LOS and a set of issues none had ever dealt with in any explicit way. I concluded that, differences notwithstanding, each would likely have construed "common heritage" as a *tensive* principle or concept, pivoting between the world as it is, finite and flawed, on the one hand, and an alternative world, a world of peace and justice on the other. I argued that Niebuhr would regard the common heritage notion as an "impossible possibility"—"possible," because

Figure 5.2. Hydro-thermal vent.
Photo: Nautilus Minerals.

this principle was just what is needed for our world, but "impossible" to fully implement due to human limitations and sin. Maritain, I conjectured, would regard common heritage as a "concrete historical ideal"—a true "ideal," but one that was beginning to be realized in this time and place. Gutierrez, for his part, I thought might view common heritage as expressive of a "utopia" that pivots between faith, with its transcendent character, on the one hand, and concrete, this-worldly social programs, on the other.

In short, it seemed to me that these three great figures would, in accord with their own insights and convictions, affirm the common heritage concept as a bridge between the world as it is and the world as it might be, a world toward which we should strive but which we could not pretend had already arrived. It turns out, however, that the tensive, heuristic, pivotal character of this concept fits well the notion of *emergence*. So here I will briefly expand on the manner in which emergence and emergent probability offer a way to understand what was and is at stake in the LOS, with relevance not only to mining, but also to certain currents of thought and practice in the world today.

The history of sea law is long and complex,[47] but for present purposes it may be simplified by saying that for several hundred years the seas were governed by two principles of customary international law. The first was that coastal states would have jurisdiction over a narrow strip of adjacent waters, often set at three miles according to the "cannon shot" rule.[48] The second principle, espoused most famously by Hugo Grotius, was that of "freedom of the high seas," which allowed for use (trade, travel, fishing, etc.) of the open seas by all so long as, in Lockean fashion, one left "enough and as good for others."[49]

By the end of the Second World War and then increasingly into the 1960s, this earlier regime was no longer deemed satisfactory. First, with decolonization numerous new states had emerged—states not always happy to abide by international rules not of their making. Second, the assumption that the oceans were a virtually inexhaustible storehouse of living resources was factually challenged. Not only did new fishing technology (sonar and refrigeration) permit larger catches, but it also allowed the fleets of one nation more easily to reach the traditional fishing grounds of others, thus giving rise to territorial disputes.

Third, 1945 saw the issuance of the Truman Proclamation, a claim of U.S. jurisdiction over its continental shelf for the purposes of hydrocarbon exploitation, with a view to U.S. postwar energy independence. This action spurred similar unilateral declarations of coastal jurisdiction, especially by some Latin American states. Among other things, these claims called into question the free passage of navies, especially through straits—a question that got the attention especially of the United States and the Soviet Union with their navies. Fourth, there were growing threats to ocean ecology—and indeed, global ecology—due to the ocean dumping of biological and other wastes, including nuclear material. Fifth, the ocean bed stood as a potential site for the placement of nuclear weapons, to go along with the nuclear weaponry already coursing beneath the ocean surface aboard nuclear-powered submarines.

Finally—and here we come back to our topic—there was the matter of seabed mining. In his 1869 futuristic novel, *20,000 Leagues under the Sea*, Jules Verne had envisioned mining on the ocean floor, and in 1873 the exploratory ship *Challenger* had dredged up from deep below strange polymetallic nodules and had made that discovery known. But only in the late 1960s did seabed mining really become a live issue, thanks in part to developing technology and to the work of John L. Mero who wrote about the extent and nature of these resources.[50]

Put in language made famous by Thomas Kuhn, these "anomalies," which the existing paradigm of ocean law and management could not handle, made pressing the need for a new ocean regime.[51] Put in Lonergan's language, there was a need at this point in history for a "creative" response to a changed situation. The probabilities that a new regime would actually emerge were greatly increased in November 1967 when Arvid Pardo, representative to the United Nations from the tiny state of Malta, galvanized the United Nations General Assembly with a lengthy speech that not only laid out in great detail the facts of the present situation, but also insisted with high rhetoric that humanity was at a turning point. "[T]he dark oceans," Pardo said,

> were the womb of life. from the protecting oceans, life emerged. We still bear in our bodies—in our blood, in the salty bitterness of our tears—the marks of this remote past. Retracing the earth, man is now returning to the ocean depths. His penetration of the deep could mark the beginning of the end of man, and indeed for life as we know it on this earth: it could also be a unique opportunity to lay solid foundations for a peaceful and increasingly prosperous future for all nations.[52]

Key to Pardo's vision of a new ocean regime was his urging that ocean space beyond national jurisdiction be declared the "common heritage of mankind."[53] This novel concept, at least as applied to ocean space, became part of the 1974 accepted set of negotiating principles which informed perhaps the most extensive negotiating process in history, a lengthy and extraordinarily complex process that culminated with a new convention opened for signing on December 10, 1982. While the common heritage concept was accepted as a heuristic principle, with its precise content to be worked out through negotiation, it did have certain initial agreed upon meanings: (1) that the area so designated could not be appropriated by any state; (2) that its resources were to be rationally managed; (3) that the area was to be used for peaceful purposes only; and, (4) significantly, that it was to benefit "mankind as a whole," with special regard for less developed nations.[54] Also associated with the principle was a concern for future generations—a point that cannot be overstressed. Put in briefest terms, if the seabed and the vast wealth sitting there is to be mined, everyone is to gain.

To retell the history of this negotiation process in the terms we have been employing would be to examine in great detail the various conditions from which the treaty eventually emerged.[55] This would include, for instance, the great skill of certain negotiators, the role that "consensus" played in the negotiations, and the "will of an overwhelming majority of nations from all parts of the world, at different levels of development and having diverse geographical characteristics in relation to the oceans, which combined to make a wind of change blow at a universal level."[56] Such analysis exceeds the scope of this chapter. But in keeping with the modest aim of prospecting for ethics, it is possible to highlight certain aspects of the process and its result that reveal both the emergent character of international law and its limitations, its lack of guarantee of success.

Figure 5.3. Mr. Arvid Pardo (right), new Permanent Representative of Malta to the United Nations, presenting his credentials to Secretary-General U Thant at UN Headquarters, January 13, 1965.
Photo: UN Multimedia.

First, while it is generally acknowledged that Pardo's U.N. speech was crucial as a catalyst for the emergence of the new law, the eventual treaty fell short of his original vision whereby all ocean space beyond national jurisdiction (and not just the deep seabed) would be declared humankind's "common heritage."[57] Second, the emergence of common heritage as a fully accepted legal concept was not a sure thing. Its early status as a legal term was vague,[58] and attempts to invest it with more meaning than it could sustain became apparent. In the midst of the negotiations, the United States passed unilateral seabed mining legislation[59] that ran counter to at least some internationalist or socialist interpretations of the common heritage principle popular especially among less developed nations. When leaders of these nations protested the U.S. action on the grounds that the common heritage principle was now an established part of international law, having attained the status of *jus cogens* (peremptory law), the United States simply denied the claim: "common heritage of mankind" was at best a heuristic principle to guide the negotiations; legally, it would mean what it meant when the negotiations were complete.[60] Put otherwise, the LOS was still emerging; just what it would be as a fully emergent law was neither guaranteed nor completely clear.

In fact, the negotiations did not come to a satisfactory end, at least in the minds of many. The United States's early involvement in the negotiations, including a generally sympathetic attitude on the part of successive administrations to the notion of common heritage and the international sharing it promised, was crucial to the success of the negotiations. But in a manner suggestive of Lonergan's analysis, this high-level support morphed into a "defensive circle" with the arrival of the first Reagan Administration. This is a third point of emphasis. Concerns about threats to laissez-faire international economic relations and the prospect of ceding national sovereignty to a centralized international authority to govern mining operations (the Seabed Authority) led to a decision not to sign the convention, just as the negotiations were wrapping up. So, as far as the common heritage concept is concerned, at least in its more egalitarian interpretations, the outcome of the negotiations was disappointing. The very concept suggestive of a *common* humanity became the flashpoint for global fissure or at least serious strain. In fact, after the convention was opened for signing the most divisive aspect of the Convention, Article XI, which dealt with deep seabed mining and which was governed by the common heritage concept, was opened for renegotiation in the hopes that dissenting nations, and the United States in particular, could be coaxed to get back on board.[61]

From a Lonerganian perspective, this turn of events is open to more nuanced interpretation in terms of the dialectics of emergence. For instance, even prior to the Reagan administration, the tide was turning toward freer trade and free enterprise—the kind of economic view skeptical of the heavily centrist and bureaucratic weight acquired by the common heritage concept in the process of the negotiations.[62] One might also suggest that the retreat of the United States from the common heritage concept and its internationalist or globalist emphasis foreshadowed, in some fashion, the resurgence of nationalism, though not necessarily the ethnonationalism we have witnessed especially of late. My only point here is that the emergence of a new ocean regime to match fully Pardo's vision would have required that certain conditions be fulfilled. They were not.

One final feature of emergence and the LOS bears emphasis, for it has much to do not only with *mining* morality, but also with mining *morality*. When the topic is international law, it is easy to get the impression that emergence is a matter simply of big, powerful nations exerting their individual or collective wills. I do underestimate the importance of this view. As just explained, the election of Ronald Reagan and the subsequent shift in U.S. policy with regard to the emerging convention were of undeniable importance. But if the "Reagan Revolution" had its effect on the LOS, it is important to recall that this revolution itself emerged on a number of levels—with lower schemes conditioning higher schemes even as the lower schemes may have been inspired from above by a vision, packaged for mass consumption, that it is "morning in America," just as a later presidential candidate would inspire many to chant, "Make America Great Again." If the Reagan Revolution served as a defensive circle inhibiting the emergence of a new ocean regime more grounded in the common heritage philosophy, it should not be overlooked that the positive thrust toward a new law was also conditioned by lower schemes inspired by a vision of a new world of international economic justice that differed in certain respects from that of the Reagan Administration.

Exemplary here was the activity of the Neptune Group, a coalition of three NGOs, with some shifting of membership. This was a visionary group. Indeed, some members were religiously inspired (the leaders, Miriam and Samuel Levering, were Quakers). But they were not so blinded by vision that they overlooked the pragmatics of successful negotiations.[63] Put in terms of emergent probability, this group was keenly attuned to the ways in which higher schemes are conditioned by the lower schemes of diplomacy at which they so adeptly worked. Or, one might say, in terms employed by the Christian Realist Reinhold Niebuhr, that the Neptune Group was comprised of "children of light," but not *naïve* children of light. As a result, this faith-inspired but very diplomacy-savvy and factually informed group was remarkably successful in gaining the trust of even those disagreeing with them. They were able to press their agenda to a relatively successful conclusion, however limited by counteractive defensive circles that conclusion turned out to be. Nor should we forget that perhaps the most important figure when it comes to the LOS, Arvid Pardo, represented the tiny country of Malta—a "microstate" that, on the world's stage, joined other microstates such as the Vatican and Nauru.

MEMORIA AND THE LAW OF THE SEA: INSIGHTS AND OVERSIGHTS

The pages above represent, in large part, an exercise in *memoria,* as I reflect now on an investigation undertaken over a quarter of a century ago, a memory refracted by my engagement over the years of a foundational and interdisciplinary thinker who aids readers in the difficult task of self-understanding that is meant to be neither self-absorption nor narcissism but rather an expansion of horizons. In terms of prospecting for ethics—in this case prospecting under the sea—I believe my early focus on the LOS exposed veins of inquiry about the ethics of mining, as well as the mining of morality, that remain valid now. Let me recall some of them here.

Direct Insights

First, sometimes at least, moral matters regarding mining, such as access and ownership and sharing the wealth, cannot be fully resolved at the level of Butte or Chuquicamata or even the individual country, large or small. Rather, they must also be worked out at regional[64] and global levels. The framers of and parties to the LOS clearly understood this, just as they understood that various issues and challenges are interlocked and cannot be separated. Thus, the LOS was negotiated as a "package" that included issues of all kinds having to do with the sea and land (such as "land-locked nations"): political, security-related, environmental, economic, and, of course, legal. Furthermore, solutions to problems of this magnitude and kind are by no means assured, and even when solutions are forthcoming (the LOS went into effect in 1994, twenty-seven years after Arvid Pardo's speech), they may be less than fully satisfactory. The LOS, it might be said, was a testament to politics as "the art of the possible."

Second, if the worldview called emergent probability can illumine the emergence of the LOS, it can also illumine much else. Indeed, as I have suggested above, it would have been possible to employ this heuristic framework more explicitly in the story of Butte and Chuquicamada (chapter 2), including the rise and fall of Anaconda, to the sad case of Nauru, or to virtually any other "moral mining" site. Third, with "insight" as the prototype of emergence, the prospect, the fact, and the frequent failure of emergence—when the "flight from insight" reigns, or for other reasons the conditions for emergence are not met—may embrace at once *both* the individual subject, such as the author or reader, *and*, recalling C. G. Weeramantry's phrase in the Nauru case, the "great historical currents that shape human events." Again, I have long been impressed with the fact that one and the same person, Saint Augustine, could, on the one hand, write something as intimate, as personal, as self-reflective as his *Confessions* and, on the other, compose something as sweeping as the *City of God* in response to the "great historical currents that shape human events" that included, among other things, the fall of the Roman Empire.

None of us may be the equal of an Augustine; we are who we are. But the clear linkage of a quiet moment of insight (the library experience) to the momentous, global event of an emerging and emergent ocean regime suggests that connections between *interiority*, on the one hand, and international affairs and those who are fully engaged in these affairs, on the other, are not the province and privilege of great minds alone. Furthermore, attempts to understand and possibly resolve for myself with the help of others what was at stake in the debates about the ocean depths and much else could not be totally separated from, in Augustinian language, a clashing of loves in the depths of my own soul. When it comes to such clashing and figuring out how we ought to live—not only with ourselves, but also with neighbors near and far (and some not yet born)—I doubt that I was, or am, alone.

Third, my exploration of the LOS led me to conclude that, even when considering a field of human endeavor (in this case international law) that is supposedly thoroughly secular, theology may still have its place. Attention to international law's past will leave exposed its Christian and, to a lesser extent, its other religious roots, such as those discussed by C. G. Weeramantry in *Islamic Jurisprudence: An International Perspective*. Furthermore, whether secularists appreciate the effort or not, theologians are free to reflect theologically, for their respective communities and beyond, on what they find in the largely secular world of international law today. This is what I tried to do as I turned to Reinhold Niebuhr, with his "Christian Realism"; to Gustavo Gutiérrez, a founder of "liberation theology"; to Jacques Maritain, whose Christian philosophy had openings for theology; and even to the constitutional legal scholar, Robert M. Cover, who understood a constitution (for instance, the LOS as a "constitution for the oceans") on the analogy of a religious creed prone to multiple and conflicting interpretations, a constitution-as-creed that splits apart as it comes into being.[65]

But fully explicit theology is not theology in its entirety. The question of God, as Lonergan puts it, is "the question that questions questioning itself,"[66] and theologians hardly have a corner on raising questions. Lawyers and marine biologists and ship captains and dockworkers and politicians and citizens of all kinds raise them, too. So, the question of God may be raised implicitly by the many questions about meaning and value that rise to the surface when anyone considers the ocean or its depths, bounded or unbounded by law. For instance, to declare a portion of the Earth's underwater crust humankind's "common heritage" leads one to ask what—or who—humanity's "benefactor" might be. Not past generations, certainly, for the ocean floor did not originate with them. Not nature, surely, for whence, ultimately, comes the natural world? If the "common heritage" is to benefit humankind "as a whole," how is that whole to be regarded except from some transcendent vantage point? Does not a meditation on the ocean depths and its resources, or anything else declared humankind's "common heritage," sooner or later assume the character of a "proof" for, or at least a question about, the existence of God? Does it not raise the "question of God" as ultimate ground of "our common home"—especially if that common home is, finally, all that is? With a convergence of questions such as these, I found it possible to write about "the theological character of the common heritage concept in the LOS" (the subtitle of the dissertation). I see now that approaching the contested issue of seabed mining with the prospector's tools found in *Laudato si'* would likewise advance a theological appreciation of what was and is at stake.

Furthermore, with "common heritage" at the center of the negotiations, the LOS may also embody some version of what Lonergan calls "the emergent religious consciousness of our time." Recall that, for Lonergan, this consciousness is intimately tied to an emerging sense of a common humanity. But vision is not realization, and direction is not arrival. So, the fact that the common heritage concept was pared down during the negotiations and was rejected altogether by some (detractors from the LOS consistently refer to the convention as the Law of the Sea Treaty, or LOST), may be evidence that an emergent consciousness of one world, of one humanity—whether that consciousness is "religious" or not—is by no means guaranteed. Recall that the title of C. G. Weeramantry's memoirs is *Towards One World*—not *One World Achieved*. A review of the LOS suggests that we are still on the way. With a resurgent and sometimes virulent nationalism threatening a more or less cooperative global order, we may be moving farther away from that goal.

But my excursions into international law convinced me of something else: that religiously and theologically inclined individuals and communities need to engage ostensibly secular realms of meaning and value, which, for various reasons (including a history of religious wars), international law tends to be. While religious traditions have much to offer international law, a conviction shared by Judge Weeramantry and others, international law has much to teach religious believers, too. At least on occasion, international law may run ahead of particular religious traditions and their moral teachings. This seemed to be the case, for instance, with an emphasis on concern for future generations that, during the 1970s and 1980s was arguably more pronounced in international law[67] than in the writings of Christian theologians.[68] So, with the strong points of international law in mind, a few years after the 1993 meeting of the Parliament of the World's Religions and its published global ethic, I was led to propose to religiously motivated colleagues earnestly seeking a "global ethic" that, as true as it might be that international law should "get religion," the religion that it used to have, it is also true that theologians and others should "get international law."[69]

Fourth, my grappling with the LOS confirmed what I thought might be a possibility: that despite the huge gap in knowledge that separated me from the international lawyers I read and tried to understand, we seemed to be dealing with much the same set of difficult, possibly intractable problems. For, as explained earlier, I had begun to look upon international law as ethics writ large. Some years later I would learn that, at the very time I was struggling to grasp the rudiments of international law with special reference to the LOS, Martti Koskenniemi, a Finnish scholar and former diplomat, was writing his own dissertation, which became *From Apology to Utopia: The Structure of International Legal Argument*,[70] widely hailed as one of the most important works in international law in the past fifty years. In his own highly sophisticated way, Koskenniemi, too, was exploring the tension—on his view, a highly unstable or indeterminate tension—between the world as it is, with all its self-interest and crude pragmatics, and the world as we might like it to be, with its lofty but possibly irrelevant moralistic norms.[71] Put otherwise, the connections I was making between theology and international law were not so much inter-*disciplinary* as they were dialogically inter-*subjective*, as I sought to engage and learn from others with their own active minds and spirit of inquiry in a field unfamiliar to me.

Inverse Insights

There is something else worth noting about the individual subject and his or her insights, in relation to world processes, whether that process be educating a generation of school children, protecting the health and safety of coal miners in West Virginia or uranium miners in Niger (chapter 6), or bringing a new law or treaty into being. It has to do with statistical knowledge. Once again, prototypical of emergence is the occurrence of insight—such as the insight described at the outset of this chapter. But insights are of more than one kind. Along with the "direct" insight that grasps some pattern of intelligibility in the data (say, when—"Ah ha!"—a detective solves a murder mystery), there is the "inverse" insight that grasps, in a particular case, a *lack* of intelligibility—a useful recognition that one is clearly barking up the wrong tree, entering a cul-de-sac, or following a false lead.[72] The point is, such an insight is at the heart of statistical knowledge. Insight into a series of coin flips will reveal that there is a lack of *systematic* pattern in the series of flips (that is, no HTHTHT—or, HHTT, HHTT, HHTT). But that does not mean there is no identifiable *nonsystematic* divergence from a norm (in this case, a .5 likelihood that any one flip will turn up heads), and thus some other kind of intelligibility to be found and respected.

Put in simplest terms, we inhabit a statistically defined universe, and that is the "real world," too. In sports, "It ain't over 'til it's over," Yogi Berra or anyone else might say. Yet, an ESPN app will help you track the probability that this or that team will win as the game gets closer to its end. Inverse insights—a grasp of a lack of connection, of pattern, of system—validate that world. While Mark Twain was certainly on to something when he declared that "there are lies, damn lies, and statistics," what he seems to have been on to is the fact that, like other modes of truth-seeking or deception, of grasping or denying the real, statistical knowledge is subject to bias and manipulation by human subjects not living up to the call to be their best selves. Since we do inhabit a statistically defined universe, answering that call to living authentically includes the realization that our own choices and actions can, within limits, shift the probabilities that good will be done and evil avoided—whether the venue for good and evil is Butte or Chuquicamata or Nauru or the high seas and what lies below. To understand better what it means to inhabit and even be citizens of a statistically defined universe, it is no doubt good to take courses in probability and statistics. But it will also help if one seeks, as an aspect of the examined life, to understand oneself.

Oversights

Finally, I would note two shortcomings (there are no doubt more than two) in my early explorations of the LOS. They have to do with ecology and natural law. Both have implications for ethical prospecting at various sites.

With regard to the first, even though I was at the time quite conscious of ecological issues as moral issues, I did not give as much attention as I could have to the ecological effects of seabed mineral prospecting and extraction. Nor did I consider fully the relationship between the fate of the oceans and climate change, even though, like climate itself, I was dealing with a "global commons." Of course, at the time seabed mining was still a future prospect, so some lack of attention to related environmental matters may be understandable. Still, if Pope Francis in *Laudato si'* keeps ever in view two concerns that must never be separated—care for humankind, especially the most vulnerable, and care for "our common home," also abused—the emphasis in the dissertation fell more to side of the first. I was concerned that, when it came to the untapped wealth on the ocean floor, especially those on the bottom get a fair share.

This is not to say that the treaty itself did not respond to environmental challenges, including those related to seabed mining.[73] Yet, as recent expert commentators stress, sea law must continue to evolve to meet new or newly perceived threats.[74] This is especially true with regard to climate change.[75] But in the specific case of seabed mining, continuing emergence (or not) of law is not without its tensions. Some today would prohibit seabed mining altogether, while others say move ahead, but in an environmentally responsible and sustainable way. So, organizations such as Green Peace sound the alarm not only about the known threats of proposed mining but also about just how little we may know about the ecosystems to be disturbed.[76] Toward the other end of the spectrum are those who emphasize the increased demand for the minerals and base metals present on the ocean floor—including those required for solar and other clean energy sources. Thus, representatives from mining companies, government officials, and academicians from various countries put their heads together, asking not whether mining should be taken off the table, but rather how best to proceed in a manner that is not only economically and technologically feasible but also ecologically responsible and sustainable.[77]

These are no longer hypothetical questions. Some fifty plus years after Arvid Pardo's pivotal United Nations General Assembly speech, Nautilus Minerals (Nautilus was the name Jules Verne gave to Captain Nemo's ship) is poised to begin mining operations off the coast of Papua New Guinea. The company's actions have met with opposition from environmentalists including indigenous people of the region—the very people Pope Francis likely has in mind in *Laudato si'*—who fear, among other things, disruption of their fishing grounds. Nautilus Minerals, whose web page included the heading "New Vision, New World, New Resources," for its part has claimed that it is setting a high standard for deep water seafloor mineral resource development by bringing into their endeavor proven practices from the offshore and resource industries. Yet, there appears to be great uncertainty even for this mining company. Nautilus Minerals has faced funding issues and has also experienced a change in company leadership.[78] At the time of this writing, the page on the Nautilus Minerals website entitled "Nautilus Cares," which formerly gave assurance about environmental and social responsibility, appears to be inoperative, at least for now.[79]

When it comes to mining-related intrusions into the deep, I have no easy way to resolve this tension between putting on the brakes (and keeping them

Figure 5.4. Saving our oceans one turtle at a time.
Photo courtesy of United States Coast Guard.

on) and proceeding but with extreme caution. Sometimes an absolute prohibition of a course of action may be the right way to go. But such absolutes are difficult to establish or maintain. In international human rights law, there is a list of rights and freedoms that can never be suspended, even in time of war, but this does not seem to discourage those who would seek exceptions. The reader might recall bitter debates in the United States over torture in the aftermath of 9/11 and the ramp-up to the "war on terror." As we shall see (chapter 6), some have argued that using or threatening to use nuclear weapons would be illegal in every and all circumstances. But even in this extreme case, with enormous environmental as well as human costs at stake, not all agree. So, it is doubtful that easy agreement can be reached about whether to halt altogether or proceed with caution when it comes to seabed mining.

In the face of this tension, our prospecting tools can be of some assistance to the moral mining that is required. One might ask, for instance, how the emerging schemes of recurrence that come under the heading of "seabed mining" are in accord with what Lonergan has called scale of values. Which values are held by those who—through their attentiveness, their cumulative insights, their sound judgments, their carefully considered actions—hope to increase the probabilities that new world processes (e.g., seabed mining in full operation, or a truly enforceable legal regime to regulate if not prohibit it) will emerge, and what meanings and values those processes will embody?

We might even ask, of lawyers, of those who run mining companies, of government officials, of citizens, what someone like Augustine or the later Lonergan or Pope Francis would surely ask: Where is the love—for "our common home," in the language of *Laudato si'*, or for our neighbors, even if far away or not yet born? Which of God's creatures (to put it theologically) will benefit from mining the seabed, and which ones stand to lose?—a question that may bring biodiversity into focus. We must also be attuned to inattentiveness, to repeated oversights, to rash or clouded judgments, to harmful actions with unintended consequences. This is especially true in this case since even science cannot seem to give us absolute certainty about what environmental and ecological costs, for instance damage due to noise pollution, seabed mining will bring. Thus, we must ask, among other things, which economic or political philosophies, explicit or operative, enlighten our minds or blur our vision. An individualistic Lockean understanding of property that seems to assume an inexhaustible world? Or a "common heritage" philosophy that means for some a more equitable sharing but portents for others an inefficient and overbearing world authority or world state? The views on property of indigenous peoples such as the early Nauruans? Or something else? Attention to these larger questions is especially crucial in times of extreme division and partisanship such as we now experience but hardly enjoy.

Or, we might return to the virtue of prudence, and ask of those who would mine the seabed and those who help to make that happen, including those who craft the law, whether such ventures are really prudent, when prudence means caution but so much besides: *memory* of past damage and disaster (think of Deepwater Horizon or the rising waters of the Berkeley Pit); careful *reasoning*, taking the time to think things through; wide consultation (including input from affected islanders with their fishing grounds or imagined future generations) with an eagerness to learn (*docility*); and *foresight*—made all the more difficult when we are peering into the darkness of the mineral-rich abyss. Of course, as Thomas Aquinas reminds us, we need to be on the lookout for vices against prudence and, more pernicious perhaps, vices that *resemble* prudence but are, in fact, anything but.

Or, one might turn to another important, if problematic approach to such issues common both to the Catholic moral tradition especially, but not exclusively, and, at least at times, to international law. I refer to *natural law*. This is a second aspect of the LOS that I may not have addressed sufficiently the first time around, even though as noted at the outset of this chapter I recognized that the LOS surely had something to do with this long-standing approach to the moral life, and even though one of my interlocutors in the dissertation, Jacques Maritain, was a natural law thinker of no little stature. But now as I review what I learned from Maritain, I see that in his own way he stressed not natural law as a static set of norms but, rather, as having much to do with the dynamics of history.

Still, one strand of natural law reasoning surely featured into the debates over the LOS and seabed mining—namely, the Lockean natural law view on property whereby property rights are attained by mixing one's labor with the natural world. We saw above how this view, however, might lead one to view the oceans as inexhaustible, a view that runs counter to the facts. Locke's notion of "leaving as much and as good for others" would seem to founder not only on the question of quantity ("as much") but also of quality ("as good"), as the ocean ecosystems are increasingly degraded. Furthermore, this Lockean view may represent a brand of "possessive individualism"[80] that runs counter to other views of natural law, such as one finds in Aquinas. No doubt these contesting theories ought to be explored further, and one recommendation of the ethical prospector is that careful, dialectical mining of the natural law tradition is one kind of mining that should continue.

Now, however, I have a somewhat different grasp of how "the eternal return of natural law," to use Heinrich Rommen's phrase, might contribute to prospecting for ethics under the sea—and in other places, too. One key question is whether natural law represents some sort of static set of "eternal verities" when it comes to the moral life, extending to international law, or whether it can be understood in a more dynamic, heuristic, operative, open-ended way. This would be in accord with the sort of emergence discernible in my library experience (insight as the prototype of emergence), on the one hand, and in the enormously complex emergent event that was the 1982 Convention on the LOS, on the other.

A clue to thinking this through comes from an intriguing observation about natural law made by Stephen Neff in his history of international law, *Justice among Nations*. As is well known, there has been in the history of international law a tension between those, on the one hand, who ground international law in some set of prior universal norms (natural law) which can serve as a standard for critique of laws made by human beings, and those, on the other, who ground law in empirically verifiable law, especially in terms of actual enacted laws and the behavior of states (positivism). Now, Neff's observation is that international law's dynamic growth should perhaps be attributed more to positivist approaches, since natural law can only offer static, unchanging norms. Under positivism, law can evolve to meet new challenges; under natural law, often it does not.[81]

One problem with this analysis, it seems to me, is that it may too easily identify natural law with a set of fixed concepts, even as it possibly underestimates the manner in which international law is the often creative, sometimes biased, work of inquiring, intelligent, and valuing human subjects. Indeed, it is striking that Lonergan, who was fully immersed in the Catholic tradition so friendly to natural law thinking, rarely invokes natural law. One reason, it would seem, is his concerns about "classicism" as distinct from historical consciousness, and a rigid normative view rather than an empirical view of culture. On a "classicist" view, one particular, time-bound culture—say, some shared set of European meanings and values—becomes *the* normative view. The reference to "civilized nations" in Article 38 of the ICJ's charter, which points to the "sources" of international law, may suggest just a residual classicism. But another reason for Lonergan's reticence for engaging the language of natural law would seem to be the danger of "conceptualism," an emphasis on concepts that derive from insights, acts of understanding, rather than the underlying grasp of intelligibility itself spurred by the spirit of inquiry. As Lonergan stresses, "concepts have dates."[82] If the natural law to which some international lawyers would appeal is reduced to a set of frozen concepts, then one can understand why Neff and others might regard it as unable to move international law forward.

This does not mean, however, that there is nothing normative in Lonergan's understanding of either nature or reason—the two traditional "sources" for natural law. As the legal scholar Patrick McKinley Brennan has argued, for Lonergan the norms, or precepts, of the natural law might be construed in terms of what Lonergan calls the "transcendental precepts," those norms intrinsic to conscious intentionality thematized, as we have seen, as Be attentive, Be intelligent, Be reasonable, Be responsible—sometimes adding, Be loving. These are the norms, Brennan argues, that should guide us—judges, lawyers, others—when it comes to formulating and interpreting the law.[83] In his "Asking the Right Questions: Harnessing the Insights of Bernard Lonergan for the Rule of Law," Brennan did not seem to have in view the *international* rule of law. But I see no reason why the work of those engaged in international law, whoever they might be, cannot be construed in terms of abiding by these intrinsic norms—or, due to biases of various kinds, failing to live up to them.

Furthermore, natural law in this sense can be related to emergent probability. Indeed, theologian Cynthia Crysdale argued years ago that we need to "revision" natural law, moving "from the classicist paradigm to emergent probability."[84] Her basic point is that, in thinking about natural law, we need to be attuned to "classical laws" (what conditions must be met to cause a rise in sea levels or black lung). But we also need to attend to "statistical laws" (what are the chances that those conditions will be met, thus resulting in coastline flooding or the increased instance of disease) that govern world processes. These may be processes in the natural world—let's say the bubbling up of mineral-rich sulfides from the earth's crust under the sea, or human processes, such as seabed mining or the establishment of a regime to regulate what industrious people ought and ought not do on the ocean floor. If we may couple this more dynamic understanding of natural-law-as-emergent probability with the virtue of prudence as applied to seabed mining, we might ask: What are the chances that, because of our actions, things will turn out well or badly—and for whom?

In this regard, *Laudato si'* includes a remarkable statement with implications for our understanding of natural law. The encyclical begins by quoting St. Francis of Assisi: "Praise be to you, my Lord, to our Sister, Mother Earth, who sustains *and governs* us, and who produces various fruit with colored flowers and herbs" (1, emphasis added). Questions about gender aside, if Mother Earth is the one who governs, who gives us the laws, then maybe being "rational" is a matter of attending to, of gaining insight into, of making judgments about just what those laws are, and responding accordingly—for instance, by shifting the probabilities that an increasingly effective earth- and ocean- and human-friendly international law will emerge. Perhaps this is the legal world to which Avid Pardo was pointing when it reminded us that, "from the protecting oceans, life emerged. We still bear in our bodies—in our blood, in the salty bitterness of our tears—the marks of this remote past. Retracing the earth, man is now returning to the ocean depths."

MARE NOSTRUM? COMMON HERITAGE AND OUR COMMON HOME

A decade after the LOS negotiations were concluded, a prominent British international lawyer and diplomat, Philip Allott, published in the *American Journal of International Law*, under the heading of "Notes and Comments," "*Mare Nostrum:* A New International Sea Law."[85] In this very densely reasoned piece, both historically and philosophically sophisticated, Allott proposed that, with the 1982 Convention as a "root stock," a truly new sea law was possibly emerging. With the common heritage principle and other features of the 1982 Convention in view, Allott put forward four principles that would inform this legal regime:

> Principle 1: The international law of the sea respects the natural integration of land and sea and air and the natural integration of all social phenomena.
> Principle 2: The systematic relationship of humanity to the sea is not merely a legal relationship of property but rather a social relationship of participation.
> Principle 3: The international law of the sea uses legal relations as a method of actualizing the international public interest and implementing international social objectives.
> Principle 4: The management of the relationship of humanity to the sea is socially and legally accountable.[86]

Informed by these principles, an emergent sea law would regard the sea no longer as the "free sea" (*mare liberum*) of Hugo Grotius or the "closed sea" (*mare clausum*) of Grotius's adversaries, but "our sea" (*mare nostrum*)—our sea *not* in the sense of possession but in terms of *participation*—and participation not just by "states" but by actors at all levels of international law. In reviewing Allott's essay now, and looking back at my own thinking about the LOS years ago, a few new insights, no doubt in need of testing, emerge.

With Allott's essay in mind, I see now how overly simplified might have been my interpretation of the LOS, especially its history and its many moving parts. I say this especially as I consider Allott's historically and philosophically detailed discussion of shifting views of "property" in relation to the sea. More positively, however, Allott seems to confirm my own intuition, if it might be put this way, about the 1982 Convention: that it represented an *emerging* but not yet fully emerged new law, an emerging *new paradigm,* a *new way* of seeing the world: "*Envisioning* Global Community" was the way I put it in the title of the dissertation (emphasis added). But Allott's construal of the emerging law, with its foundational principles, perhaps does something more: With its four informing principles of *integration*, *participation*, *public interest*, and *accountability*, he arguably points to the vision and practical plea that one finds in *Laudato si'*. Allott's principle of *integration*, which is scientifically as well as socially attuned, echoes Francis's *integral ecology*; his emphasis on *participation* is not far from *Laudato si'*s emphasis on conversation involving all; his *public interest*—to say nothing of what he means by *mare nostrum*–suggests care for our common home; his calls for accountability echoes Francis's invitation to conversion. Given this international lawyer's vision of an emergent law in keeping with an emerging consciousness, it is striking that, in his annotated bibliography to *Justice among Nations,* Stephen Neff finds in Philip Allott affinities to someone who had much to say about the melding of religion and science, and about an emerging world, namely, the Jesuit Pierre Teilhard de Chardin.[87] Perhaps this is another connection to be explored, another vein to be traced at another time.

INTERIM PROSPECTOR'S REPORT

These are some of the fruits of my first encounters with the LOS and my reflections since, and I hope that they may contribute to prospecting for ethics not only under the ocean, but in other places, too—such as outer space, the topic of chapter 7. As one considers, for instance, the agenda proposed by Pope Francis is *Laudato si'* to care for our common home, but also the many other matters about which human beings might care—including, to use older vocabulary, the state of their souls—it seems that there is much to learn from seabed mining and the emergence of the Law of the Sea.

The Third United Nations Law of the Sea Conference (UNCLOS III), from which the LOS emerged, was an enormously complex process that addressed a spate of such often contentious issues as property, ecology, security, economic equality and access, the notion of state sovereignty, and the relationship between "developed" and "less developed" nations. With common heritage of humankind as a pivotal, controversial concept in the law, the very notion of human community and diversity was at issue as well. The question of mining on the ocean floor provoked the negotiations' deepest rifts. If these legal issues are also moral issues, then exploring the LOS, even in a limited way as has been the case here, should advance our ethical prospecting in several ways that are not limited to seabed mining, or to mineral extraction of any kind.

First, by trying to connect a concrete personal experience in a library to an historical event of a truly global scale, I wanted simply to draw attention to connections between *interiority*, on the one hand, and the *world(s)* we inhabit, on the other. Mining morality must somehow include both self and world—a world mediated by meaning. In my own case, which may point to others in the reader's experience, the connections are obviously many, and even the ones I have made deserve more comment than I could offer here. But let me at least stress again the notion of emergence, with its lack of guarantees. Assuming a commitment to value and values, even if one is not entirely sure what one is seeking (for questions of values are, indeed, questions), one can ask: What will make it more rather than less likely, more rather than less probable, that, in Aquinas's simple phrase, I "do good and avoid evil"? Or, together with others, what will increase the likelihood that *we* not only do well but also good? What will make it more rather than less likely that a negotiation process will have a good outcome, that the health of the oceans will not be worsened, that the sort of paradigm shift in the hearts and minds of many that Pope Francis hopes for in *Laudato si'* will actually occur?

The stress on lack of guarantee urges another question. What if we fail? This is a second ethical prospecting point on which to report. My investigation of the LOS was a foray into an imperfect world. Not unlike the Gospel story of the Wheat and the Tares, the highest ideals for a common humanity and vices of various kinds dwell together. If the "common heritage" concept was central to the emergent law, it was a concept not fully embraced by all. Long before the Trump Administration sought to withdraw from the 2015 Paris Climate Accord, the United States turned its back on formal adoption of the LOS even as they accepted most of it as binding customary law. Reinhold Niebuhr's Augustinian-inspired attention to limits and the human fault, on which I drew in part for my investigation, is a good reminder of the seemingly stubborn fact of not only finitude, of falling short, but also what the Christian tradition has called sin—especially sin as "contraction," a turning away from the other with regard only for oneself or one's tribe.

But neither Lonergan nor the Catholic tradition he represents are blind to the human condition or the human fault. For instance, decades before the LOS emerged, Jacques Maritain warned about inflated notions of national sovereignty, whereby individual nations fail to recognize in *law* what they are in *fact*: "imperfect" societies that live in an interdependent world—the very sort of recognition that informs the LOS.[88] As for Lonergan, he wrote not only of progress and decline but also of redemption, not only of creating but also of healing in history. He was attuned not only to the "shorter" cycle of decline, but also of the "longer" cycle, which is so long because its lessons are so difficult to learn. The LOS was, in my view, a remarkable achievement, a creative venture of the first order and of a global order, but the LOS is neither perfection nor panacea. Whether or not Pope Francis's remark about the world becoming an immense pile of filth is fully accurate, the oceans are in deep trouble, ecologically and in other ways. Refugees die at sea, piracy is not a thing of the past, and the seas remain a possible theater of war, perhaps of a nuclear kind.

With not only uncertainty but also actual failure, including moral failure, both a sad fact of history and a troubling prospect for the future, it would seem all the more crucial that mining morality be open to a transcendent response to the human fault and open to some sort of eschatological hope to animate efforts in the concrete. The barons of Butte, despite all their creativity, left in their wake the need for healing. The nation's largest Super Fund site, the Berkeley Pit, stands under the watchful eye of Our Lady of the Rockies as a reminder. The Nauru case raised the question of reparations for a broken island and for broken trust that was supposed to be "sacred." Now we ask whether the oceans—for instance, the Great Barrier Reef—can be the receiver of restorative justice, too.[89] Perhaps each such sad situation or crisis is a parable raising the question of what true redemption might entail, and where justice—legal, economic, ecological, intergenerational, divine—converges with the human and divine mercy of which Pope Francis often speaks. Mining morality invites and requires raising these questions anew.

A third item to include with this prospector's report regards the "inter" dimension of ethics: *inter*-disciplinary, *inter*-national, *inter*-faith, *inter*-cultural, *inter*-subjective. In reviewing my own exploration of the LOS, I stressed the role of international law, and at least pointed to the latent theological dimensions of the treaty especially with the common heritage concept as a key element. What I did not stress enough is how ethics, dealing with some form of the question "How ought we to live?" is best understood not as a separate academic discipline so much as an ongoing conversation involving multiple disciplines and perspectives, multiple levels of analysis, multiple philosophies and theologies—all leading to "cumulative and progressive results." To cite two examples: In my dissertation on the LOS, I viewed the international law of the sea through the lens of four Western figures—three theologians and one constitutional lawyer, all males, and three of them dead. This was difficult and fruitful enough, and one needs to finish such things and move on. But I did not attempt to incorporate into my study, in any depth, other perspectives—for instance African views on the "common heritage of mankind"[90] (despite my having spent time in Africa), or Asian perspectives on the same.

But also lacking was sufficient engagement of "natural" sciences of various kinds (earth science, oceanography, geology, marine biology, climatology, etc.). When considering mining morality with the ocean as a focal point, conversation partners of all kinds need to be involved. Illustrative here is Woods Hole Oceanographic Institution, which announces as its goal "Understanding the ocean. For the planet, for the future."[91] This institution is attentive to seabed mining, including its legal dimensions, but its overall orientation is toward the sciences that would help us achieve understanding necessary for what is, implicitly, a moral goal (*for* the planet; *for* the future).

Furthermore, this institution is fully devoted to education, and thus it returns us to some form of the question, raised by such masters as Plato and Aristotle, but also by people like C. G. Weeramantry who inspired law students and others over the years: can such things as open-mindedness, judiciousness, integrity be taught? Put in terms of emergent probability, it appears that the Woods Hole founders and directors are hoping, through their vision and educational efforts, to shift the probabilities that humanity (including future generations) as well as the planet, "our common home," will enjoy progress rather than decline and, wherever necessary, be healed.

The heavy focus on ocean sciences, not only at Woods Hole but elsewhere, raises at least two further questions that an ethical prospector should consider. First, just as aspiring lawyers "learn to love the law," one wonders whether scientists who immerse themselves for years in the sciences of the sea learn to love the sea and all that it holds in ways that exceed the science they profess. In other words, whether scientists are "religious" or not, might not science—or, rather, scientists—be informed by that love for and reverence toward creation which Pope Francis, and long before him St. Francis of Assisi, preached? This seems plausible at the very least.

Given the concern today regarding "science deniers," especially related to climate change, it is important to emphasize the great contribution science and scientists make to an ocean ethic, if we may call it that. But this raises a second question. Why assume that scientists, who are human beings, are any lest prone to biases of various kinds, or at the very least a plurality of moral points of view, some on shaky ground? Those opposed to seabed mining, warning of its ill effects, are hardly "science deniers." Then again, commercial mining ventures have their own committed STEM representatives on board their mining vessels and on their payrolls. Who is to say what counts as the just and prudent way to proceed? Perhaps it is not a question science can answer, at least not on its own. In the next chapter, where everything begins with mining, the mining of uranium, we will face this question again in a more dramatic, possibly explosive, way.

NOTES

1. For a relatively comprehensive account, see Richard Pallardy, "Deepwater Horizon Oil Spill of 2010: Environmental Disaster, Gulf of Mexico," *Encyclopedia Britannica* (n.d.), at https://www.britannica.com/event/Deepwater-Horizon-oil-spill-of-2010.

2. For an autobiographically-based reflection on "participation" as a key category in ethics, see James M. Gustafson, "Participation: A Religious Worldview," *Journal of Religious Ethics*, 44/3 2016): 148–75.

3. This is evident in Augustine's *Confessions*, but the psychological approach one finds in *De Trinitate* is, in its own way, also rooted in self-knowledge.

4. Mark Morelli, "Horizontal Diplomacy," in Matthew L. Lamb, ed., *Creativity and Method: Essays in Honor of Bernard Lonergan* (Milwaukee: Marquette University Press, 1981), 459–74.

5. Duncan Snidal was at the time the chair of the Committee on International Relations in the Department of Political Science. He suggested among other things that I attend weekly meetings of the Program on International Politics, Economics, and Security (PIPES), a funded discussion group with guest presenters from around the country.

6. See James Brown Scott, *The Catholic Conception of International Law: Francisco de Vitoria, Founder of the Modern Law of Nations; Francisco Suárez, Founder of the Modern Philosophy of Law in General and in Particular of the Law of Nations* (Washington, DC: Georgetown University Press, 1934).

7. Lonergan, *Insight*, 28.

8. That is, the metaphysics to which I refer takes into full account the "turn to the subject." See Lonergan, "Metaphysics as Horizon," in *Collection*, Collected Works of Bernard Lonergan, vol. 4 (Toronto: University of Toronto Press, 1998), 188–204.

9. For a discussion of this isomorphism, see Lonergan, *Insight*, 470–71, 473–74.

10. For some further reflections on isomorphism between the act of deciding and the good to be achieved, see George, "Anticipating Posterity."

11. Lonergan, *Insight*, 506.

12. On emergent probability, see Lonergan, *Insight*, 146–51; and Melchin, *History, Ethics, and Emergent Probability*.

13. Recall that Lonergan was influenced by Toynbee's examination of the rise and fall of civilizations in his twelve-volume *A Study of History*.

14. Lonergan, *Method*, 13.

15. Lonergan, "Healing and Creating," 103.

16. On this assimilative capacity in relation to education, see Richard Liddy, "Bernard Lonergan on a Catholic Liberal Arts Education," *Catholic Education: A Journal of Inquiry and Practice* 3/4 (June 2000): 521–32. Or, to invoke Michael Polanyi again, it is a matter of "dwelling in" all sorts of insights, judgments, and decisions accumulated earlier and by others, and possibly "breaking out" with some new insight, some new idea or plan, of one's own. Think, for instance, of all the mining knowledge that Marcus Daly had assimilated by the time he recognized the great copper potential of Butte, or all the legal and other knowledge Christopher Weeramantry had assimilated by the time he signed on as investigator in the Nauru case.

17. The Thomist roots of Lonergan's work are fully evident. When it comes to international law, I have in mind Aquinas's influence especially on early shapers of international law such as Vitoria, Suaréz, and Grotius. See also E. B. F. Midgley, *The Natural Law Tradition and the Theory of International Relations* (New York: Harper and Row, 1975).

18. Jack L. Goldsmith and Eric A. Posner, *The Limits of International Law* (Oxford: Oxford University Press, 2005).

19. Mary Ellen O'Connell, *The Power and Purpose of International Law: Insights from the Theory and Practice of Enforcement* (Oxford: Oxford University Press, 2008).

20. The oft-cited listing of these sources is Article 38 of the Statute of the International Court of Justice. "Subsidiary" sources are "judicial decisions and the teachings of the most highly qualified publicists of the various nations."

21. For this distinction, see Charlotte Ku and Paul F. Diehl, eds., *International Law: Classic and Contemporary Readings* (Boulder, CO: Lynne Reinner Publishers, 1998), 3–16.

22. Louis Henkin, *How Nations Behave: Law and Foreign Policy*, 2nd ed., Council on Foreign Relations Books (New York: Columbia University Press, 1968; 1979), 47.

23. The fact that diverse forms of international law emerged over the course of history is emphasized by Philip Bobbitt in *The Shield of Achilles: War, Peace, and the Course of History* (New York: Random House, 2002). Stephen C. Neff, in *Justice among Nations*, similarly emphasizes the multiform character of international law over the centuries.

24. Geoffrey Best, *War and Law since 1945* (Oxford: Oxford University Press, 1994). I am doubtful that this situation has turned around since Best wrote some twenty-five years ago.

25. See Ian Urbana, "The Outlaw Ocean," *New York Times*, Five-Part Series, July 25, 2016, https://www.nytimes.com/interactive/2015/07/24/world/the-outlaw-ocean.html.

26. Lonergan, *Insight*, 118.

27. Gustafson, "Participation."

28. Lonergan, *Insight*, 144f.

29. Ibid., 141.

30. On the good of order and its broader context, the human good, see Lonergan, *Method*, 27–56; *Topics in Education*, 34–39.

31. For a discussion of values, see Lonergan, *Method*, especially chapter 2, "The Human Good."

32. On the various conversions, see Lonergan, *Method, passim*.

33. See Lonergan, *Insight*, 232–69.

34. Since Catholic social thought constitutes one set of prospector's tools, and since such tools can require sharpening or revision, it is worth considering why it took so long for a formal condemnation of slavery as an institution to emerge from the heart of the Catholic Church. For an insightful analysis of this tragic if not truly reprehensible oversight, see John Francis Maxwell, *Slavery and the Catholic Church* (Chichester and London: Barry Rose, 1975). Maxwell treats this oversight as a "disaster" that needs to be investigated lest it recur.

35. On development from "below" and "above," see Lonergan, "Healing and Creating in History." Note that this "bottom up" and "top down" imagery—already limited—should not be construed as the equivalent of "grassroots" and "halls of power." People working at the grassroots may be informed by a love that reorients all, by inherited values, and by visions of an alternative world, just as people at the

highest level may be working from the bottom up, seeking to chart truly new territory, step by step, one insight or solid judgment or sound decision at a time.

36. Robert Heilbroner, *The Worldly Philosophers: The Life, Times, and Ideas of the Great Economic Thinkers*, 7th ed. (New York: Touchstone/Simon and Schuster, Inc., 1999).

37. A perhaps overly functionalist view of religion notwithstanding, this point is made at some length by James A. R. Nafziger, "The Functions of Religion in the International Legal System," in Mark L. Janis and Carolyn Evans, eds., *Religion and International Law* (The Hague: Martinus Nijhoff Publishers, 1999), 155–76.

38. Thus the U.N. Charter begins: "We the peoples of the United Nations determined to save succeeding generations from the scourge of war, which twice in our lifetime has brought untold sorrow to mankind, ..."

39. Reinhold Niebuhr, "The Myth of World Government," *The Nation*, October 21, 1944: 313; and "The Illusion of World Government," *Foreign Affairs* 27 (April 1949): 379–88.

40. Lonergan, *Topics in Education*, 29.

41. See International Covenant on Political and Civil Rights, https://www.ohchr.org/EN/ProfessionalInterest/Pages/CCPR.aspx; and International Covenant on Social, Economic, and Cultural Rights, https://www.ohchr.org/en/professionalinterest/pages/cescr.aspx

42. See, especially, John XXIII, *Pacem in Terris*.

43. Mary Ann Glendon, *A World Made New: Eleanor Roosevelt and the Universal Declaration of Human Rights* (New York: Random House, 2001).

44. John Haughey discusses this problem and draws upon Lonergan to address it. See John C. Haughey, S.J. "Responsibility for Human Rights: Contributions from Bernard Lonergan," *Theological Studies* 63/4 (December 2002): 764–85.

45. The fact that the dissertation was not explicitly "Lonerganian" was, in part, itself a function of unmet conditions. None of the directors/readers available to me was fully conversant in Lonergan's thought, while individually or collectively these same scholars had a superb understanding of the figures, and the issues, on which I chose to focus.

46. "Envisioning Global Community: The Theological Character of the Common Heritage Concept in the Law of the Sea," Ph.D. diss., University of Chicago, 1990.

47. See D. P. O'Donnell, *The International LOS*, 2 vols., ed. I. A. Shearer (Oxford: Oxford University Press, 1981, 1984); and Lawrence Juda, *International Law and Ocean Use Management: The Evolution of Ocean Governance,* Ocean Management Policy Series (London: Routledge, 1996).

48. H. S. K. Kent, "The Historical Origins of the Three-Mile Limit," *The American Journal of International Law*, 48/4 (October 1954): 537–53.

49. On the connection between Grotius's freedom of the seas doctrine and Locke's view of property and government, see Alexandra Merle Post, *Deepsea Mining and the Law of the Sea* (The Hague: Martinus Nijhoff Press, 1983), 93. Traditional sea law included, of course, principles besides these two. Some, such as proscriptions of piracy, remain crucial today.

50. John L. Mero, *The Mineral Resources of the Sea* (Elsevier Publishing Co., 1969).

51. The 1958 and 1960 Conventions left unresolved especially the crucial question of the width of the territorial sea.

52. *Official Record*, United Nations General Assembly, Twenty-second Session, First Committee, 1515th meeting, 1 November 1967.

53. For a succinct summary of this concept and its history in international law, see Prue Taylor, "The Common Heritage of Mankind: A Bold Doctrine Kept within Strict Boundaries," in *The Wealth of the Commons: A World beyond Market and State*, http://wealthofthecommons.org/essay/common-heritage-mankind-bold-doctrine-kept-within-strict-boundaries.

54. "Declaration of Principles Governing the Seabed and the Ocean Floor," United Nations General Assembly, 1933rd plenary meeting, Resolution 2749 (XXV), December 1970, *Official Records of the General Assembly*, Twenty-fifth Session, Supplement No. 28 (New York: United Nations, 1971). One might argue that there are affinities between the clause regarding less developed nations and the "preferential option for the poor" of the Catholic social tradition.

55. Juda, *International Law and Ocean Management.*

56. "International Law is Irrevocably Transformed," Statement by Javier Pérez de Cuéllar, Secretary-General of the United Nations, December 10, 1982, *The Law of the Sea: United Nations Convention on the Law of the Sea with Index and Final Act of the Third United Nations Conference on the Law of the Sea* (New York: United Nations, 1983), xxx.

57. See Arvid Pardo, "An Opportunity Lost" in *LOS: U.S. Policy Dilemma*, ed. H. Oxam, David D. Caron, and Charles L. Buderi (San Francisco: ICS Press, 1983); and Aaron Danzig, "A Funny Thing Happened to the Common Heritage on the Way to the LOS," *San Diego Law Review* 12 (1975): 655–64.

58. Steven Gorove, "The Concept of 'Common Heritage of Mankind': A Political, Moral, or Legal Concept?" *San Diego Law Review*: 9 (1972): 390–403.

59. H.R. 2759 (96th): Deep Seabed Hard Mineral Resources Act.

60. H. Roberto Herrera Caceres, "La sauvegarde du patrimoine commun de l'humanité," in *The Management of Humanity's Resources: The LOS*, Workshop, The Hague, 29–31 October 1981, ed. René-Jean Dupuy (The Hague: Martinus Nijhoff Publishers, 1982), 125–34.

61. The LOS took full legal effect in 1994. The United States has since signed the Treaty but has yet to ratify it. It does, however, recognize the vast majority of its provisions as codification of binding customary law.

62. Christopher C. Joyner and Elizabeth A. Martell, "Looking Back to See Ahead: UNCLOS III and Lessons for Global Common Law," in Ku and Diehl, eds., *International Law: Classic and Contemporary Readings*, 245–72.

63. Ralph B. Levering and Miriam L. Levering, *Citizen Action for Global Change: The Neptune Group and the Law of the Sea* (Syracuse: Syracuse University Press, 1999).

64. Consider, for instance, the Regional Seas Programme of the United Nations Environment Programme, a program that grew out of the LOS. See United Nations

Environment Programme, "Working with regional seas," https://www.unenvironment.org/explore-topics/oceans-seas/what-we-do/working-regional-seas.

65. Robert M. Cover, "*Nomos* and Narrative," Forward to "The Supreme Court 1982 Term," *Harvard Law Review* 97 (1983): 4–68.

66. Lonergan, *Method*, 103.

67. See Edith Brown Weiss, *In Fairness to Future Generations: International Law, Common Patrimony, and International Equity* (Dobbs Ferry, NY: Transnational Publishers & Tokyo, Japan: United Nations University, 1989.

68. A 1986 dictionary of Christian ethics includes an entry on "Future Generations, Obligations to." After reviewing the issues and the literature, all philosophical, Ronald Greene observes that "in view of the urgency of these basic questions and the attention given them in the philosophical literature, it is remarkable that to date they have received so little treatment at the hands of theological ethicists." See *The Westminster Dictionary of Christian Ethics*, ed. James F. Childress and John Macquarrie (Philadelphia: The Westminster Press, 1986), 242–43.

69. William P. George, "Looking for a Global Ethic? Try International Law," 483–504.

70. Martti Koskenniemi, *From Apology to Utopia: The Structure of International Legal Argument,* Reissue with a New Epilogue (Cambridge: Cambridge University Press, 2005).

71. I attempted to respond to the challenges posed by this recent classic in George, "Neither Apology nor Utopia," Paper delivered at the meeting of the Society of Christian Ethics, January, 2014.

72. Lonergan, *Insight*, 43–50.

73. Article 145 prescribes "Protection of the marine environment."

74. In accord with Article 145, "the Mining Code" developed in recent years by the International Seabed Authority "has a strong environmental focus." See Donald R. Rothwell and Tim Stephens, *The International Law of the Sea*, 2nd Edition (Oxford and Portland, OR: Hart Publishing, 2016), 148.

75. Rothwell and Stephens, *International Law of the Sea,* 25–27.

76. Green Peace, "Deep Seabed Mining: An Urgent Wake-Up Call to Protect Our Oceans," March 2014, http://www.greenpeace.org/international/Global/international/publications/oceans/2013/Deep-Seabed-Mining.pdf.

77. See the 7th Deep Sea Mining Summit at https://www.deepsea-mining-summit.com/index. The 2017 Summit includes a session entitled "A Holistic Approach to Deep Sea Mining" that includes: "(1) focusing on deep sea mining projects in a holistic way; (2) analysis of existing and proposed seabed mining and processing systems; (3) looking at seafloor production equipment, vertical transport systems, as well as metallurgical processing; and (4) *addressing the issues regarding environmental studies and looking for more efficient solutions*" (emphasis added).

78. Nautilus Minerals, Press Release: Change in Directors and Officers, http://www.nautilusminerals.com/irm/PDF/2086_0/NautilusMineralschangeindirectorsandofficers.

79. Nautilus Minerals, "Nautilus Cares," http://cares.nautilusminerals.com/.

80. See C. B. Macpherson, *The Political Theories of Possessive Individualism: Hobbes to Locke* (Oxford: Oxford University Press, 1962).

81. Neff, *Justice among Nations*, 258.

82. See Robert M. Doran, "System and History: The Challenge to Catholic Systematic Theology," *Theological Studies* 60 (1999): 652.

83. Brennan "Asking the Right Questions."

84. Cynthia Crysdale, "Revisioning Natural Law: From the Classicist Paradigm to Emergent Probability," *Theological Studies* 56/3 (1995): 464–84.

85. Philip Allott, "*Mare Nostrum:* A New International Law of the Sea," *The American Journal of International Law*, 86/4 (October 1992): 764–87.

86. Ibid., 766.

87. Neff, *Justice among Nations*, 465.

88. Jacques Maritain, "The Problem of World Government," in *Man and the State* (Chicago: The University of Chicago Press, 1951), 188–216.

89. For an incisive theological reflection on damage to the Great Barrier Reef, see Denis Edwards, "Ecological Theology: Trinitarian Perspectives," *Proceedings of the Catholic Theological Society of America* 72 (2017): 14–28.

90. See, for example, Edwin Egede, *Africa and the Deep Seabed Regime: Politics and International Law of the Common Heritage of Mankind* (Heidelberg: Springer Verlag), 2011.

91. Woods Hole Oceanographic Institution, http://www.whoi.edu/#goto.

Chapter Six

Uranium in Africa and Beyond: A Matter of Being and Time

Once near a small village in Zambia, a mining country, a secondary school student explained to me, "Before the Europeans came, we did not have time." But surely that cannot be true. Different conceptions, perhaps conflicting conceptions, but no conceptions of time at all?[1] What of that other dimension, space? Might not the Plateau Tonga, or any distinct grouping of people, have a distinctive conception of space? Or, what about "being"? In 1945, Placide Tempels, a missionary in the Belgian Congo, published *La philosophie bantouen* (*Bantu Philosophy*), a book that may be read as a European's honest attempt to appreciate the richness, depth, and distinctiveness of Bantu ways of thinking and doing.[2] In it, Tempels proposed that "force" may be for Bantu peoples what "being" is in the philosophy that Tempels inherited from the West.

"Everything begins with mining." So says the law of Butte. According to Pope Francis, "everything is connected." Tempels's *La philosophie bantouen* was published in the same year atomic bombs were dropped on Hiroshima and Nagasaki. Uranium for Hiroshima came from the Belgian Congo, Tempels's adopted land. Everything and everywhere—including Hiroshima and the Belgian Congo (since independence in 1960, the Democratic Republic of the Congo)—may be in some way connected, but whether any one of us can fully grasp even a fraction of those connections is another question. But we should try. So, again taking refuge in the notion of prospecting for ethics rather than presenting a finished ethics of mining, this chapter will take up some mining-related connections that may otherwise go unnoticed. They have much to do with *being* and *time*.

Figure 6.1. Universal Nuclear Warning Symbol.

Being and *time* are two fundaments of reality. At least thinkers and writers from ancient Greece to Martin Heidegger have thought this to be so.[3] Following their lead and for the sake of organizing this phase of ethical prospecting, with the help of Gabrielle Hecht's illuminating study, *Being Nuclear: Africans and the Global Uranium Trade*,[4] the first part of this chapter considers "being" and what Hecht calls the "ontologies"[5] of the nuclear age. Put briefly, which "things"[6] (uranium, yellowcake, radiation poisoning, cancer, trade relations, individual nations, nuclear power plants, nuclear bombs, nuclear medicine, etc.) are considered "nuclear," and which things are not, can make a difference—politically, economically, medically, and in other ways. To add concreteness to Hecht's and our considerations, we will be more mindful of uranium mining in one particular African country, the vast land of Niger.

Then, in the latter part of the chapter, the emphasis shifts to "time." Here, we will consider mining not so much as where everything begins, say, in the uranium mines of Africa, but rather in terms of where it can lead—in this case, to nuclear weapons or to more peaceful if still problematic uses, such as nuclear power. With a focus on weapons of mass destruction as one of uranium's purposes or ends, in the shadow of the *Bulletin of the Atomic Scientists'* Doomsday Clock,[7] we will ask what "deciding in time" might mean. But we will also ask that question against the horizon of God understood, but never fully, in terms of an "eternal now." Here, Thomas Aquinas's understanding of prudence, especially with its time-sensitive elements of "memoria" and "foresight," can again aid us in our ethical prospecting. While we will not be bringing new figures such as Heidegger into this discussion of *being and time* in relation to mining (others may surely do so), I hope to show that reflections on the development and use of the atomic bomb, and at least mention of threats to future generations in the case of nuclear power, can lead to philosophical and theological considerations of the most basic kind. Such reflections on time may place mining and morality in a distinctive if not entirely new light.

BEING NUCLEAR IN AFRICA AND ELSEWHERE

Gabrielle Hecht, a University of Michigan historian and specialist on Africa, begins her award-winning *Being Nuclear: Africans and the Global Uranium Trade* by recalling the role of "aluminum tubes" and "yellowcake from Niger" in the events and decisions leading up to the 2003 invasion of Iraq.[8] This starting point in Niger adds to our ethical prospecting in several ways. First, it brings closer to the center of moral consciousness mining in *Africa*—an enormous and enormously complex continent, with over 1.2 billion people speaking over two thousand languages or dialects and facing challenges on multiple fronts. Recalling God's concern recorded in the Book of Jonah not only for the "more than a hundred and twenty thousand people" living in Nineveh, at the edge of the world, but also "the cattle" living there (Jonah 4:11), we must not forget all the other wonderful living creatures that inhabit this incredibly vast and varied land.

Second, not unlike the case of Nauru, by considering uranium mining in such countries as Gabon, Namibia, and South Africa, or, in our case especially, Niger, we are, in the words of C. G. Weeramantry, drawn into the often roiling "historical currents"—and crosscurrents—"that shape the course of human affairs." Here, the human affairs include colonization, decolonization, and the emergence of new African states; South African apartheid; the Cold War (and its proxy wars, some in Africa); the nuclear arms race; the emergence of the nuclear power industry and its accidents (Three Mile Island, Cherynobl, Fukusima-Daiimichi); efforts to halt or slow nuclear proliferation; today's nuclear flashpoints of Iran and especially North Korea; environmental crises and global climate change; terrorism (including the threat of nuclear terrorism)—the list goes on.

Third, coupling Niger with the invasion of Iraq calls to mind the importance of international law and relations. For the Iraq war had, and continues to have, significant international legal as well as geopolitical implications—just as the presence on our planet of nuclear weapons remains fraught with legal and other challenges. Finally, we will pay attention to Niger, rather than, say, South Africa, which occupies a more central place in Hecht's study, for the simple reason that this vast, lesser known country is one of the poorest in the world. Implicitly at least, the welfare of people on the margins is of great concern to Hecht as it is, of course, to Pope Francis and many others around the globe.

Ontologies in Africa

In certain respects, Hecht's thesis is relatively simple. Against the backdrop of all the threats and fantasies that emerged with the nuclear age—the nightmare of a nuclear war on the one hand, the once rosy prospect of nuclear-generated electricity "too cheap to meter," on the other—Hecht argues that there is something *exceptional* about "being nuclear." By comparison, things that do not fall under this ontology, this category of "being," may be considered *banal*. This ontology, Hecht argues, has immense implications for economics and politics, and deeply affects the lives of those involved in the extraction and initial processing of uranium. For instance, if uranium, once it is turned into yellowcake for shipment and further processing, is considered *nuclear*, then it may be treated as *exceptional* when it comes to trade; special rules and regulations and prices may apply. On the other hand, if it is treated as *banal*, that will have trade implications, too—for instance, it will be of less concern to whom the uranium is sold. This is the sort of issue that Hecht takes up in the first part of her book. Consider another question: if the mining of uranium is pretty much like mining of other kinds (say, gold or copper), if the extraction of uranium is *banal* rather than *exceptional,* then special protection of miners exposed to radiation, and the complexities of testing for radiation and its effects, becomes less of a priority. The welfare especially of those doing the initial extraction and processing occupies Hecht in the book's latter part.

In other respects, however, there is nothing at all simple about the story that Hecht tells. In fact, if a close analysis of the relatively simple Nauru case could fill ten volumes, one can only imagine what a truly comprehensive understanding of "Africans and the Uranium Trade" (the subtitle of her book) might entail. Indeed, Hecht confesses that there are matters she does not discuss—for instance, "environmental contamination produced by mine [sic] and mine tailings. There is much say about all these topics," she explains, "but I must leave those challenges for later—or for others."[9] Since there is arguably a strong moral impetus behind Hecht's research and writing, it would seem that she herself is engaged in a sort of "ethical prospecting," exposing important veins of inquiry to be taken up later or by others.

But these limitations do not diminish the importance or the nuance of her historical analysis, an analysis that has a dramatic beginning. Recalling the origins of the nuclear age, she observes how nuclear weapons were viewed as

> fundamentally different from any other human creation. The rupture in nature's very building blocks, wrought during fission, propelled claims of a corresponding rupture in historical time and space. . . . "Nuclear" scientists and engineers enjoyed far more prestige, power, and funding than their "conventional" colleagues. Morality-speak inevitably accompanied debates, rendering nuclear things either sacred or profane.[10]

With the atomic breakthroughs, Hecht continues, "apocalypse, no longer the preserve of religion, now lay within humanity's techological grasp." Utopian but also dystopian dreams took hold of nations of diverse ideological persuasion. Yet, immutable as the ontology distinguishing the two realms may have seemed at the dawn of the nuclear age, "nuclear exceptionalism was full of contradictions. For all the efforts at making nuclear things exceptional, there were opposing attempts to render them banal." [11] This mutability of the supposedly immutable ontology is Hecht's main point. It turns out that "this unreflexive reflex, this certainty about which things do or don't fall into the domain of the 'nuclear,' simply doesn't correspond to historical realities."[12]

To exemplify her point, she turns to Niger and observes that, in 1995, Niger and Gabon together accounted for one-fifth of the fuel for nuclear power plants in Europe, the United States, and Japan. Yet, a U.S. Government report on proliferation stated that neither of these countries had any "nuclear activities."[13] By contrast, in 2003, Hecht points out, "yellowcake from Niger made Iraq nuclear."[14] Times—and categories—had changed. Or, to come at this from another angle, "[*r*]*adiation* is a physical phenomenon that exists independently of how it is detected or politicized. *Nuclearity*," on the other hand, "is a *technopolitical* phenomenon that emerges from political and cultural configurations of technical and scientific things, from the social relations where knowledge is produced."[15] And it is these sorts of configurations that Hecht explores in her detailed research. Nuclearity is not the same everywhere; it is not the same for everyone; it is not the same at all moments in time. It will mean one thing when Africa is seen as the "dark continent" early in the nuclear age, when Africans themselves had little say in mining matters; it will mean something else in South Africa under apartheid, when those in power want to hold their seat on the International Atomic Energy Commission, and thus seek to depoliticize the mining of uranium, so affected by racial distinctions; it may mean something else again when Africans themselves exercise an increasing degree of agency; it may change meanings yet again when the question has to do with the adverse health effects on miners.

Bernard Lonergan, had he paid attention to Hecht's field of inquiry, might have said much the same thing, for in his view "concepts [such as nuclearity] have dates."[16] That is, to explore ontology—and ontologies—requires what Lonergan calls "historical consciousness." So, before narrowing our focus on "being nuclear" to Niger, it will be helpful to give some sense of how the tools provided by Lonergan especially can illumine the ethical prospecting that Hecht has undertaken and which we may join.

Since her focus is on "being" and a plurality of "ontologies," we might stress, first of all, that for Lonergan "being" is not some "concept," but rather "the supreme *heuristic* notion; prior to every content, it is the notion of the to-be-known."[17] But this notion is not some abstraction, substituting for particular insights, particular judgments, or their accumulation—say, the kinds of insights and judgments made by a crew chief in a uranium mine, by the board of directors of a mining company, by members of the International Atomic Energy Agency, or by a member of an NGO fighting to rid the earth of nuclear things, including nuclear power. On the contrary, the notion of being as the "to-be-known" impels human subjects to think and act in certain ways, just as the "transcendental precepts" impel the individual subject, and communities, to be attentive, to be intelligent, to be critical, to be responsible in the world—and worlds—in which we find ourselves. The later Lonergan stresses especially not only the notion of *being*, but also the notion of *value*, and thus judgments of value and decision-making. Since values are apprehended in feelings, affectivity is very much in play.[18] Of course, the notion of being as a heuristic notion may, in individuals or in groups, be impeded by bias as well.

In "Natural Right and Historical Mindedness," Lonergan clarifies the notion of historical mindedness by relating it to the notion of "collective responsibility," the very sort of responsibility, one might suggest, that is of interest to Hecht and others when it comes to things deemed nuclear, or not—including the mining of uranium. Lonergan begins with the distinction in a "contemporary ontology" between "on the one hand, a constant human nature; on the other hand, a variable, human historicity."[19] Such historicity is discernible in the educational process, where a person's mental horizons change over time, but it is discernible in other facets of life as well—for example, mining in Butte or Chuquicamata, on the island of Nauru, in the deserts of Niger. As these and any number of other mining sites and their respective contexts illustrate, in Lonergan's words,

> [t] he family, the state, the law, the economy, are not fixed and immutable entities. They adapt to changing circumstance; they can be reconceived in the light of new ideas; they can be subjected to revolutionary change.
>
> Moreover . . . all such change is in its essence a change of meaning—a change of idea or concept, a change of judgment or evaluation, a change of the order or the request.[20]

When one adds to this the various functions of meaning that Lonergan describes elsewhere—cognitive, constitutive, and so on[21]—it becomes even more apparent how Hecht's exploration of "nuclearity" with regard to Africa might be receptive to these particular prospecting tools.

The fact of this variability, a variability in meaning, Lonergan continues, has long been obvious—and troublesome. Is *everything* relative, context bound, peculiar to time and place? To counter the notion that all was "convention," without any guiding norm, the Greeks posited a notion of "natural right." But such a notion may be construed as an abstract reality, or it may be understood as "concretely operating." Lonergan opts for the latter construal, and by "concretely operating," he has in mind the dynamism of human conscious intentionality, of individuals and groups attending to data of various kinds, of raising questions that seek satisfaction in insights, of raising further questions about whether those insights are more than bright ideas, and of raising yet further questions for deliberation—questions of the good, of value, of not only what's in it for me and us but what's in it for others, including, as one might stress along with Pope Francis, future generations.

But there is something else in play, namely, love—of spouses, of families (recall Finn's interviews with women), of citizens of nations newly independent or well-established. There is God's love which, in Christian terms, "is flooding our hearts by the Holy Spirit that is given us" (Romans 5.5). Love, for Lonergan, is "a new principle [that] takes over, and as long as it lasts we are lifted above ourselves and carried along as parts within an ever more intimate yet ever more liberating dynamic love."[22] This is the very sort of thing one might expect Pope Francis to say. But it also has relevance to what Hecht is about.

To see this more clearly, we must stress that, for Lonergan, this constant self-transcendence, this "progress," is by no means assured—a point made repeatedly in previous chapters. For along with attentiveness and understanding and good judgment and responsible decisions, there is also oversight, bad or rash judgments, pursuit of satisfactions of every kind rather than choices to do the arduous good in the concrete. So not only is there a humane progression in history as individuals and groups move from a very practical world of common sense, to a plateau of theory, and then to a plateau of interiority and integration whereby persons may move back and forth easily between the two realms. There is also a problematic mixing of plateaus at any given time, such that commonsense folk and heady theoretians may speak past or be suspicious of one another. But there is also a sometimes very harsh "dialectic" in history, between insight and oversight, between pursuit of the worthwhile and settling for what is worthless, between love and hatred. Each person must grapple with this dialectic in his or her own history, but "what before could be dismissed as, in each [individual] case, merely an infinitesimal in the total fabric of social and cultural history, now has taken on the dimensions of collective triumph or disaster."[23]

We saw in the case of Nauru and its phosphate plunder one version of "disaster" to which many (the Germans, the Japanese, the Mandate nations of England, Australia, and New Zealand—and perhaps the Nauruans, too) contributed over time with their oversights, their shortsighted judgments, their irresponsible acts, their lack of love, or at least understanding, of neighbor. It is the very sort of downward spiral, but reaching a global scale, about which Pope Francis warns us in *Laudato si'*. As an historian, Hecht herself is arguably engaging this complex dialectic between human progress and human decline with regard to "being nuclear." One might, for instance, posit that a recurring piece in the puzzle that she calls "nuclearity," namely, South African apartheid and the racism behind it, is the sort of collective "disaster" that fits Lonergan's analysis. So, too, may be the collective state of uranium miners in those cases in which the oversight needed to protect human welfare has been replaced by oversight of another kind—in this instance, the failure to grasp that, relative to other kinds of mining, uranium extraction may be exceptional, with exceptional dangers to miners and to others, such as those nearby seeking potable water, needing special care.

But again, insight into insight mixed with oversight, especially when it is widespread, is no simple matter. Africa is not just one big place, and mining, even when limited to uranium (think of what prospecting for ethics in the case of African "blood diamonds" might yield) is not just one thing. To make some sense of this complexity, Hecht turns to the anthropologist Anna Tsing, who "uses the notion of *friction* as a metaphor for the creative and destructive power generated by 'universal' concepts and practices when they travel. This friction," Hecht explains,

> calls attention to the unevenness with which knowledge travels, the inequalities that shape its motion, the always-local circumstances that change its content along the way, and the material consequences of its motion. The production and dissolution of nuclear things in African places, I argue, occurred in the friction between transnational politics and (post)colonial powers, between abstract prescription and embodied, instrumental practices.[24]

It is no wonder that "being nuclear" in Africa has generated so much friction. Or, rather, it is no wonder that those human subjects who generate and sometimes manipulate concepts such as "nuclearity," cause so much friction, sometimes to the point of a massive explosion. The human subjects involved in "nuclear things," in Africa and beyond, have been so numerous, their meanings and values so diverse and sometimes at odds, how could such friction be avoided? To aid the reader of *Being Nuclear*, Hecht lists at the outset no less than sixty-eight acronyms and abbreviations for institutions and movements that are so many collective characters in a 350-page narrative about Africa and uranium. These range from financial firms, such as ADL (Arthur D. Little, Inc.), to governmental agencies, such as AECB (Atomic Energy Board [South Africa]), to international organizations, such as the WHO (World Health Organization), to service organizations such as MDM (Médicins du Monde). Even apart from the fact that this listing is short on mining companies (e.g., Aleva in Niger) with their economic interests, it takes little imagination to suspect that not all of these institutions, with their individual leaders and agents, with their mission statements, are in full agreement as to what "nuclearity" might or should mean in the concrete—say in the mines of a particular country such as South Africa or Niger. Indeed, each of these institutions is, recalling the words of Janet Finn, a potential but also distinct vein of ethical inquiry begging to be traced.

There is something else worth pointing out. Given what Lonergan says about love, including love of God and its transformative power, or given Pope Francis's explicit theology in *Laudato si'* or his frequent stress on mercy, it is noteworthy that none of Hecht's acronyms or abbreviations hints of anything explicitly religious. This contrasts with the visibility of religious figures and bodies that spoke out against the apartheid that receives so much attention in *Being Nuclear*, or of the religious leaders in Africa who have indeed turned their attention to the plight of miners, uranium and other.[25] To an extent, this is to be expected. Religion has in recent decades often been "the missing dimension of statecraft,"[26] and, as noted previously, religion has been relatively absent from international law, including laws dealing with things nuclear—this despite the fact that, functionally, religion can serve international law in several positive ways.[27]

Nor, recalling what was said above about Bantu philosophy, neither does there seem to be in *Being Nuclear* extended attention given to indigenous wisdom traditions that might have something to say about mining, even though Hecht does discuss appeals to the rights of indigenous peoples in the antinuclear movement to the point of finding in Navaho culture an ancient choice between two "yellow substances"—corn and uranium—as a basis for life.[28] The fact that Hecht is keenly attuned to the misunderstandings of, and condescension toward, African indigenous beliefs and practices during the beginnings of the atomic age is indicative of her respect for traditional ways of life.

Here, it might be good to pause and stress that our prospecting tools have much to say about the intersection of nuclearity and Africa that cannot be said fully here. When Pope Francis expresses concern about marginalized people in such places as Niger, he is building on the Catholic social tradition, for instance on notions of "integral development" found in Pope Paul VI's important theologically grounded encyclical on the development of peoples, *Populorum Progressio,* and on Pope Benedict's *Caritas in veritate* with concerns about global justice. As for Lonergan, in a thorough and insightful way, Joseph Ogbonnaya has drawn heavily on his many works, along with those of Lonergan scholars such as Robert M. Doran, to discuss social transformation and sustainability. Ogbonnaya does this in ways that take seriously the *transcendent* realm of meaning and, on the scale of values, *religious* value.

His work is an excellent example of moving from the sort of prospecting for ethics found in these pages to a serious attempt at mining morality, with a focus on the same Africa about which Hecht writes. He does so with an insider's knowledge to complement his appreciation and understanding not only of Lonergan but of other sources as well.[29]

None of this is to meant to delegitimize or underestimate Hecht's analysis, or to assume that those taking an ostensibly secular approach are any less morally converted than those claiming religious belief and practice. But it does say something about the intellectual and moral horizon that someone like Hecht brings to her exploration of "being nuclear." That is, for Hecht, as for Lonergan, "ontology" is a matter of meaning and of missed or distorted meanings, of judgments and misjudgments of fact and value by a multitude of agents in multiple contexts.

What may be less apparent in the case of Hecht, however, is what Lonergan calls the *notion* of being. A notion is not a concept deriving from insight, or even a shifting set of concepts. Rather, it is preconceptual, heuristic, anticipatory, and operative. It is closer to an open question than to the settled answers that it seeks. The notion of being assumes, along with a rich and subtle realm of common sense and a bracing realm of theory, also a "transcendent" realm of meaning.[30] In this realm, the question of God is raised, a question that questions questioning itself, a question that does not eliminate or minimize the very sorts of questions of fact and of value that Hecht assiduously pursues, but rather affirms and grounds the meaning and value that these questions seek.

As noted above, early in her book Hecht observes that "apocalypse, *no longer the preserve of religion,* now lay within humanity's technological grasp."[31] In certain respects, this appraisal is understandable and defensible. Again, we may live largely in a secular age—even if abandonment of rationality and even truth, replaced by magical thinking or conspiracy theories, is an alluring option for many. But there is no reason to assume that religious discourse that is serious about meaning and value cannot still share the stage of inquiry, about apocalypse and so much else, with historians and others who express little or no explicit thoughts or passions about "being religious," but do seek to know the real and to do the good. After all, Hecht herself seems not to abandon religious language altogether: she aligns the split between the "exceptional" and the "banal" with the distinction between the "sacred" and the "profane."[32]

The Case of Niger

To highlight the sorts of questions of concern to Hecht, raised in particular contexts—geographical, cultural, historical—we can say more about the case of Niger. One starting point is with the aluminum tubes incident with which Hecht begins her book, and which the reader may recall had much to do with the highly questionable rationale for the 2003 invasion of Iraq. But another which she provides is France's explosion of a nuclear bomb in Algiers in February 1960, not far from a massive uranium deposit in another colony, Niger.[33] This event alerts us to the fact that there is no way to understand the "ontology of nuclearity" as it affects Niger without some attention to Niger as a one-time colony of France. This is a complex relationship, and there is no hope of doing justice to that relationship here. But on the premise that prospecting for ethics when it comes to mining will require, again in Finn's terms, "tracing the veins" of colonialism and postcolonialism, we can at least highlight a few points.

One is the question of personal agency and leadership, on the side of both the French and the Nigeriens. Just as in *The Battle for Butte* Michael Malone stressed his interest in the political forces at play but inevitably discussed the outsized personalities of the copper kings, so, too, Hecht is attuned to "technopolitics" with its systemic characteristics, but she does not overlook the key role of highly-placed individual decision-makers with their visions, their ambitions, their loyalties, their failings. Put in Lonergan's terms, she does not overlook individual "subjects" and their acts. To give but one example, she reports in some detail on the important work of Barbara Rogers, a member of the UK Foreign and Commonwealth Office, in exposing and seeking to address highly questionable pricing and other practices involving the Rössing uranium mine in Namibia.[34]

In the case of Niger, she pays heed to a key agent of France around the time of decolonization, Jacques Foccat. She also focuses on the first president of Niger, Hamani Diori, along with his successor, Seyni Kounché, who ousted Diori in a coup. While this may be, in its own way, a "great men" approach to history (in other places Hecht is very attentive to often nameless laborers in the mines), the fact is that it made a difference—and not only for themselves—just where these highly placed individuals stood with regard to "nuclearity." Decision-making affecting the lives of others is not only about who has the power (the French? the Nigeriens?); it is also about what people who have that power do with it—and why.[35]

One point at which these decision-makers, and their decisions, mattered in the emergent postcolonial world was on the abiding question of sovereignty. In fact, one could no doubt reflect at length on the relationship between "being nuclear" and "being sovereign," for it is doubtful that, under scrutiny, the "ontology of sovereignty" would sit still for long. It is very likely that a particular country's "being nuclear," or not, would have something to do with the shifting concept of "being sovereign." In any event, as we saw in our discussion of the Law of the Sea, powerful nations such as the United States can be reluctant to cede their sovereign authority to an international regulatory body such as the Seabed Authority. But emerging nations, too, make strong claims of national sovereignty to protect themselves not only from the powerful nations of the world, but also from powerful transnational corporations with designs on their resources. In this case, Hecht explains, sovereignty "was distributed through technopolitical systems that turned nature into resources, and resources into commodities."[36] But these were systems in which a young nation's—or an old nation's—leaders could make a difference.

In the case of uranium and uranium mining, there were at least three ways an emerging nation such as Niger could assert its sovereignty. One was through development demands, asking of the French with their interest in uranium to ensure that, with that mining, came "the financial, social, and infrastructural dimensions of mine capacity."[37] In this regard, Gabon's president, Omar Bongo, was seemingly more successful, than was Niger's Diori, in getting these demands met. A second way to express sovereignty was through *pricing*. Who—Niger or some foreign power(s)—would set the price for the mined uranium? Here, the success of OPEC in determining the price of oil inspired uranium-rich countries like Niger and Gabon to focus on pricing as well. As the best way to assert Niger's sovereignty, given France's attachment to things nuclear, President Diori pushed the *nuclear* status of uranium; President Bongo, on the other hand, found reason to stress the *banality* of Gabon's uranium as a way to affirm the sovereignty of Gabon.

A third way to strengthen claims of sovereignty would be to assert authority over who a nation's business partners will be. In Niger's case, under President Kounché this meant selling yellowcake to neighboring Libya, and its president Muammar Qaddafi, who in turned served as a broker to other states. Anyone the least bit aware of Libya's and Qaddafi's role in the "great historical currents that have shaped human affairs" will understand that this was not without its controversy. Here, the point is not to sort all this out, even to the degree that Hecht does, but simply to stress that the ethics of mining, in so far as it involves uranium and Africa, cannot ignore the conflicts in that part of the world. If Butte was a "moral morass," certainly the greater Middle East region is that and more.

The complexity, or friction, that Niger's "nuclearity" entails appears only to have increased since independence in 1960. Here, the plan is not to resolve that friction so much as to identify a few of its contributing elements. Some of these are discussed in Hecht's concluding chapter, "Uranium in Africa." She notes, for example, the challenge of governance over the years, which included at various times corruption and dictatorship, but also reform movements. She also discusses the ongoing tension between mining ventures, such as Areva, and NGOs such as Greenpeace who, in her view, tend to paint the behavior of the companies like Areva with too broad a brush—for instance, "reducing Arlit's [one of Areva's mines] history to racist neocolonialism," when in fact radiation-related health issues challenge both Niger and France alike.[38] Hecht points out that, while *nuclearity* often discriminates along axes of class, race, and geography," with the element of power mixed in, "*radiation* . . . doesn't discriminate" along such axes.[39] She also notes that cries for an end to nuclearity by certain NGOs are not particularly welcome by those in Niger who find employment in the mines.

A Recent Snapshot of Friction

Before independence in 1960, and then for several years after, the context for uranium mining in Niger was largely the colonial and then postcolonial relationship between Niger and France with its strong commitment to both nuclear energy and nuclear weaponry. A 2014 Reuters report provides a good sense of the friction that has played out over the years.[40] This Reuters' snapshot of "nuclearity" in Niger was taken as Areva and Niger were negotiating new contracts. The two were at loggerheads over complaints that Niger had gained far too little from the relationship in terms of worker benefits, infrastructure, and the pricing of uranium that determines taxation. As Mining Minister Tchiana put it, "Instead of mountains of waste in Arlit, we want buildings, homes, hospitals and investment." The mayor of the regional capital Agadez, Rhissa Feltou, complained that "these companies are not paying enough in tax. We are bitter about the presences of extractive industries here. . . . Mining is not responding to the expectations of the people."[41]

Figure 6.2. Uranium mine, Arlit, Niger.
Photo by David François, published under the Creative Commons Attribution-Share Alike 3.0 Unported license.

Areva, for its part, stressed its own difficulties in a time of depressed uranium markets, and thus the limits of what they could do—certainly not "everything." The market situation affected the opposing sides' views on pricing. While Niger wanted a political basis for price, Areva wanted "spot pricing" to be a major criterion for price agreements. Areva also pointed to what it had done—for instance, the free clinics it provided and the construction and renovation of schools. Alleged corruption may also have accounted for the fact that taxes paid to the government of Niger did not come back to the local level. Security issues resulting from the presence of Al Qaeda was also a matter for mutual blame. Furthermore, since matters of fact are certainly relevant to the ontology of nuclearity, it is worth noting that a lack of transparency was a problem in this case. At the same time, there were organizations in place seeking to improve accountability regarding nature resources. This would include, for instance, the Extractive Industries Transparency Initiative, a global coalition of companies and governments, including Niger. These entities aimed for greater transparency all around. Finally, since we do not want to overlook the place of the individual subject in a leadership position, it is striking that the president of Niger in 2014, Mahamadou Issoufou, who pressed hard against Areva, had a background in mining and was once employed by that very firm.

This 2014 snapshot tells too little about uranium mining in Niger. But it tells enough to illustrate that, if, as Pope Francis insists, "everything is connected," then the connections in Niger are complex and are becoming increasingly so. The World Information Service on Energy's Uranium Project (an organization highly critical of nuclear energy) lists some forty companies currently performing or planning to engage in "uranium prospection and/or exploration in Niger,"[42] although just how extensive the actual prospecting is, or how firm the plans are for that prospecting, is not clear.[43] The list includes, among others, mining companies from Canada, Great Britain, Russia, India, and China.

A brief consideration of Chinese involvement may be particularly instructive for understanding what being nuclear means in Niger today and into the future, but also for the light it sheds on the more general topic of prospecting for ethics. The two major uranium mines in Niger, a country with some 7 percent of the world's recoverable reserves, are near the remote town of Arlit. The mines are run by Areva, under 70 percent French ownership. Areva is the second largest employer in Niger after the government, and the mines account for about one-third of the country's exports, supplying France with about a third of its electrical power. As noted above, over the years, the relationship between this company and Niger has been contentious, with complaints that the Nigeriens themselves are not benefiting sufficiently from the mining, especially given generous tax breaks and other corporate benefits.

Consideration of a contentious negotiation of an agreement a few years ago would no doubt elucidate the sort of "friction" about which Hecht writes. For instance, the company was being pushed to negotiate better terms at the very time that the uranium market was depressed in the aftermath of Fukushima and Japan's shutdown of numerous commercial nuclear reactors. In other words, "nuclearity" cannot prescind from historical realities, such as the fact that plans for a third mine, at Imouraren, were put on hold due in part to these market factors. But a fourth mine, in Azelik, situated in a marginal region populated by the Tuareg people, is also of interest. Under a joint partnership called Somina, the mine is operated by Chinese companies, in partnership with Niger, which holds a 33 percent share. According to a 2015 *Business Insider* report, the Azelik mine is "an instructive guide to the future of Niger's uranium and the global nuclear energy at large."[44] As of May 2017, the mine was closed, with its future uncertain. But from the beginning, there were problems. A 2010 report told of local protests about lease of local land "for uranium exploitation without permission or compensation." For some in northern Niger, the uranium concession bespoke "a Chinese colony," without respect for local laws and regulations—a complaint voiced elsewhere in Africa—for example, in Zambia.

While it is difficult to verify the claim, the seminomadic Tuareg, who are heavily dependent on water for their flocks, believe that the mining operations have lowered the water table in the area. Lack of health care and improper disposal of mining waste are other complaints. As the mayor of In'gall put it, "There isn't any benefit for the population that lives here. They're just afraid of contamination."[45] In a scenario that would fit well into the warnings of *Laudato si',* population growth, environmental degradation, and broken promises of a better life through mining have conspired to alter the Tuareg culture itself. As one resident explained, "Younger people don't believe they need to take care of the animals. They want to go to town and change their lives. They have another idea in their heads."

But "another idea" often goes unrealized. While Tuareg revolts led to an increased voice in the affairs in northern Niger (one more not so small chapter in the story of Niger), and while mining regulations were shored up, the Chinese were accused of operating "well outside of accepted industry norms as Nigerien employees understood them," a charge that would be heard elsewhere in Africa. Just as the labor unions in Butte feared informants for the company in their midst, so workers at Azelik feared being overheard with their complaints and thus losing their jobs. The situation was so dire, and the people working in the mines so poor, that, in the view of one employee, "slavery's back in the north of Niger, but with another face." As explained above, Areva had faced similar charges of being uncaring, but the *Business Insider* reporter remarks on the comparison: "Areva, for all of its occasional tensions with the Nigerien government and society, had at least turned Arlit into one of the country's most desirable places to live with modern hospitals, schools, and a comfortable workers' village." Janet Finn might have said something similar about Chuquicamata when the Anaconda Copper company, easily demonized, ran the show.

The point here is not to demonize the Chinese; the available reportage is spotty, and the situation of the Chinese in Africa is no doubt rife with complexity. But in terms of prospecting for ethics, for asking within the context of nuclearity in Africa how we ought to live, the "historical currents that have shaped human affairs" can no longer be only about Eurocentrism and its penchant for domination, demonstrated or alleged. An ethics of mining must take into account actors from other sectors of the globe. In Butte, and elsewhere in the United States, Chinese workers did not fare very well, victims of the group bias that Longeran describes. Now, with the global tables partially turned in Africa and elsewhere, the Chinese, too, will need to ask—and be asked—where they stand with regard to nuclearity and the responsibilities that it brings. They will need to be fully in the conversation, the sort of conversation envisioned by Pope Francis and others who share his broad and deep concerns.

DECISION TIME IN THE NUCLEAR AGE

If *being* nuclear, in Africa or anywhere else, presents extensive conceptual and practical challenges, then we should hardly expect less if we try to join nuclearity, including uranium mining, and *time*. Saint Augustine was succinct in stating the problem: "What then is time? If no one asks me, I know: if I wish to explain it to one that asks, I know not."[46] I begin with these words for at least two reasons: First, there is clearly much about time that I do not understand—here, again, I am prospecting rather than producing a finished idea. Second, just as Augustine's *Confessions* open with question after question posed to God, questions that make evident that Augustine is dealing with a mystery that he will never fully understand, so, too, here I will raise questions that I cannot answer in full but that might nevertheless be good to ponder.

Morality and Time: Prospecting for Connections

The virtue of prudence seems like a promising place to start, for prudence, as Thomas Aquinas explains, is that virtue which enables us to realize the ends of the other virtues, such as justice, in the here and now[47]—"in history," as Gabrielle Hecht or Michael Malone might put it.

The introduction to our prospector's tools discussed this virtue in some detail and we have picked up the tools of prudence from time to time. Here, I want simply to stress that this virtue, with its quasi-integral parts, has much to do with time. *Memoria* looks to the past, and *foresight,* or *providentia,* looks ahead. If as the philosopher Josef Pieper insists, *memoria* means "true to *being* memory,"[48] then maybe we are moving into the realm captured by the title of Heidegger's *Being and Time.*

There is reason to assume that the other quasi-integral parts have something to do with time as well. For instance, *reasoning* to a right judgment sometimes takes time—as we clearly saw in the Nauru case. If, in Aquinas's world, we were angels, who know everything they know in an instant, we would not have this problem. But, alas, we are not they.[49] True, some judgments come quickly, and maybe they should. Sometime *shrewdness,* which has to do with "alacrity," leads us to strike while the iron is hot, for he or she who hesitates is lost. But sometimes it is good and necessary to look before leaping, and sometimes for a very long time, for one might be staring into the abyss. Surely, too, *circumspection* can be time-sensitive. What was appropriate yesterday may not be appropriate today; circumstances have changed.

Second, according to modern theories of relativity, perhaps there is no such thing as absolute "simultaneity," of two things happening absolutely at the same time.[50] If that is the case, then perhaps everyone and everything has a distinct time zone. But to this proposition, a theologian of a rather traditional bent might respond: What about God's activity? What of God's grace? From God's point of view, from the point of view of God's "eternal now," aren't all of God's graceful acts—the call of Abram to be the father of a great nation; the conversion of Saul on the road to Damascus; the changed heart of the slave ship captain, John Newton, author of the hymn "Amazing Grace"; the subtle graces during the "long loneliness" of Dorothy Day—happening at the same time? From God's point of view, does not each of these acts take place at the very same moment, that is, God's moment? This assumes a view of God as unbounded by time and space, or spacetime, with its past and future, its hither and yon, its "from this perspective" and "from that point of view"—a rather traditional view of God as enjoying an "eternal now." Since we are at least considering a view of God as outside of time, with time—whatever it might mean—as tied to God's creation (about which Pope Francis says a great deal), we might recall that Augustine, who asked about time, also asked and thought a lot about God as Trinity. So we may have occasion below to suggest some connections between time, mining, morality, and a Triune God.

Third, it should be stressed that international law, that vast and extremely complex carrier of meaning and value, and one set of ethical prospecting tools, is largely about time as well as space. Who has territory and who does not (and what counts for "territory") makes a difference. Does a country's "airspace" have a certain limit, say ninety miles, or does it extend *ad caelum*—"to the heavens," allowing nations to tax satellite use of that space? International law considers such things. As for time, international law has its "epochs," and treaties have timelines and dates. *Custom*, another source of, or evidence for, international law, develops over time—sometimes centuries, sometimes within a few years or less. As we saw in our discussion of the Law of the Sea, international law encompasses, or at least considers quite seriously, *future* generations. Perhaps in sum, when we consider that international law comprises a certain kind, or certain kinds, of juris-*prudence*, a jurisprudence that may have real affinities to the prudence of Aquinas, then clearly that prospector's tool called international law has much to do with *time.*

Gathering these initial considerations together, we might conclude that moral judgments and decisions about mining or anything else, with the virtue of prudence serving as a prime way to understand those judgments and decisions, have much to do with time. Such decisions take time. Some come quickly, almost instantaneously; some are agonizingly slow. Some know and choose their life's path when still a child; others seem ever at the crossroads of a calling. It took well over fifteen years for the LOS to emerge from the cocoon of countless insights, judgments, and decisions by negotiators—and, of course, the United States has yet to become a party despite the time that has since passed. This is to say nothing of Arvid Pardo's timeline for the law, as he looked back to the primordial watery abyss which we retain in the saltiness of our tears. Lest we veer off topic, we must stress that the copper of Butte and Chuquicamata, the phosphate of Nauru, and the uranium of Niger have their geological timelines, too.

In making moral decisions, we reach into the past, but never just the past, through memory; we touch the future, but never just the future, through foresight. Even when we do our best, neither past nor future may be altogether clear. In short, moral decisions are conditioned and contextualized—perhaps even defined—by time, whatever that might mean. But, at least from one point of view, shared by Augustine, Aquinas, and others, moral decisions are also made against an ultimate horizon not of the temporal but of the eternal, of the divine. In this sense, each and every decision in time is relative, not just to some fast but still finite constant like the speed of light, and not only to individuals' and groups' particular moral time zones or horizons—as critically important as these sorts of relativity might be. Rather, moral decisions are made—or can be made—against the horizon that I have called, following others, an "eternal now" that embraces in a single act of knowing and loving all that has happened, say, under the watchful eyes of Our Lady of the Rockies or Rio's *Cristo Redentor*, and all that will ever happen long after those human artifacts are no more.

Does Time Have a Moral Meaning?

So, morality—in Montana's Silver Bow County, on Nauru or in Niger, on the high seas or far below—is conditioned or contextualized by time, for instance times of war and times of peace. But I want to raise another possibility. Is there a way in which *time itself* might be conditioned, even defined, by morality? With regard to Augustine, what if we linked his understanding of time found in Book XI of the *Confessions* not only to the intellectual and religious conversions on display in earlier books—for example, his intellectual breakthrough that God is not a "body" (and thus not finite, restricted to space and time)—but also to the *moral* conversions so central to his life's story? With regard to Aquinas, in trying to relate time and space to eternity, what if we looked not to the first part of the *Summa Theologica*, which deals with God and creation, but rather to the second part, which deals with sin and grace, and with such earthly matters as theft and murder and bribery and debauchery—that is, the kinds of moral matters we came across in the story of Butte?

Turning to the more recent past, what if we associated theories of relativity not with Einstein the physicist but rather Einstein the moralist? To help people to get the point of Einstein's theories, those who understand these things may use images of moving trains and people standing on train station platforms.[51] It appears from these theories that large objects like the stars can bend time and space. But what if the train in the picture was given a destination? Let's say it was bound for Auschwitz or Bergen-Belsen or the salt mines of Siberia or the gold mines of South Africa under apartheid? Might not that image alter our understanding of time and space, or of spacetime? Might we not regard time as movement in the direction of the truly good, or of moral failure and possibly of redemption? What if, like large bodies, moral decisions can bend time itself?

Recent and not so recent discussions of time—from Augustine to Einstein, let's say—seem to require that we move beyond what Bernard Lonergan calls the realm of common sense, wherein things are related to us, in an immediate, simplified sort of way, and into the realm of theory, wherein things are related to one another.[52] So, for instance, in the realm common sense, acceleration can mean the feeling of "going faster" as the airplane takes off, while in the realm of theory, it can be expressed by a mathematical formula. Yet, common sense, that with which we are familiar—such as the experience of watching a train pass by—does not fall away altogether. So with regard to deciding in time, we might begin with some "commonsense" expressions: What do we mean when we say, "I had a *good* time"? Or, more generally—whether one lives in Butte, Montana, or in the deserts of Niger—"Those were *good* times." "Those were *bad* times." What is it that makes those times *good* or *bad*?" What is it that makes those times *morally* good or *morally* bad? When a mining company gives its employees a "hard time," and if working conditions are a moral matter, as the Catholic social tradition would insist, what is it that makes that time "hard"? Or, to take a larger example drawn against the moral backdrop of the industrial revolution and laissez-faire capitalism that has no little relevance to mining, what is the moral meaning of Charles Dickens's novel, *Hard Times*?

In short, can our judgments, our choices, our decisions make time itself good or bad, hard or not so hard? If Martin Luther King's "arc of history bends towards justice," then, first of all, is the arc of history imbued with moral meaning—such that time has a moral shape, a moral definition—and, secondly (recalling what we've said about emerging probability), can we bend that arc through our actions? To put it most succinctly, does morality have anything to do with the very *being* of time?

I should say right away that the sort of thing I am getting at has relevance not only for momentous moral decisions but for more mundane ones, too. But it may better elucidate the moral dimensions of time if we focus on a truly big moral problem rather than on a lesser one, a problem that begins with mining in places like Niger but surely does not end there. Furthermore, while here the topic of time and morality is addressed from the perspective primarily of a theologian, I want to proceed in such a way that science and scientists, especially as moral agents, are fully in view. Thus, I propose to turn to a moral pivot, if not *the* moral pivot, of the last century, and maybe of ours, a process and series of events that involved and revolved around science—the same science that has so helped us to rethink the notion of time. We want to ask about the "ends of mining," or more specifically, just what happened to some of the uranium from the Belgian Congo. Where did it end up? Having taken it from the ground, where did we take it? With it, where did *we* go? So we turn our attention to the atomic bomb.

Morality, Time, and the Manhattan Project

I am told that a newly arrived graduate student met with the Divinity School professor at the University of Chicago with whom she had come to study. They talked of their shared love of New York City, and the professor mused, "Well, Chicago is a lot like New York. Just without Manhattan." But in fact, Manhattan had come to Chicago, and, more precisely, to the University of Chicago—founded in part by John D. Rockefeller, of Standard Oil—some years before. Or, at least the Manhattan Project, aimed at producing an atomic bomb, had come to this gathering point of physicists and technologically inclined academics. It was a time-sensitive project: the Germans were reportedly working on a powerful new weapon; the goal of the Manhattan Project was to get there first. So under the south bleachers of old Stagg Field, where the original "Monsters of the Midway," the University of Chicago football team, had played its games, Enrico Fermi and his colleagues successfully engineered the first self-sustaining nuclear chain reaction at 3:25 p.m., December 2, 1942—an important step on the way to building a monster of a different kind.

Near the corner of 57th and Ellis Avenue, a Henry Moore sculpture now stands to commemorate that momentous event. But commemorate is a verb. So, in the spirit of what Augustine and Aquinas called *memoria*, it is worth our thinking back to what transpired under those bleachers and in hearts and minds of the human agents huddled there. For while this first nuclear reaction generated barely enough energy to power a single lightbulb, it was an essential link in a huge cooperative effort that would lead to results probably beyond the imagination of the participants—not only nuclear power plants that light so many offices and homes—but nuclear-powered submarines coursing under the seas today, carrying nuclear firepower far surpassing that of the bombs dropped on Japan.

It is worth thinking about this effort as cooperative, since the Manhattan Project involved at its peak, in one way or another, about 125,000 employees. The biblical Tower of Babel story (Genesis 11: 1–9), wherein people sought to build a city and reach heaven apart from God, is perhaps instructive here. As the bible tells it, God's punishment for this offense was to multiply the languages of the builders, so that they would no longer be able to understand one another. But the punishment may be viewed also as a saving act to keep them from future cooperation in evil and destruction. For we must recall the often-overlooked obvious: cooperation, the Atlantic slave trade, let's say, or human trafficking today, can be a morally wretched thing, just as cooperative efforts such as the Underground Railroad or *Medicins Sans Frontiers* can be moral on a heroic scale, making for morally better times.

In the case of the Manhattan Project, with the language of mathematics and the sciences now serving as a common tongue, we might ask whether the nuclear bomb was a failure of memory, a failure to recall what can happen when people put their heads together, especially if the objective is to demoralize and destroy the enemy—as was arguably the case with obliteration bombing of World War II. Through forgetfulness, Aquinas warned, prudence may be lost.[53] Here is where science and scientists as moral agents feature in. A rhetorical question from the peace movement, decades ago, often ran: "Suppose they gave a war, and no one came?" But one might ask a more modest question: "Suppose they gave a war and all the scientists, technicians, engineers, and mathematicians—all the STEM people (so crucial to mining of every kind)—decided to stay home?" If, as Sherman said to Atlanta as the

Northern army was burning it down, "War is hell," might not war be a lesser hell if all scientists refused to get involved?

When the fruit of the Manhattan Project was ripe and ready for testing in New Mexico, J. Robert Oppenheimer, the scientist chosen to head the project at Los Alamos, was asked to name the testing. He named it "Trinity." Why Oppenheimer, a secular Jew, made this choice is not entirely clear.[54] One explanation is that he was deeply influenced by Hindu thought, especially the *Bhagavad-Gita*. So, it has been argued, Oppenheimer would have "associated 'Trinity' with Brahma the Creator, Vishnu the Preserver, and Shiva the Destroyer."[55] But it is just as likely, if not more so, that Oppenheimer drew inspiration from the poems of John Donne, which he was reading at the time. Holy Sonnet 14 begins:

> Batter my heart, three person'd God; for, you
> As yet but knocke, breathe, shine, and seeke to mend;
> That I may rise, and stand, o'throw mee, and bend
> Your force, to breake, blow, burn, and make me new.

Indeed, this poem features prominently in John Adams's 2004 opera, *Doctor Atomic,* which focused on Oppenheimer and the few hours leading up to the nuclear test.

Given the close connection that Oppenheimer has given us between what happened in the New Mexico desert, but beginning with mining in Africa, and Christian imagery and theology, it seems reasonable, from the inside as it were, to follow through on that imagery and theology. That is what I would like to do. But not without a comment about the great impact of Hindu thought upon Oppenheimer. After all, the words of Oppenheimer most often quoted are those he is said to have thought to himself when he saw the effects of that first nuclear explosion—namely, the words of Krishna found in the *Bhagavad-Gita*: "I am become Death, the destroyer of worlds." Relevant to our topic, the word translated here as "Death" is often rendered as "Time."[56] Thus, "I am become *Time,* the destroyer of worlds."

Figure 6.3. Albert Einstein and J. Robert Oppenheimer.
Photo courtesy of US Govt. Defense Threat Reduction Agency.

Now, I am in no position to discuss Hindu thought with

any authority, but relying on others, I will make one crucial point: Oppenheimer had strong pacifist leanings, and yet he never backed away from his conviction that developing, testing, and even dropping the bomb on Japanese population centers was the right moral path to follow. From the *Gita* he reportedly gained a sense of duty to fight. Moreover, this sense of duty was coupled with his commitment to science. To oversimplify but not by much: We are engaged in a great war, and science must play its part; science can build the bomb, and thus it should; it is up to others, those in authority, to decide whether and how to use it. Only with such convictions to drown out all moral ambiguity and hesitation—moral ambiguity and hesitation evident among other Manhattan Project participants—only with such clear focus could the project succeed.

The project did succeed. Whether it succeeded morally, especially with the dropping of the bomb, first on Hiroshima and then on Nagasaki, is another question. At this juncture one could turn for guidance to the just war tradition—especially with its set of *jus in bello* criteria for how a war, once deemed justifiable (*jus ad bellum*), could be morally fought. This approach would be quite in keeping with resources provided by Augustine and Aquinas, by Francisco de Vitoria and Hugo Grotius (those key contributors to international law), and many others in the Christian tradition and beyond. One thinks especially of the Jesuit moral theologian John C. Ford's classic 1944 article on obliteration bombing, which, prior to Hiroshima, made a compelling argument that the American and British bombing policies and practices were morally wrong.[57]

But even apart from the protests of some that the Just War tradition should be abandoned, at least by the Catholic moral tradition,[58] here we may take a more explicitly theological approach, the sort of approach one finds in the great war articles that appeared in the *Christian Century* some seventy-five years ago, written by the Protestant theologian H. Richard Niehbuhr—someone who arguably shared in the "emerging religious consciousness of our time" of which Lonergan would later write. Here, we will simply recite their titles, but titles can be telling. So they run: "War as God's Judgment,"[59] "War as Crucifixion,"[60] and, simply, "Is God in the War?"[61]

Healing the Hell of Hiroshima

With such theological themes and questions in mind, one cannot help but ask: Should the name "Trinity" apply only to the *testing* of the Bomb? Might "Trinity"—Father, Son, Holy Spirit; Creator, Redeemer, Sanctifier—also name the fiery explosions in Japan? After all, Christians confess that they believe in "God, the Father almighty, maker of heaven and earth." Richard

Rhodes entitled his classic historical study *The Making of the Atomic Bomb*, and Gabrielle Hecht refers to the Bomb as a "human creation." Are those who think theologically, at least those who are Christians, to say there is no connection whatsoever, even a skewed connection, between God's creative power, shared with human beings, and the "creativity" required to build the Bomb? After all, Lonergan thought that it was quite possible, sometimes with horrendous results, to disconnect "creativity" in history from sorely needed "healing" love.

What about the Son? Could we not say that the unspeakable suffering that was Hiroshima and Nagasaki was an extension of the suffering of Christ? Since we have mentioned Augustine, who wrote about time but also, in the *City of God* and elsewhere, about the fate of the Roman Empire, we might note that the film *Gladiator* begins with the Roman army poised to pacify the rebellious northern tribes. The Roman general, later to become a slave and gladiator, instructs his officers: "At my command, unleash hell." Could not those words have been spoken by the commander of the Enola Gay, as the plane approached its target? Does not the Christian creed say something about the crucified Christ descending into hell before he rose from the dead? Could not God have been, as Niebuhr suggests, "in the war" in that way? If the founder of Black Theology, James Cone, could write a book entitled *The Cross and the Lynching Tree*, linking the horrendous, unconscionable killing of blacks in the United States to the suffering and death of Christ, could not someone write a book entitled *Hiroshima as Hell*, the hell into which the Crucified Christ descended in order to save?

What of the Holy Spirit? The last chapter of Richard Rhodes's *History of the Atomic Bomb* is entitled "Tongues of Fire." It is a chapter filled with the most horrifying accounts, some by children, of human suffering, death, and grief. If, as H. Richard Niebuhr theologized, God, whom Christians believe can bring good out of evil, was "in the war," could it be that Hiroshima was also a twentieth-century Pentecost, when the Holy Spirit descended like tongues of fire, with people from diverse lands and languages each hearing the word of God in his or her own tongue? Could not the war, including Hiroshima as God's "judgment" and as "crucifixion," also be a new beginning?

If, as H. Richard Niebuhr's brother Reinhold insisted, the doctrine of original sin was empirically verifiable, maybe there is also empirical evidence that the Holy Spirit hovered over Hiroshima. Father Pedro Arrupe, SJ, was, as anyone who met him could attest, a man of great holiness and joy—a sign, the Bible would say, of the Holy Spirit. Years before his move to Rome to serve as Superior General of the Society of Jesus, he was a missionary living on the outskirts of Hiroshima, and he was there when the bomb fell. Trained as a physician before entering the Jesuits, he responded immediately, and for the rest of his life, to God's call to care, to accompany, and to heal in the "field hospital" that Pope Francis says the church should be.

Surely Arrupe was not and is not alone. One thinks of Mike Mansfield, who after years as Senate Majority Leader, where he opposed the Vietnam war early on, served with great distinction as ambassador to Japan. When during his tenure a U.S. Navy ship accidently sank a Japanese freighter with loss of life, Mansfield knew just what to do. He went to the Emperor and, with cameras rolling at his insistence, apologized with a below-the-waist bow. An international incident was defused.[62] Is it too much to suggest that this humble, deeply principled statesman was also apologizing for the hell that the United States and its allies had unleashed on Hiroshima and Nagasaki, to say

Figure 6.4. Hiroshima—atomic effects.
Photo by U.S. Government employee, in the public domain.

nothing of Tokyo and other population centers that felt the full deadly weight of conventional weapons? Mansfield no doubt knew what the culture asked of him because he had taught Asian history at the University of Montana, where a library now bears his name. But maybe it was also because, earlier still, after returning from the Marines without a high school diploma, he had learned about the human condition when he worked with the copper miners of Butte.

Hiroshima was a horrible, horrible time—made horrible by human beings who started with uranium mined in the Belgian Congo. From a Christian theological perspective, it was arguably also a time relative to God's time, that is, God's eternal now. It was relative to the Trinitarian God's creative, saving, and sanctifying presence, drawing good out of evil, the awful evil of war.

Since this is a book on ethics, even if it is mostly ethical prospecting, one might expect at this point clear assignations of blame for Hiroshima and other cruel acts of war, and the horrible times they brought and bring. But perhaps there should be reluctance even here. The blame seems to be spread so far. When it comes to war, it seems almost an accident if we are on the side of the angels, if there is such a side.[63] Maybe this is the sort of thing that Abraham Lincoln was trying to convey in his Second Inaugural Address, in which he depicted the Civil War as the self-inflicted punishment brought down upon the heads of the North as well as the South for the great sin of enslaving fellow human beings. Maybe Ulysses S. Grant reflected on these things when he retired to Galena, Illinois, with its lead mines and its rolling hills.

When one thinks of the Manhattan Project, that vast cooperative effort of modern science wedded to the waging of war, it seems the bomb was almost inevitable, beyond any one person's control. It is not unlike Lincoln's profound words, devoid of singular blame: "And then the war came." One might have said of Hiroshima: "And then the bomb fell." I say, "*almost* inevitable." Individual and communal human judgments, prudent or imprudent decisions, counted then and they count now, bending time in one direction or the other. Good judgments, prudent judgments, informed by memory and foresight and so much else are still required, when it comes to mining—as a beginning but also with its beneficial or destructive ends—and to endeavors of every kind. Even if we limit our discussion to the nuclear realm, momentous decisions face the human community today.

We might cite, for instance—to return for a moment to international law and its juris-prudence—consider the World Court's 1996 advisory opinion on the legality of the use or threat to use nuclear weapons.[64] Despite wide agreement with respect to many aspects of the question of legality, the Court could not quite bring itself to pronounce such use or threat to use these weapons illegal under all circumstances. In his remarkable dissent of over one hundred pages, Judge Weeramantry, the same Sri Lankan lawyer who thought so much about mining on Nauru, sharply disagreed.[65]

It would be possible to read Weeramantry's dissent in light of what Aquinas says about prudence—about such things as memory and foresight—for these are surely to be found there.

For instance, Weeramantry's *memoria*, recorded in his dissent, includes accounts of the profound suffering of war in general and Hiroshima in particular. Indeed, he uses some form of the word "suffering" about forty times.[66] He also lays out in much greater detail, and with greater *foresight* than had the Court itself, the devastation that a future nuclear exchange would bring. We might also note that while Hindu literature influenced Oppenheimer's views on war and the atomic bomb, in his dissent Weeramantry similarly draws on ancient Indian epics, the *Ramayana* and the *Mahabharatha*, but with different effect. The *Ramayana* includes a clear denunciation of a weapon, the use of which could "destroy the entire race of the enemy, including those who could not bear arms."[67] Arguably, Weeramantry's recourse to texts some three thousand years old was an instance of what Pieper called "true to being" memory, such that being and time, mining and megaweapons, are morally joined.

The Moral Challenge to Scientists and Technicians

Now, none of us is in quite the position of a Robert Oppenheimer in the New Mexico desert, testing the results of a massive project, or of a Judge Weeramantry in The Hague. Then again, maybe we are. Each of us, in smaller ways, may be called to test the results of our individual and communal thoughts and actions thus far. Each of us is a member of a world court, asking what kind of world and what kind of times lie ahead, and thus deciding now what should be done and what should be disallowed.

This is particularly true, but of course not only true, of the extended STEM community, which has such power to affect the future, to make for good times or for bad. In light not only of Hiroshima and Nagasaki, but also, say, the tsunami-caused Fukushima Daiichi disaster, STEM representatives especially may need to ask just how prudent their actions might be, or whether their magnificent creations have the power to heal and not destroy. When it comes to "nuclear things," we might inquire especially about the weal or woe of future generations. This is a concern that, in the context of uranium mining, takes on a troubling twist: the dangers associated with buried nuclear wastes stretch so far into the future, reaching thousands of years, that responsible people strain to figure out how best to warn far-off unknown future generations: "Don't dig here!"[68]

It may well be that, in terms of prudence, the nuclear power industry does reasonably well. It is not as though nuclear power companies and governing agencies have not considered the downsides and the enormous risks of what Eisenhower called "Atoms for Peace," or have learned nothing *(memoria)* from nuclear accidents. There are in place regulations and policies and practices meant to meet the challenges,[69] and, when it comes to nuclear safety, there are no "trade secrets," for a serious accident anywhere is an accident affecting all. Besides, in the face of climate change some argue that nuclear power must be at least one alternative to fossil fuels to meet energy demands.[70]

Then again, one might posit that, like many scientists and engineers, those involved with nuclearity have an intense desire to see how the world works, to discover new things, and to try them out. This desire to know, to test, to build, may indeed be good in itself. After all, especially in *Insight* Lonergan stresses in the "intellectual pattern of experience" a "pure and unrestricted desire to know," and we might extend this to knowing how things work or could be made to work. Michael Polanyi made a great deal of what he called "intellectual passions."[71]

The problem is, what if this "pure" desire or these passions mix with other desires, maybe also insatiable? Augustine's *libido dominandi,* the desire to dominate, for one; "the desire for profit," which Aquinas says, "knows no limit and tends to infinity,"[72] for another. Or, pure desires may get overmixed with other noble desires, such as the desire to serve one's country. Thus, Fritz Hamer gave us nitrogen-based fertilizers to feed a hungry world. But Haber was also unapologetically engaged in gas warfare, and for that he relied on his dictum: "During peace time a scientist serves humanity; in war, the Fatherland"[73]—a sentiment that might collide with a poet's bitter appraisal, informed by vivid memories of gas warfare, of "the old lie" told to school boys: "*Dulce et decorum est pro patria more.*"[74] With mixed sentiments and motives like these, it is no wonder that Lonergan could write of "the longer cycle of decline" with its lessons so hard to learn, or that Hans Jonas thought that we must be guided by a "heuristics of fear" as we engage and enact the future that is ours but not ours alone.[75] We might note here, too, the strong, arguably too strong, judgment of C. G. Weeramantry, whose views we have heard on other matters. With his deep concern for future generations and protection of the environment, in the aftermath of Fukushima he called for the abolition of nuclear reactors worldwide.[76]

Time and the Essence of Decision

Even as "big questions"—the grand scheme of things, the very meaning of time—await final answers, we cannot shirk our responsibility to make judgments and decisions in the here and now. We cannot give up on prudence, with its memory and its foresight and its caution, with its boldness tempered by an eagerness to learn from others, with its need to reason things out. What we decide will shape the future. Our decisions will, in part at least, define the times—and perhaps even determine what we mean by "time." But good moral judgment in the concrete, the stuff of prudence, is no easy matter, and is often less than crystal clear.

There is nothing like a crisis, perhaps, to bring this point home—a crisis such as that which was spread out over thirteen days in October 1962. Even a moment's reflection on such crises might leave us a little more circumspect, or humble, in our very necessary judgments about the thinking and acting of others, and even of ourselves. In his classic study of the Cuban missile crisis, *The Essence of Decision,* the political scientist Graham Allison argues that what transpired during those perilous days cannot be so easily stated, for it cannot be understood in only one way.[77] Most revealing, perhaps, is the source for the title of his book, a speech by John F. Kennedy, in which Kennedy remarked, "The essence of ultimate decision remains impenetrable to the observer—*often, indeed, to the decider himself*" (emphasis added).

Against the backdrop of obscurity of this kind, one is reminded of another Graham, Graham Greene. This Graham also wrote a book about Cuba—a semicomical book, entitled *Our Man in Havana*, about spying and operatives and fabricated information or "intel." More to the present point, however, is the ending to *The Heart of the Matter*—a dialogue between a Catholic priest and Mrs. Scobie, grappling with her husband's suicide, a most grievous sin in the eyes of the Church:

> [Mrs. Scobie says]: "At the end of this—horror. He must have known that he was damning himself.
>
> "Yes, [said Fr. Rank] he knew that all right. He never had trust in any mercy—except for other people."
>
> "It's no good praying" [said Mrs. Scobie].
>
> Father Rank clapped the cover of the diary to, and said furiously, "For goodness sake, Mrs. Scobie, don't imagine you—or I—know a thing about God's mercy."
>
> "The Church says."
>
> "I know the Church says. The Church knows all the rules. But it does not know what goes on in a single human heart."[78]

Mindful of decisions that in some way begin with mining but do not end there, moral decisions that can decide and define the times for one's children, one's children's children, and the planet itself, decisions that may even verge on the suicidal, perhaps this is a good place not to end but to pause: on a note not of optimism but of hope. For the Christian tradition, hope is a "theological virtue," given as a gift. It has to do with matters of ultimacy—of salvation or damnation—or, as Kennedy put it, with the essence of ultimate decision. It is a virtue that situates us between presumption and complacency, on the one hand, and despair and paralysis, on the other. It is within the ambit of hope that we may face the decisions of the day but not simply for the day.

The Doomsday Clock of the *Bulletin of the Atomic Scientists* creeps ever closer to midnight,[79] and for the sake of argument or meditation, a meditation on mining and more, we may assume that that clock also runs on African and on other cultures' time. If the "foresight" represented by that clock is anywhere near the mark, we live in not only interesting but also very dangerous times. If, as Aquinas taught, grace builds upon and perfects human nature and its capacities, then we will need to do what is humanly possible to grow in prudence: to better our memories, to learn from others, to think things through, to look ahead. But we will also need to call upon God's grace and love—a love which casts out the fear that, Aquinas says, can be a bad counselor. Pope Francis, who in his own way has been saying and doing much about these things, encouraging more dialogue between science and religion in the process, seems to agree with Father Rank who places mercy—God's mercy and our mercy toward one another—at the heart of the matter. Indeed, before he issued *Laudato si'*, he called for a year of mercy, for mercy appears to be the quality of God's time.

Everything may begin with mining, but not everything ends there. Will our decisions lead to, indeed constitute, better—morally better—times? Will, say, the seminomadic Tuareg of Niger be better off? Aware of the difficulties that face and sometimes engulf or overwhelm the human community, but aware, too, of God's eternal present and presence of love and justice and mercy without separation, we cannot know with anything more than what the Catholic tradition, at least, has called "moral certainty." We cannot know for sure. But, like the best prospectors of yesterday and today, we can hope that this is so and thus carry on.

INTERIM PROSPECTOR'S REPORT

When the mining-as-beginning is uranium mining, and the end-of-mining is a possible nuclear nightmare, the prospects for further ethical investigation are many. Here I will point to three veins of further inquiry to be explored.

First, in this chapter, we entered increasingly wider moral spheres: not only the vast continent of Africa in the nuclear age, but also the mysterious realms of being and time. The latter are philosophical- or theological-sounding realms, but they are not realms restricted to those with academic degrees in those fields. If "everything begins with mining," then anyone who thinks much about mining may sooner or later meet questions seemingly impractical at first: just what that "everything" that begins with mining is, from whence it came, and just where it might go. Or, to put it another way, one might simply ask, Why is there something—such as uranium—rather than nothing? Wouldn't nothing be so much simpler?

One finds this sort of deep questioning in great philosophical and theological works—given the controlling ideas for this chapter, we can let Heidegger's *Being and Time* stand for all the rest. But the reader or anyone else may find such questions arising from within one's own consciousness, just as mineral-rich sulfide vents bubble up from the ocean floor. Sooner or later, such questioning might be required whether one's initial focus is on mineral extraction, as has been the case for much of this book, or whether one's moral gaze is focused elsewhere: the taking of human life and care for the same; the relationship between human beings and other creatures; the questions of war and destruction that have occupied many, such as the authors of those ancient texts that spoke both to Robert Oppenheimer, who built a bomb, and to Judge Weeramantry, who argued against its use.

Second, while mining morality may, and arguably must, extend to questions of a most basic, let us say metaphysical, sort, still, the stress on the virtue of prudence is meant to bring attention to the particular case, the timely act, the best possible judgment in the here and now—a nexus joining past and future, *memoria* and foresight. Recall once more Shefa Siegel's comment: "There is a maddening futility about speaking of 'mining,' as if it were singular or coherent. It is like talking about 'Africa' or addressing the 'international community' in the fashion of humanitarians, as if it is all one big thing."[80] This chapter alone should dispel the notion that "Africa" is "one big thing." But what Siegel says about mining applies elsewhere—for instance, to education wherein moral formation is at stake and questions of an ethical nature abound. Education may have its common goals, even its "best practices," but that does not mean that all schools are alike, or that what proves to be the best practice here will necessarily be the best practice there. The example of education also highlights a dimension of ethics that is immensely challenging. If prudence has its "spheres," at what level, in what sphere should the prudent judgments affecting the lives of students be made: the home? the local public or charter school? the state? the Department of Education with its common standards? the education for profit sector? the dojo? the *madrasa*? the Hebrew theological school?

Such questions of spheres and levels, even hierarchies, and their interconnections will not go away. Prospecting for ethics can point to the problem, but not offer the solution, for that solution must be enacted, not just envisioned or proposed. The Law of the Sea, with its pivotal common heritage concept, worked out over many years, was one attempt to address the problem of sometimes cooperating sometimes conflicting spheres—in this case of states, of regions, of coastal waters, of the seabed, of the high seas. Attempts to corral the nuclear genie, released from its bottle by human beings and spread across the globe, is another. Multilateral treaties are just one problematic example of efforts to keep good relations alive and evil in check. The reader may have in mind other attempts to live together justly and in peace in a diverse and diversely leveled world, and thus contribute to the healing and creating in history that, it seems, is constantly required anew.

Third, when it comes to "nuclear things," I have put special stress on the roles and responsibilities of the STEM community, crossing borders of various kinds. But nuclearity is but only one STEM issue area; the promises but also the moral perils faced by such gifted people are spread very wide. No doubt "science deniers," prone to what Lonergan calls the general bias of common sense, impede "healing and creating in history," and humanists often remain too much in the scientific dark. But there is also a danger that, educationally and in other ways, those who live by science and technology and numbers just may lose sight of what is humane.

Films, along with other conveyers of meaning and value, can remind us of that. So, for instance, *The Insider* probed questions of conscience facing a chemist, the tobacco industry, and the corporate media, and an older movie about the end of a college education says more than perhaps it knew about the STEM community's considerable, if unintended, contributions to the ecological crisis we face. In *The Graduate* a young man trying to find himself is advised by one of his elders that his future is to be found in a single word: "Plastics." Sure enough, it is reasonable to assume that a sizable portion of the estimated "5 trillion pieces [of plastic] weighing over 250,000 tons . . . now floating in the world's oceans"[81] have settled there since that film was released in 1967, the same year Arvid Pardo, as we saw last chapter, urged the nations of the world to turn their full attention to the sea before it was too late.

But if filmmakers can feed the moral imagination extending to science and technology, then maybe we can feast for a moment on the fact that one and the same film actor could play not only the Roman general-become-gladiator who unleashed upon the enemies of the empire the fiery technological hell of his time, but also a conscience-stricken chemist, and a Nobel Prize-winning but tortured steward of a beautiful mind.[82] In other words, we have choices when it comes to roles and responsibilities. When it comes to STEM matters, the stakes for getting things right—how do we best use math and science?—are high not only on the screen. A few years after *The Graduate* appeared, at the University of Wisconsin, where graduates abound, four young men blew up Sterling Hall, where on three floors the Army Mathematics Research Center was housed. That was during the Vietnam War—a war that the Butte miner turned college professor and then statesman, Mike Mansfield, questioned early on. It was among the "great historical currents" that should lead the moral miner, of whatever community, political party, or educational bent or discipline to stop and to ask: "How ought we to live? Where have we been? How did we get to where we are? Where should we go from here?"

The great currents—or, recalling the Law of the Sea, the tides—"that shape the course human affairs" still ebb and flow. It is a constant challenge for each and all to decide when to go with the flow and when or how to try to divert or reverse that flow without doing more damage in the end. In the Sterling Hall bombing, more than the Army Mathematics Research Center was destroyed, and one researcher, a physicist with a young family, was killed.[83] A quiet, brilliant, unassuming man, not associated with the targeted research center, but probably attuned to Einstein's thoughts about time, or spacetime, he was caught in the cross fire between a horrible war and the violence meant to bring it to an end. He was interested in superconductivity and high-speed trains. In view of our next chapter's mining site, maybe he was also interested in speeding asteroids and the stars.

NOTES

1. John Mbiti discusses African notions of time, with its tendencies to stress the past over the future, in *New Testament Eschatology in an African Background: A Study of the Encounter between New Testament Theology and African Traditional Concepts* (New York and London: Oxford University Press, 1971).
2. For an English translation, see Placide Tempels, *Bantu Philosophy*, Présence africaine, Collection (Paris: Présence africaine, 1959).
3. Martin Heidegger, *Being and Time* (New York: Harper and Row, 1927; 1962).
4. Gabrielle Hecht, *Being Nuclear: Africans and the Global Uranium Trade* (Cambridge, MA: The MIT Press, 2012).
5. For present purposes, "ontology" may be defined simply as the study of being.
6. Lonergan defines a "thing" as a "unity-identity-whole." "Things" are not to be confused with "bodies." *Insight*, 275–79. Hecht's references to "things" would seem in line with Lonergan's definition.
7. The clock remains perilously close to midnight due to threats involving, among other things, nuclear weapons proliferation and insecurity, climate change, a resurgent nationalism, and the rise of autocracies. Meanwhile, threats to a shared commitment to truth and facticity create a "a new abnormal" that makes it increasingly difficult to address big problems. See "It is *still* 2 minutes to midnight," 2019 Doomsday Clock

Statement Science and Security Board, *Bulletin of the Atomic Scientists*, https://thebulletin.org/doomsday-clock/current-time/.

8. See, for example, David Barsto, William J. Broad, and Jeff Gerth, "The Nuclear Card: The Aluminum Tube Story—A Special Report; How White House Embraced Suspect Iraq Arms Intelligence," *The New York Times,* October 3, 2004.

9. Hecht, *Being Nuclear*, 5.

10. Ibid., 6.

11. Ibid., 8.

12. Ibid., 13.

13. Ibid.

14. Ibid., 3.

15. Ibid., 15.

16. Doran, "System and History," 652.

17. Lonergan, *Insight* (emphasis added), 380.

18. Lonergan, *Method*, 38, 66.

19. Bernard J. F. Lonergan, "Natural Right and Historical Mindedness," in *A Third Collection: Papers by Bernard Lonergan*, SJ, ed. Frederick E. Crowe, SJ (Mahwah, NJ: Paulist Press/London: Geoffrey Chapman, 1985), 170–71.

20. Ibid., 170.

21. Lonergan, *Method,* 76–81.

22. Lonergan, "Natural Right," 175.

23. Ibid., 176.

24. Hecht, *Being Nuclear*, 46.

25. See, for example, MAC: Mines and Communities, "Mining, Communities, and Sustainable Development," http://www.minesandcommunities.org/article.php?a=9925; and Vatican Radio, "South African bishops issue statement on mining industry," at http://en.radiovaticana.va/news/2015/08/20/south_african_bishops_issues_statement_on_mining_industry/1166273.

26. Douglas Johnston and Cynthia Sampson, eds., *Religion the Missing Dimension of Statecraft* (New York: Oxford University Press, 1994).

27. Nafziger, "Functions of Religion in the International Legal System."

28. Hecht, *Being Nuclear*, 289.

29. See, for example, Joseph Ogbonnaya, *Lonergan, Social Transformation,* and *Sustainable Development*, foreword by Robert M. Doran (Eugene, OR: Pickwick Publications, n.d.?); "Theology, Culture and Sustainable Development in Africa," ACUHIAM *Journal* 3 (2012): 1–30; and "Religion and Sustainable Development in Africa: The Case of Nigeria," *International Journal of African Catholicism* 3/2 (2012): 1–22.

30. On realms of meaning, including the transcendent realm, see *Method*, 81–85.

31. Hecht, *Being Nuclear*, 8 (emphasis added).

32. Ibid., 6.

33. Ibid., 106.

34. Ibid., 97–100; 143; 149–53.

35. Let us not forget that an early "nuclear" U.S. president, Harry S. Truman, need not have used his power to order the dropping of the Bomb. To recall Malone's reflection on Butte: "It need not have been that way." But he did use his power in this way.
36. Hecht, *Being Nuclear,* 115.
37. Ibid., 115–16.
38. Ibid., 323.
39. Ibid., 324.
40. Daniel Flynn and Geert De Clercq, "Areva and Niger's uranium fight," *Reuters*, February 5, 2014, https://www.reuters.com/article/niger-areva/special-report-areva-and-nigers-uranium-fight-idUSL3N0L44UW20140205.
41. Ibid.
42. World Information Service on Energy (WISE), "New Uranium Projects—Niger," http://www.wise-uranium.org/upne.html. WISE is highly critical of nuclear power and looks toward a nuclear-alternative world.
43. A few of the websites listed are invalid.
44. Armin Rosen, "One Uranium Mine in Niger Says a Lot about China's Huge Nuclear-Power Ambitions," *Business Insider*, October 24, 2015, https://internationalreportingproject.org/stories/view/one-uranium-mine-in-niger-says-a-lot-about-chinas-huge-nuclear-power-ambiti.
45. Ibid.
46. Saint Augustine, *Confessions,* Bk XI, viii.
47. Aquinas, *ST* II–II 4, 6.
48. Pieper, *The Cardinal Virtues*, 15 (emphasis added).
49. George, "Angelism and Its Devilish Effects on Education."
50. John D. Norton, "Spacetime and the Relativity of Simultaneity," http://www.pitt.edu/~jdnorton/teaching/HPS_0410/chapters_2017_Jan_1/spacetime_rel_sim/index.html.
51. For a visual illustration, see MyEarbot, "Simultaneity–Albert Einstein and the Theory of Relativity," May 5, 2007, https://www.youtube.com/watch?v=wteiuxyqtoM.
52. Lonergan, *Method*, 81–85.
53. Aquinas, *ST* II–II 47, 16, "Whether Prudence Can Be Lost Through Forgetfulness?"
54. Here, I am following James A. Hijiya, "The *Gita* of J. Robert Oppenheimer," *Proceedings of the American Philosophical Society* 144/2 (June 200): 123–67.
55. Hijiya, "*Gita,*" 163. Hijiya is referring to Marjorie Bell Chambers, "Technically Sweet Los Alamos: The Development of a Federally Sponsored Scientific Community" (Ph.D. diss., University of New Mexico, 1974), 142.
56. Hijiya, "*Gita,*" 131, n. 51.
57. John C. Ford, SJ, "The Morality of Obliteration Bombing," *Theological Studies* 5 (September 1944): 261–73; 308–9.
58. Joshua J. McElwee, "Landmark Vatican Conference Rejects Just War Theory, Asks for Encyclical on Nonviolence," *National Catholic Reporter*, April 16, 2017, https://www.ncronline.org/news/vatican/landmark-vatican-conference-rejects-just-war-theory-asks-encyclical-nonviolence.

59. *The Christian Century*, May 3, 1942.

60. Ibid., April 28, 1943.

61. Ibid., August 5, 1942 (an exchange with Virgil Aldrich).

62. Eulogy by Charles Ferris, October 10, 2001, http://www.mansfieldfdn.org/backup/tribute/tributes.htm.

63. When I was a teenager, I once overheard my younger sister talking with her friend, Alice Barth, as they watched TV. There was some sort of war movie on and Alice asked, "What was your father in the war? A German, or what?" I thought it was a funny thing to say. Looking back, I see how unknowingly profound was the question of this young girl, who bore the last name of the great Karl Barth, a theologian who, in the shadow of World War I, had grave doubts about the capacity of human beings to do—or even to know—the right thing, the prudent thing, apart from God's revealed guidance and grace.

64. International Court of Justice, "Advisory Opinion on the Threat or Use of Nuclear Weapons," 1996, http://www.icj-cij.org/en/case/95.

65. "Dissenting Opinion of Judge Weeramantry," http://www.icj-cij.org/files/case-related/95/095-19960708-ADV-01-12-EN.pdf.

66. By contrast, the same word count in the American Catholic Bishops' well-known 1983 peace pastoral, *The Challenge of Peace*, ends at five.

67. Cited in "Dissenting Opinion of Judge Weeramantry," III, 2, p. 429.

68. Scott Beauchamp, "How to Send a Message 1,000 Years to the Future," *The Atlantic*, February 2015, https://www.theatlantic.com/technology/archive/2015/02/how-to-send-a-message-1000-years-to-the-future/385720/.

69. See, for example, World Nuclear Association, "Safety of Nuclear Power Reactors (Updated May 2018)," http://www.world-nuclear.org/information-library/safety-and-security/safety-of-plants/safety-of-nuclear-power-reactors.aspx; United States Nuclear Regulatory Commission, "NRC Regulatory Guides," https://www.nrc.gov/reading-rm/doc-collections/reg-guides/; and *Regulatory Control of Nuclear Power Plants: Part A (Textbook)*, Training Course Series No. 15 (Vienna: International Atomic Energy Agency, 2002).

70. See Richard Rhodes (author of *The Making of the Atomic Bomb*), "A Sensible Climate Change Solution, Borrowed from Sweden," review of Joshua S. Goldstein and Staffan A. Qvist, *A Bright Future: How Some Countries Have Solved Climate Change and the Rest Can Follow*, in *New York Times: Book Review,* February 9, 2019, https://www.nytimes.com/2019/02/05/books/review/bright-future-joshua-s-goldstein-staffan-a-qvist.html.

71. Polanyi, *Personal Knowledge,* 133–202.

72. Aquinas, *ST* II–II, 77, 4.

73. For one overview of Haber and his work, see István Furó, "Fritz Haber—A 'Dr. Evil' Who Has Accomplished Much Good," KTH Royal Institute of Technology (Stockholm), https://www.kth.se/en/che/archive/arkiv/haber-1.83967.

74. This is the closing line of Wilfred Owens's World War I poem, "*Dulce et Decorum Est*." The Latin phrase, the poem's note explains, is taken from the Roman poet Horace: "It is sweet and fitting to die for one's country." See Poetry Foundation, https://www.poetryfoundation.org/poems/46560/dulce-et-decorum-est.

75. Hans Jonas, *The Imperative of Responsibility: In Search of an Ethics for the Technological Age* (Chicago: University of Chicago Press, 1984), 26–27, 202–3.

76. C. G. Weeramantry, "Nuclear Reactor Catastrophe in Japan: An Open Letter to the World's Environmental Ministers," Weeramantry International Centre Peace Education and Research, March 14, 2001, https://ratical.org/radiation/radioactivity/C.G.Weeramantry.html.

77. Graham Allison, *The Essence of Decision: Explaining the Cuban Missile Crisis* (Boston: Little, Brown and Company, 1971).

78. Graham Greene, *The Heart of the Matter* (New York: Penguin Books, 1971), 271–72.

79. *Bulletin of the Atomic Scientists*, Doomsday Clock, at https://thebulletin.org/doomsday-clock/.

80. Siegel, "The Missing Ethics of Mining."

81. This is the estimate recorded by the organization Parley for the Oceans. See http://www.parley.tv/oceanplastic/#parley-air-strategy-1.

82. The actor was Russell Crowe, who played the lead in *Gladiator, The Insider*, and *A Beautiful Mind.*

83. Deborah Zifland and Ron Seely, "Sterling Hall Bombing: 40 Years Later, Family Members Celebrate Physicist's Life," *Wisconsin State Journal*, August 17, 2010, at https://madison.com/wsj/news/local/education/university/sterling-hall-bombing-years-later-family-members-celebrate-physicist-s/article_ba113d78-a980-11df-9db0-001cc4c03286.html.

Chapter Seven

Asteroid Mining: Ethics for Aliens or for Us?

In 2014 Dr. Brian May, an astrophysicist better known as the lead guitarist for the rock group Queen, and Grigorij Richters, director of a then-recent fictional film about an asteroid strike on London, initiated a global movement to increase awareness of the danger that asteroids posed to Planet Earth. Together with two others, they began pushing for recognition of what they called Asteroid Day.[1] Joining forces with B612, an American-based nonprofit organization created to promote early detection of dangerous asteroids, they attracted the interest of well-known scientists and astronauts and produced the 100x Declaration,[2] the aim of which was to speed up dramatically the detection of asteroid threats to the planet. Some forty thousand concerned citizens from around the globe would eventually add their names to the declaration.

By 2016, the group had garnered sufficient support for its cause that the United Nations General Assembly officially declared June 30 of each year "Asteroid Day."[3] In its statement about this UN action, the four Asteroid Day founders explained: "We founded the annual event to raise awareness of the asteroid threat and opportunity to unite the human species behind a simple goal: Protect our planet from asteroid impacts. It is the only natural disaster we know how to prevent if we work together towards a global solution. We are all crew members of Spaceship Earth. We hope you will join us."[4]

Now, attention to Asteroid Day and the efforts and organization behind it may seem an odd way to introduce a chapter on asteroid mining. For one thing, the high-profile and less-well-known signatories of the 100x Declaration do not seem particularly interested in the asteroid mining to which others are so drawn. On the contrary, the whole purpose of this organized effort, reaching to the level of the UN General Assembly, has to do with protecting the planet from a potentially devastating event. In fact, Asteroid Day seems to portray asteroids as the mortal enemy of Spaceship Earth—the group's clear intent to identify and deter only the dangerous ones notwithstanding. For the Asteroid Day cause, at least some asteroids seem to have a bad name.

Yet, this statement may indeed be a fitting place to begin a discussion of mining morality, with asteroids as a focal point—or, better, as focal *points*, since asteroids number in the millions. Note the phrase chosen by the founders: "awareness of the asteroid threat and opportunity to unite the human species." "Threat and opportunity"—does this not have a "mining morality" ring to it? "Opportunity to unite"—is this so different from something Pope Francis might have said about another threat at once global and local, namely, ecological devastation and climate change?[5] Is the phrase "opportunity to unite the human species" not in keeping with the "emerging religious consciousness" discussed by Lonergan and so closely tied to an awareness of a common humanity? Is it so different from the vision of "one world" that animated the work of C. G. Weeramantry when he turned his attention to the Nauru case (chapter 4), or when he wrote on the nuclear weapons threat (chapter 6), which, like everything else, begins with mining?

In short, this statement does offer some guidance for discussing asteroid mining. Keeping in mind that we are prospecting for ethics and not discussing asteroid mining in all its complexity, here I propose to think about asteroids first under the heading of "opportunity," especially opportunity related to mining, and then, to balance Spaceship Earth in its moral trajectory, under the heading of "threat." By threat is meant not so much the physical impact of an asteroid crashing into our planet, but rather threat in metaphorical senses that involve the moral life. Someone with Hegelian leanings might view this approach in the familiar terms of "thesis" (opportunity) and "antithesis" (threat) awaiting a "synthesis" of some kind. Recourse to Hegel may or may not be fitting. But in the latter part of the chapter I return to our prospecting tools, with a special emphasis on international space law, to emphasize that, when it comes to ethical prospecting with asteroids as a focus, there is no such thing as an easy spaceflight into all good or all bad. The prospects for a moral meeting place between opportunity and threat, some moral synthesis if you will, must be sought if not found once and for all.

ASTEROIDS AS OPPORTUNITY

Gabrielle Hecht began her study of African uranium mining and trade (chapter 6) with an insightful historical review of "the Atomic Age," especially as it involved uranium and Africa—a review I did not attempt to capture in full. Ideally, the topic of asteroid mining would be similarly prefaced with an analysis of "the Space Age," beginning, let's say, with Sputnik—the one Russian word that many Americans in the late 1950s knew.[6] But the Space Age is a topic so vast I can hardly do it justice in this chapter, or likely anywhere else. Here, I wish simply to highlight some more optimistic or opportunistic[7] aspects of the Space Age that are readily apparent before we turn to the more restricted topic of asteroid mining.

Rocket Boys and Other Optimists

One should not make too much of a single film and what it has to say. But if an inspiring, feel-good movie such as *October Sky* cannot tell us everything important about our topic, that does not mean it cannot tell us anything important at all. So, to recall from our earlier reference to this historically based if also Hollywood-embellished film,[8] Homer Hickam and his schoolmates are growing up in Coalwood, West Virginia. Surely, coal country has its virtues and its honor, and these are on full, rugged display in the person of Homer Senior (Homer's father's name in real life if not in the film). But a young boy's future in the mines has its limits. Ultimately, Homer's father cannot compete with the inspiration of rocketing pioneer Werner von Braun, who stirs the boy's admiration, or of his high school science teacher who fills his head with thoughts of the beyond. Homer and his friends, obsessed with rockets and outer space, overcome the requisite adversity of inspirational stories and win the national science fair. Homer, eventually ends up with NASA, with the coal mines presumably left behind.

While this is mostly the Rocket Boys' story, it is worth pausing on two background characters just mentioned. Von Braun (1914–1977), along with many of his scientist-colleagues, was brought from Germany to the United States after the Second World War. Once in the United States, he became a leader in military rocketry and U.S. space programs, including the Apollo missions. He also popularized the achievements of the Space Age and was a lifelong advocate for missions to Mars. Somehow, in all of this, the fact that he had once belonged to the Nazi Party and had made rockets meant for war faded from view.[9] Those perceived as truly evil might be rounded up and tried for their horrendous Nazi-sponsored crimes. But others escaped punishment of any significant degree. In the case of von Braun, it appears that embracing the Space Age for the right country now—von Braun gladly accepted U.S. citizenship—could cover a multitude of possible sins less grave than, say, those associated with Eichmann in Jerusalem.[10] With the right commitments and national allegiances, the Space Age apparently had its powers to redeem.

Then there is Miss Riley, the boys' science teacher. Given the fact that the central characters—father and son and the other Rocket Boys—are male, *Oc-*

tober Sky would seem hardly to rate as a feminist film. But that's not entirely so. At a key point in the film, Homer's mother stands up to her husband for not supporting their son at a moment of crisis. In a less dramatic but no less significant way, Miss Riley effects a change in the boys' minds as well as their hearts, turning their eyes upward toward the October sky and downward to the pages of books on science and rocketry. When even today the ratio of young women to men entering the STEM fields is not encouraging, the potential of women to be scientifically minded mentors and intellectual models is arguably a subtheme of the film.[11] So, from that point of view, this movie about mining and the Space Age brims with moral prodding and even optimism. But that is not all. Miss Riley is suffering from Hodgkin's lymphoma. So, it may not be too much to suggest that the film raises the question of whether escape not only from the coal mines of West Virginia and its health and safety hazards, but from the earth's bounds altogether, might offer an escape from very serious illness and even death. Indeed, no less an intellectual icon than the late Stephen Hawking envisioned space as the salvation of a dying planet and an extinction-bound human race.[12]

In all such stories there are crises to be met and overcome. When one of the boys' rockets apparently goes astray and starts a fire, the boys are held responsible and their launches come to a halt. But with the help of a book from Miss Riley, Homer calculates the trajectory of their own rocket and concludes that they are not at fault. Sure enough, the culprit is a flare from a nearby airfield. So the message is seemingly clear: Not unlike Eisenhower's "Atoms for Peace," the rockets of this new Space Age generation are aimed only at the good. The young men's rockets are pointed at and beyond the higher reaches of humanity, and away from destruction and despair.

At least, that's the sort of happy thought from this film that one might take away. Lest anyone doubt that the enthusiasm of the Space Age remains today, recall the excitement when, in February 2018, Elon Musk, the fabulously wealthy founder of SpaceX, launched into space one of his Tesla Roadsters aboard Falcon Heavy, the most powerful rocket in the world—even if David Bowie's "Major Tom," looping on the car's radio, offered a subtle reminder that not all space shots have endings that are happy or even clear.[13] NASA, it might be noted, began tracking the roadster to make sure that it would not be confused with an asteroid come too near.[14]

Asteroids and Cosmology

The context for asteroid mining is surely greater than October Sky—or maybe any visible sky, let's say the Big Sky over Butte, Montana. In terms of mining morality, even the move from coal country to near-Earth asteroids (prime candidates for mining in space) seems too small. After all, the very designation "near-Earth" implies that there is much beyond, as indeed there is. There are the "millions" and "billions" and "trillions" of things out there to which Carl Sagan referred in his popular 1970s television show *Cosmos*. There was and is "a galaxy far, far away" in a filmmaker's fertile imagination and on theater and TV screens. There was and is the imaginative, and often moral, journey of the Starship Enterprise, with countless television and, later, film-watching Trekkies hopping on board with the nationally, ethnically, racially, and even specially diverse starship crew. For those who want less imagination and more that meets the eye, if quite indirectly, there are the awe-inspiring images of deep space returned from the Hubble Telescope. The name Hubble may stand for all of those who, from ancient times until today, have gazed up at the stars—all who, looking up, have wondered and tried to understand, even if, like the early Greek philosopher Thales, they have risked momentarily losing sight of reality at their feet.[15]

If these examples favor secular or only implicitly religious events and themes, there are always Biblical references to the stars. Their number was to be the measure of God's promise to Abraham (Genesis 22:17), and one special star was there to guide the journey of the Magi (Matthew 2:1–12), those noble yet humble subjects of medieval paintings and more recent poetry.[16] Skipping past biblical times—but not really, since the Bible was always there to inspire—one recalls the example of St. Ignatius of Loyola, who founded the Society of Jesus because he found God in all things, but certainly in the stars he gazed upon from the rooftops of Rome. This kind of star-gazing was later pursued by Jesuit astronomers in China and India,[17] and is carried forward today by Guy Consolmagno, the Jesuit brother who directs the Vatican Observatory.[18]

From that same Vatican, Pope Francis in *Laudato si'* quotes the Psalmist: "Praise him, sun and moon, praise him, all you shining stars! Praise him, you highest heavens, and you waters above the heavens! Let them praise the name of the Lord, for he commanded and they were created" (Ps 148:3–5). If, as Aristotle insisted in the very first line of his *Metaphysics*, all human beings desire to know, it is not surprising if star-gazing leads one to wonder and to question, compelling one science writer to posit that immersion into modern physics and astrophysics may be paramount to "Reading the Mind of God."[19] On this vast topic of astronomy and cosmology in relation to questions of a religious or theological sort, I have at this point little more to say. I simply stress, as I did in chapter 6 with some references to being and time, or spacetime, that prospecting for ethics may expose a profoundly rich vein of thought and desire beyond the temporally and spatially immediate, a rich vein of human inquiry that should not be suppressed or obscured.

Such suppression or obscurantism is always a risk. In urban settings, for instance, star-gazing is not so assured. Just as the Jesuit poet Gerard Manley Hopkins observed that feet, "being shod," have lost touch with the earth,[20] it is all too easy to forget that the stars and the blackness beyond are always there. It is no wonder that Sedona, Arizona, has a city ordinance meant to curb light pollution. Nor should it be a surprise that a total eclipse of Earth's own star in the summer of 2017 seemingly tapped Americans' and others' deepest yearning for something beyond this planet and the endless news cycles that threaten to depress further an already dour and divided collective soul.

Asteroid Mining 101

Despite the premise of an old TV show, *Lost in Space,* it may be good to get lost in space and in the stars, if it means forgetting oneself to find oneself. But now it is time to be more focused, to return to Earth, or at least near-Earth, and turn more directly to the topic of asteroid mining and to the sense of awe and excitement it can bring. In this regard, the subtitle of John S. Lewis's *Asteroid Mining 101*, is instructive: *Wealth for the New Space Economy*.[21] Wealth and newness—two optimistic themes, two possible correctives to the old ways of Earth and its deep pockets of poverty and want. Or, at least that is one way to read this fine primer on the topic of this chapter.

The book is remarkable in several ways. For one thing, the range and amount of information it provides might pose a challenge to some readers. The "101" designation notwithstanding, this is a demanding book, with forays into astronomy, physics, geology, engineering, robotics, and other STEM areas that are at times quite detailed. Yet, this very challenge may be construed in another, more optimistic way. *Asteroid Mining 101* reminds one that there are in fact people who *do* understand these things and are learning more all the time, people who know a great deal about asteroids and their location—the asteroid belt, certainly, but also nearer to earth. They have scouted out various kinds of asteroids and what they have that earthlings and space travelers might want or need: not only valuable metals such as platinum, but also water, which, once broken down, can provide spaceship fuel that otherwise would need to be brought from earth. The abundant water could also provide hydration as well as badly needed protection from radiation for humans in space.

There are many such aspects of *Asteroid Mining 101*—and no doubt related works—that deserve discussion. Here, I would focus on three. First is a clear awareness that mining in space is not quite like mining on earth. For the most part, asteroid miners would not be people, at least not directly on the scene, but rather machines—closer, it would seem, to deep seabed min-

Figure 7.1. Four largest asteroids.
Photo courtesy of NASA.

ing than to the extraction of copper from the mines of Butte or Chuquicamata in the days of Anaconda, or of uranium unearthed in South Africa or Niger, where mine workers are at risk. There are also the physical factors that alter one's earthbound notion of speed and its effects—after all, the mining would be undertaken on asteroids speeding along at thousands of miles per hour. Very attractive from the entrepreneurial miner's point of view, for astronomical and geological reasons that Lewis explains, unlike the earth with its troublesome layers covering over the target ores, asteroid ore lies close to the surface, with levels of purity that can surpass the best ratios of ore to other materials found on earth. Conceivably, platinum retrieved from a single asteroid could equal our earthly reserves.

Second, Lewis's account of asteroid mining directs the mind not only to mining in space but to living there as well. These space communities would be sustained in large part by processes that, like everything else, begin with mining, but move beyond it with such activities as in situ 3-D printing of useful products. If, on earth, colonization has all too often meant exploiting the resources of one country only to ship those resources elsewhere so that they might be turned into marketable products that are then sold at inflated prices to the country of origin, asteroid mining envisions communities sustained by space mining and manufacturing, not back on earth but there in space. All the science fiction about Earthlings' life in space may not be fiction for long. With asteroid mining in the offing, the International Space Station may be but one small chapter of a new story about realms beyond our earthly home.

This is not to say, of course, that nothing will be returned to earth. This leads to a third, and perhaps the key, point of discussion: the near unbridled optimism about the wealth to be gained from asteroid mining. In his preface to *Asteroid Mining* 101, Rick N. Tumlinson, cofounder of the Space Frontier Foundation, asks the reader to

> Think about it. Real companies with staffs of talented engineers, scientists and businesspeople, funded in part by very smart and in some cases incredibly wealthy people who are themselves very successful business people, who want to send machines and possibly people to fly millions of miles into space and 'dig up' the rocks floating up there to make even more money.[22]

Perhaps the most widely recognized voice of space science today, Neil DeGrasse Tyson, affirmed this sentiment when he speculated in 2015 that space ventures could bring the first trillionaire.[23]

DeGrasse Tyson's vision, shared by others, might be a stretch. Still, *Asteroid Mining 101: Wealth for the New Space Economy* was, after all, published by Deep Space Industries, the very sort of enterprise Tumlinson has in mind. It is worth pausing to stress further the kind of vision that grounds his strong endorsement of Lewis's *Asteroid Mining 101.* The Credo for Tumlinson's Space Frontier Foundation reads:

> The Space Frontier Foundation is an organization of people dedicated to opening the Space Frontier to human settlement as rapidly as possible.
>
> Our goals include protecting the Earth's fragile biosphere and creating a freer and more prosperous life for each generation by using the unlimited energy and material resources of space.
>
> Our purpose is to unleash the power of free enterprise and lead a united humanity permanently into the Solar System.[24]

The foundation's further description of Who We Are reads in part:

> The Space Frontier Foundation is transforming the space industry into a dynamic and inclusive frontier open to free enterprise. We are determined to convert the image held by many young people that the future will be worse than the present, and we reject the idea that the world's greatest moments are in its past.
>
> Founded in 1988, the Space Frontier Foundation is an organization committed to realizing the vision of a greatly expanded and permanent human presence in space. Space alone offers the resources necessary to ensure the survival and prosperity of our species for numerous generations to come. To realize this vision, the Foundation is fundamentally transforming the conception of space into a widely accessible frontier, ripe with opportunity.

In short, the Space Frontier Foundation exemplifies the sort of transformative optimism, if we may call it that, that propels initiatives on asteroid mining by such start-up enterprises as Deep Space Industries, or DSI, the website of which at one time announced that they were "Opening Deep Space for Business." Notably, Tumlinson was once DSI board chairman, and John S. Lewis was identified as the company's chief scientist. Perhaps they may be viewed as chief optimists as well.

But if optimism is the operative word, it is optimism in flux if not descent. References to Deep Space Industries are now in the past tense. In early 2019, DSI was acquired by Bradford Space, "a U.S.-owned space systems manufacturer with locations in the Netherlands and Sweden."[25] There is continuity and discontinuity in the move. DSI is now Bradford Space, Inc., or BSI, to keep the continuity, but its focus is no longer so clearly on asteroid mining. In two respects, Deep Space Industries is not alone. A competitor entrepreneurial group with early eyes on space and its opportunities has been Planetary Resources.[26] This company, supported by founding entrepreneurs such as Sir

Figure 7.2. Arm prototype.
Photo courtesy of NASA.

Richard Branson and Google founder Larry Paige, emphasizes exploratory missions to advance asteroid mining. Headquartered in the high-technology-rich Seattle area, Planetary Resources sees asteroid mining as the very key to our future expansion in space. In fact, their website suggested that, true to their name, they are "redefining natural resources." It is no wonder. As they remind visitors to their website, there are some sixteen thousand near-Earth asteroids "rich in resources" and "two trillion tonnes of water available for life support and fuel in space." Furthermore, the kind of asteroid exploration and eventual mining they envision promises a "95 percent reduction in space exploration cost."

There are surely other aspects of this company that could be targeted for discussion. Here, I would mention three. First, since I have repeatedly returned to the notion of prospecting rather than mining, it is remarkable how much emphasis Planetary Resources gives to this preliminary work, taking special pride in the probes developed to detect water and other resources on target asteroids. Second, while it may be the case that Planetary Resources wishes to redefine "natural resources," thus emphasizing the conceptual, physical, and practical distances between Earth and space, it is striking that, on one of their webpages, they discuss meeting with those who mine for gold some five thousand feet beneath the earth's surface to learn about shared or similar challenges facing both asteroid and deep-earth miners.[27] Such meetings suggest a larger point. In this chapter we want to stress mining in space. But as the people at Planetary Resources apparently understand well, this cannot mean leaving behind all the lessons and laws, physical and other, typical of Earth.

Third, it is noteworthy that one of Planetary Resources' shareholders is the Grand-Duchy of Luxembourg. According to Étienne Schneider, Deputy Prime Minister and Minister of the Economy, this partnership demonstrates Luxembourg's "strong commitment to support the national space sector by attracting innovative activities in space resource utilization and other related areas."[28] Now, it might seem a little odd for such a small country rather than, say, France or Germany or China, to be so invested in asteroid mining. But just as Liberia once found it in its interest to encourage so many ocean-going vessels to sail under its flag, so, too, a very small country might see its future in the skies above.

But it is difficult to know whether this optimism, or the even the paragraphs above, are any longer current. Much like DSI become BSI, Planetary Resources has been acquired by another company, this time a blockchain firm. ConsenSys, Inc., which uses its software platforms to engage in crypto-currency and other ventures, apparently sees Planetary Resources' space technology fitting into its own future.[29] There is no speculation here as to just where these companies and others like them are headed, and with them the prospects of mining asteroids any time soon. For the moment, asteroid mining seems to be coming "down to earth."[30] But it might be suggested that slowing down might not be such a bad thing. For we want to consider that human interaction with asteroids speeding through space may include dangers that counsel space entrepreneurs to go slow.

Space Age Learning

But before turning to possible asteroid-related threats, we want to stress that the optimism of the Space Age, at least in the late 1950s and the 1960s, had much to do with education. Books and classes and science fairs and the hands-on learning of model rocketry were integral to the Rocket Boys' lives. The mines of Coalwood no doubt had lessons to impart, but they could not teach Homer Hickam everything he wanted to know about escaping the bounds of earth. So on his way to NASA and other ventures (including a tour in Vietnam and a life as writer), Homer attended Virginia Polytechnic Institute. Today, a Rocket Boy or Girl with eyes set on space, and especially on asteroids and what they have to offer, might enroll in the Massachusetts Institute of Technology, where freshmen, with a little help from their mentors, engage in cooperative-learning and problem solving to offer a fine overview of asteroid mining and its issues—technical, economic, legal, and political.[31] Or, maybe a latter-day Homer Hickam will find his or her way to the STEM professors in the Colorado School of Mines, where they have initiated the first full program in space mining.[32] Located in Golden, Colorado, the home of Coors Beer, this campus might be just the place to enter the gold rush into space. In any event, when it comes to asteroid mining and other mining as well, it seems that education and its "can do" problem-solving attitude can add to the optimism that all will be well.

ASTEROIDS AS THREAT

If a movie like *October Sky* can suggest that space is our future, maybe even our salvation, there are several films to remind us that space is not without its perils, and that asteroids pose a special threat. By their titles alone, two films released in 1998—the same year that Hickam's *Rocket Boys* was published—get right to the point. *Armageddon*, bad science and all, suggests a final battle with religious overtones. It is a band of misfits, some with criminal records, who save the day and the world by planting a nuclear bomb (with uranium from Niger?) on an in-bound asteroid. *Armageddon* recalls a theme at least as old as the 1970s *Dirty Dozen,* when the enemy to be thwarted by a group of scoundrels was not an asteroid headed towards Earth, but rather mere malicious Earthlings, in this case the Nazis—the Nazis of Werner von Braun's Germany in his earlier years, when many subscribed at least for a time to an ideology that, it seems today, simply will not die.

The other 1998 release was *Deep Impact.* The double-entendre is simple enough: Were a giant asteroid, or, in this case a comet—basically an asteroid composed mostly of ice rather than metals and rocky material—to strike the earth, its destructive effects would be immense. But great, too, is the impact that the impending event would have on the lives of individuals and of families, of whole nations and of friends. The film also raises the not so subtle question of who will escape doom by being among the chosen allowed to enter caves designed to survive the ordeal. Only these elected few will be saved. The others, to recall the title of a popular Christian book and film series, will be left behind.

Other asteroid films carry other plots and themes. Maybe the asteroid cataclysm will be due to human error, such as an errant rocket flying into and disturbing the asteroid belt, with a flock of asteroids heading toward earth as a result (*The Day the Sky Exploded*, 1958). Maybe moving the earth off its axis will save the planet from certain death (*Asteroid v. Earth,* 2014). Or, maybe an inbound asteroid can simply help you to know who you want to be with until the end and at the end (*Seeking a Friend for the End of the World*, 2012). While it may be cheating to cite a film in which the threatening body is not an asteroid but rather a newly discovered rogue planet—but not really cheating, since large asteroids are "planetoids" by another name—the critically acclaimed *Melancholia* (2011) brings into alignment deep personal depression and doom of a larger kind, with no last-minute heroics or narrow escape in the final scene. There is something to be said for unhappy endings to arouse from their slumber those who want simply to be entertained.

Space Ethics and Alienation

Sure enough, asteroid movies may simply counter boredom, but even the bad ones might make us think. I do not want to downplay the threat of an asteroid crashing into the planet. The founders of Asteroid Day and all their followers do not dismiss the dangers. Nor does NASA, with its asteroid diversion strategies. But when it comes to films with something to say about mining morality, about asteroids as a metaphorical threat, it is worth reaching back to the 1979 film *Alien.* Against the backdrop of scenes such as a nasty little creature emerging from a human thorax, it might be forgotten that the Nostromo, the spaceship traveling back to Earth with Ridley and her crewmates aboard, is a tug ship, in this case hauling 20,000 tons of refiner ore. At least some of it has come from asteroids, let us assume. Thus, the connection to space mining is clear. To secure the connection, the early scenes include a back-and-forth familiar to mining, namely, a labor dispute—in this case whether the crew members will get a bonus for their work beyond what is stated in their contract with "The Company."

The film's plot raises further issues relevant to mining morality. When the crew is awakened from its cryogenic sleep, they are surprised to learn that they are only halfway home. They have been awakened, according to protocol, to respond to a distress call from a distant moon. They dutifully follow up but fail to recognize before it is too late that the signal is likely not a distress call at all, but rather a warning to stay clear of this dangerous dot in galactic space. So we learn that really bad things can come from good intentions and following the rules. After a rough landing that damages the ship, Executive Officer Kane, the most inquisitive of the investigating team, disturbs some eggs on the strange vessel they encounter. From one of them, a creature emerges and attaches itself to the face mask, and then the face, of this overly curious citizen of space.

But rules and regulations can also protect and even save. Fearing contamination from the attached creature, Warrant Officer Ridley, the ranking officer onboard since Captain Dallas is off ship with Kane and the others, refuses entry of the crew to save Kane, even against the captain's order, until they have been properly quarantined. But Science Officer Ash, Ridley's subordinate, defies her order, and lets them in. The alien eventually detaches from the comatose Kane (but only after an attempt to cut the creature off his face reveals a truly deadly acid instead of blood) and is nowhere to be found. Once Kane awakens and seeks nourishment, the creature bursts forth from his chest, escapes into the ship and, with its remarkable adaptive capacities marveled at by the science officer, quickly grows to human size. It appears that not following protocol and the orders of a woman not to be cowed by her male crewmates can have very bad results.

As the film reaches its climax, Ridley in desperation blows up the gigantic tug ship and its cargo. With the ship's cat Jones, she narrowly escapes in a pod where she finally overcomes the alien that has come on board, and she expels it into space. She puts Jones and herself into cryo-sleep for the journey home with the hope that someone will find her in space. But that's the ending—and a beginning for sequels. Earlier, the alien had set its deadly sights on all the other crew members except Science Officer Ash, who, it turns out, is an android programmed by The Company to ensure, with the highest priority, that the alien is returned safely for study. All others on the Nostromo are expendable. Disabled by the crew members, his (its?) head left hanging by wires, the robot is sufficiently reassembled to tell them more about the alien and how it can be destroyed. He says it can't. The nearly severed head of the android Ash admits to admiring the creature "for its purity . . . a survivor, unclouded by conscience, remorse, or the delusions of morality." With such qualities, it is perhaps understandable why, as one of the engineers observes, the alien must be of interest to The Company's weapons division.

The testimony of this android perhaps captures in the extreme the threat that hovers over the Space Age in general and asteroid mining in particular. Alien terror, abetted by human technology, has gained the upper hand. But here it must be pointed out that, at least for present purposes, this film is only secondarily about extraterrestrial life—whether such life exists and just what that life might be, even as there are many, including theologians, who rightly wonder about such things.[33] Rather, for the sake of our ethical prospecting, *Alien* is about human beings and whether their ventures will end in *alienation* for space travelers, for space miners, and for all on Earth who send them there. It is about whether human beings will return to Earth—if they do not simply stay in colonized space—not only with recovered resources but also with their humanity intact.

Alienation to the Point of War

What might that loss of humanity, that alienation, entail? At this point, one could of course turn to Marx and Marxism, since alienation is in this tradition such a central theme. Given the role that The Company plays in this film, it would be easy to view alienation in terms of capitalistic domination. If one is prospecting for ethics, surely this is one rich vein of critical inquiry to pursue, as many rightly have.[34] But here I would emphasize also an extreme form or feature of alienation: the penchant for war and violence. Again, the conscience-less alien seems especially fit for war, and war, we might recall, features prominently in space-related films.

Here, art and entertainment all too readily imitate life, or at least the human condition at its bloodiest.

But it may be that the fantasies of space films and fiction, because they are so entertaining, tend to blunt the reality of war. So it is that the Reagan Administration's Strategic Defense Initiative, proposed twenty years after the 1963 Cuban Missile Crisis, considered briefly in the previous chapter, quickly assumed the name of "Star Wars" in part to emphasize the near fantastic technological demands of the program.[35] But the nickname, apt as it might have been, likely also detracted from the seriousness of what was at issue: against the backdrop of the Cold War deterrence paradigm of Mutually Assured Destruction (MAD), a possible nuclear exchange between the Soviet Union and the United States. The militarization of space is not a thing of the past. The Trump Administration has envisioned and pushed for a Space Force as a new branch of the military.

In short, one question posed by the film *Alien* is whether mining in space brings those who so engage in this activity closer to war or closer to peace and the prosperity that asteroid entrepreneurs envision and promise. The alien that terrorizes the Nostromo and its crew was, as the admiring android science officer puts it, a "survivor" in the extreme, "unclouded by conscience, remorse, or the delusions of morality." For human beings, the coupling of war and survival is an ancient and not so ancient theme. We might note that, toward the end of his lengthy dissent from the ICJ nuclear weapons advisory opinion discussed in the previous chapter, Judge Weeramantry laments, "A world order dependent upon terror would take us back to the state of nature described by Hobbes in *The Leviathan,* with sovereigns in the posture of Gladiators; having their weapons pointing and their eyes fixed on one another . . . which is a posture of Warre."[36] It is perhaps unfair to compare the denizens of Hobbes's state of nature with the conscienceless Nostromo invader. But for the sake of prospecting for ethics, it is wise to remember (and *memoria* is crucial for prudence) that humanity, whether engaged in space mining or most any other activity, including the rituals of religion, may certainly lean in that direction.

ASTEROIDS AND AUTHENTICITY

The Space Age, it would seem, can engender the optimism not only of the Rocket Boys growing up in coal country but of also of space entrepreneurs, some with vast wealth, who see asteroids as our future. On the other hand, the possibility may loom that greed and alienation, terror and war and other kinds of destruction await us in space because we will have brought them or found them there. And if the human-constructed and programmed android science officer in *Alien* is right, such impulses cannot be killed. Theologians from Saint Augustine to Reinhold Niebuhr might have put such impulses under the heading of Original Sin.

But there is also reason to think that the difficult truth is to be found somewhere in between—between wild optimism and darkest pessimism and dread, between the companies now embarking on asteroid mining and promising the brightest future for humanity and The Company in *Alien* that echoes Glasscock's harsh judgment on Standard Oil as "the greatest, most powerful, most ruthless and conscienceless trust on earth." After all, recall that "the company" that was once the Anaconda Copper Mining Company was not without its merits and showed at least a modicum of compassion and concern for its workers and the community, in Butte and Chuquicamata and beyond. Anaconda's sister company, Montana Power, could be judged by some to be an example of capitalism at its best before it gave way to new get-rich schemes and optimum shareholder satisfaction, before it imploded with losers all around. As was noted with reference to the story of Butte, even John D. Rockefeller of Standard Oil, the *bete noire* of the populists when the Copper Kings reigned, but also a philanthropist and a founder of one of the world's great universities with a chapel that bears his name, had certain standards that, had they been followed by his minions, might have left the people of Butte and other places a little less bereft.

In short, between wild optimism and a world at war with itself lies the human condition, or, to quote Heilbroner again, the human prospect. As Lonergan might put it against the backdrop of his studies on grace, it is a condition in urgent need of healing and a prospect requiring creativity. This in-between, I suggest, is where mining morality mostly occurs. Preliminary to that task, at least in the present case, is prospecting for ethics. In the remainder of this chapter we will return to our prospecting tools to see what veins of inquiry might be uncovered on the way to near-Earth asteroids and the moral mining sites they represent.

The Notion of Authenticity

One place to start is with the notion of alienation itself, as discussed by Lonergan. For we might recall that, even if the term is most closely associated with Marx's exploited worker—a reality that is all too relevant to mining—the term is not Marx's alone. In his essay on the "emerging religious consciousness of our time," Lonergan emphasizes that the experience of alienation is integral to the emergence of this consciousness. Even as he refers to "our time," Lonergan may not be saying anything radically new. After all, Lonergan's own Christian tradition has long stressed estrangement from God and self that is at once highly personal and yet global in scope. "In Adam's fall, fell we all," is one way the Christian tradition has put it. Systematically, Anselm's *Cur Deus Homo* stresses the fall of the whole human race from justice and grace. Dramatically, Shakespeare's Portia in *The Merchant of Venice* argues that "the quality of mercy is not strained," for all are in need. Or, one thinks of the meditation on the Incarnation in St. Ignatius of Loyola's *Spiritual Exercises* where the Trinity is imagined looking down on all the people on the surface of the earth, in all their variety—"some white and others black; some in peace and others in war; some weeping and others laughing; some well, others ill; some being born and others dying, etc."—and desiring to save them all.[37] As for the more personal to match the more structural dimensions of the problem of alienation, Lonergan's prime mentor, Thomas Aquinas, points out that it would seem that "love of self" is the basis of every sin.[38] But in fact in Aquinas's order of charity "love of self" comes right after "love of God" and ahead of "love of neighbor."[39] So the "love of self" that is at the root of every sin is not true self-love at all, but "rather an *inordinate* love of self,"[40] or love of a false self, a separation or alienation from who we really are and are meant to be.

If, for Lonergan, alienation is the problem, the response would be the ongoing, difficult task of authenticity. No less than alienation, authenticity is a malleable sort of term. But in the context of the prospector's tools that provide some guidance here, authenticity necessarily has a breadth and depth of meaning. Authenticity is a matter of conversion—religious, moral, intellectual, and, some would add, psychic. Or, summing these up, "ecological," Pope Francis might say. It is a matter not of human effort alone, the sort of Pelagianism rejected by Augustine and others, but also of grace; human beings do not achieve authenticity on their own.

Yet, if it is a matter of grace, and if, in traditional terms, grace builds on nature and elevates it, then authenticity is a matter of human capacities, too. These include capacities for anticipating through feelings the values that constitute a fully human life, as well as the dynamic capacities for knowing and loving detailed not only in the pages of *Insight* and *Method in Theology* but in literature and in art, in history and in heroic human examples, often close to home and hidden from public view. Authenticity is a matter of heeding in this moment and that, in practical undertakings and theoretical forays, the transcendental precepts—Be attentive, Be intelligent, Be reasonable, Be responsible, Be loving, and, if necessary, Change—that are intrinsic to intentional consciousness informing every endeavor. It is a matter of the highly personal and the systemic, indeed the global, as we will emphasize below. It is a matter of progress under threat of decline, the progress spurred by authentic knowing and doing, the decline quickened by succumbing to biases of various kinds and the drag of sin.

Authenticity may also be a matter of an emergent probability, with its lower and higher schemes of recurrence, that is no guarantee that all will be well but is rather a feature of the world in which human beings thrive or sometimes barely survive. It is a world in which the odds can be improved that there will be peace rather than war, health rather than sickness, nutrition rather than starvation, ecological care rather than devastation, an economy and polity that serves all rather than the few, asteroid aversion rather than earthly impact. Such improvement can come from thoughtful human activity in tune with the notion that the cosmos is not about to bend to human command but, rather, as Pope Francis and Saint Francis put it, "sustains and governs" us. In terms of the functional specialties that Lonergan proposes as central to method in theology—a method that is applicable to international law and much else besides—authenticity is in part a matter of finding out for sure where we have been, or shouldn't have gone, where we might rightly go now, and how to join others in following the right path.

When it comes to asteroid mining, we cannot use our prospecting tools to the full. But since they are interconnected—here, with authenticity as their nexus—let me at least suggest a few lines of inquiry. First, I would note the obvious: No less than the Atomic Age, with its Manhattan Project and its Atoms for Peace, the Space Age is remarkable for its cooperative schemes. One thinks back to the recurrent *Challenger* missions: a space vehicle goes up, does its business, then returns to earth, only to take flight again—unless some mechanical failure or human short-cut brings disaster. Or, one thinks of the film *Apollo 13* with engineers huddled in an urgent cooperative effort to save the crew through improvisation, and the raucous scene at the end when a roomful of NASA workers at their computers hear the voices of the astronauts re-entering the bounds of earth. It was, the operations director claims, NASA's "finest hour." Saving Apollo 13 was a cooperative effort to be sure, everyone doing his—and, later, we will learn from the film *Hidden Figures* and elsewhere with regard to earlier missions, her—job so that the lower cooperative schemes can condition the emergence of a space program of immense complexity, immense cost, immense success, and, occasionally, immense and tragic loss. Now, it seems, those cooperative schemes are located increasingly in the private sector.

Second, we recall that the good of order, with its cooperative schemes, is good only in a restricted sense. Whether these schemes are good in a richer, fully moral sense depends on the values they serve. They may, for instance, simply bolster the bank accounts of the already fabulously rich and powerful. Or, they may spread the wealth—economic and other—around. They may increase the likelihood of a more peaceful world, or they may prepare the way for war, which, incidentally, is sure to violently interrupt the good of order even when, perhaps especially when, that order helps human communities and nations to thrive.

Third, the prospector's tools found in Lonergan's writings are oriented to the concrete, for, as Lonergan points out, the good is always concrete. The good "in its every instance and every aspect" is his concern. Thus, the ethical prospector is called to attend to the particularities of asteroid mining, ever the while asking where and how asteroid mining is connected to other kinds of mining and to other realms of thinking and doing, of meaning and value: politics and economics, engineering and astrophysics, education and religion, and, as we'll see below, the world of law. If what Lonergan calls "generalized empirical method" cuts across boundaries of various kinds, I would stress that he discerned its dynamic presence in theology or, better, in theologians, including theologians of the everyday. Indeed, one might argue that attentiveness, understanding, judgment, and responsibility are tailor-made for what some call "contextual theology," since, as we have emphasized from the beginning, not all mining is the same. Butte is not Nauru, the uranium of Niger is not the platinum found in outer space. But the context of each may, at a deeper level, be similar or the same: The question of God, Lonergan, observes, is the question that "questions questioning itself." This is true whether the questioning regards labor relations in Chuquicamata, uranium-related health issues in Africa, or, as we shall see, the legal regime that should govern mining in space—also "our common home."

Asteroids and Our Common Home

When we turn to *Laudato si'* in order to aid our ethical prospecting, it will be good to recall that the prospecting tools, including those embedded in *Laudato si'*, are meant to be "self-sharpening." The effort to apply them may expose weaknesses in the tools and thus the need for expansion or refinement that can occur precisely as the tools are employed. So, for instance, while *Laudato si'* discusses mining in several places, it makes no mention of asteroid mining or, for that matter, of asteroids or of space travel of any kind. This may be construed as a weakness in the text. Yet, even as ores of various kinds require refinement to reach full value, so linking *Laudato si'* to asteroid mining may reveal valuable but unforeseen shades of meaning in this chapter of Catholic social thought.

While asteroids are to be found nowhere in *Laudo si'*, Pope Francis most certainly counts the stars as creature-inhabitants of "our common home." Francis writes, "When we see God reflected in all that exists, our hearts are moved to praise the Lord for all his creatures and to worship him in union with them" (87). Then, true to his chosen papal name, he goes on to recite the hymn of Saint Francis of Assisi, with its prayerful ode to "Sir Brother Sun" and "Sister Moon *and the stars*" (emphasis added). What are asteroids, etymologically, but starlike beings?[41] So, even as one might assume that, in *Laudato si',* it is our planet that is "our common home" in need of care, the boundaries of that home in fact extend far beyond the ends of the earth—to "the heavens," to "the cosmos," to the entire "universe" to which Francis so frequently refers.[42]

We might say, then, that the expanded context for Pope Francis's theological reflections on our common home is the entire universe. Morally speaking, the starting point appears to be not obligation or even repentance but rather praise. The opening words of the letter, "'*Laudato si', mi Signore*'—'*Praise be to you, my Lord,*'" tells us so. In this regard, what Francis presents is in line with certain aspects of Lonergan's thought: the sense of wonder that is "the pure and unrestricted desire to know" found in *Insight*; the "consolation that has no cause" found in the Ignatian Spiritual Exercises that touched the Jesuit lives of both Lonergan and Jorge Mario Bergoglio;[43] the transforming "Love of God flooding our hearts by the Holy Spirit given to us" (Romans 5.5), a verse to which Lonergan often returns; the emphasis on grace that marked Lonergan's early writings and hovers over the rest.

But if praise of God for the entire universe, an attitude so in keeping with gazing at the stars and starlike heavenly beings, is the ultimate context for the pope's encyclical—sometimes ode to, sometimes lament on—our common home, there are also in *Laudato si'* other contexts more immediate for ethical prospecting in space.[44] Let us focus briefly on three.

First is Francis's commitment to "integral ecology," wherein everything is connected, and thus the need for "ecological conversion,"[45] a profound and effective recognition that as human beings we are emmeshed in ecosystems larger than ourselves. A focus on outer space, on asteroids and asteroid mining, affirms this fact but adds a reminder that these ecosystems in no way end at earth's edge. Put in language deeply embedded in Catholic social thought and teaching, the "common good"—the shared good—at issue and to be cared for is not just the local, the regional, the national, the global, not even the planetary good. Rather, what is also at issue is the *cosmic* common good—and goods—that we share. By "we" I mean not only leaders of powerful nations, not only the CEOs and superrich board members and shareholders of asteroid mining companies, not even the relatively well off and secure. I mean also impoverished stargazers of whatever culture, those on the margins who do not enjoy the "true wealth of nations,"[46] the very persons embraced by Pope Francis's vision and concern. But I also mean all those creatures, living or not, that inhabit and constitute and share the universe brought into being by God.

Second, this enlarged notion of a common good—grounded in the Common Good (God) encountered through praise—affirms and extends certain norms regarding property—for instance, the considered conviction that even if possession is "private," its use is not. Or, to return to understandings of property one finds in Thomas Aquinas, private property is a dynamic development of, the "natural law," not one of its basic precepts That is, experience—but also understanding, sound judgments, and responsible decision-making—has shown that things are thus better cared for, that there is more order in society, and that the chances for peace are improved.[47] Within the Catholic social tradition, the *universal destination of goods* is a moral starting point for thinking about the earth and its beyond. In an emergency, Aquinas maintains, the moral tilt is to the original position—not of John Rawls,[48] but of *creation* as understood by Francis and others who have come before. Those who steal out of stress of need, when there really is no other option, are availing themselves of what, primordially, is to be held in common. Technically speaking, such actions do not count as theft.[49] In short, in terms of Catholic social thought, asteroids belong to all of us, as gifts to be shared. Even if, for good reason, near-earth asteroids—or their riches—are in some way provisionally parceled out, to this mining company, to that state-sponsored enterprise, still they belong to all and should benefit all, especially those who labor under "stress of need."

At this point we might emphasize that, for Francis, those affected by "stress of need" includes "earth herself." For our planet is "among the most abandoned and maltreated of our poor" (2). Thus, if the asteroids ultimately belong to all and should benefit all, it follows that gains from asteroid mining—with its possibly first "trillionaire"—should be used to relieve that "stress of need" that so affects a possibly dying planet. In short, asteroid mining should in some way contribute to the planetary "healing and creating in history" to which Lonergan refers.

Third, key to effective care of our common home, extending way into space, will be a shift away from the "technocratic paradigm" that links technology with power, especially economic power, with too little thought of human and other beings caught in the operative paradigm's sometimes unreflective and uncaring maw. As Francis makes clear, he is not espousing some sort of Ludditeism as an alternative; technology can be life-giving and even beautiful in its own way. Surely, the Rocket Boys thought this to be so. But precisely because in the case of space exploration and even habitation, the technological advances are so awe-inspiring, so promising, so brilliant, the need for caution may be greater. The late Stephen Hawking speculates that space could be humanity's salvation, but only because of the mess—or, in Pope Francis's words, "the immense pile of filth"—we have made of the earth.[50] When it comes to asteroid mining, no doubt many of the obstacles are technical—the kind of problems that practically minded people working in the STEM fields are so adept at solving. But Francis's larger point, it would seem, is closer on a communal scale to what St. Augustine recognized in his own case—that "I had become to myself a vast problem."[51] As the film *Alien* warns, this problem, the problem of alienation, is one that even technicians of unusual aptitude are not apt easily to solve.

This problem—the problem of the human fault—may be obscured by the expanse of space. For Pope Francis, the earth is approaching a pile of filth from which we can no longer divert our eyes. But the space that awaits mining expeditions is vast. If, as we were told during the Great Recession, certain banks were too big to fail, maybe outer space with its asteroids is simply too big to pollute or pillage to death, even if the endangered oceans once seemed the same. After all, the metals to be retrieved, we are told, will never run out, and unlike the case of Pleasant Island become the pillaged island of Nauru, there are, so far as we know, no indigenous peoples to disparage or displace. Then again, already over five hundred thousand pieces space debris present a real and growing problem.[52] Whether we can do irreparable harm to this outer sector of our common home is a legitimate question. In terms of the foresight and caution that prudence demands, it is a question that must be faced.

But even as it is addressed, it is good to remember that, for Aquinas at least, the caution that is integral (or "quasi-integral") to prudence considers possible consequences of another kind. Caution, the last of the quasi-integral parts of prudence, is meant to avert moral damage to ourselves. For Francis and for the tradition he represents, a concern for moral ecology, no less than Elon Musk's red Tesla Roadster, must be on board mineral-retrieving rockets heading into space. Even now before the mining begins, the cube satellites prospecting for ore must be programmed for ethical prospecting as well. The alternative is likely alienation from who we are and are meant to be.

Asteroids, the Ocean, and Emergent International Law

For the sake of ethical prospecting, it is worth asking people where they would like to go if they had a choice, without worry about safety or cost: into outer space or to the bottom of the sea? Some undergraduates, I have found, somewhat surprisingly opt for the ocean floor. Why wish to go maybe a mile or two down, when one could fly to Mars? But should it be such a surprise that the ocean floor holds such appeal? Do not the ocean depths have much to offer and to teach? Surely, they do, even if here we make no attempt to plumb those depths in ways that would lead us into mystery. Rather, there is another reason to consider once again ocean space. Everything in history is connected, Pope Francis claims. Our chapter on the Law of the Sea and seabed mining focused in part on *inner* space, hoping to bridge the gap between interiority and global issues, between insight as a highly personal matter and international affairs as a matter of wide complexity and deep concern. But connections between, say, the authority of personal conscience, on the one hand, and the International Seabed Authority, on the other, are not the only ones germane to ethical prospecting. It so happens that there are striking connections between the LOS and the legal regime that governs, or might govern, mineral extraction in the world far above. To bring this chapter to an end, we will review a few of those connections now.

Figure 7.3. Signing of the Space Treaty by the United States.
Photo: UN Multimedia.

First, recall that one way to understand international law is in terms of "ethics writ large," an ongoing attempt to grapple with an implicit question: How ought we to live together as a human community? This question was surely alive during debates over the LOS with its multiple foci—geographic, economic, security, environmental. The question arises again when it comes to mining in space. Second, the LOS presented a remarkable if imperfect case of emergence, in this case of new law to keep pace with emerging technologies, newly emergent states, and emerging threats to peace and the global environment. So, too, the emergence of asteroid mining through the vision, financial backing, and technical skill of Deep Space Industries, Planetary Resources, and others, is giving rise to the need for a suitable legal regime to match. Just as there was no guarantee that the LOS would in fact emerge (the law as envisioned by some never quite did), so, too, there is no guarantee that a suitable law to govern asteroid mining will be found, widely affirmed, and obeyed.

Third, my own inquiry into the LOS led to the conclusion that, at least in the case of a key and highly contested principle in the 1982 Convention, the "common heritage of mankind," the emergent law seemed to be holding in tension the world as it is, with its finitude and self-interest and contested jurisdictions, and the world as it might be, a world of human solidarity, prosperity and peace, of justice for all, including future generations, and genuine care for the countless, sometimes threatened denizens of the sea. So, too, in ways to be explained below, emergent space law also seems to pivot between, or hold in uneasy tension, accomplishment and aspiration, *lex lata* (established law) and *lex ferenda* (law as it might be but is not yet), political realities and high principles, private profit and shared benefits, self-interested nations and a global community with its "commons" to be enjoyed by all, especially those most in need.

Fourth, sea law and space law, it turns out, are in fact mutually dependent in the law-making process. The reader may recall that, in the *Trail Smelter Arbitration Case* (discussed in chapters 3 and 4), the arbitrators lacked legal guidance for settling a case of pollution travelling across the border between Canada and the United States. So, they looked for assistance in *existing* law. In U.S. federal law, which can deal with the relations between individual member states, they found examples of how one "state" (Canada) might be liable for environmental damage done to another "state" (the United States). Similarly, in crafting a new ocean regime, certain negotiators looked to existing law, in this case space law (the Moon Treaty, and the Outer Space Treaty), for precedents and legal meanings regarding "common heritage." What, they asked, did international law have to say about the moon and celestial bodies as global commons? How might that legal meaning translate into a new law of the sea and the global commons with which it deals? Now, the questions run partly in the other direction: With the language and legal meanings of common heritage more fully embedded and specified in the Law of the Sea, a law now in force, what might those legal understanding have to contribute to space law, which, when enacted, was vague on the kind of mining that is now on the horizon?

Unilateral Claims to the Ocean Floor and Outer Space

At this point, to clarify and to expand on what is at stake, it might be helpful to highlight two legislative initiatives on the part of the United States, one regarding the LOS, the other asteroid mining. The first we have already seen in chapter 5: H.R. 2759 (96th): Deep Seabed Hard Mineral Resources Act. Signed into law in 1980, it was designed to allow the United States to move forward with seabed mining even as the U.N. Convention on the Law of the Sea was still being negotiated. This unilateral move was controversial because it was seen by some, especially nations on the economic margins, as a way for the United States to preempt the emerging LOS and international governance of the deep seabed, with its "common heritage" designation. So, some protested that U.S. legislation fell short of the "common heritage" principle, which had assumed the status of *jus cogens*, or peremptory law—that is, law that would invalidate any domestic law that contravened it. But proponents of the U.S. legislation denied that the common heritage norm could be considered *jus cogens*, which is a problematic legal term to begin with, since the meaning of the principle would not be clear until the negotiations had been completed and the treaty would be open for signing, ratification, and eventual legal effect. Put otherwise, while some saw common heritage, with robust, some might say "socialist," interpretations, as an accomplished legal reality, others treated it as a heuristic notion at best, with its precise legal meaning yet to fully emerge.[53]

The case of space law with special reference to space mining seems not so different. Just as the movement toward an emergent sea law was interrupted—or, some might argue, given a push—by H.R. 2759, so, too, the United States provoked international discussion about the legality of asteroid mining by its enactment of the 2015 U.S. Commercial Space Launch Competitiveness Act,[54] Title IV of which addresses, among other topics, asteroid mining within a domestic United States context. A key passage from that section of the Act reads:

> A United States citizen engaged in commercial recovery of an asteroid resource or a space resource under this chapter shall be entitled to any asteroid resource or space resource obtained, including to possess, own, transport, use and sell the asteroid resource or space resource in accordance with applicable law, including the international obligations of the United States.

But just what that "applicable law" is and what those "international obligations" are is not so clear. True, as any international law textbook, especially designed for students in the United States, will attest, according to the U.S. Constitution, "international law is a part of our law." But as Paul De Man points out, this provision of the U.S. Commercial Space Competitiveness Act "complicates matters significantly in light of the current state of international space law and the ratification status of the Outer Space Treaty."[55] That is, the United States, as a party to that treaty, is bound by its prescriptions, and the treaty does state that "[o]uter space, including the Moon and other celestial bodies, is not subject to national appropriation by claim of sovereignty, by means of use or occupation, or by any other means." But as De Man continues, "[n]atural resources are neither explicitly included in, nor expressly excluded from the text of this provision; indeed, they are not even once mentioned in the set of the United Nations (UN) space treaties binding upon the United States."[56]

Now, the Moon Treaty does add some legal language about "common heritage" and other issues relevant to asteroid mining. While the United States and other major nations are not a party to that treaty, the United States was instrumental in the drafting of the agreement, and in the absence of other space law to give guidance, the Moon Treaty is important for aiding the law-making process. For instance, as Von der Dunk points out, the Moon Treaty distinguishes between "celestial bodies" and "extraterrestrial materials which reach the surface of the earth by natural means" (Art. 3).[57] Thus, one might argue that it is one thing to say that nonappropriation applies to the Moon or another such body in space; it is another thing to say that nonappropriation would apply to a much smaller asteroid on which mining robots might land.

But even if that distinction does not hold, Von der Dunk continues, when it comes to nonappropriation international lawyers light upon another clause in the Moon Treaty: "Neither the surface nor the subsurface of the moon, or any part of thereof or natural resources *in place*, shall become property of any State, international intergovernmental or non-governmental organization, national organization or non-governmental entity or of any natural person" (Art. 11[3], emphasis added). The distinction between natural resources *in place* and resources extracted gives rise to argument that legal prescriptions about nonappropriation applied to asteroids and their resources cease to obtain once the resources have been removed.

Whether this is a solid legal argument or the crassest sort of casuistry, I leave to international lawyers to sort out and the reader to ponder in the movement from ethical prospecting to mining morality. Certainly, the charge of crassness might be rebuffed by appeals to a Lockean view of property: the goods of the earth become one's property by mixing in one's labor. But that simply begs the question: Why a Lockean view of property, and not some other view? In any event, arguments and counterarguments over a couple of words—"in place"—does seem to be indicative of the tension between, on the one hand, "common heritage," "common home," the "universal destination of goods," and, on the other hand, near absolute commitments to private possession and the quest for profit that, Aquinas warns, extends to infinity—which is more than a trillion, as in "trillionaire."

Just as some nations objected to the 1980 U.S. legislation on seabed mining, believing it to be out of sync with emergent (or still emerging) international law, so, too, some have objected to the 2015 U.S. Commercial Space Launch Competitiveness Act. At least one commentator objects to the "provincialism" of the act. That is, it does not recognize the laws of other nations to govern space mining and assumes that the only ones doing the mining in space will be U.S. citizens or corporations such as Planetary Resources and Deep Space Industries.[58] Frans G. von der Dunk notes especially two of Brazil's objections to the act:

- that multilateral interests should take precedence over unilateral ones; and
- that domestic legislation is a poor substitute for a multilateral instrument.[59]

Another space law expert, Ram Jakhu, expresses the opinion "that natural resources [in space] should not be allowed to be appropriated by anyone—states, private companies, or international organizations." But to this Thomas Gangale responds, as the last words in his commentary on the legality of mining celestial bodies, that "Jakhu's statement merely expresses his preference of a *lex ferenda*; it is not a pronouncement of the *lex lata.*" Gangale's almost mocking retort to another critic of the U.S. action is particularly relevant to our discussion. To Gbenga Oduntun's objection that the act "goes against a number of treaties and international customary law which already apply to the entire universe," Gangale replies that "if human law applies 'to the entire universe,' one cannot choose but wonder how this presumption of human jurisprudence is viewed by nonhuman sentient beings elsewhere in the universe."[60] Now, maybe by "entire universe," Oduntun simply meant all the nations of the world. But by his choice of words, he may have done better than he knew. That is, he has come close to stating the problem of emerging law in ways that approach the vision of *Laudato si'* which holds that, when humans act—and this would include enacting laws—they ought indeed to act with the entire universe in mind. For the universe is our common home.

So the arguments go—back and forth. Argument is arguably a good thing. It is needed to spur the emergence of a legal framework adequate to match the challenge of asteroid mining and other space activities. Just what that framework will or should be is at this point an open question. Von der Dunk suggests various ways in which the question might play out. "The worst-case scenario," he says, "is a continuing fragmentation of the legal situation," leading to "commercial uncertainty, *mala fide* entrepreneurs going ahead regardless, or politically-motivated land grabs" (a little like the relatively lawless times of Bannock and early Butte). Another possibility is a top-down treaty regime which to von der Dunk does not seem likely. A third possibility is a bottom-up approach whereby other nations will follow the U.S. example of enacting their own laws while "ensuring compliance with the Outer Space Treaty and other relevant elements of international law, and thus gradually coming to a common understanding of what should be considered legitimate or legally allowed."[61]

Asteroids and Islands in the South China Sea

Whether Von der Dunk is on target with his speculations, I do not know. But I will say that the "land-grabs" in the absence of a suitable space regime to which he refers are reminiscent of the kind of language ("under-water land-grabs" were President Lyndon Johnson's fear) that gave impetus to the LOS. So it is not surprising that, given the exploits of Elon Musk and others that hasten human

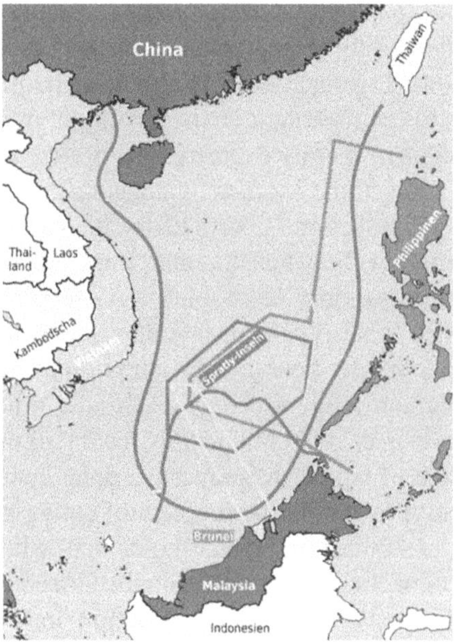

Figure 7.4. South China Sea Claims.
Courtesy of Voice of America.

ventures into the beyond, space law expert Roncevert Ganon Almond looks to the LOS for legal guidance with regard to a future in space. He explains that "[a]s technology can propel us beyond the boundaries of our earthly domain, we cannot escape our human nature and the attendant consequences. However, the international community can learn from and improve upon our history by anticipating the coming legal and geopolitical debates in outer space."[62] A chapter in that history from which we can learn, Almond believes, is the way in which the LOS has helped the international community, through arbitration, to meet a recent and current challenge: Chinese expansion in the South China Sea and the conflict it provoked.

Just what Almond means by "our human nature" is not entirely clear. But the "consequences" that worry him in the absence of a sound legal space regime are evident enough from what has transpired here on earth. With one eye on the South China Sea and the other on outer space, he lists five areas of concern: (1) increased proprietary claims, facilitated by technological advancement; (2) novel legal claims arising from legal uncertainty; (3) militarization and enforcement; (4) environmental impact; and (5) peaceful dispute resolution. Issues falling under these headings were very real in the South China Sea crisis. For instance, Almond cites the rise in military presence, on the part of the Chinese and the United States, to press claims and protect interests, and he cites the damage to the coral reefs resulting from Chinese island construction to further their territorial claims. The presence of an established legal framework was key to dealing with challenges in these and each of the other areas. Such a framework will be key for living peacefully and prosperously in space. "[W]ith sufficient political will," Almond counsels, "the international community can learn from and improve upon our history by anticipating the coming legal and geopolitical debates in outer space."

"Learn from and improve upon our history." Does this not sound like a call to engage in that quasi-integral part of prudence called *memoria* coupled with *docility*—or eagerness to learn? Is it not akin to applying the "functional specialities" of *research*, *interpretation*, *history*, *dialectics* to existing law to make sure we head in the right direction as we head into space? "*Anticipating* the coming legal and geopolitical debates in outer space" (emphasis added). Does this not signal the need for *foresight*, that part of prudence from which that virtue gets its name? Does it not suggest the need to establish our *foundations*, to clarify *doctrines*, such as "common heritage," to make sure that the *system* of space law is relatively coherent and comprehensive, to *communicate* the "cumulative and progressive results" of our best efforts so that they may be put into practice?

More broadly, is not Almond urging us implicitly to look at who we are and where we have been (the coal mines of the Rocket Boys' West Virginia, the phosphate mines of Nauru, the uranium mines of Africa, the multiple rounds of the Third United Nations Conference on the Law of the Sea, to name a few visited moral mining sites) so that we might know the way forward? Does he not also want us to think ahead so that we might see more clearly and to assess where we have been and where we might have gone astray? This may indeed be what Almond intends. Still, his very reference to "human nature," even if relatively optimistic, may suggest that the way to a truly just and effective legal regime will not be easy. There is always the possibility that an alien to human nature will sneak itself on board.

Interim Prospector's Report

The vastness of space is so great, and the asteroids that could be mined so many, that it is difficult to limit this ethical prospector's interim report to just a few observations and recommendations. Still, I will stop at three.

First, we should not shy away from the vastness. There may be even in international law, with its reference to "heavenly bodies" and the notion of airspace extending "*ad caelum*" (to the heavens), some residual religious consciousness, some tacit transcendent realm of meaning, some religious or quasi-religious notion of a "common home" that includes the cosmos with its asteroids and its stars. The proper response would seem to be wonder or awe or, for *Laudato si'*, praise. Yet other, less generous responses are possible, too. The Copernican Revolution may yet be incomplete, as humans continue to revel in the privileged place of their power to conquer and to colonize even space, and, in the process, become trillionaires. But, then again, might not the stars and starlike bodies be instruments of conversion, of "amazing grace," helping humans to learn to love their finitude and to share with one another the gifts of the beyond? In reflecting on the LOS, I wondered if immersing oneself in matters of the deep, as, say, marine biologists do, might lead one not only to greater knowledge but also genuine love of all creatures of the sea, whether living or simply held in existence by Neptune or some other gods or goddesses of the deep. Now, since Neptune (along with Mars and Jupiter and others) is by human naming a heavenly or godly orb, perhaps this is a sign that, at the very least, human beings still regard space as, in some respect, a realm of the divine. Thus, when the question of ethics comes up, the question of how we ought to live, it is possible that this is a question of cosmology and maybe of theology, too.

Second, if a focus on space and its riches is a welcome opening to transcendence, there are also, as the story of Thales reminds us, immediate and urgent matters of earth to which to attend. Visionaries are wonderful and sorely needed, but they must also be asked how their vision is to be attained. If this is a fair question to ask of someone like Pope Francis, so is it a fair question to pose to those who undertake or support asteroid mining. Consider again statements made by Rick Tumlinson's Space Frontier Foundation:

> Our goals include protecting the Earth's fragile biosphere and creating a freer and more prosperous life for each generation by using the unlimited energy and material resources of space.
>
> Our purpose is to unleash the power of free enterprise and lead a united humanity permanently into the Solar System.

Now, Pope Francis and many others would surely affirm the goal of "protecting the Earth's fragile biosphere," and they would be all for "creating a freer and more prosperous life for each generation." But whether unleashing "the power of free enterprise" is sufficient to "lead a united humanity permanently into the Solar System" is not so sure. After all, one might argue that such "unleashing" gave us Standard Oil and the copper kings of Butte, and, today, a world of nearly unfathomable disparities of wealth—and now, Tumlinson asks us to think about

> incredibly wealthy people who are themselves very successful business people, who want to send machines and possibly people to fly millions of miles into space and 'dig up' the rocks floating up there to make even more money.

Just how such ventures will engender "a united humanity" needs to be stated and spelled out, lest what Lonergan calls the general bias of common sense, with its quick and easy judgments, rule the day. The need for fuller explanation is especially acute when divisions can be so pernicious and so pronounced. If we cannot simply assume that unity is automatic, then those who promise it, for instance by picking up and moving to space, ought to be asked to offer a fuller account. After all, gold rushes on other frontiers did not always produce peace and prosperity for all. The town of Bannock had its robbers and its vigilantes that hung the bad guys without trial. Maybe things will be different this time. But if so, why and how?

Third, if neither unbridled optimism nor unbounded pessimism is an acceptable option (I do not deny that they are attractive and acceptable to many), we need to seek alternatives in between. In the present case, and in others, our prospecting tools may expose some suitable veins. Perhaps to clarify their own programs and projects, students of Lonergan often quote his words about dealing with a crisis of meaning—and, one might add, a crisis of value—a crisis that is arguably as acute as when Lonergan wrote "Dimensions of Meaning" some fifty years ago. There he submits that

> There is bound to be formed a solid right that is determined to live in a world that no longer exists. There is bound to be formed a scattered left, captivated by now this, now that development, exploring now this and now that new possibility. But what will count is a perhaps not numerous center, big enough to be at home in the old and the new, painstaking enough to work out one by one the transitions to be made, strong enough to refuse half measures and insist on complete solutions even though it has to wait.[63]

All along I have suggested means for making the requisite "transitions": What Lonergan calls the functional specialties, with a mediated phase and a mediating phase; what Aquinas understood as the virtue of prudence, with its *memoria* and its foresight, its shrewdness and its willingness to learn; what is known as the Catholic social tradition, grounded in the past but increasingly concerned about future generations; and what goes under the name of international law, with its ancient roots and its up-to-date applications and explorations, with its *lex lata* and its *lex ferenda* regarding such things as the world ocean and outer space, and in between a range of human rights. What Lonergan's words may not capture is the urgency of the situation we face, a sense of urgency captured by *Laudato si'*, but not only there. If Lonergan is correct that we may need to wait for "complete solutions," that does not mean we can or should wait to begin to mine morality, whether on earth or in space, with the aid of self-sharpening prospecting tools—those found in these pages but also those that others might bring, or have already brought, to a critical if daunting task.

NOTES

1. See "Our Story," on the Asteroid Day: 30 June website, at https://asteroidday.org/our-story/.
2. For a text of the declaration, explanations, and option to sign, see 100x Declaration, https://asteroidday.org/declaration/.

3. This date was chosen because on the morning of June 30, 1908, the largest recorded asteroid impact on Earth occurred near the Stony Tunguska River in Yeniseysk Governorate (now Krasnoyarsk Krai).

4. The founders are, along with Brian May and Grig Richters, Danica Remy, the COO at B612, and Rusty Schweickart, an American aeronautical engineer and an astronaut.

5. The Asteroid Day group's claim that the asteroid threat is "the only natural disaster we know how to prevent if we work together towards a global solution" might come as news to the Intergovernmental Panel on Climate Change, or to parties to the Paris Accord on Climate Change.

6. The Russian word *sputnik* means "fellow traveler." Whether during the Cold War the Russians intended any political meaning, I am not sure.

7. I do not at this point mean "opportunistic" in any negative sense. But the fact that the word lends itself to moral suspicion is also suggestive of the opportunity/threat/resolution framework guiding this chapter.

8. The film is based on Homer H. Hickam Jr.'s best-selling memoir, *Rocket Boys* (New York: Random House, Inc., 1998).

9. For NASA's own brief biography of von Braun, which does not fail to mention his problematic Nazi past (including the fact that one rocket program he worked on used slave labor), see https://www.nasa.gov/centers/marshall/history/vonbraun/bio.html.

10. See Hannah Arendt, *Eichmann in Jerusalem: A Report on the Banality of Evil,* Introduction by Amos Elan (New York: Penguin Books, 2006). The Eichmann trial was also a significant case in the history of international law.

11. *October Sky* came out in 2006. A decade later, *Hidden Figures*, another historically based film featuring rockets, space travel, and lots of math, would add race as well as gender to the narrative of suppression, belated recognition, and future promise.

12. See, for instance, David Shukman, "Hawking: Humans at risk of lethal 'own goal,'" *BBC News*, January 19, 2016, https://www.bbc.com/news/science-environment-35344664.

13. https://www.theguardian.com/science/2018/feb/07/space-oddity-elon-musk-spacex-car-mars-falcon-heavy.

14. Jackin Wattles, "NASA Is Keeping Tabs on Elon Musk's Roadster," *CNN Tech*, February 12, 2018, http://money.cnn.com/2018/02/10/technology/future/nasa-elon-musk-spacex-tesla-roadster/index.html.

15. Lonergan recalls the story of Thales falling into a well, only to be mocked by a milkmaid, in his discussion of "common sense and its subject." "Still," Lonergan observes, "Thales could have seen the well for he was not blind, and, perhaps, the milkmaid could have been interested in the stars, for she was human" (*Insight*, 182).

16. See T. S. Eliot's "The Journey of the Magi."

17. Augustín Udías, "Jesuit Astronomers in China and India," chapter 4 of *Jesuit Contributions to Science: A History* (New York: Springer Cham, 2003), 79–104.

18. For a brief profile of Brother Consolmagno, SJ, and his work that discusses both the Star of Bethlehem and the Vatican Observatory's uncompromising commit-

ment to science, see Elizabeth Pavalato, "Searching for the (Star) Light at the Vatican Museum," Saturday Profile, *The New York Times*, December 22, 2017, A6.

19. See James Trefil, *Reading the Mind of God: In Search of the Principle of Universality* (New York: Anchor Books/Doubleday, 1989). When I read this book years ago, I was impressed by its content (much of which I've forgotten) and yet was left wondering whether, in the end, the author had really gotten to the most basic question, "the question of God," as Lonergan puts it, or even to the question of the philosopher Leibniz: "Why is there something rather than nothing?"

20. Gerard Manley Hopkins, SJ, "God's Grandeur."

21. John S. Lewis, *Asteroid Mining 101: Wealth for the New Space Economy* (Deep Space Industries, 2015).

22. Lewis, *Asteroid Mining 101,* 1.

23. Katie Kramer, "Building the Economy Here on Earth by Exploring Space: Tyson," CNBC, *On the Money*, May 3, 2015, https://www.cnbc.com/2015/05/01/build-the-economy-here-on-earth-by-exploring-space-tyson.html.

24. "Credo of the Space Frontier Foundation," https://newspace.spacefrontier.org/about/.

25. Bradford Space, http://bradford-space.com/.

26. Planetary Resources, https://www.planetaryresources.com/.

27. "Ever Been 5000 Feet Below Earth's Surface? Asteroid Miners Explore Barrick's Hemlo Mine," Planetary Resources, https://www.planetaryresources.com/2017/09/ever-been-5000-feet-below-earths-surface-asteroid-miners-explore-barricks-hemlo-mine/.

28. "Planetary Resources and the Government of Luxembourg Announce €25 Million Investment and Cooperation Agreement," Planetary Resources, https://www.planetaryresources.com/2016/11/planetary-resources-and-the-government-of-luxembourg-announce-e25-million-investment-and-cooperation-agreement/.

29. Jeff Foust, "Asteroid Mining Company Planetary Resources Acquired by Blockchain Firm," Space.com, November 2, 2018, https://www.space.com/42324-asteroid-mining-company-planetary-resources-acquired.html.

30. Andrew Zaleski, "How the Space Mining Industry Came Down to Earth," *Fortune*, November 24, 2018, http://fortune.com/2018/11/24/asteroid-mining-space-planetary-resources/.

31. MIT, Mission: The Future of Strategic Resources: Asteroids, http://web.mit.edu/12.000/www/m2016/finalwebsite/solutions/asteroids.html. The educational program (Terrascope) resulting in this "solution" is described as follows: "Solving Complex Problems (12.000) is a unique learning opportunity for MIT freshmen. Focused around a single 'unsolvable' problem, students must delve deep into a global issue to compose a comprehensive solution that is beneficial and acceptable worldwide. Students must work together and guide themselves through this unique interdisciplinary endeavor, and emerge with a greater understanding of teamwork, leadership, and skills necessary to solving complex problems."

32. Colorado School of Mines, Space Resources Program, https://space.mines.edu/.

33. See, for example, Christopher L. Fisher and David Fergusson, "Karl Rahner and the Extra-Terrestial Intelligence Question," *Heythrop Journal* 47 (2006): 275–90.

34. See, for example, Naomi Klein, *This Changes Everything: Capitalism and the Climate* (New York: Simon and Schuster, 2014).

35. For a short analysis that links the technology requirements of SDI to the technology depicted in the film *Star Wars*, see "The Strategic Defense Initiative (SDI): 'Star Wars'" on the Cold War Museum's website: http://www.coldwar.org/articles/80s/SDI-StarWars.asp.

36. "Dissenting Opinion of Judge Weeramantry," http://www.icj-cij.org/files/case-related/95/095-19960708-ADV-01-12-EN.pdf.

37. The First Day of the Second Week, and the First Contemplation, *Spiritual Exercises of St Ignatius of Loyola*, trans. Father Elder Mullen, SJ (New York: J.P. Kennedy & Sons, 1914).

38. Aquinas, *ST* II–II, 84, 2 obj. 3.

39. On the order of charity, see Aquinas, *ST* II–II 26, 1–12.

40. Aquinas, ST I–II 77, 4 (emphasis added).

41. Greek *asteroeides*, "star-like." From *aster* "star" + *-eidos* "form, shape."

42. "Heavens" appears in the text four times, in quoted scripture passages; "cosmos" appears three times; and "universe" appears twenty-four times, occasionally with explicit equation to "our common home."

43. See Lonergan, *Method*, 106.

44. I say "seemingly," for I would argue that *theologically* the farthest reaches of the cosmos are every bit as immediate as a mineshaft one might enter or an asteroid crashing into the earth.

45. I have noted above that Francis's "ecological conversion" is arguably in sync with Lonergan's three- and possibly fourfold notion of conversion: religious, moral, intellectual, and psychic.

46. Finn, ed., *The True Wealth of Nations*.

47. Aquinas, *ST* II–II, 66, 2.

48. In making this point, I am not denying the heuristic value of Rawls's "original position," which indeed may aid our understanding of and judgments about the just society.

49. Aquinas, *ST* II–II 66, 7.

50. Shukman, "Hawking: Humans at Risk of Lethal 'Own Goal.'"

51. *Confessions*, Bk IV, iv (9).

52. "Space Debris and Human Spacecraft," NASA, September 26, 2013, https://www.nasa.gov/mission_pages/station/news/orbital_debris.html.

53. H. Roberto Herrera Caceres, "*La sauvegarde du patrimoine comun de l'humanité,*" in *La gestion des ressources pour l'humanité: le droit de la mer*," Workshop, The Hague, October 29–31, ed., René-Jean Dupuy (The Hague: Martinus Nijhoff Publishers, 1982), 125–34.

54. U.S. Commercial Space Competitiveness Act, Pub. L. 114-90 129 Stat. 704 (November 25, 2015).

55. Paul De Man, "The Exploitation of Asteroids and the Non-Appropriation Principle: Reflections on the Nature of Property Rights in Light of the US Space Resource Act of 2015," *Journal of Space Law* 40/1–2 (2015–2016): 2 [1–55].

56. Ibid., 3.

57. Frans G. von der Dunk, "Asteroid Mining: International and National Legal Aspects," *Michigan State International Law Review* 26/1 (2017): 90.

58. Thomas E. Simmons, "The Unfortunate Provincialism of the Space Resources Act," *The Space Review: Essays and Commentary about the Final Frontier* (online), January 25, 2016. http://www.thespacereview.com/article/2910/1.

59. Von der Dunk, "Asteroid Mining," 99.

60. Thomas Gangale, "The Legality of Mining Celestial Bodies," *Journal of Space Law*, Vol. 40:1–2 (2015–2016): 189.

61. Von der Dunk, "Asteroid Mining," 100.

62. Roncervert Ganon Almond, "Building a Durable Legal Framework in Space: The Extraterrestrial Impact of the South China Sea Dispute," *Yale Journal of International Law,* October 24, 2017, http://www.yjil.yale.edu/building-a-durable-legal-framework-in-space-the-extraterrestrial-impact-of-the-south-china-sea-dispute/.

63. Bernard J. F. Lonergan, "Dimensions of Meaning," in Frederick E. Crowe and Robert M. Doran, eds., *Collection*, Collected Works of Bernard Lonergan, vol. 4 (Toronto: University of Toronto Press, 1998), 245.

Part III

A PROSPECTOR'S REPORT

Chapter Eight

From Prospecting for Ethics to Mining Morality

The reader may recall that I began this project with Shefa Siegel's complaint about the "missing ethics of mining." An extended exercise in ethical prospecting, spread over several chapters, was meant to respond to that complaint. I know that others have also been responding, and perhaps more effectively, even if their direct concern has not been mining, as in "resource extraction." To give but a single example, I think of those philosophers who, years before I hit on the topic through exposure to the Law of the Sea, wondered about our obligations to future generations, even when mining was not on their minds. I did, however, stress the limits of this contribution, placing my efforts under the heading of "prospecting" for ethics, rather than mining morality in full. But there may be other ways to explain what I have tried to do.

THE KNOWN-UNKNOWN

One is in terms of Lonergan's distinctions between and among the "known-known," the "known-unknown," and the "unknown-unknown."[1] These may seem a clever or even silly distinctions. The reader may recall that they invited derision when used by then Secretary of Defense Donald Rumsfeld to describe progress in the war in Iraq.[2] But the distinctions can, in fact, be quite helpful. We begin to read something that we know right away tells us nothing new (the known-known), so we set it aside. Or, we commit ourselves to some project and then panic when we realize we didn't have a clue as to what we were getting ourselves into (the unknown-unknown) when we said, "Yes, you can count on me."

When it comes to ethics, Plato, it seems, stated a version of the problem long ago.[3] Socrates asks whether virtue can be taught. In seeking an answer together with his dialogue partner Meno, Socrates notes that, first, we need to find out just what virtue is. But here's the snag: If we already *know* what virtue is, and we *know* we know it, why waste our time asking what it is? What is there to find? If on the other hand we really *don't* know what virtue is, how will we even know what we're looking for, or know when we have found it? Socrates' own answer in *Meno* is that we already know such things as the truths of geometry from before we were born; we just need to remember them in our present life—which, of course, can be quite a challenge. A lot of dialogue will be required (or, in *Meno*, a lot of drawing squares and triangles on the ground) to jar our memories. Even then, some may resist coming out of the cave of forgetful bliss.

Socrates' answer about a pre-existent soul that knew but then forgot may or may not be satisfactory. But his presenting problem is very real. An answer would seem to be a middle ground between the "known-known" and the "unknown-unknown," namely, the "known-unknown." We don't know something—say, what the full-blown ethics of mining that Seifel is looking for would be—but we *know* we don't know it. *And* we may have some ways of seeking it out, some means of moving from the unknown to the known. The "operator" that moves us along, step by step, or occasionally by leaps and bounds, is the spirit of inquiry, informed by the heuristic, open-ended, transcendental notions of being and value, of the real and the good. Of course, we will need to be very mindful along the way of impediments to our search—bias of various kinds, and what the Christian tradition calls sin. But we are not totally helpless in our quest. Our human capacities may not be totally wrecked, and there remains the possibility of healing and elevating grace.

Now, it seems that the "known-unknown" is the sort of thing I have been dealing with in these pages. With the help of certain prospecting tools, I have been suggesting ways of moving toward better and more complete answers to the question, "How ought we to live?"—first of all when it comes to mining, with which everything begins, but also in those various spheres and phases of life that make up the "everything" that has begun with mining or will begin. But, as Lonergan reminds us, the notions that guide us are not abstract. They are not some static, heavenly ideas. Rather, they are concrete and comprehensive. The notion of being is unrestricted, leading us to seek to know all that is; the notion of value leads us to seek the good in its every aspect and its every instance: now in Butte and Chuquicamata, now on the island of Nauru, now in the deserts of Niger, now beneath the sea or the bleachers of Stagg Field in the days of the Manhattan Project, now in the Hague or the United Nations, now in outer space—and in every other place and time under the sun and the stars or shaded from view. As *transcendental,* these notions lead us into a transcendent realm of meaning and value, beyond our full grasp, without in any way disparaging other realms of meaning—the common sense of the everyday, or our forays into theory—or other values on the scale of values. For as someone like Pope Francis would insist, these, too, are diverse instances of God's creation, diverse aspects of "our common home."

When I have had occasion to explain to students what I think Lonergan means by the "known-unknown," I use the example of a course description: It should give one a pretty good idea of what is to be learned. But reading the description with a degree of understanding is hardly the same as completing a course in calculus or literature or geology or astrophysics, for learning is sometimes a slow and arduous task. It can also be boring—as in the saying about politics, that it sometimes requires "slow boring of hard boards." Or, maybe we should say, "slow boring of solid rock to reach the ore we seek." Some students may be allergic to anything "boring," and we are all students at times.

The "known-unknown" may be arduous enough when we're talking about a single course, but when it comes to mining morality, that's not what we're talking about. While colleges and universities should offer courses in ethics, with their theories and cases, it is doubtful that ethics can be taught in a single course. In prospecting for an ethics of mining, I have, for instance, treated international law as ethics writ large. But some very astute international lawyers remind us that international law is not a course. It is a curriculum. Even this may be an understatement. Manfred Lachs, of high esteem, insisted that international law, to be authentic and effective, must reach beyond its own disciplinary bounds, even to theology. Stephen Neff insisted that to understand international law, that oh so "Western" invention, we should probably start in India and China. Christopher Weeramantry, as we have seen, thought that if his students were to move international law into the realm of the "known," they should learn something about Islamic jurisprudence.

What I have suggested with the help of selected tools are some possible ways forward, some ways to move from the "known-unknown" to at least a better-known ethics. Lest we despair that our prospecting tools themselves are nothing more than disconnected fragments of knowledge, or a pile of puzzle pieces that will never interlock, it might be helpful to bring into the discussion a dictum passed on from someone I consulted years ago on the Law of the Sea. Jacques Maritain stressed that, in our philosophizing, it is important that we "distinguish to unite."[4]

I believe our fellow prospectors have done just that. Thus, Lonergan distinguishes four distinct levels of cognitive activities (experience, understanding, judgment, decision) that anyone may identify within oneself and for oneself, but together they constitute one dynamic method of knowing and doing leading to cumulative and progressive results. In line with those distinct yet interconnected levels of conscious intentionality, he distinguishes eight "functional specialties," which I have extended not only to international law but also to the efforts of, say, those seeking to tell the story of Butte and, later, Chuquicamata. But each of these specialties, while distinct, is a part of a single way to the true and the truly good, with its mediated phase (where we have been?) and its mediating phase (where do we go from here?). Further, Lonergan writes of a scale of values, but it is an *integrated* scale—the higher levels, say, the personal or the religious, do not pooh-pooh the vital value of clean air or water or safety in the mines.

While emergent probability has its distinguishable higher and lower schemes, the lower condition the higher and cannot be dismissed. Whether in an evolving natural world that gave us "the Richest Hill on Earth" with its copper or "Pleasant Island" with its phosphate, or in the "great historical currents that shape the course of human affairs" (Weeramantry), the lower schemes are in the picture, too. Or again, for Lonergan, economics needs to be distinguished from politics and especially moralistic bromides, but the distinctions involved are not a separation. Finally, development can be from below or from above, and these are not the same. But it is really one development—even when, especially when, the development from above means being in love with God who grounds every other value on the scale, every sort of good.

So, too, Aquinas discusses distinct "spheres" of prudence, and I have stressed how problematic this can be. But it is still one virtue. Prudence may be one virtue, but it has eight "quasi-integral parts." Each part is necessary; none is sufficient on its own. They need each other to function well. Further, prudence is but one cardinal or "hinge" virtue connected to the rest. It is especially connected to love or charity, the "mother and root of all the virtues."[5] As for international law, it is so vast that it seems bound to splinter into a thousand parts. The problem is very real. Yet international lawyers and others, such as diplomats, continue to meet and discuss, seeking to address problems of every kind. The more optimistic ones like C. G. Weeramantry think that, imperfect as it is, international law can play a part in moving toward "one world." Stephen Neff can show how varied, how changeable international law has been and still is. Yet he has managed to fit a lot of intelligibility between the covers of a single volume with a simple title: *Justice among Nations*. Perhaps in his own way, he, too, has been distinguishing to unite.

Of course, in the Catholic social tradition as reflected in *Laudato si'* definitions, distinctions, developments abound. But it is one tradition, of which *Laudato si'* is but one significant chapter. But even this tradition is but a part of a larger whole that includes the everyday and the stars. For as Pope Francis insists, "everything is connected."

Such dynamic equilibria among parts and wholes would seem to say a lot about how we ought to live. But if such equilibria, such interdependence among parts of larger wholes—for instance, almost two hundred nations sharing the same globe—should be the norm, it often is not the fact. Imprudent persons or groups or nations may limit *memoria* to the good old days that never were or distort it to the point of Holocaust denial. They may use their *reason*, a quasi-integral part of prudence, to get people to purchase a claim to a deposit of fool's gold or to invest in a deviously clever Ponzi scheme. In a cruel twist on *foresight*, like that copper-king-become-U.S. senator, William Clark, imprudent and arguably unjust (as in "intergenerationally" unjust) people can look to future generations and cynically leave them to fend totally for themselves. In short, any of the parts of prudence can get distorted, and if one part is messed up, it messes up the rest.

The problem of bias and distortion can be pervasive, affecting both individuals and groups, leading to shorter and longer cycles of decline. Lonergan's integral scale of values may break down when the skewed meanings and disvalues of a culture lead to a dysfunctional society, when personal value turns into egoism or narcissism or autocracy, when religion writes a recipe for domination or conquest and says it was written by God. In other words, we are prospecting for ethics in, at best, a wounded world, a world out of whack and sometimes out of control.

The prospect of presenting a finished product called "the ethics of mining" thus seems so daunting that one may wonder if such is even possible, especially in a world speeding along in cyberspace and not quite sure where it is going. True moral landing spots seem hard to find. After all, as Seigel points out, mining isn't all one thing. Neither, Stephen Neff will point out, is international law. For Lonergan, a classicist understanding of "culture," with a single shared set of meanings and values setting the norm, must give way to historical mindedness and an empirical approach to viewing the world. If, especially with Pope Francis, we have spent more time with a single religious tradition, Catholic Christianity, even that tradition does not stand still when it comes to moral matters.[6]

This is to say nothing of traditions in dialogue with other traditions, religious and other, sometimes divided against themselves. There may exist something that Lonergan calls "the emerging religious consciousness of our time," but given religion-related strife, on top of the sheer diversity of religious traditions, communities, and sects, to say nothing of new forms of atheism that demand a hearing, one may wonder if "our time" will ever come. Then, of course, there is the ecological devastation, the global climate change, the abuse of "our common home," that is so often abuse of those most vulnerable in the human community, to say nothing of other species. Mining practices around the globe have something to do with that.

CATCHING ETHICS IN THE ACT

Yet, maybe there is another way to think about these things. Maybe when it comes to possibly finding an "ethics of mining," a tried-and-true way to answer the question of how to live, the fact proves the possibility. Maybe we have not been engaged in *prospecting* for ethics after all—or, engaged in only that. Rather, by visiting Butte and Chuquicamata, Nauru and Niger, the International Seabed Authority and asteroids in outer space, maybe we have been catching ethics in the act—ethics not as some grand theory, and not in an ideal world, where the *ceteris* are always *paribus*, where no one lies, where "self-interest" is closer to true "self-love" than it is to a domesticated version of what was once called avarice.[7] Rather, in these pages maybe we have caught people in the act of living an examined life in the world as it is: an "immense pile of filth," a world heating up, too often to the point of war. A complex and confusing world, a wounded world in need of healing.

So, for instance, three Montanans seek to tell the story of Butte—and the world—as best they can. In so doing, they help us with *memoria* so that we might make better decisions, more prudent decisions from now on, for, as Michael Malone points out, "It need not have been this way." A commission seeks to find out just who was and is accountable for what happened to Nauru, that microcosm of the "great historical currents that have shaped the course of human affairs." In the process the commission and its student helpers contribute to "healing and creating in history." Arvid Pardo, from the tiny state of Malta, gets the world, or at least the United Nations, to think about the oceans from whence we came, eons ago. With the help of seasoned diplomats and ordinary citizens, he plants the seeds for a legal paradigm shift: no longer the *mare liberum* (the free sea) of Hugo Grotius, nor the *mare clausum* (the closed sea) of Thomas Seldon, but now *mare nostrum,* "*our* sea," not in the sense of possession but in ways that bring to mind "our common home."

Or, again, an American scholar turns our attention to uranium and nuclearity in Africa, a huge continent that is too rarely mentioned in the daily news in America. Her insights surely say something about the "we," as in, "How ought *we* to live?" In one mining country, Zambia, a secondary school student gets us, or at least me, to think about time "before the Europeans came," and a Protestant theologian, H. Richard Niebuhr, helps us to make some theological sense of Hiroshima—and that is no easy thing. In the book's penultimate chapter, an international lawyer asks us to turn our attention to problems in the South China Sea. He thinks that by looking there and learning what international law can do, limited though it may be, we will be better able to negotiate with peace and justice the frontiers of space so special to the Rocket Boys, but also to asteroid miners seeking to become the world's first trillionaires.

MINING MORALITY WITH OTHERS AND THE OTHER

Each of these and others may help us to heed Socrates' dictum, that the unexamined life is not worth living. Each may help us to answer the question of ethics, "How ought we to live?" If someone like Judge Weeramantry concludes that those who turned Pleasant Island into phosphate plunder cannot rightly claim, "We didn't know. There were no laws," he may be exposing a problem flagged by many: the problem of moral impotence, the problem of knowing the good but without follow-through, the problem of sin and thus the need for a "higher power" if we are to repent and change our errant ways. Just as no one really mines alone, so, too, ethics is a cooperative effort, with both the living and the dead pitching in to help us out. We have seen some examples in these pages. But there is also that "Amazing Grace" of which both a one-time slaver and the first black American president could sing, the former after abandoning his slave ships, the latter after a massacre in a place of prayer.

When we think about ethics in terms of the examined life, we are likely to think about a personal inventory, an examination of conscience, a taking stock of one's own life. Surely that is essential. Certainly, that is key. But if our starting point for such an examination is mining, where everything begins, we soon find by visiting various mining sites the truth of Pope Francis's claim, that everything—and everyone—is connected. So the question "How ought I to live?" grows into the question of how ought *we* to live, and the "we" is very wide: From the Irish and Chinese of Butte, over a hundred years ago, to the Chinese and Zambian workers in the copper mines of today, from sea creatures disrupted by seabed mining to minerals on speeding asteroids, now *in situ* but maybe not for long. At least for people like Pope Francis and Saint Francis, *all* creation matters, for it is our common home. Of creation, Saint Augustine stresses in the opening to his *Confessions,* humanity is but "a small piece."[8] An examination of personal and collective conscience may, like everything else, begin with mining. But it may also begin with praise for all that is.

By stressing the magnitude and complexity of it all, I do not mean to drive us into the sort of paradoxes for which Zeno was famous: since everything is connected, we must comprehend everything before we can know anything at all; or, because the whole world is in peril, each one of us must be a superhero and save it all. That is to miss the point—the theological point, at least—that we are not God.

But neither are we alone. The university in which I have taught for many years has a descriptor for what we hope to do: "[E]ducate one student at a time in the company of others." When it comes to the questions of ethics, each of us is different, with different gifts and different callings, different starting points, different social roles, different spheres of justice and prudence within which decisions must be made. Still, we share one thing in common. None of us learns totally on our own. We learn from others, living and dead. To deny this fact is to risk becoming, as one leading Lonergan scholar puts it, "a self-made man or woman who worships his or her maker."[9] Lonergan himself spent years "reaching up to the mind of Aquinas," and Janet Finn learned from the women of Butte and Chuquicamata. Christopher Weeramantry, a Sri Lankan Catholic, found wisdom and warnings not only in Shakespeare and Hobbes and Hugo Grotius but also in the ancient texts of India and Sri Lanka; and Robert Oppenheimer looked to those ancient texts, too. Homer Hickam learned from Miss Riley, with her cancer, but also from his parents and from Werner von Braun. Fritz Heinze learned about mining and metallurgy in universities. Marcus Daly learned about mining from others in the mines.

We can learn from the mistakes of others, as well as from our own, for Malone's observation that "it need not have been this way" surely applies beyond Butte. One thinks of genocide, chattel slavery, the Holocaust, inquisitions and crusades, wars and war crimes, the abuse of children, and apartheid not yet gone—and those are just near the top. Black lung and radiation poisoning and crippling debt to the company store—or to foreign banks—are in there somewhere, too. Meanwhile tons of plastic in the warming oceans are floating to the surface, just as toxins rose from one of the tallest smokestacks in the world that I saw near Anaconda, Montana, many years ago. By seeking to understand our own situation even as we broaden our moral horizons, by asking where we have been and where we go from here, by asking others and the Other to help us to find our way, by asking how we need to change and by following through, we may shift ever so slightly, but maybe much more, the probabilities that true healing and creating in history will occur. Even a "self-made man" like Dennis Washington surely learned from others and from disaster. His company's mining safety record is about as close to perfect as you can get, even as the toxic water in the nearby Berkeley Pit continues to rise.

Bernard Lonergan, whose tools, among others, I have enlisted here, describes his book *Insight* as "an essay in aid of personal appropriation of one's own rational self-consciousness,"[10] an appropriation that opens to new vistas that both embrace and extend beyond one's own time and place and social location. With less profundity and precision, to be sure, the aim of this book has been not so different. By turning attention to mining, the reader has been invited to answer, from perhaps new angles and distant vantage points the invitation to live more fully what Socrates called the examined life, a self-understanding that reaches beyond the self to the bottom the sea, to the nucleus of the atom, to deep space and beyond.

Thus, the simple conclusion of this prospector's report: Without going to court or even filing a claim, without even traveling by car or boat or plane or spacecraft to any of the mining sites we have visited, we can avail ourselves of a revised version of the "apex rule": Whatever moral ground upon which each of us presently stands is in fact the apex of hidden veins of meaning and value, spreading out far and wide beneath the surface, intersecting with meaningful and valuable veins claimed by others, some no longer living, others not yet born. They are rich veins, ready to be mined if only the veins can be shared. The recovery process will be no less arduous than the challenges faced by miners of copper or coal or uranium or asteroids speeding through space. But the payoffs can be immense. The ore will not be depleted. We will better care for one another and for our common home. We may discover that, even in our darkest moments, we are never truly alone.

NOTES

1. Lonergan, *Insight*, 555–58.
2. For a brief discussion of Lonergan's distinctions, with references to Rumsfeld and Iraq, see Joseph A. Komonchak, "Horizons," *Commonweal*, April 10, 2014, https://www.commonwealmagazine.org/horizons.
3. Plato, *Meno*, in *Five Dialogues* 2nd ed., trans. G. M. A. Grube; rev. John M. Cooper (Indianapolis: Hackett Publishing Co., 2002), especially 80a–e.
4. Jaques Maritain, *Distinguish to Unite: or, The Degrees of Knowledge*, trans. under the supervision of G.B. Phelan (New York: Charles Scribner's Sons, 1959).
5. *ST* I–II 62, 4.
6. John T. Noonan, *A Church that Can and Cannot Change: The Development of Catholic Moral Teaching* (Notre Dame, IN: University of Notre Dame Press, 2005).
7. See Albert O. Hirshman, *The Passions and the Interests: Arguments for Capitalism before Its Triumph,* Twentieth Anniversary Edition (Princeton: Princeton University Press, 1977), 20–21.
8. Saint Augustine, *Confessions,* Bk I,i (1).
9. Fred Lawrence. "The Fragility of Consciousness: Lonergan and the Postmodern Concern for the Other," *Theological Studies* 54 (1993): 60.
10. Lonergan, *Insight*, 764.

Bibliography

Allison, Graham. *The Essence of Decision: Explaining the Cuban Missile Crisis*. Boston: Little, Brown and Company, 1971.

Allott, Philip. *The Health of Nations: Society and Law beyond the State*. Cambridge: Cambridge University Press, 2002.

———. "*Mare Nostrum:* A New International Law of the Sea." *The American Journal of International Law*, Vol. 86, No. 4 (October 1992): 764–87.

Almond, Roncevert Ganan. "Building a Durable Legal Framework in Space: The Extraterrestrial Impact of the South China Sea Dispute." *Yale Journal of International Law*. October 24, 2017. http://www.yjil.yale.edu/building-a-durable-legal-framework-in-space-the-extraterrestrial-impact-of-the-south-china-sea-dispute/

Anand, R. P. *Development of International Law and India*. Published under the auspices of the Max Planck Institute for European History, Frankfurt, Germany. Frankfurt, 2005; New Delhi 2007.

Anghie, Antony. *Imperialism, Sovereignty, and the Making of International Law*. Cambridge: Cambridge University Press, 2004.

Appiah, Kwame Anthony. *Cosmopolitanism: Ethics in a World of Strangers*. New York: W.W. Norton, 2006.

Aquinas, Thomas. *Summa Theologica*. Translated by Fathers of the English Dominican Province. New York: Benziger Brothers, Inc., 1948; reprinted by Westminster, MD: Christian Classics, 1981.

Arendt, Hannah. *Eichmann in Jerusalem: A Report on the Banality of Evil*. Introduction by Amos Elan. New York: Penguin Books, 2006.

Aristotle. *Nicomachean Ethics*. Translated with introduction and notes by Martin Oswald. New York: Macmillon Publishing Company, 1962.

Augustine, Saint. *Confessions*. Translated by Henry Chadwick. Oxford: Oxford University Press, 1991.

Barsto, David, William J. Broad, and Jeff Gerth. "The Nuclear Card: The Aluminum Tube Story—A Special Report; How White House Embraced Suspect Iraq Arms Intelligence." *New York Times,* October 3, 2004.

Beauchamp, Scott. "How to Send a Message 1,000 Years to the Future." *The Atlantic*, February 24, 2015. https://www.theatlantic.com/technology/archive/2015/02/how-to-send-a-message-1000-years-to-the-future/385720/.

Benedict XVI. *Caritas in Veritate*. http://w2.vatican.va/content/benedict-xvi/en/encyclicals/documents/hf_ben-xvi_enc_20090629_caritas-in-veritate.html.

Berman, Harold J. Review of *Religion and International Law*, ed. Mark W. Janis and Carolyn Evans. *American Journal of International Law* 94/4 (October 2000): 800–803.

Best, Geoffrey. *War and Law since 1945*. Oxford: Oxford University Press, 1994.

Bevins, Vincent. "As Brazil Mine Spill Reaches Ocean, Its Catastrophic Extent Becomes Clear." *Los Angeles Times*, December 20, 2015. http://www.latimes.com/world/brazil/la-fg-brazil-spill-20151220-story.html

Bianchi, Andrea. *International Law Theories: An Inquiry into Different Ways of Thinking*. Oxford: Oxford University Press, 2016.

Brennan, Patrick McKinley. "Asking the Right Questions: Harnessing the Insights of Bernard Lonergan for the Rule of Law." *Journal of Law and Religion* 21 (2006): 1–38.

Brown Weiss, Edith. *In Fairness to Future Generations: International Law, Common Patrimony, and International Equity*. Dobbs Ferry, NY: Transnational Publishers & Tokyo, Japan: United Nations University, 1989.

Bulletin of the Atomic Scientists. Doomsday Clock. https://thebulletin.org/doomsday-clock/.

Byrne, Patrick. *The Ethics of Discernment: Lonergan's Foundations for Ethics*. Toronto: University of Toronto Press, 2016.

Byrne, Patrick H. "The Thomistic Sources of Lonergan's Dynamic World View." *The Thomist* 46 (1982): 108–45.

Caceres, H. Roberto Herrera. "*La sauvegarde du patrimoine commun de l'humanité*." In *The Management of Humanity's Resources: The Law of the Sea*, Workshop, The Hague, 29–31 October 1981. Edited by René-Jean Dupuy, 125–34. The Hague: Martinus Nijhoff Publishers, 1982.

Cassese, Antonio. "States: Rise and Decline of the Primary Subjects of International Law." In *The Oxford Handbook of the History of International Law*. Edited by Bardo Fassbender and Anne Peters, 49–70. Oxford: Oxford University Press, 2012.

Charlesworth, Hillary. "Law-making and Sources." In *The Cambridge Companion to International Law*, edited by James Crawford and Martti Koskenniemi, 190–92. Cambridge: Cambridge University Press, 2012.

Clouse, Carol J. "Can Deep-Sea Mining Avoid the Mistakes of Mining on Land?" *The Guardian*, June 28, 2017. https://www.theguardian.com/sustainable-business/2017/jun/28/deep-sea-mining-environmental-mistakes.

Conway, Elliot. Online review of Antony Anghie, *Imperialism, Sovereignty, and the Making of International Law*." https://classicliberalchap.wordpress.com/

Crowe, Frederick E. "The Genus 'Lonergan and' . . . and Feminism." In *Lonergan and Feminism*, edited by Cynthia S. W. Crysdale, 13–32. Toronto: University of Toronto Press, 1994.

Crysdale, Cynthia. "Horizons That Differ: Women and Men and the Flight for Understanding." *Cross Currents* 44/3 (Fall 1994): 345–61.

———. "Revisioning Natural Law: From the Classicist Paradigm to Emergent Probability." *Theological Studies* 56/3 (1995): 464–84.

Daley, Jason. "Brazilian Mine Disaster Leaves 58 Dead, 200 Missing." Smithsonian .com, January 28, 2019. https://www.smithsonianmag.com/smart-news/brazilian-mine-disaster-kills-dozens-and-covers-town-mud-180971358/#D6EbeHXuYjbluEXg.99.

Damrosch, Lori F., Louis Henkin, Richard Crawford Pugh, Oscar Schachter, and Hans Smit. *International Law: Cases and Materials,* 4th ed. American Casebook Series. St. Paul: West Group, 2001.

Danielsen, Dan. Review of Antony Anghie, *Imperialism, Sovereignty and the Making of International Law. American Journal of International Law* 100/3 (July 2006): 757–62.

Danzig, Aaron. "A Funny Thing Happened to the Common Heritage on the Way to the LOS." *San Diego Law Review* 12 (1975): 655–64.

De Man, Paul. "The Exploitation of Asteroids and the Non-Appropriation Principle: Reflections on the Nature of Property Rights in Light of the US Space Resource Act of 2015." *Journal of Space Law* 40/1–2 (2015–2016): 1–55.

Doherty, Ben. "The Nauru Files: A Brief History of Nauru, Australia's Dumping Ground for Refugees." *The Guardian,* August 9, 2016. https://www.theguardian.com/world/2016/aug/10/a-short-history-of-nauru-australias-dumping-ground-for-refugees.

Doran, Robert M. "System and History: The Challenge to Catholic Systematic Theology," *Theological Studies* 60 (1999).

Edwards, Denis. "Ecological Theology: Trinitarian Perspectives." *Proceedings of the Catholic Theological Society of America* 72 (2017): 14–28.

Egede, Edwin. *Africa and the Deep Seabed Regime: Politics and International Law of the Common Heritage of Mankind.* Heidelberg: Springer Verlag, 2011.

Emmons, David M. "The Socialization of Uncertainty: The Order of Hibernians in Butte, Montana, 1880–1925." In *Montana: A Cultural Medley*, edited by Robert R. Swartout, 146–75. Helena: Faircountry Press, 2015.

Finn, Daniel. *"Centesimus Anno."* In *Modern Catholic Social Teaching Commentaries and Interpretations*, 2nd ed., edited by Kenneth R. Himes, O.F.M., and Associate Editors Lisa Sowle Cahill, Charles E. Curran, David Hollenbach, S.J., and Thomas Shannon, 450–81. Washington, DC: Georgetown University Press, 2018.

Finn, Daniel K. *Christian Economic Ethics: History and Implications*. Minneapolis: Fortress Press, 2013.

———. "Recycling Isn't Enough: A Defense of Responsible Mining," *Commonweal Magazine,* May 2, 2017: 12–14.

———, ed. *The True Wealth of Nations: Catholic Social Thought and Economic Life*. New York: Oxford University Press, 2010.

Finn, Janet L. *Tracing the Veins: Of Copper, Culture, and Community from Butte to Chuquicamata*. Berkeley: University of California Press, 1998.

Fisher, Christopher L., and David Fergusson. "Karl Rahner and the Extra-Terrestrial Intelligence Question." *Heythrop Journal* 47 (2006): 275–90.

Flynn, Daniel, and Geert De Clercq. "Areva and Niger's Uranium Fight." *Reuters*, February 5, 2014. https://www.reuters.com/article/niger-areva/special-report-areva-and-nigers-uranium-fight-idUSL3N0L44UW20140205

Ford, John C., SJ. "The Morality of Obliteration Bombing." *Theological Studies* 5 (September 1944): 261–73; 308–9.

Furó, István. "Fritz Haber—A 'Dr. Evil' Who Has Accomplished Much Good." KTH Royal Institute of Technology (Stockholm). https://www.kth.se/en/che/archive/arkiv/haber-1.83967

Gangale, Thomas. "The Legality of Mining Celestial Bodies." *Journal of Space Law*, Vol. 40:1–2 (2015–2016).

Garner, Eric L. "International Treaties Governing Mineral Exploration." *Environmental and Engineering Geology*, Vol. III. http://www.eolss.net/sample-chapters/c09/E6-65-05-04.pdf

Gebarra, Ivone, and Maria Claire Bingemer. *Mary, Mother of God, Mother of the Poor.* Translated by Philip Berryman. Theology and Liberation Series. Maryknoll, NY: Orbis Books, 1989.

George, William P. "Angelism and Its Devilish Effects on Education." *Chicago Studies* 29 (2000): 194–210.

———. "Anticipating Posterity: A Lonerganian Approach to Contingent Future Persons." In *Contingent Future Persons: Philosophical and Theological Challenges*, edited by Jan C. Heller and Nick Fotion, 191–208. Theology and Medicine Series. Kluwer Academic Publishers, 1997.

———. "Catholic Theology, International Law, and the Global Climate Crisis." In *Confronting the Climate Crisis: Catholic Theological Perspectives*, edited by Jaime Schaefer, 177–200. Milwaukee: Marquette University Press, 2010.

———. "Envisioning Global Community: The Theological Character of the Common Heritage Concept in the LOS." Ph.D. dissertation, University of Chicago, 1990.

———. "Grotius, Theology, and International Law: Overcoming Textbook Bias." *Journal of Law and Religion* 14 (Winter 2001): 101–25.

———. "International Law as Horizon." In *Lonergan Workshop*, vol. 23: *Ongoing Collaboration in the Year of St. Paul*, edited by Frederick Lawrence, 195–226. Boston: Boston College, 2012.

———. "International Regimes, Religious Ethics, and Emergent Probability." *Annual of the Society of Christian Ethics*, 1996: 145–70.

———. "Learning Alone: Solitude and Undergraduate Education." *America Magazine*, September 15, 2008, 16–18.

———. "Looking for a Global Ethic? Try International Law." *Journal of Religion* 76/3 (1996): 353–82. Reprinted with slight emendations in *Religion and International Law*, edited by Mark W. Janis and Carolyn Evans, 483–504. The Hague: Martinus Nijhoff Publishers.

———. "Murder, He Wrote: Introducing Christian Ethics through One Question in the *Summa*." *Teaching Theology and Religion* 11/4 (2008): 222–29.

———. "Neither Apology nor Utopia: A Lonerganian Approach to International Law." Paper delivered at the annual meeting of the Society of Christian Ethics, January, 2014.

———. "Regarding Future Neighbours: Thomas Aquinas and Concern for Posterity." *The Heythrop Journal* 33/3 (July 1992): 283–306.

———. "Why Catholic Universities Should Engage International Law." *Journal of Catholic Higher Education* 27/1 (Winter 2008): 173–93.

Gerhart, Mary. "Bernard Lonergan's 'Law of the Cross': Transforming the Sources and Effects of Violence." *Theological Studies* 77/1 (March 2016): 77–95.

Glasscock, C. B. *The War of the Copper Kings: Greed, Power, and Politics: The Billion-Dollar Battle for Butte, Montana, the Richest Hill on Earth*. Helen, MT: Riverbend Publishing, 2002.

Glendon, Mary Ann. *A World Made New: Eleanor Roosevelt and the Universal Declaration of Human Rights*. New York: Random House, 2001.

Goldsmith Jack L., and Eric A. Posner. *The Limits of International Law*. Oxford: Oxford University Press, 2005.

Gorove, Steven. "The Concept of 'Common Heritage of Mankind': A Political, Moral, or Legal Concept?" *San Diego Law Review*: 9 (1972): 390–403.

Green Peace. "Deep Seabed Mining: An Urgent Wake-Up Call to Protect Our Oceans." March 2014, accessed at http://www.greenpeace.org/international/Global/international/publications/oceans/2013/Deep-Seabed-Mining.pdf.

Greene, Graham. *The Heart of the Matter*. New York: Penguin Books, 1971.

Grewe, Wilhelm. *The Epochs of International Law*. Translated and revised by Michael Byers. New York: Walter de Gruyter, 2000.

Grotius, Hugo. *The Free Sea*. Richard Hakluyt with William Welwood's Critique and Grotius's Reply, edited by David Armitage. Indianapolis: Liberty Fund, 2004.

Guarino, Ben. "Thousands of Montana Snow Geese Die after Landing in Toxic, Acidic Mine Pit." *Washington Post*, December 7, 2016. https://www.washingtonpost.com/news/morning-mix/wp/2016/12/07/montana-snow-geese-searching-for-pond-land-in-toxic-mine-pit-thousands-die/?utm_term=.536a19871f8c

Gustafson, James M. *Ethics from a Theocentric Perspective*. Vol. 1: *Theology and Ethics*; Vol. 2: *Ethics and Theology*. Chicago: University of Chicago Press, 1981; 1984.

———. "Participation: A Religious Worldview," *Journal of Religious Ethics* 44/1 (March 2016): 148–75.

———. *Varieties of Moral Discourse: Prophetic, Narrative, Ethical, Policy*. Grand Rapids: Calvin College, 1988.

Hartman, Howard L., and Jan M. Mutmansky, eds. *Introductory Mining Engineering*, 2nd ed. John Wiley & Sons, 2002; reprint New Delhi, Wiley India Pvt. Ltd., 2007.

Haughey, S.J. John C. "Responsibility for Human Rights: Contributions from Bernard Lonergan." *Theological Studies* 63/4 (December 2002): 764–85.

Hecht, Gabrielle. *Being Nuclear: Africans and the Global Uranium Trade*. Cambridge, MA: The MIT Press, 2012.

Heidegger, Martin. *Being and Time*. New York: Harper and Row, 1927; 1962.

Heilbroner, Robert. *An Inquiry into the Human Prospect*. Updated and Reconsidered for the 1980s. New York: W.W. Norton and Company, 1980; 1974.

———. *The Worldly Philosophers: The Life, Times, and Ideas of the Great Economic Thinkers*, 7th ed. New York: Touchstone/Simon and Schuster, Inc., 1999.

Henkin, Louis. *How Nations Behave: Law and Foreign Policy*, 2nd ed. Council on Foreign Relations Books. New York: Columbia University Press, 1968; 1979.

Hirshman, Albert O. *The Passions and the Interests: Arguments for Capitalism before Its Triumph*. Twentieth Anniversary Edition. Princeton: Princeton University Press, 1977.

Hickam, Homer H. Jr. *Rocket Boys*. New York: Random House, Inc., 1998.

Hijiya, James A. "The *Gita* of J. Robert Oppenheimer." *Proceedings of the American Philosophical Society* 144/2 (June 200): 123–67.

Human Rights Watch. "Zambia: Workers Detail Abuses in Chinese-Owned Mines." November 3, 2011. https://www.hrw.org/news/2011/11/03/zambia-workers-detail-abuse-chinese-owned-mines

International Labor Organization. "Learn More about Child Labour in Mining." http://www.ilo.org/ipec/areas/Miningandquarrying/MoreaboutCLinmining/lang—en/index.htm

"International Law Is Irrevocably Transformed." Statement by Javier Pérez de Cuéllar, Secretary-General of the United Nations, December 10, 1982. *The Law of the Sea: United Nations Convention on the Law of the Sea with Index and Final Act of the Third United Nations Conference on the Law of the Sea*. New York: United Nations, 1983, xxx.

Johnston, Douglas, and Cynthia Sampson, eds. *Religion the Missing Dimension of Statecraft*. New York: Oxford University Press, 1994.

Jonas, Hans. *The Imperative of Responsibility: In Search of an Ethics for the Technological Age*. Chicago: University of Chicago Press, 1984.

Jonsen, Albert R., and Stephen Toulmin. *The Abuse of Casuistry: A History of Moral Reasoning*. Berkeley: University of California Press, 1986.

Joyner, Christopher C., and Elizabeth A. Martell. "Looking Back to See Ahead: UNCLOS III and Lessons for Global Common Law." In *International Law: Classic and Contemporary Readings*, edited by Charlotte Ku and Paul F. Diehl, 245–72. Boulder, CO: Lynne Reinner Publishers, 1998.

Juda, Lawrence. *International Law and Ocean Use Management: The Evolution of Ocean Governance*. Ocean Management Policy Series. London: Routledge, 1996.

Kaltenborn, Carl von. *Zur Geschitche des Natur- und Völkerrechts sowie der Politik*. Volume 1: *Die Vorläufer des Hugo Grotius auf dem Gebiete des Ius naturae et gentium sowie der Politik*. Leipzig: Verlag von Gustav Mayer, 1848.

Kaveny, Cathleen. *Law's Virtues: Fostering Autonomy and Solidarity in American Society*. Washington, DC: Georgetown University Press, 2012.

Kennedy, David. "Images of Religion." In *Religion and International Law*, edited by Mark W. Janis and Carolyn Evans, 145–54. The Hague: Kluwer Law International, 1999.

Kent, H. S. K. "The Historical Origins of the Three-Mile Limit." *American Journal of International Law*, 48/4 (October 1954): 537–53.

Klein, Naomi. "A Radical Vatican?" *The New Yorker*, July 10, 2015. http://www.newyorker.com/news/news-desk/a-visit-to-the-vatican.

———. *This Changes Everything: Capitalism and the Climate*. New York: Simon and Schuster, 2014.

Kohn, David. "Who Killed Montana Power?" CBS *Sixty Minutes*, February 6, 2003. https://www.cbsnews.com/news/who-killed-montana-power-06-02-2003/

Koskenniemi, Martti. *From Apology to Utopia: The Structure of International Legal Argument*. Cambridge: Cambridge University Press, 2005.

Kramer, Katie. "Building the Economy Here on Earth by Exploring Space: Tyson." CNBC. *On the Money*, May 3, 2015. https://www.cnbc.com/2015/05/01/build-the-economy-here-on-earth-by-exploring-space-tyson.html

Lachs, Manfred. "The Grotian Heritage, the International Community, and Changing Dimensions of International Law." In *International Law and the Grotian Heritage: A Commemorative Colloquium*, edited by T. M. C. Asser Instituut. The Hague: T.M.C. Asser Instituut, 1985.

Lawrence, Fred. "The Fragility of Consciousness: Lonergan and the Postmodern Concern for the Other." *Theological Studies* 54 (1993): 55–94.

Leavy, Jane. *The Last Boy: Mickey Mantle and the End of America's Innocence*. Harper Collins Publishers, 2011.

Lehr, Dick. "The Racist Legacy of Woodrow Wilson." *The Atlantic*, November 27, 2015.

Levering, Ralph B., and Miriam L. Levering. *Citizen Action for Global Change: The Neptune Group and the Law of the* Sea. Syracuse: Syracuse University Press, 1999.

Lewis, John S. *Asteroid Mining 101: Wealth for the New Space Economy*. Deep Space Industries, 2015.

Liddy, Richard. "Bernard Lonergan on a Catholic Liberal Arts Education." *Catholic Education: A Journal of Inquiry and Practice* 3/4 (June 2000): 521–32.

———. "Changing Our Minds: Bernard Lonergan and Climate Change." In *Confronting the Climate Crisis: Catholic Theological Perspectives*, edited by Jaime Schaefer, 253–75. Milwaukee, WI: Marquette University Press, 2011.

Lonergan, Bernard J. F. "Dimensions of Meaning." In *Collection*, Collected Works of Bernard Lonergan, vol. 4, edited by Frederick E. Crowe and Robert M. Doran, 233–45. Toronto: University of Toronto Press, 1998.

———. "Healing and Creating in History." In *A Third Collection: Papers by Bernard J. F. Lonergan, SJ*, edited by Frederick E. Crowe, SJ, 100–109. New York: Paulist Press, 1985.

———. *Insight: A Study of Human Understanding*, 5th ed. revised and augmented. Collected Works of Bernard Lonergan, Vol. 3, edited by Frederick E. Crowe and Robert M. Doran. Toronto: University of Toronto Press, 1992.

———. *Lonergan's Macroeconomic Dynamics: An Essay in Circulation Analysis*. Edited by Frederick G. Lawrence, Patrick H. Byrne, and Charles C. Hefling Jr.

Collected Works of Bernard Lonergan, vol. 15. Toronto: University of Toronto Press, 1999.

———. “Metaphysics as Horizon.” In *Collection*, Collected Works of Bernard Lonergan, vol. 4, edited by Frederick E. Crowe and Robert M. Doran, 188–204. Toronto: University of Toronto Press, 1998.

———. *Method in Theology*. Toronto: University of Toronto Press, 1990.

———. “Natural Right and Historical Mindedness,” in *A Third Collection: Papers by Bernard Lonergan*, SJ, edited by Frederick E. Crowe, SJ, 169–183. Mahwah, NJ: Paulist Press/London: Geoffrey Chapman, 1985.

———. “Prolegomena to the Study of the Emerging Religious Consciousness of Our Time.” In *A Third Collection*, edited by Frederick E. Crowe, SJ, 55–73. Mahwah, NJ: Paulist Press/London: Geoffrey Chapman, 1985.

———. *Topics in Education, Collected Works of Bernard Lonergan,* vol., 10, edited by Robert M. Doran and Frederick E. Crowe. Toronto: University of Toronto Press, 1993.

Lovin, Robin W. *Christian Ethics: An Essential Guide*. Nashville: Abingdon Books, 2000.

MAC: Mines and Communities. “Mining, Communities, and Sustainable Development.” http://www.minesandcommunities.org/article.php?a=9925

Macpherson, C. B. *The Political Theories of Possessive Individualism: Hobbes to Locke*. Oxford: Oxford University Press, 1962.

Malone, Michael P. *The Battle for Butte: Mining and Politics on the Northern Frontier, 1864–1906*. Seattle: University of Washington Press, 1981.

Martin, Joan. *More Than Chains and Toil: A Christian Work Ethic of Enslaved Women*. Louisville, KY: Westminster John Knox Press, 2000.

Maritain, Jacques. *Distinguish to Unite: or, The Degrees of Knowledge*. Translated under the supervision of G. B. Phelan. New York: Charles Scribner’s Sons, 1959.

———. *Man and the State*. Chicago: The University of Chicago Press, 1951.

Maxwell, John. *Slavery and the Catholic Church*. Chichester and London: Barry Rose, 1975.

Mbiti, John. *New Testament Eschatology in an African Background: A Study of the Encounter between New Testament Theology and African Traditional Concepts*. New York and London: Oxford University Press, 1971.

McElwee, Joshua J. “Landmark Vatican Conference Rejects Just War Theory, Asks for Encyclical on Nonviolence.” *National Catholic Reporter*, April 16, 2017. https://www.ncronline.org/news/vatican/landmark-vatican-conference-rejects-just-war-theory-asks-encyclical-nonviolence

Melchin, Kenneth. *History, Ethics, and Emergent Probability: Ethics, Society and History in the Work of Bernard Lonergan*. Lanham, MD: University Press of America, 1986.

Mero, John L. *The Mineral Resources of the Sea*. Elsevier Publishing Co., 1969.

Mich, Marvin L. Krier *Catholic Social Teaching and Movements*. New York: Twenty-Third Publications, 1998.

Midgley, Mary. “Trying Out One’s New Sword.” In *Heart and Mind*, 80–87. New York: Palgrave Macmillan, 1981.

Mill, John Stuart. "Inaugural Address Delivered to the University of St. Andrews." February 1, 1887. London: Longmans, Green, Reader, and Dyer, 1867.

Milsom, John. "Geophysical Methods." In Charles J. Moon et al., eds., *Introduction to Mineral Exploration*, 2nd ed. Malden, MA: Blackwell Publishing, 2006 127–54.

Montana Resources. https://www.montanaresources.com/

Moon, Charles J., Michael K. G. Whately, and Anthony M. Evans, eds. *Introduction to Mineral Exploration*, 2nd ed. Malden, MA: Blackwell Publishing, 2006.

Morelli, Mark. "Horizontal Diplomacy." In *Creativity and Method: Essays in Honor of Bernard Lonergan*, edited by Matthew L. Lamb, 459–74. Milwaukee: Marquette University Press, 1981.

Nafziger, James A. R. "The Functions of Religion in the International Legal System." *Religion and International Law*, edited by Mark L. Janis and Carolyn Evans, 155–76. The Hague: Martinus Nijhoff Publishers, 1999.

National Public Radio. "Trump Disparages 'Dumb' Deal with Australia on Refugees." February 2, 2017. http://www.npr.org/sections/thetwo-way/2017/02/02/513012395/trump-disparages-dumb-deal-with-australia-on-refugees

Neff, Stephen. *Justice among Nations: A History of International Law*. Cambridge, MA: Harvard University Press, 2014.

Newman, John Henry. *An Essay in Aid of a Grammar of Assent*. Introduction by Etienne Gilson. New York: Doubleday and Company, 1955.

Niebuhr, Reinhold. "The Illusion of World Government." *Foreign Affairs* 27 (April 1949): 379–88.

———. "The Myth of World Government." *The Nation*, October 21, 1944: 312–14.

Nijman, Janne Elisabeth. *The Concept of International Legal Personality: An Inquiry into the History and Theory of International* Law. The Hague: T.M.C. Asser Press, 2003.

Noonan, John T. *Bribes: The Intellectual History of a Moral Idea*. Berkeley and Los Angeles: University, 1984.

Norton, John D. "Spacetime and the Relativity of Simultaneity." https://www.pitt.edu/~jdnorton/teaching/HPS_0410/chapters/spacetime_rel_sim/index.html

Obregón, Liana. "The Civilized and the Uncivilized." In *The Oxford Handbook of International Law*, edited by Bardo Fassbender and Anne Peters, 917–42. Oxford: Oxford University Press, 2012.

O'Connell, Mary Ellen. *The Power and Purpose of International Law: Insights from the Theory and Practice of Enforcement*. Oxford: Oxford University Press, 2008.

O'Donnell, D. P. *The International Law of the Sea*. 2 vols. Edited by A. Shearer. Oxford: Oxford University Press, 1981; 1984.

Ogbonnaya, Joseph. *Lonergan, Social Transformation,* and *Sustainable Development*. Foreword by Robert M. Doran. Eugene, OR: Pickwick Publications, 2013.

———. "Religion and Sustainable Development in Africa: The Case of Nigeria." *International Journal of African Catholicism* 3/2 (2012): 1–22.

———. "Theology, Culture and Sustainable Development in Africa." ACUHIAM *Journal* 3 (2012): 1–30.

Ormerod, Neil, Paul Oslington, and Robin Koning. "The Development of Catholic Social Teaching on Economics: Bernard Lonergan and Benedict XVI." *Theological Studies* 73 (2012): 391–421.

Ormerod, Neil, and Cristina Vanin. "Ecological Conversion: What Does It Mean?" *Theological Studies* 77/2 (June 2016): 328–52.

Pallardy, Richard. "Deepwater Horizon Oil Spill of 2010: Environmental Disaster, Gulf of Mexico." *Encyclopedia Britannica* (n.d.). https://www.britannica.com/event/Deepwater-Horizon-oil-spill-of-2010

Pardo, Arvid. Address to the U.N. General Assembly. *Official Record.* United Nations General Assembly, Twenty-second Session, First Committee, 1515th meeting, 1 November 1967.

———. "An Opportunity Lost." In *The Law of the Sea: U.S. Policy Dilemma*, edited by H. Oxam, David D. Caron, and Charles L. Buderi, 13–26. San Francisco: ICS Press, 1983.

Paul, Jesse. "Animas River Fouled by 1 Million Gallons of Contaminated Mine Water." *Denver Post,* August 6, 2015. http://www.denverpost.com/2015/08/06/animas-river-fouled-by-1-million-gallons-of-contaminated-mine-water/

Paul VI. *Populorum Progressio: Encyclical of Pope Paul VI on the Development of Peoples*. Libreria Editrice Vaticana, 1967. http://w2.vatican.va/content/paul-vi/en/encyclicals/documents/hf_p-vi_enc_26031967_populorum.html.

Pavalato, Elizabeth. "Searching for the (Star) Light at the Vatican Museum." *The New York Times*, Saturday Profile, December 22, 2017, A6.

Peppard, Christiana Zenner. "*Laudato si'*." In *Modern Catholic Social Teaching Commentaries and Interpretations*, 2nd ed, edited by Kenneth R. Himes, O.F.M., and Associate Editors Lisa Sowle Cahill, Charles E. Curran, David Hollenbach, SJ, and Thomas Shannon, 515–52. Washington, DC: Georgetown University Press, 2018.

Peppard, Christiana Z., and Andreaa Vicini, eds. *Just Sustainability: Technology, Ecology, and Resource Extraction*. Maryknoll, NY: Orbis Books, 2016.

Phillips, Kerri. "How Nauru Threw It All Away." Australian Broadcasting Corporation (ABC). RN, March 11, 2014. http://www.abc.net.au/radionational/programs/rearvision/how-nauru-threw-it-all-away/5312714.

Pieper, Josef. *The Cardinal Virtues*. New York: Harcourt, Brace, & World, Inc., 1965.

Plato. *Apology*. In *Essential Dialogues of Plato*. Edited by Pedro de Bals. Translated by Benjamin Jowett. New York: Barnes and Noble, 2005.

———. *Meno.* In *Five Dialogues,* 2nd ed. Translated by G. M. A. Grube. Revised by John M. Cooper. Indianapolis: Hackett Publishing Co., 2002.

———. *Republic*. Translated by Francis MacDonald Cornford. New York: Oxford, 1945.

Pogge, Thomas. "Divided against Itself: Aspiration and Reality of International Law." In *The Cambridge Companion to International Law*, edited by James Crawford and Martti Koskenniemi, 373–97. Cambridge: Cambridge University Press, 2012.

Polanyi, Michael. *Personal Knowledge: Towards a Post-Critical Philosophy*. Chicago: University of Chicago Press, 1958; corrected version 1962.

———. *The Tacit Dimension*. Garden City, NY: Doubleday & Company, Inc., 1966.

Pontifical Council for Justice and Peace. *Compendium of the Social Doctrine of the Church.* http://www.vatican.va/roman_curia/pontifical_councils/justpeace/documents/rc_pc_justpeace_doc_20060526_compendio-dott-soc_en.html.

Post, Alexandra Merle. *Deepsea Mining and the LOS*. The Hague: Martinus Nijhoff Press, 1983.

Pring, George (Rock). "International Environmental and Human Rights Law Affecting Mining Law Reform." Presented at the Mining Law Seminar Northern Institute for Environmental and Minority Law (NIEM) Arctic Centre, University of Lapland Rovaniemi, Finland, 25–26 September 2008.

Ratner, Steven, and Anne-Marie Slaughter, eds. *The Methods of International Law*. The American Society of International Law, 2004.

Rawls, John. *A Theory of Justice.* Cambridge, MA: The Belknap Press of Harvard University Press, 1971.

Raymaker, John, with Ijaz Durrani. *Empowering Climate-Change Strategies with Bernard Lonergan's Method.* Lanham, MD: University Press of America, 2015.

Rhodes, Richard. Review of Joshua S. Goldstein and Staffan A. Qvist, *A Bright Future: How Some Countries Have Solved Climate Change and the Rest Can Follow. New York Times: Book Review*, February 9, 2019. https://www.nytimes.com/2019/02/05/books/review/bright-future-joshua-s-goldstein-staffan-a-qvist.html.

Rosen, Armin. "One Uranium Mine in Niger Says a Lot about China's Huge Nuclear-Power Ambitions." *Business Insider*, October 24, 2015. https://internationalreportingproject.org/stories/view/one-uranium-mine-in-niger-says-a-lot-about-chinas-huge-nuclear-power-ambiti.

Rothwell, Donald R., and Tim Stephens. *The International Law of the Sea*, 2nd. ed. Oxford and Portland, OR: Hart Publishing, 2016.

Schmitt, Carl. *The* Nomos *of the Earth in the International Law of the Jus Publicum Europaeum*. New York: Telos Press Publishing, 2003, 101–25.

Schuck, Michael. *That They Be One: The Social Teaching of the Papal Encyclical 1740–1989.* Washington, DC: Georgetown University Press, 1991.

Schumacher, E.F. *Small Is Beautiful: Economics as if People Mattered.* London: Blond and Briggs, Ltd., 1973.

Schwibold, Dennis L. *Copper Chorus: Mining, Politics, and the Montana Press, 1889–1959*. Helena: Montana Historical Society, 2006.

Scitovsky, Tibor. *The Joyless Economy: A Psychology of Human Satisfaction.* Revised Edition. New York: Oxford Unversity Press, 1976; 1992.

Scott, James Brown. *The Catholic Conception of International Law: Franciso de Vitoria, Founder of the Modern Law of Nations; Francisco Suárez, Founder of the Modern Philosophy of Law in General and in Particular of the Law of Nations.* Washington, DC: Georgetown University Press, 1934.

Shukman, David. "Hawking: Humans at Risk of Lethal 'Own Goal.'" *BBC News*, January 19, 2016. https://www.bbc.com/news/science-environment-35344664

Siegel, Shefa. "The Missing Ethics of Mining." *Ethics and International Affairs*. 27/1 (February 2013).

Simmons, Thomas E. "The Unfortunate Provincialism of The Space Resources Act." *The Space Review: Essays and Commentary about the Final Frontier*. Monday, January 25, 2016. http://www.thespacereview.com/article/2910/1

St. Amour, Paul. "An Introduction to Lonergan's Macroeconomic Theory." Marquette University Lonergan Colloquium, February 28, 2013.

Swartout, Robert R. "From Guangdong to the Big Sky: The Chinese Experience in Frontier Montana, 1864–1900." In *Montana: A Cultural Medley*, edited by Robert R. Swartout, 94–120. Helena: Faircountry Press, 2015.

Taylor, Charles. *A Secular Age.* Cambridge, MA: The Belknap Press of Harvard University Press, 2007.

Taylor, Prue. "The Common Heritage of Mankind: A Bold Doctrine Kept within Strict Boundaries." *The Wealth of the Commons: A World beyond Market and State.* http://wealthofthecommons.org/essay/common-heritage-mankind-bold-doctrine-kept-within-strict-boundaries

The Guardian. "The World's Most Toxic Town: The Terrible Legacy of Zambia's Lead Mines." May 28, 2017. https://www.theguardian.com/environment/2017/may/28/the-worlds-most-toxic-town-the-terrible-legacy-of-zambias-lead-mines.

The Westminster Dictionary of Christian Ethics. Edited by James F. Childress and John Macquarrie: Philadelphia: The Westminster Press, 1986.

Trefil, James. *Reading the Mind of God: In Search of the Principle of Universality.* New York: Anchor Books/Doubleday, 1989.

Udías, Augustín. "Jesuit Astronomers in China and India." Chapter 4 of *Jesuit Contributions to Science: A History*, 79–104. New York: Springer Cham, 2003.

United Nations Convention on the Law of the Sea. https://www.un.org/Depts/los/convention_agreements/texts/unclos/unclos_e.pdf

United States Conference of Catholic Bishops. "Global Climate Change: A Plea for Dialogue, Prudence, and the Common Good." June 15, 2001. http://www.usccb.org/issues-and-action/human-life-and-dignity/environment/global-climate-change-a-plea-for-dialogue-prudence-and-the-common-good.cfm

———. "Seven Themes of Catholic Social Teaching." http://www.usccb.org/beliefs-and-teachings/what-we-believe/catholic-social-teaching/seven-themes-of-catholic-social-teaching.cfm

Urbana, Ian. "The Outlaw Ocean." *New York Times*, Five-Part Series, July 25, 2016. https://www.nytimes.com/interactive/2015/07/24/world/the-outlaw-ocean.html

Vatican Council II. *Pastoral Constitution on the Church in the Modern World: Gaudium et spes*. Promulgated by Pope Paul VI, December 7, 1965. http://www.vatican.va/archive/hist_councils/ii_vatican_council/documents/vat-ii_cons_19651207_gaudium-et-spes_en.html

Vatican Radio. "South African Bishops Issue Statement on Mining Industry." http://en.radiovaticana.va/news/2015/08/20/south_african_bishops_issues_statement_on_mining_industry/1166273

Vitoria, Francisco de. *De Indis* (On the American Indians). In *Francisco de Vitoria, Political Writings.* Cambridge Texts in the History of Political Thought. Edited by Anthony Padgen and Jeremy Lawrence, 231–292. New York: Cambridge University Press, 1991.

von der Dunk, Frans G. "Asteroid Mining: International and National Legal Aspects." *Michigan State International Law Review* 26/1 (2017): 83–99.

Walzer, Michael. *Spheres of Justice: A Defense of Pluralism and Equality.* Basic Books, 1989.

Wattles, Jackin. "NASA Is Keeping Tabs on Elon Musk's Roadster." *CNN Tech*, February 12, 2018. http://money.cnn.com/2018/02/10/technology/future/nasa-elon-musk-spacex-tesla-roadster/index.html

Weeramantry, C. G. *Islamic Jurisprudence: An International Perspective*. Kuala Lumpur: The Other Press, 1988.

———. *The Lord's Prayer: Bridge to a Better World.* Ligouri, MO: Liguri/Triumph, 1998.

———. "Nuclear Reactor Catastrophe in Japan: An Open Letter to the World's Environmental Ministers," March 14, 2001. http://www.wagingpeace.org/wp-content/uploads/2012/11/2011_03_16_weeramantry.pdf

———. *Towards One World: The Memoirs of Judge C.G. Weeramantry,* 3 vols. Moratuw: OPRO Printing and Publishing Solutions (Pvt) Ltd. Vol. I: *The Sri Lankan Years* (2010); Vol. II: *The Australian Years* (2012); Vol. III: *The International Court of Justice and Thereafter* (2014).

———. *Tread Lightly on the Earth: Religion, the Environment and the Human Future*. A Report for the World Future Council. Pannipitiya, Sri Lanka: Stamford Lake (Pvt.) Ltd., 2009.

——. *Universalising International Law*. Leiden: Martinus Nijhoff Publishers, 2004.

Weeramantry, Christopher. *Nauru: Environmental Damage under Trusteeship*. Melbourne: Oxford University Press, 1992.

Weeramantry, Judge Christopher, and John Burroughs. "International Law: A Peace Lesson," Peace Lessons from around the World," 2005. A web-based part of Hague Appeal for Peace. www.haguepeace.org

White, Lynn Jr. "The Historical Roots of Our Ecological Crisis." *Science* 155/3767 (10 March 1967): 1203–7.

Wills, Gary. *Under God: Religion and American Politics*. New York: Simon and Schuster, 1990.

World Information Service on Energy (WISE). "New Uranium Projects—Niger." Last updated January 30, 2019. http://www.wise-uranium.org/upne.html

Xenophon. *The Memorabilia: Recollections of Socrates*. Translated by H. G. Dakyns. Macmillan and Co., 1897.

Zifland, Deborah, and Ron Seely. "Sterling Hall Bombing: 40 Years Later, Family Members Celebrate Physicist's Life." *Wisconsin State Journal*, August 17, 2010. https://madison.com/wsj/news/local/education/university/sterling-hall-bombing-years-later-family-members-celebrate-physicist-s/article_ba113d78-a980-11df-9db0-001cc4c03286.html. Accessed April 9, 2019.

Index

Page references for figures are italicized.

About the Author

William P. George is emeritus professor of theology at Dominican University, River Forest, Illinois. He holds a PhD in Ethics and Society from the University of Chicago Divinity School, where his dissertation focused on the 1982 UN Convention on the Law of the Sea. His teaching has focused on such topics as property and debt, Catholic social thought, slavery, war and peace in Christianity and Islam, and the politics of Saint Augustine. He has also taught international law for the Department of Political Science, along with integrative seminars in the Honors Program and the Core Curriculum, the latter of which he directed for eight years. His many articles and book chapters have focused on such topics as international law and religion, gun violence, climate change, concern for future generations, global ethics, and education. He was named the President's Distinguished Service Professor for 2018–2019.

Ingram Content Group UK Ltd.
Milton Keynes UK
UKHW021321300323
419412UK00007B/123

9 781978 707924